"Li's well-paced account of the ensuing cloak-and-dagger episodes that lead to his defection to the West adds suspense to a tale already full of adventures, but there are no conventional bad guys to be found in it. Indeed, he writes with fine compassion for the Chinese consul who attempts to dissuade him from becoming an outcast: 'unlike me, he had to go back and would probably never manage to get out again.' Nicely written and humane: for anyone interested in modern Chinese history or for fans of dance."
—*Kirkus Reviews*

"Honest and refreshing."
—Adeline Yen Mah, author of *Falling Leaves*

"A moving, true story of family love and a boy's great courage on his journey from terrible poverty to the world stage—one of the books of the year."
—*Women's Weekly* (Australia)

"It is in large part this book's resemblance to good fiction that renders it so readable. The scene in the Chinese consulate after Cunxin defects is fraught with real menace, charged with potential for violence and even international incident, and could hardly be better described . . . a crackling yarn."
—*The Sunday Independent* (Ireland)

"Li Cunxin has written a remarkable book about his own remarkable journey. It is really about the nature of family love, courage, and obsession. *Mao's Last Dancer* is told with simplicity, but Li's style is deceptive. It takes skill to write simply, just as it takes years of backbreaking work to make ballet look elegant and effortless."
—*The Sydney Morning Herald*

"Very evocative."
—*Financial Times*

continued . . .

"Remarkable." —*The Sunday Telegraph* (London)

"His autobiography traces profound political change, from the disastrous results of Mao's Great Leap Forward in the late 1950s to China's gradual opening after 1978, under new paramount leader Deng Xiaoping." —*Gold Coast Bulletin* (Australia)

"Anything but boring." —*Houston Press*

"*Mao's Last Dancer* is not a typical dancer's story. Yes, Li triumphs over physical pain. More important, he illustrates the sustaining power of deep cultural roots and enduring familial love. Evoking a vivid sense of life's evolution in communist China and the stark contrast of Western society, he also crosses chasms of the heart. And while *Mao's Last Dancer* is not a self-improvement book, Li's courage and perseverance ultimately make his story more inspiring than a dozen tomes by the likes of Dr. Phil." —*Houston Chronicle*

"His story will appeal to an audience beyond Sinophiles and ballet aficionados." —*Publishers Weekly*

"He is an expert storyteller, and his memoir—which includes his struggles to perfect his art in the tense political framework, the complex events surrounding his defection, and the heartbreaks and joys of his professional and personal lives—makes for fascinating reading. The portions dealing with his childhood and loving family in Qingdao are especially poignant, and the work as a whole unfolds with honesty, humor, and a quiet dignity. This book has wide appeal, for it concerns not only a dancer's coming-of-age in a turbulent time but also individual strength, self-discovery, and the triumph of the human spirit." —*Library Journal*

MAO'S LAST DANCER

LI CUNXIN

BERKLEY BOOKS

NEW YORK

THE BERKLEY PUBLISHING GROUP
Published by the Penguin Group
Penguin Group (USA) Inc.
375 Hudson Street, New York, New York 10014, USA
Penguin Group (Canada), 90 Eglinton Avenue East, Suite 700, Toronto, Ontario M4P 2Y3, Canada
(a division of Pearson Penguin Canada Inc.)
Penguin Books Ltd., 80 Strand, London WC2R 0RL, England
Penguin Group Ireland, 25 St. Stephen's Green, Dublin 2, Ireland (a division of Penguin Books Ltd.)
Penguin Group (Australia), 250 Camberwell Road, Camberwell, Victoria 3124, Australia
(a division of Pearson Australia Group Pty. Ltd.)
Penguin Books India Pvt. Ltd., 11 Community Centre, Panchsheel Park, New Delhi—110 017, India
Penguin Group (NZ), 67 Apollo Drive, Rosedale, North Shore, 0632, New Zealand
(a division of Pearson New Zealand Ltd.)
Penguin Books (South Africa) (Pty.) Ltd., 24 Sturdee Avenue, Rosebank, Johannesburg 2196,
South Africa

Penguin Books Ltd., Registered Offices: 80 Strand, London WC2R 0RL, England

The publisher does not have any control over and does not assume any responsibility for author or third-party websites or their content.

PRINTING HISTORY
G. P. Putnam's Sons hardcover edition / April 2004
Berkley trade paperback edition / March 2005
Berkley trade paperback movie tie-in edition / August 2010

Berkley movie tie-in edition ISBN: 978-0-425-24030-4

The Library of Congress has catalogued the G. P. Putnam's Sons hardcover edition as follows:

Li, Cunxin, date.
Mao's last dancer / Li Cunxin.
p.   cm.
ISBN: 0-399-15096-X
1. Li, Cunxin, date.   2. Ballet dancers—China—Biography.
3. Defectors—China—Biography.   I. Title.
GV1785.L475A3   2004   2003047199
792.8'092—dc21
[B]

PRINTED IN THE UNITED STATES OF AMERICA

10 9 8 7 6 5 4 3 2 1

To the two special women
in my life—my mother and my wife

献给我一生中最亲爱

以及对我影响最大的两位女人：

我的母亲方瑞庆

和我的妻子玛丽。

CONTENTS

PART THREE
THE WEST

PART FOUR
MY STORY CONTINUES

囍

A WEDDING
QINGDAO, 1946

On the day of her marriage, a young girl sits alone in her village home. It is autumn, a beautiful October morning. The country air is cool but fresh.

The young girl hears happy music approaching her house. She is only eighteen, and she is nervous, frightened. She knows that many marriage introducers simply take money and tell lies. Some women from her village marry men who don't have all their functional body parts. Those women have to spend the rest of their lives looking after their husbands. Wife beating is common. Divorce is out of the question. Divorced women are humiliated, despised, suffering worse than an animal's fate. She knows some women hang themselves instead, and she prays this is not going to be her fate.

She prays to a kind and merciful god that her future husband will have two legs, two arms, two eyes and two ears. She prays that his body parts are normal and functional. She worries that he will not be kindhearted and will not like her. But most of all she worries about her unbound feet. Bound feet are still in fashion. Little girls as young as five or six have to tuck four toes under the big toe and squeeze them hard to stop the growth. It is extremely painful, and the girls have to change the cloth bandages and wash their feet daily to avoid infection. The tighter the feet are bound the smaller the feet will become. Eventually all five toes grow together. Infections often occur, and the girls are so crippled they have to walk mostly on their heels. But when this bride was about eight and her mother tried to bind her feet, two or three years later than was usual, she defied her and ran away. Her mother eventually gave up, but secretly she was pleased. A daughter with unbound feet could help do the hard chores. But would her future husband and in-laws think the same?

The groom is a young man of twenty-one. He leaves home before sunrise. Sixteen strong men are hired to carry two sedan chairs for the three-hour journey from his village to the bride's. There are trumpets, cymbals, gongs and bamboo flutes, and the bride's sedan chair is covered with red and pink silk banners and flowers. The groom's is a simple blue sedan chair, which will leave from the east side of the village and reenter from the west.

As soon as the groom's entourage leaves home, the women of his family start to prepare the house and the wedding feast to follow. They glue colored-paper cuttings all over the walls, doors and windows—different shapes, with lucky words on them, to symbolize happiness and good fortune. They place a square table in the center of their courtyard and cover it with a red cloth. In the center they place nine huge bread rolls, called mantos, in the shape of a pagoda. There is also a metal bowl, with candlesticks and incense holders on either side. On the ground are two round bamboo mats.

The bride is in such a panicked state by the time her groom arrives. He wears a dark blue cotton mandarin gown and a big tall hat, with silk flowers pinned over his heart. He kneels, and kowtows three times, bowing his head all the way down to the floor, always facing north, always in the direction of the god of happiness.

Tea, sweets, roasted sunflower seeds and peanuts are then served. A lunch feast follows, but the cost of the meal will break the bride's family finances. Many relatives and friends chip in to help, but the favors and debts will have to be repaid in years to come. The groom's entourage has to be satisfied, however. The meal will affect her new family's attitude toward her. It will determine whether she will have a smooth or bumpy ride on the way to her in-laws' house. The young bride remembers that a friend of her mother's was married a year before—at her wedding, the musicians played funeral music and the carriers walked her around in circles, making her dizzy and sick. Even worse, the carriers lowered her sedan chair to the ground, which is very unlucky: that bride would end up with a life of hard work instead of a life of luxury. All this was caused by the in-laws' dissatisfaction with the food that was served at her house.

While the groom's people drink their wine and eat their food, the bride sits on her bed, her kang, away from everyone, with her silk veil concealing her face. This is called the "quiet sitting." She wears a long dark maroon gown, with pink silk flowers sewn onto it. Her hairpiece is full of beautiful colored hairpins and flowers, and is very heavy. She has no jewelery because her family is too poor.

Soon, her second brother secretly whispers to her through a crack in the door, "My brother-in-law has all his moving parts!" This is news from heaven. The young bride sobs with joy.

Toward the end of the meal, the bride's mother brings her a bowl of rice, a double-sided mirror and ten pairs of red chopsticks. The bride has to eat three mouthfuls of rice, and the last mouthful she spits into her mother's pocket. She has to keep some rice in her mouth to last all the way to her in-laws' house before she can swallow, symbolizing that she will never starve along the entire journey of her life. Then she puts eight pairs of chopsticks into her mother's pocket. The remaining two pairs she keeps, the ones with chestnuts and dates tied on them, symbolizing the early arrival of sons.

The bride cannot stop shaking. Tears stream from her eyes as she spits the rice into the pocket. Soon she will become someone's wife and another family's daughter-in-law. She grabs her mother's hand, as if clutching onto a life-saving straw.

"You silly girl," her mother says to her. "Don't cry! You're going to a family with enough food. Do you want to be poor for the rest of your life?" She takes out her handkerchief and gently wipes her daughter's tears and hugs her long and tight for the last time. "My girl, I'll always miss you and love you. Take good care of your husband and he'll take good care of you. Obey him and make him happy. Bear many of his sons. Look after your mother-in-law like you've looked after me. Be kind to her until she dies." She lowers the veil over her daughter's face, and leaves, feeling nothing but pain.

The bride sobs quietly for the first half of her journey to the groom's village. She has never left home before. She is terrified. At the halfway point one of the carriers shouts, "Halfway point, flip your mirror!" So she takes the mirror she's been given and flips it over: now she should forget her past and look forward to the future. Then she is met by a group of four carriers from the groom's village, to make the changeover. She doesn't touch the ground. The musicians continue their happy wedding tunes, and the carriers walk carefully along the uneven dirt road.

When she arrives at the groom's gate, the metal bowl on the table is already flaming with fire. The candle and incense are lit. The groom gets out of his sedan chair and waits for his bride, her face still concealed by her thick silk veil as she is assisted out of her sedan chair by two of his sisters. They walk together toward the table while a local wise man reads loudly an ancient poem. Few people understand it because few of them have ever gone to school, but the bride and groom kneel on the two round bamboo mats while they listen, and afterwards kowtow. The groom then takes his new bride's hands and helps her up. She cannot see the flames from the bowl on the table, but she can feel the intense heat. This fire is the fire of passion, the fire of love.

Before the bride takes her first step with her husband, the groom's fourth brother gently brushes the soles of the bride's shoes with a time-worn iron filled with burning coals, to give her warmth from the end of her body right up to her heart. Led by her husband, she walks slowly toward the door, where there is a horse's saddle. They have to cross over it together. The bride cannot see anything through her veil and she is so afraid that she will trip, but the saddle symbolizes hard times in life and they have to overcome it together. She hesitates. Her husband squeezes her hand. "Stop. Now lift your foot," he whispers. She pulls up her gown to her knees and steps over safely. But as soon as her second foot touches the ground, her heart sinks. She has shown her unbound feet to the entire world! Her in-laws will be disgusted. She wants to scream, to go home to her mother. She will be laughed at, humiliated for the rest of her life. Her husband's family will think she's brought them disgrace and shame.

Her husband feels her hesitation. "Are you all right?" he asks quietly.

She doesn't answer. What can she say?

"Let's go to the kang," he says gently.

On one of the inside corners of the kang sits a triangular wooden box called *doo*. Glued onto it is a diamond-shaped "double-happiness" paper sticker, and inside are different kinds of grains: wheat, corn, rice, millet, sorghum . . . they represent the hope that the newlyweds will have plenty of food throughout their lives. There is a pair of axes too, called *fu*, meaning "fortune," with chestnuts and red dates tied to their wooden handles, and there are also two thin quilts handmade by the groom's sisters, folded into square sitting mats.

First the bride hands her husband the red handkerchief that her mother had given her. He puts it inside the *doo*. Then she hands him the pair of chopsticks with chestnuts and dates attached, and he carefully sticks them upright into the grain.

After a few awkward moments, the groom says in his gentle voice, "Reiqing, *bu yao pa, wu bu hui shang ni*." Don't be afraid. I won't hurt you.

All day the bride has longed to remove her veil. Now she hesitates. She is afraid. Her husband might not like her appearance. But she is reassured by his gentle tone.

She nervously lifts her veil and, for the first time in their lives, they are able to look at each other.

Both cannot believe their luck. The bride sees he is handsome. There is something honest and humble about him too, and he immediately captures her heart.

The groom keeps looking at his bride and is stunned by her beauty. They sit there, speechless, until their "widen your heart" noodles arrive, made by the bride's mother, to comfort the newlyweds' hearts, to symbolize acceptance of each other's fortunes and faults, the bride letting go of her old family values and adopting her new family's ones. Then comes the "warming your heart" rice wine, and they drink from each other's cups with crossed arms.

The groom's brothers, their wives and his sisters come forward one by one to wish the newlyweds a happy life together, until their silver hairs and beard touch the ground. Then the groom's youngest sister, about the same age as the bride, whispers to her, "I'm so happy to see your big feet! I've got them too!" She gives her new sister-in-law a wink and flies out of the room, giggling. The young bride is overjoyed.

The groom is soon called away to the wedding banquet to drink with his friends and relatives, while the bride begins her "sitting through the time." For three days she sits, legs crossed in a lotus position, back straight, for every waking hour. She eats and drinks little, to avoid frequent trips to the toilet.

Many relatives, friends and neighbors visit during those three days, and on the first night people come to "make chaos." The newlyweds have to withstand much teasing and tricking, especially the bride. She is expected to pour visitors' drinks, light their cigarettes and peel the peanuts to feed into their mouths. "Making chaos" will go on until very late into the night, and by the time the last visitor leaves, both bride and groom will be exhausted.

On the fourth day, by tradition, the bride takes her new husband to visit her own family. They like their new son-in-law, and they are happy for their daughter. "My girl, count your blessings," her mother tells her. "Don't look back. It's only starvation and a hard life here. You're now a Li's girl. Make him love you."

She knows her mother is right. When she gets into the back of the cart and looks back at her familiar village for the last time, she has no tears. She knows her family will no longer be her main source of comfort. Her name and place are changed forever. Her destiny lies ahead.

So it was for this bride and groom, my mother and my father, in Qingdao in 1946. My mother looked at her strong husband in the front of the cart and felt lucky and proud that day. Her new husband seemed dependable, like a rock. He seemed gentle, kind and considerate. She felt the urge to know him, understand him, and care for him. She leaned over to my father in the front of the cart and asked him if she could sit beside him. Without a single word, he moved over to the side and let his new bride sit close.

PART ONE

MY CHILDHOOD

1

HOME

My parents, as newlyweds, lived with my father's six brothers, their wives, his two sisters and their children, a total of over twenty people crammed into a six-room house. My mother was the youngest daughter-in-law, so her status in the Li family was the lowest. Family hierarchy had to be respected: she would work hard to prove her worth.

Often my mother would not see my father until late in the evenings, because he worked at two jobs, either away in the fields or carting building materials, all day long. Then the family would sit for dinner under the candlelight (there was no electricity in the village then), with men eating at one table, women and children eating at others. My parents hardly set eyes on each other during that first year of marriage. Sometimes, in the dim candlelight, my mother would even mistake one of her brothers-in-law for her own husband.

The women of the house would sew, wash, clean and cook. My mother was meticulous and efficient, and the speed and quality of her work won her mother-in-law's approval. To cook well was a sign of love and care. My mother was often the one sent to deliver the food to the men in the fields too, because of her unbound feet. Then she could see her husband in the daylight, and her sisters-in-law secretly envied her such freedom.

My mother's mother had died within the first year of my parents' marriage, so my mother would visit her father once a year with gifts and special food she cooked, even though she was never loved by her father in the same way as he loved his sons. A son could work in the fields. A son could bring home a daughter-in-law. A son could carry on the family line. To fail to have a son was considered the greatest betrayal of one's ancestors.

The people who lived in the New Village had been forced to move there during the Second World War from another village about twenty miles north. The Japanese had occupied Qingdao and built an airport where my father's family used to live. The New Village was still small then, with just over three hundred and fifty families, a two-roomed office and an open square. Later, loudspeakers, from which Mao's official revolutionary doctrines were broadcast, would hang from poles or sit on people's rooftops. The houses were attached to each other in long rows with a gap of about four feet between each row.

My parents continued to share a house with my father's family—as the family grew and more children arrived, they simply built more adjoining rooms. Their first son had arrived about a year after their marriage, their second just over two years later, their third two years after that, and then their fourth, Cunsang, in 1955. But Cunsang was lucky to have survived his first week in the Li family. When he was only a few days old, there was an accident. Two of the bigger brothers were playing, stacking up chairs, and the chairs crashed down upon Cunsang's head. He started having seizures. My mother took him immediately to the hospital where the doctor told her that he most likely had brain

4

damage, but was too young to have any treatment. All my mother could do was take him home.

For several days he did not feed, he cried nonstop and the seizures continued. Finally, in desperation, my mother wrapped him in a little handmade blanket, took him out into the snow, and left him on the Northern Hill, close by our village. She thought somebody with magic power might save him. She cried all the way home.

My father's mother, Na-na, came by later to check on her new grandson. Na-na was a kind, tiny little woman. When she found the baby missing, she begged my crying mother to tell her where he was. Eventually she did, and Na-na rushed on her crippled, bound feet to the Northern Hill. She found Cunsang and took him home. He was blue all over, nearly frozen to death, and had a severe fever for several days. But then, miraculously, Cunsang stopped crying. The seizures ended and he seemed to recover. He too grew up with the rest of his brothers in that crowded house, and my mother eventually came to be known as "that lucky woman with seven sons."

My family's house looked into the back of someone else's house, and that house looked directly into theirs. It had a small front courtyard which was enclosed, in years to come, by six-foot stone walls. People with money had the stones delivered and secured with mortar, but my family was too poor, so my father and some of the older sons went to the mountains to bring those stones back themselves, by horse and cart. You could see through the holes in the wall and spy on the neighbors, and once part of the wall fell apart.

My family's property had no backyard. The house itself was built with big stones and bricks, with German-style terra-cotta tiles, made locally. Inside, my parents and their sons had four rooms: two small bedrooms about eight feet square, a slightly larger bedroom about ten feet square and the kitchen-cum-living-room,

5

which was about the same size as the larger bedroom. It had two built-in woks with big wind boxes attached to make fire. Those woks occupied three-quarters of the space in that room. Crockery cupboards were built into the walls, and a small freestanding wooden pantry, made by my father, stood in one corner. There was no refrigeration and no running water, only a huge clay pot for storing drinking water. If both woks were in use at the same time, there would be no space for people to pass through that room without having to move aside whoever was operating the wind box.

The woks backed onto the bedroom walls, which were covered with newspaper "wallpaper," and which contained the chimneys. Fire and smoke would travel through under the mud-brick beds and escape through the walls on the other side. The mud-bricks were supposed to retain heat, but they were not very effective: as the night wore on the beds became colder.

The floor was a reddish earth. During the wet weather, water always seeped through the earth and my father would have to take out the wet floor and wait for a dry day to replace it, every inch with new earth, pounding it down with a huge wooden hammer. The harder the floor, the less chance there was for the water to penetrate.

There were no wardrobes in the house. Clothes were stored in papier-mâché boxes my mother made, stacked on the two small beds during the day and moved onto the floor at night. There was also a main bed about the size of a small double bed, and eventually my parents and all their sons had to share those three beds. The main bedroom was also the room where my family ate, and the only room with an attic: it was my father's secret hiding place for important things like money. Others were forbidden to go there.

After waking each morning on the freezing beds, everyone would fold the blankets into rolls and tuck them neatly away.

What remained was a bamboo mat. A wooden tray about two by four feet, passed down from my father's ancestors, would be placed on top of the mat and the family would sit around it, cross-legged, knee to knee, to eat each meal. Three of the older sons had to sit on wooden stools by the edge of the bed because there wasn't enough room around the tray for everyone.

My family had to go to one of the village wells to fetch water, carrying it back in two buckets that hung from either end of a bamboo pole balanced across the shoulders. The adults and the big boys would carry big buckets, and the little boys had smaller buckets. Water was heated in the big wok, and wooden or clay basins about three feet wide and a foot deep were used for baths. There was one public bath in the commune shared by over ten thousand people, which my family couldn't afford, and no bathroom in the house, only a toilet, which was a hole in the ground in the front courtyard. You had to stand or crouch on two wooden boards, one on each side of the hole. There was no roof, so it was freezing cold in the winter. Half of the toilet was inside the wall, and half outside, to allow the lowest class of laborer in the village to collect the waste, which was used in the fields as fertilizer. He'd use a wooden spoonlike scooper and pour the waste into two wooden barrels that sat on each side of his wheelbarrow. The shit man pushed his wheelbarrow through the narrow streets every day, and if people were coming toward him, they'd move aside and allow him to pass. One day the shit man had a collision with a bicycle. The foul contents of the wheelbarrow ran all over the street. What a smell! Even after the neighbors washed the shitty area over and over with water, the dreadful smell remained and everyone avoided that street for a long time. Neighbors complained to the head of the village and tried to have the shit man replaced, but no one else wanted to be the next shit man.

My family had to utilize every inch of their front yard. There was a small vegetable patch, climbing beans on the stone walls, and a pigsty with a couple of pigs, but there was never enough food to feed the people, let alone the pigs, so the pigs were always very thin. Eventually they were sold to the commune. There was also a chicken yard, but again, the chickens never received enough food to produce many eggs, and the few they did lay were sold in the market for badly needed cash.

The commune allocated each family in the village a piece of land. My family's was one twentieth of an acre, halfway up the Northern Hill, about fifteen minutes from home. It was so small that it could only be used to grow essential foods, such as corn and yams. On Sundays, which was the only day my father could spend at home, the entire family, including the children, worked on this land with him. All the land in Li Commune was divided into small, stepped terraces, and everything was done by hand using shovels, picks, hoes, sickles and plows. At one stage the village had the luxury of two old, starved oxen, which were used for plowing, but they were slow and often refused to walk, despite constant whipping. They too eventually died, one after the other.

My mother's earnings, as with all the peasants', depended on the weather and luck. They had no say in what to plant: the central government in Beijing decided that. My family planted mainly wheat in the winter, corn, yams and sorghum the rest of the year. The government would get the first and biggest portion, at the government-set price, and the rest was divided among the peasants according to the number of members in each family and how many points the family earned during the year. This apportioned food would be counted against your earnings at the end of that year. Every day, the head of each working group in the village would register who worked and for how many hours. Then, at the end of each month, all the peasants would gather and decide how many points each person was entitled to. The most a man could earn in a single day was ten points, which was about one yuan or roughly seventeen U.S. cents then. Women normally received about half of a man's earnings.

One year, there was a severe drought and nobody was paid a single yuan for a whole year. The village had to borrow some money from the Qingdao government to lend every family so they could buy food to survive. It took the people in the village more than two years to repay that loan, and still the peasants had to eat anything that moved, and some things that didn't. Often they couldn't even find any bark to eat.

My family was very poor, but there were even poorer people than the Li family in our commune. By the time I was born there was deprivation and disease everywhere. Three years of Mao's Great Leap Forward and three years of bad weather had resulted in one of the greatest famines the world had ever seen. Nearly thirty million people died. And my parents, like everyone else, were desperately fighting for survival.

I was my parents' sixth son. I was born on 26 January 1961. By then my parents had been married for fifteen years, and the Li family had grown to become a large extended family. Our na-na, my father's mother, lived next door, and his fourth brother (we called him Fourth Uncle) lived next to her. Our third uncle's family lived in front of us, but he died of an unknown disease in his early thirties and left four young girls and a boy. My father, whom we called Dia, and our fourth uncle became their de facto fathers.

It's a Chinese custom that the mother stays in bed for a month after giving birth. Their babies are delivered at home by a local midwife. To get out of bed and work before the month's end was supposed to be bad for the mother's health, and it could

9

do unthinkable harm in her later years. But I was born just twenty days before the Chinese New Year, and this was the busiest time of the year for my mother, my niang. Because of my birth she was far behind in her preparations for the feast. She had no daughter to help her. Our na-na tried to help, but she had bound feet. So my niang didn't have the luxury of staying on her kang for that first month.

My life began with near tragedy for my parents. When I was just fifteen days old, my niang left me on our kang and wrapped me in a cotton quilt before going to the kitchen to make her bread rolls for the Chinese New Year. Mothers in China always wrapped their babies' arms tightly against their bodies and laid them facing up, so the baby's head would grow to the normal shape. That day my niang had so many rolls to steam that the kang where I was lying got boiling hot. I was probably suffocating in the tightly wrapped quilt. I struggled my right arm loose, and the kang badly burned the middle of my arm.

When my niang first heard my screams, she thought I was crying for milk. She had none left in her breasts, so at first she did not respond. By the time she came to check on me, the whole elbow area of my right arm was severely burned and blistered.

The burn quickly became infected. Two days later, my entire right arm had swollen up and turned bright red. My parents had no appropriate medication. They could not afford to take me to the hospital. The burned area gradually became full of pus, and I developed a dangerously high fever. I screamed constantly day and night.

They finally had to borrow some money from our relatives and friends to take me to the hospital. "Your son has a severe infection," the doctor informed my parents. "He is too young to take any medication. You should have come earlier. Your only alternative is to apply some herbal medicine. But I can't guarantee this will work."

"What will happen if it doesn't work?" my niang asked, desperately afraid.

"He may lose his right arm. As soon as you see the infection spread, bring him in and we will have no choice but to cut his arm off," he replied.

My parents looked at their tiny son and couldn't believe that he might grow up with only one arm. My niang's guilt was beyond description. My dia kept telling her that there would be a cure somewhere. They took the doctor's prescription and purchased the herbs from a local medicine shop. My niang followed the doctor's instructions and stewed the herbal ingredients in the wok. They applied the dark liquid to my arm. It didn't help. It made the infection worse, and the redness began to travel away from my arm.

My niang started to panic. She took me to see many healers who lived in our area and tried their different secret family recipes, to no avail. Then my fourth aunt said to my niang, "An old healer told my mother once that bai fang helps infections. Why don't you try it?" Bai fang was a meat tenderizer that looked like white rock salt. It was full of acid. At first my niang didn't take the suggestion seriously, but with all other options exhausted she decided to give it a try.

When she first applied the bai fang I screamed like a stuck pig. She couldn't bear to see her son suffering such pain and she seriously doubted whether a meat tenderizer would ever work, so after a few tries she stopped the treatment.

But my fourth aunt believed strongly it would work. "*Ni tai sin yuen la!*" You are too soft-hearted, she said to my niang. She locked her door, crushed the bai fang into a powder and rubbed massive amounts onto my raw, exposed muscles. She was literally rubbing salt into an open wound. I screamed nonstop the whole day. Every hour she would wash my arm with warm water and reapply masses of bai fang.

Years later my niang confessed, "I was outside your fourth aunt's door and my heart bled each time you screamed. The sound of your cries was like a thousand sharp knives cutting into my guilty heart! Several times I banged on your fourth aunt's door, trying to take you away. Thank the gods for your fourth aunt's determination. She just ignored me."

My fourth aunt wasn't really sure whether this bai fang would work either. She nearly gave up many times that day. But she knew this was the last chance they had to save my arm.

By the end of that day I had lost my voice completely from screaming. But my aunt's determination saved my arm. The infection slowly went away. A large scar remained, and in years to come, in moments of crisis, I would always touch it. It would become my link to my niang and a reminder of her love.

Three years later, my niang gave birth to her seventh son, my youngest brother, Cungui, who we called by his nickname Jing Tring. My parents knew they couldn't provide enough food to feed the sons they now had, and as far as I can remember there was never enough food. Meat, seafood and eggs were all on a strict quota system, along with oil, soy sauce, sugar, salt, wheat and corn flour, rice and also coal. Every family was allocated a very small quantity of these items each month, but often they were not available at all.

We ate a lot of dried yams. They were the easiest things to grow, so most of our land was used for yams. I was often woken up at five o'clock in the morning by my niang to go to the yam fields with my big brothers before they started school for the day. We each carried a shovel and a bamboo basket made by our dia, to dig for any yams that might have been overlooked by the peasants during harvesting. We were cold and hungry but the hope of those yams for breakfast always kept us going. Often the fields had already been turned over by others in equally desperate circumstances, and we returned home with empty baskets.

During summer, every family's front yard and roof were covered with slices of these yams drying in the sun. They looked like snowflakes. Some people even laid them out on the street. But if rain came, you had to quickly pick them all up, for if they got wet they soon went moldy. Once they were dried, the sliced yams would be stored in a huge clay pot in my older brothers' bedroom or in our dia's attic.

Dried yams were our basic food for most of the year. We occasionally had flour and corn bread for a treat, but those were my niang's special reserves for relatives or important visitors. We had dried yams, steamed or boiled, almost daily, week after week, month after month and year after year. Dried yams were the most hated food in my family, but there were others in the commune that could not even afford dried yams. We were luckier than most. We were luckier than the thirty million who starved to death. Dried yams saved our lives.

One year, I remember that our commune experimented with growing peanuts on a few small pieces of land, but it was a disappointingly meager crop. After the peanut field had been harvested, a group of boys my age, about five or six years old, followed some of the older boys with spades and bamboo baskets, trying to find peanuts in the ground that, like the yams, might have been missed by others. None of us found many peanuts after hours of earth churning, but on the edge of the field one of the boys discovered a rat hole, a lucky find for starving boys! He immediately started digging. We gathered around him as if he were a magnet: rats always stored food for winter, so we were all excited and envious of the boy's find. We knew not to kneel by the rat hole because local superstition told us that if we did the rat tunnel would disappear. So the boy dug as fast as he could, with his ass in the air. Several times he nearly lost the tunnel because the rats tried to block it. Then he found that it branched out in different directions, and soon he discovered three stores: one of peeled peanuts, one of half-peeled and the third of unpeeled peanuts. We never saw the rats; we thought they had a secret escape route.

That lucky boy gathered almost half a basketful of peanuts, but secretly I felt sad for the rats, losing their food like that. They too might die of starvation that winter. What a cruel world, I thought, where we had to compete with the rats for food.

Mealtimes in my family were always sad for my niang. There was often nothing for her to cook. We would look at what little food there was on the wooden tray and, out of respect for our elders, always wait for our dia to start. One day, when my niang served dinner, it was clear there was not enough food for everyone.

"I don't feel hungry," our dia said casually. "I had a rather big lunch today. You all go ahead."

Each of us had our chopsticks in hand, ready to swarm on the food. But we hesitated. Our niang was next in line. She quickly gave our dia an annoyed look and made "*zhi, zhi, zhi*" sounds with her tongue. "Don't you dare not eat! Your health is our entire family's security. We will all only be drinking water if you starve yourself to death!"

"I really mean it. I'm not hungry," our dia protested innocently.

"Don't annoy me, you liar!" our niang admonished, and she picked some food up with her chopsticks and put it in our dia's bowl. We started to eat only once he took the first bite. Our parents always ate their food slowly to allow us more food. On many occasions our niang told us to leave the best food for our dia because he was our main breadwinner. But our dia always made excuses and told us we should give the best food to our niang: if not for her we would all have only "northwest wind" for dinner.

We rarely ate meat. Once a month we would wait in long lines at the market for the fattest piece of pork available. Our niang would extract lard from it to use for cooking later, but

14

everyone else wanted the fat pork too, so we didn't get it very often.

One afternoon, my niang heard that the meat shop in our commune was selling pork, but only for a few hours. She borrowed one yuan from my fourth aunt and told me to run to the meat shop as fast as I could in case they ran out, which they often did. It was a good half hour away. There were three long lines of people waiting by the time I arrived. An hour later I handed the cashier my money and our ration card, and I was given a small piece of fatty pork. I was so excited! I knew my niang would be happy with such a fatty piece.

She was ecstatic. She immediately cut the pork into small pieces and started to cook them to extract the lard. I was her wind-box pusher. The delicious fragrance and the sound of sizzling pork made my tummy rumble. She was in high spirits. "What a good piece of pork! This amount of lard will last us a while," she said, and handed me a bowl with a small piece of pork crackling in it. "Don't burn your tongue," she warned. The crackling melted in my mouth—nothing in the world could taste as good.

My niang also cut up a cabbage to cook. "This will be a nice surprise for your dia!"

That night, when the cabbage dish was served, we could actually *see* the traces of precious oil floating in the sauce! My second brother found a small piece of pork in the cabbage too, and put it into our dia's bowl. Our dia immediately passed it to our niang. Our niang passed it back to him. "Don't be silly!" she said, "I especially cooked this for you. You need it for your strength at work."

My youngest brother was sitting next to our dia. Our dia turned to him and said, "Jing Tring, let me see your teeth." Before our niang could say anything, he put that piece of pork into my brother's mouth. There was silence, and a long, sad sigh from our niang.

15

It was always like this. Often a small piece of meat in a vegetable dish would be passed from person to person because it was so scarce. Seven pairs of hungry eyes would look at our parents, begging for more. But no begging words were ever spoken because we all knew how difficult it was to get any food at all. There was simply nothing more to cook. My parents didn't know where the food for our next meal would be coming from.

To survive, my niang worked every spare hour she had in the fields, as well as cooking and looking after her boys. She cooked three meals a day, every day. We never dreamed of going to a restaurant. There was only one restaurant in our area anyway, and it mainly served the government officials. Often my niang had to bury her pride and borrow food from relatives or neighbors. She was an extremely resourceful cook and could make delicious dishes from anything, except dried yams. I hoped never to see another piece of dried yam as long as I lived. They looked whitish before cooking and turned pale gray afterwards. They had no taste and stuck in our throats, so we normally had a bowl of hot water to help get them down, or if we were lucky we would get a bowl of watery rice, wheat or corn congee. Congee is like thin porridge, with very few grains in it.

I loved watching my niang cook while I pushed the wind box. This was a special time for me. I could talk to her alone then, and have a little bit of undivided attention. I was her favorite wind-box pusher, the fastest among my brothers to make the fire. I was also the most patient. My joy and sadness fluctuated along with my niang's. She would be in such a happy mood when she had oil, seafood or especially if she had a piece of pork. I would ask her many questions about the cooking, and I learned when to add certain spices and how to be a good cook.

Food wasn't our only problem of course. Even the water we used had to be boiled. We were not allowed to drink unboiled water. We were told that unboiled water from the village wells could give us worms. My brothers and I all had worms many times throughout our childhood. We would get knotted stomachs and bad pains, and our parents would wake us up and give us some sweet medicine to chew. We called them "the vomitable worm killers." They came in the form of candies shaped like miniature pyramids. The first taste was bearable, with some sweetness, but after five of them I wanted to vomit. And I was only halfway there: I had to eat ten of them! My poor older brothers suffered even more, because the older you were the more worm killers you had to chew. We took them at night while our stomachs were empty and the worms had nothing to eat except the vomitable worm killers. After that, for the next few days, we had to be on a strict diet of warm food, warm water, no sweet, salty or oily food, and no seafood. That meant only one thing—dried yams, meal after meal. Sometimes the worms didn't come out for days and we had to repeat the whole process. Most of the time the worms came out still alive, usually many of them and all about a foot long. The older brothers hated their younger brothers for this horrible ordeal because we, most likely, caused the annual drama by not washing our hands regularly. They had no choice but to go through this process each year.

But despite our poverty, our parents always taught us to have dignity, honesty and pride. Never to steal or do things that would harm others. Our good family name was most sacred and should be protected with all our might.

I tested this one day when I was playing at a friend's house. I was about five. Sien Yu was the same age, and his uncle, who lived in the city, had brought him a small toy car when he'd visited the day before. It was the first time I had ever seen a toy car. I had never seen anything more beautiful in my life! Sien Yu let me play with it for a while. I loved it so much. When he went inside to get a drink, I took it and ran home.

17

"Where did you get that?" my niang asked suspiciously.

"I . . . I found it on the street."

She knew I was not telling the truth. No one in our area could afford to spend money on a toy. "Who did you just play with?"

"Sien Yu," I replied.

She took my hands firmly and pulled me back to Sien Yu's house. She said to his mother, "Sien Yu's niang, is this your son's toy car?"

Sien Yu's mother nodded.

"I'm sorry, I think my son has stolen your son's toy car," my niang said.

"Don't get upset," Sien Yu's mother replied. "Your son is too young to understand."

"I'm ashamed, I'm ashamed of what my son did!" said my niang, and apologized profusely. She tried to make me do the same, but I felt too embarrassed and refused, and wished I had never seen that toy car. I wished for a hole in which to hide. I wished for thick skin to cover my face. I felt the blood rushing to my neck. I tried to escape from my niang's firm grip. I wanted to run away and never come near Sien Yu's house again. I hated my niang for embarrassing me like this. She shouted. She wanted the entire world to know I had stolen my friend's toy car. I screamed and kicked as she dragged me home. "I want a car! I want a car!" I yelled.

As soon as we went inside our house, with despair in her eyes, she pulled me to her chest, hugged me tightly in her arms and sobbed. It was as though she had suffered as much humiliation as I had. "I'm so sorry to do this to you," she whispered tenderly. "I'm so sorry we are too poor to buy you a toy car." After a brief moment she continued. "I'm too stupid to have all of you in this cruel world! You don't deserve this suffering!" I felt her tears streaming onto my hair. "We are too poor! The gods in heaven won't answer our prayers, and even the devil below has abandoned us. We are born with a hopeless fate," she sighed.

"Stop saying that! Don't say anything!" I begged her. I hated to see her so sad.

She continued as though she hadn't heard me. "How I wish I had the money to buy you a toy car! But we don't even have enough money for food."

"I'll have enough food for you one day! I swear!" I said to myself.

She hugged me tighter as she sobbed. I didn't know how long she hugged me, but I didn't want her to stop.

That evening, at dinner, after she had told everyone what I had done, my dia started lecturing us. "Although we have no money, no food, and can't buy clothes, and although we live in a poor house, one thing we do have is PRIDE. Pride is the most precious thing in our lives. Throughout our forefathers' struggles, the Li family always had our pride and dignity. We have always had a good reputation. I want every one of you to remember this: never lose your pride and dignity no matter how hard life is."

二

2

MY NIANG AND DIA

Memories of my niang and my dia are always related to how hard they both worked. Our dia was often up before five-thirty in the morning, which meant my niang had to be up even earlier to cook him breakfast. With all the cooking, washing and sewing she had to do, she hardly had time or energy to pay each of us much attention. We all fought over her love and affection, and she was constantly exhausted. She cooked every meal, made all our clothes for every season and made all our quilts and blankets too. She carried the laundry either to the stream about twenty minutes south of our house or to a dam about half an hour away up on the Northern Hill. The stream often had little water in summer, and our big clay water pot would be covered with ice in the winter. Yet she had no alternative for washing the dishes and clothes.

We always had to be extra careful that we didn't run out of coal for cooking and heating in the middle of winter. There was a great shortage of black coal throughout China, so we never had enough, not even half-burned coal, to heat the water for my niang's huge amounts of washing. Each family was apportioned a small quota of black coal on strict rations, but we only used it to ignite the half-burned coal, which looked like little pieces of gray sponge. This coal had already been burned once by factories or power stations, and if we saw some on the side of the road or in the garbage we would pick it up and take it home. Half-burned coal was very hard to light. It needed black coal to keep it burning. Using the wind box, my niang first lit some dried grass, which was gathered and stacked during summer. Sometimes it could take up to fifteen minutes to light the fire. On windy days, the smoke from my niang's cooking would fill the house, and we would all wake up in the morning coughing.

The small amount of black coal that was allocated to us we would try to keep for winter heating. The temperature in Qingdao could go as low as minus fifteen degrees Celsius, and often the inside of our house felt colder than the outside. We'd mix the black coal with some dirt to make it last longer. Even heating up some water for the washing was a luxury for my niang. But our patched clothes were always clean. She took immense pride in making her seven sons look well cared for.

Every aspect of life was hard for my parents. We even had to sleep in the same bed. Jing Tring and I slept with them until I was eleven. All four of us, head-to-toe. I hated my brother's smelly feet right by my face, and he must have hated me more since I was taller than he was. Sometimes he'd end up on my side of the kang with the quilt all to himself, and I'd have to grab the quilt back. But I loved sleeping with my parents. It felt so safe. I often wondered why my niang always looked for her hairpins on my dia's side in the mornings and imagined what they were up to while we were asleep. So often I tried to pretend that I was asleep in order to find out their secrets, but I never managed to stay awake.

I rarely saw a smile from my niang, but when I did, my heart would blossom like a lotus flower. I would have given anything to make her smile. Occasionally, in my naïve way, I tried to cheer her up with stories. When I was only little, my second brother had done some jobs for someone in the village and he'd paid my brother with a young goat. We put all our prayers into that goat, hoping that when she grew up she might produce some milk for us which we could sell for cash. I loved that goat. I took her anywhere I could to feed her grass and I brought grass home for her every day.

As I passed our main bedroom window one day, I overheard one of my niang's friends telling her, "I heard there is a rare and special goat that will sneeze out a worm sometimes. This worm can cure some rare diseases. The government in Beijing would pay a lot of money for it!"

Not long after, as I was going to take the goat to eat some grass before sunset, my niang said, "Just look at this skinny goat! Do you think anyone in their right mind would give away a milk-producing goat?" I knew she was in despair over our shortage of food that day, and she was short-tempered. I tried to think of something that would cheer her up and suddenly remembered her friend's tale about the goat.

I put on my best innocent face. "Niang, I saw our little goat sneeze out a worm the other day."

She looked alarmed, and asked me excitedly, "What does the worm look like?"

"A whitish caterpillar about the size of my finger." I stuck out my second finger.

"What happened to the worm?" she asked eagerly.

"The goat ate it very quickly," I replied casually.

"Next time when she sneezes out the worm you must pull the goat away from it and try to capture it. This kind of worm is worth a lot of money!" She became happier then, and seemed to dream. "Maybe this is our savior goat," she murmured to herself, and she would forget about her despair for a while.

But one day I told the same story once too often and she realized I had been making it up all along. "Get lost! Don't think you can fool me again!"

What a shame, I thought. Now I would have to think of a cleverer tale to cheer her up.

And the goat? She eventually died, from starvation, the following winter.

My niang was also recognized as one of the best seamstresses in the village. Sewing was one of the most important pastimes for the ladies. My parents simply had no money to buy ready-made clothes, and my niang didn't have a sewing machine. So the older ladies would teach the younger ones, and they often gathered together as a sewing group in our small, crowded house, even though they knew we were very poor, to share their secrets, drink tea and gossip. The women of the village loved to come and share their happiness or their problems with my niang, and her sewing skill was admired by many. Her stitches looked as if they *were* made by a sewing machine—small and perfect. Once she was asked by a friend to redo some machine-sewn zippers because he preferred my niang's delicate stitchwork.

My niang's warm personality was well liked and respected by people of all ages in the surrounding villages. Like my dia, she always tried hard to help others. Besides that "lucky woman with seven sons," she was also known as "the live treasure." Men occasionally stopped by our gate to have a chat with her: most women would have been intimidated and embarrassed, talking to men other than their own husbands, but not our niang. For this, Na-na often fondly called her "that wild girl."

But my niang was also an open-minded person, receptive to new ideas. Mao's Cultural Revolution boasted that one of the great achievements of the Red Guards had been the establishment of evening schools. These were especially aimed at teaching the uneducated peasants Mao's communist ideas. We were all given copies of Mao's Red Book. I was six years old then, and I remember two enthusiastic young Red Guards coming to teach my niang to read. She never learned to recognize individual words, but she could memorize entire paragraphs of Chairman Mao's sayings. She would practice while she was washing, cleaning, sewing and cooking: I often saw her lips moving as she silently recited passages from her book. She was considered a model student.

One day, while my niang was trying to make a fire to cook dinner, two young Red Guard girls came into our house to check on her reading progress. She was having a terrible day and couldn't get the half-burned coal to light. Smoke filled the whole room. My niang was a sensible, fair woman: she was polite and explained that she didn't have time to talk just then and asked them to come back another time. So the girls left and she pulled all the unlit half-burned coals out and tried again. She asked me to push the wind box for her. But just as she was going to start cooking, the two girls came back. They kept insisting on testing my niang on her understanding of Mao's Red Book. They had to report back to their group leader that evening they said.

I could see my niang's anger growing. Eventually, she told me to get up off the floor and asked one of the girls to push the wind box. She handed the second girl her wok flipper and asked her to take over the cooking. The two girls just stood there and looked at each other, very confused. By now my niang was frustrated and at the end of her patience. She roared at them. "I could learn Chairman Mao's sayings every day, all day long, until I die, but who is going to do my cleaning, washing and cooking? Who will bathe my sons, sew their clothes, provide my entire family with three meals a day, every day of the year? Who will cook things out of thin air? Do you think Chairman Mao's words will fill our stomachs? If you can come back every day to help me do all of *these* things, I will learn whatever you want me to learn—and more!"

The two girls left, red faced. That night my niang told my dia what she'd said to the two girls. He just smiled. That was the end of my niang's educational adventure, and the two girls never returned to our house again.

By the time I was eight, the hard work and poverty had begun to wear down even my niang, strong as she was. She woke up one morning complaining of dizziness and a headache, and she didn't eat any breakfast. My youngest brother, Jing Tring, and I were home with her. She had planned to do a lot of washing that day but found the water in our storage pot frozen hard. So she packed up a heavy clay washing basin full of clothes and, carrying a wooden washing board under the other arm, she headed to the man-made dam on the steep Northern Hill.

I knew she didn't feel well. I begged her not to go. "I'll fetch you some water so you can do your washing at home."

"It will be slippery at the well with all the ice around it! Do you want to die in the well?" she replied impatiently. "I have to finish these clothes, or your brothers will have to wear filthy clothes to school tomorrow." She walked out the door. "If I don't get back before your dia gets home, tell him to come and help me carry the clothes back."

A couple of my friends came over to our house to play that morning. Then, around noon, a neighbor rushed to our house, shouting, "Hurry! Your niang has fainted halfway between the dam and your house!"

My dia was not yet home from work and often he had to finish his quota of lifting heavy materials for the morning before he was allowed to take his lunch hour. Most of the time he wouldn't come home for lunch, but that morning he'd said he would try to get back because he knew our niang wasn't well.

I asked my friends to look after Jing Tring, then rushed to my fourth uncle's house to see if he was home. The door was locked. In a panic I rushed to another neighbor's house, but realized immediately that she would not be able to help: she had tiny bound feet. It would take her all day to walk up the Northern Hill on the rough dirt road.

I ran to a couple more houses and found no one to help. Then I ran as fast as I could toward the dam. Tears streamed down my face. I was afraid that I would be too small to be of any help.

I found my niang lying on the side of the road, her clay washing basin broken in pieces, the pile of washed clothes scattered around in the dirt. She looked so pale. I threw my body on top of hers and shook her violently. "Niang! Niang, wake up!" I shouted, panicking, fearing she was dead. When my face touched hers, I felt it burning and she lay in my arms, motionless.

A few minutes later she slowly opened her eyes and asked me, in a weak whisper, "Where is your dia?"

"He is not home yet!" I replied, frightened, but relieved she was still alive.

She sighed. "Where are your elder brothers?"

"They are not home from school yet."

She sighed again. It seemed hopeless. "Help me up," she said.

My earlier fears were correct: I was too small to be of much help. I held one of her hands to support her but it was not enough and after a few slow wobbling steps, she crashed to the ground again. I felt useless. I wished that I was big and strong enough to carry her on my back. I wept in desperation.

"I'm going to have a little rest here," she said. "Go home and see if your dia and any of your brothers are back."

I flew home. No one was there. I rushed out of our house in all directions trying to find help. Eventually I saw a middle-aged man riding his bike home. "*Da . . . Ye!* Are you in a hurry?" I stuttered, the words like bullets out of a machine gun.

"Not particularly. Why?" he replied, puzzled.

"My niang fainted on the Northern Hill and can't get home. Please help her. She is dying! Please! I beg you!" I spoke so fast and stuttered so much that he had to ask me to repeat myself, but when I tried my stutter just got worse. I wanted to show him my urgent heart inside my chest. Finally, out of desperation, I began to stamp my feet. That helped the rhythm of my speech and he eventually understood.

"Where is she?" he asked.

I pointed toward the hill.

"Don't worry, leave it to me." He hopped onto his bike and pedaled off as fast as he could, with me running behind. He reached my niang before me and was already on the way down with her, motionless, propped on the back of his bike. I quickly went back to gather all the clothes but found nothing to carry them with. What to do? I wrapped all the long pieces of clothes around my neck, waist and arms, and carried the small pieces against my chest on the wooden washing-board. The muddy clothes were extremely heavy, and made me twice as big, but I was going downhill, and I managed to get everything home.

By the time I arrived, my fourth aunt and some other women had already begun to put cold wet towels over my niang's forehead. One of the ladies told me to get some boiled water to make a ginger drink, to help with her high fever. I took two thermal bottles and a coupon and headed for the hot-water depot. The village shared one hot-water boiler. I paid one fen for every water bottle filled, and the old shopkeeper stamped two little red squares on our coupon.

That was the first time I ever saw my niang ill. She couldn't get out of bed for nearly a week. The "barefoot doctor" in our village gave her a dozen different kinds of medicine, and she had to take a handful three times a day with warm water. We were always told to take medicine with warm water. The barefoot doctor was one of Mao's inventions, a product of the Cultural Revolution. They were supposed to live among the peasants, live *like* peasants. Their precious shoes wouldn't be useful in the muddy fields, so they were known as barefoot doctors. By the early 1970s, facing a severe shortage of doctors and nurses in the countryside, Mao ordered clinics and hospitals to train as many people as possible and send them to the countryside. He criticized the medical profession for avoiding the communes and refusing to share the experience of the peasants' lives. Many people were rushed through a short training course. They read *The Barefoot Doctor's Manual* and were declared qualified doctors.

But despite the barefoot doctor's medicine, my niang's fever wouldn't recede, and she kept having dizzy spells. Her lips became covered with white blisters, she lost weight and her eyes sank deep under her brows. I often placed my hands onto the frosted window and then onto my niang's burning forehead to help cool her down.

That week, my dia had to cook, wash, clean and get my brothers ready for school. He didn't have a minute to himself. He rose very early to cook us breakfast and rushed home to see my niang and cook us lunch. Dinner was always late since he had to finish his day's quota before he could come home. My dia's cooking was basic and often flavorless, but nobody complained. We knew how serious my niang's illness was and how hard it was for my dia. I was so frightened that my niang might die. "Look after your dia if I don't make it," she said. "Maybe I will die young, just like my mother."

Everyone in the family, all the way down to five-year-old Jing Tring, was expected to pull his weight. My niang was so worried that my dia might get sick from overworking: we would not survive if he got sick. He was the breadwinner, the rock and spine of our family. But he never showed any signs of frustration or fatigue. He spoke even fewer words than usual that week. He just worked and worked and worked.

We had no money to take my niang to the hospital, and the medicine from the barefoot doctor was cheap and ineffective. So my dia chopped huge amounts of ginger and garlic into tiny pieces, boiled them in the wok with some sugar borrowed from my fourth aunt, and gave it to my niang. She drank massive amounts of this steaming-hot mixture and immediately covered herself from head to toe with layer upon layer of thick cotton quilts to make herself sweat. Then Cunfar and I were sent to the big grain grinder about five minutes away in the eastern section of our village to grind some wheat to make her some noodle soup as a treat. The grain grinder was a round platform pieced together from several thick granite stones. On top was a huge heavy stone ball with a hole in the middle and a strong bamboo stick through it. A person on each side would push the stone ball around to crush the wheat. My brother and I pushed the ball in a circle until the wheat was finely crushed, and when we returned with the bowl of cracked wheat, my dia used a fine wire sieve, which he'd made himself, to separate the flour from the cracked wheat shells. He mixed the flour with some water and rolled it into a thin pancake, then patiently folded it into many layers. Then he cut the pancake into noodles with a big cleaver. He even used a few drops of my niang's precious oil—and *two* eggs! But my niang noticed immediately that the color of the soup was rather strange and after the first taste she asked my dia, "Have we run out of salt and soy sauce?" At first my dia didn't understand, then all of a sudden he realized he'd forgotten the most important ingredients. They burst into laughter. Even in sickness my niang had a sharp sense of humor, and a brilliant, contagious laugh.

It was wonderful to hear my parents laugh again. Niang called Jing Tring and me over. "Help me eat some of these noodles. Your dia has made too much." We all knew that she'd hardly eaten anything the entire week. We all knew she could have eaten twice as much as our dia had made. "Get out of here!" our dia said. "Your niang will never eat her noodles in peace while you're here." Our niang protested, but our dia gently pushed us out of the room and forced her to finish her soup.

Over the next few weeks, my niang gradually recovered, but we never found out what she'd had, though exhaustion and starvation were the likely causes. Her health was never quite the same, and she suffered from dizzy spells ever after. My dia wanted my niang to stop working in the fields, but in her usual strong way she argued back. "We can't afford for me to stay home! Your wage is not enough for all of us to survive."

"If we only have water to drink," he said to her, "it would still be better than you working yourself to death. Our family could never survive without you, either."

But the reality was that our family couldn't live on my dia's wage alone. He eventually agreed to my niang working in the fields only part-time, to ensure our survival.

Every day except Sundays, my dia would ride his old bike to work in the town of Laoshan. It was a good half hour away. He paid someone in the flea market ten yuan for that beloved second-hand bike. It needed a lot of fixing before he could ride it, but he was a resourceful handyman and could fix anything. It was so precious to him that we were never allowed even to touch it. He had to carry all kinds of heavy materials—huge grain sacks, big pieces of stone—as part of his job. He was the tallest and strongest among the crew of five, so he was called upon to carry the heaviest materials. He was also the driver's right-hand man: when the truck had to reverse he would guide the driver, sitting alongside. I was very proud of him. A truck was impressive—most transport was still done by horse and cart in the communes. His job was also considered one of the better-paid jobs in the county and many people were envious of him. He was paid thirty-five yuan per month, almost U.S. $4.20 then! I wished that I could be a truck driver one day, but I knew at the bottom of my heart that my destiny lay in the fields as a laborer, like hundreds of millions of others.

It was often well after seven in the evening before our dia came home in those days. He would be worn out, and my niang often had to massage him at night to prepare him for the next day. As long as I could remember, he never missed one single day's work, even when he didn't feel well.

Apart from my dia's few brief days with a teacher, my parents never went to school when they were children, so they could not read to us. But nighttime was still story time, and our dia would tell us his stories and fables, always simple and basic, but we constantly begged him for them and we always listened eagerly.

My brothers also played their own version of I-spy. One of them would select a word from the newspapers glued all over the walls and ceiling, and whoever spotted this word first would have a turn to select the next. Sometimes we would not find the word for days. Later, once I'd learned to read a little, one of my words held the record for the longest time it took to find. We always thought it was sad that our parents couldn't join in because they couldn't read.

One year, a friend of our dia's who worked in a Qingdao printing factory gave us some Deer cigarette labels. They were green, and we used them as wallpaper for the ceiling. Our dia could not afford cigarettes. Instead he smoked a wooden pipe and cheap tobacco, but he often joked to his friends that he had the luxury of enjoying Deer cigarettes every day because of the labels on our ceiling.

My dia was always patient and emotionally controlled, sometimes stubborn, and always good-tempered. The only time I remember him losing his temper with us was when my fourth brother's teacher came to report to our parents about his bad school marks that year. Cunsang knew his teacher's report wouldn't be good. He gathered together my fifth brother, Cunfar, my youngest brother, Jing Tring, and me and said to us, "Let's make chaos! I hate her, and she doesn't like me either!" We thought the teacher was a disruption to our nightly playtime anyway, so we needed little encouragement. The teacher sat on one end of the kang and my niang on the other. Our dia poured them a cup of tea each. As soon as the teacher started to tell my parents of my brother's poor school progress, my fourth brother gave us the signal, and we began running from side to side on the kang and yelling at the tops of our voices.

Our dia gave us a dark look. "Be quiet," he said.

"I'm sorry about our misbehaving children," our niang apologized. "They are tired tonight."

After a few quiet seconds, Cunsang whispered in our ears. "She let out a loud fart the other day and pretended it wasn't her! It was the worst smelling bomb!" We laughed uncontrollably. "Farter, farter, smelly farter!" we shrieked.

The teacher pretended she didn't hear, but our parents were so embarrassed. As usual, our dia left all the talking to our niang. "You will be in trouble if you make any more noise!" she threatened. She turned to the teacher. "I'm very sorry. I can't wait to send these boys to school, so you can teach them proper manners, but they are too young right now."

"Not only yours," the teacher replied. "All boys are wild. I don't know how you're coping with so many of them."

A few minutes later I knocked the teacher's cup over and spilled some tea onto her clothes. We were like three wild animals. We even broke one of the supporting mud bricks on the kang because we were jumping up and down like monkeys. My parents kept warning us, and apologizing to the teacher.

Eventually the teacher had had enough humiliation. "I have to go now. I have other families to visit tonight," she said, giving us a disgusted look. By now we were completely out of control and sensed victory. My parents continued apologizing to the angry teacher on her way out and begged her to come back another day.

As soon as the teacher was gone, my niang turned to my dia. "Lock the door!" she screeched. "Kill these wicked boys! I can't believe how bad they are!"

Jing Tring started to cry, so she removed him from the kang. "The little one is too young to understand. It's not his fault. Just kill the big ones! See if they dare do it again!"

My dia stormed into the room with a broomstick in his hand and closed the door. I had never seen him so angry. He was tall by Chinese standards, and a scary sight. His face was frightening enough, let alone the flailing broomstick, and he shouted as he swung it at us. "See if you dare to behave like this again!" He hit us with that broomstick so hard that I wanted to dig a hole in the ground and hide.

My niang kept urging him on from the other side of the door. "Hit them harder, hit them harder!"

We kept screaming, "Wouldn't dare do it again! Wouldn't dare do it again! We promise!" We screamed so loud that some of our neighbors came and knocked on our door, begging for leniency, but my niang explained what had happened and our neighbors finally left the matter to our parents.

Our niang's head popped in and out of the room like a yo-yo. "Hit them harder! Teach them a lesson! See if they will ever dare to do it again!" I thought it was strange that her head came in and out like that. We didn't know then that she thought we looked so comical she was laughing her head off outside, but she had to at least pretend she was angry with us and was on our dia's side. What a lesson that was: we never misbehaved like that again.

I can only remember my parents fighting once, and it turned our family upside down. Our dia was invited to a relative's wedding and after a drink or two of highly alcoholic rice wine, he would open up and become a chatterbox. He stayed longer than usual that afternoon, which worried my niang. She was afraid he would lose dignity from overdrinking. She sent us to collect him several times, and he kept assuring us that he would be home soon. Finally, she sent her three youngest sons to get him. He'd clearly had too much to drink by that time and was angry when he got home. He was embarrassed by her sending us so many times and felt that he had lost face in front of his friends and neighbors. They argued quietly at first, trying to keep it to themselves. But neither of them would back down, and it soon became a shouting match.

I was so scared by their raging at the tops of their voices that I ran to our na-na's house next door. She followed me back, hobbling quickly on her bound feet, and shouted at my dia, calling him by his nickname. "Jin Zhi! Jin Zhi, what do you think you are doing? Stop that! You'll bring shame to Li's name." Our na-na adored both her youngest son and daughter-in-law. My parents had enormous respect for her, and in her presence they temporarily stopped their argument. But the bickering continued all week.

That week, even though the house was small and they had to sleep on the same bed, they refused even to look at each other. I could see both of them were miserable, but nobody knew what to do. My dia got up even earlier than usual and left the house without breakfast on those days. The atmosphere was tense and all of us behaved extremely well, with the older boys looking after the younger ones. Our kindhearted na-na was concerned about us. She came to help out. She tried to be the mediator, but to no avail. "I can't believe I have such a stubborn son and daughter-in-law!" she'd utter to herself. "It's hopeless, it's hopeless!"

During the day, little things would trigger my niang's tears, and her eyes became swollen from crying. Life was hard enough for my niang, I thought, but this only added more sadness. I kept asking her what I could do for her, but she would just look at me and shake her head. "If only you could help," she said.

Once she suddenly slumped down to the ground and sobbed, and I rushed to her and hugged her as tightly as I could, and tried to wipe her tears away with my small dirty fingers. She gently brushed my hands away from her face and sat me on her lap. She hugged me, and I felt her warmth seep through my whole body. For a while there were no words spoken, just her sad sighs. I wished that our hug alone would give her enough comfort to get her through the day. "My fate was meant to be unlucky from the day I was born," she said eventually. "I was born poor and will die poorer. My life will be as short as *my* niang's. Promise me that you'll burn enough incense and money for me when I'm in my grave."

"Niang, stop! Please stop saying that!" I cried, and quickly put my little hand over her mouth. I cried, not only with tears, but also with my heart. I was soaked with sadness. I didn't want my niang to leave me, ever. The thought of losing her made me feel utterly wretched. The only thing I wanted was her happiness. I wished I had magical powers to grant her that happy life. But if my parents couldn't solve their differences, what could I do? I was just a little boy.

But I did think of something. Later that day, I waited at the entrance to our village for my dia's return. I waited until it was pitch black. He'd finished work late and was surprised to see me standing there by myself. Before he could ask me why, I said to him, "Niang is worried about you and she sent me here to wait for you." Of course this was not true, but I wanted him to know that she loved and cared for him. Without a word he lifted me onto the backseat of his bike and pedaled home.

My niang was already waiting anxiously by the gate. She was relieved to see us both. "Thank you for sending Jing Hao to meet me," my dia said.

My niang was surprised. She looked at him, then at me, and suddenly understood what I had done. She lifted me off the bike and hugged me so tight that I felt my bones crack. She burst into tears and laughter. "You little smart devil! You little smart devil!" she kept saying.

My dia was puzzled. "What's all this about?"

"I didn't send him to meet you!" my niang said, laughing her contagious laugh. "Who cares about you? It's all his doing!"

"I thought it was strange that you didn't send one of the older boys," my dia said with a rare smile. "I'm starving, what's for dinner?"

"Northwest wind!" my niang joked.

My parents were speaking to each other again, the first time in over a week. The next morning Niang was looking for her hairpins on my dia's side of the bed again.

三

3

A Commune Childhood

By 1969, when I was about eight years old, the poverty around Laoshan and our commune had worsened. I remember going with several of my friends to the beach one day, an hour's journey away by foot, to find clams and oysters or, if we were lucky, a dead fish that was washed up on the shore. We each carried our own bamboo basket in our arms and a small spade over our shoulders. My parents always warned us never to go into the water because of the rips.

Many people were already there, also searching, by the time we arrived. After about half an hour, we'd found nothing except empty seashells. The beach was so clean and bare it was as if even the sea creatures had abandoned us.

Halfway home I suggested to my friends that we should make a slight detour and sneak into the nearby airport to try and find some half-burned coal. During the Second World War the Japanese had built this airport as one of their main cargo facilities. Now there were only a few People's Liberation Army guards and some old cargo planes left. The Japanese used coal and half-burned coal as part of the filler under the runway, and the outer part of the runway had already been dug away by desperate people. Since then the guards had tightened security.

I had only been there once before, with one of my older brothers. There was a line of big trees along the edge of the airport and a small ditch for water drainage. The ditch was dry at that time of the year and we crept along it for about fifteen minutes, bending our bodies down into the ditch so the guards couldn't see us.

There was still evidence of half-burned coal there, about half a yard below the surface, and very hard to loosen. But digging half-burned coal was like digging gold for us. We had no sense of time and we eventually had our baskets full. Carrying heavy baskets with a bent body, though, proved too difficult for us eight-year-olds. About halfway out, one of the boys slowly straightened up and was spotted by the military guards. They immediately fired bullets into the air and started to chase us. We were scared witless. We dumped our baskets and spades, and ran for our lives.

I rushed breathlessly home. It was half past one in the afternoon. "There is some food in the wok for you," my fifth brother, Cunfar, said. Niang had left some dried yams and pickled turnips for me.

"Where is Niang?" I asked him as I ate my lunch.

"She went back to work in the fields," he replied. Cunfar only had morning classes at school that day. There weren't enough classrooms for everyone to go for a full day.

"Where have you been?" he asked me.

I told him what had happened at the airport. He frowned. "You dropped your basket and spade there?"

"Yes, I had no choice! The soldiers would have killed us if they'd caught us!"

"No, they wouldn't," he replied.

"Yes, they would! They even fired bullets at us!"

"You have to go back and get your basket and spade. We cannot buy new ones—our parents have no money," he said.

"I'll never go anywhere near that airport again!"

But he did eventually talk me into going back. At the edge of the ditch I refused to go any further and pointed to where we'd dropped our baskets and spades. He went to look, but the guards had confiscated them. Only some half-burned coals were left scattered around the ditch.

Our winters in those days were bitterly cold in Qingdao, but as well as having to cope with the lack of coal, we also had to deal with lice. They lived with us in our cotton quilts, coats and pants. Unlike our summer clothes, which our niang washed regularly, our quilted winter coats and pants couldn't be washed because they were painstakingly made with loose cottonwool pieces that would have shriveled into balls in the water. The only proper way to wash our winter clothes was to take them apart and restart the whole messy, tiring, time-consuming process of making them all over again. Our niang would spread the cottonwool on our kang and the fibers would fly everywhere, like white dust. She'd have white fibers all over her black hair and clothes. She'd look like a white cotton ball herself. But once they were made, our winter clothes would last the entire season.

The only real way to combat lice was to keep clean. Every weekend our niang would heat up huge woks of water for us and tip the water into an old wooden washing basin. Each of us had a piece of thin washing cloth, and we'd soap our bodies and help to wash each other's backs. If one family member had lice, the rest of the family would too: they bred and multiplied so quickly. It wasn't just our family—lice were everywhere in China. Everyone scratched constantly. In the evenings after we took off our clothes and got under the quilts, our niang always flipped our clothes inside out, trying to kill the lice with her thumbnails. By the end of the evening her thumbnails would be covered in blood. She was such an expert at killing those little bloodsuckers: she had the most incredible eyesight, despite the dim light. We had a single twenty-watt bulb hanging down from the ceiling in each room (electricity had come to our village the year before I was born). Generally, the commune would cut off power at eight every night. Then Niang would light a small kerosene lamp and patiently continue her work. But she could never get rid of the lice completely because they lived inside the seams of the fabric. They only came out to suck our blood during the day when we wore our clothes.

I have so many vivid childhood memories like these, but I do not ever remember going to a doctor or hospital as a child: not that I didn't get sick, but we could never afford it. The only time I got close to a medical person was waiting in line for a barefoot nurse to give us smallpox shots. We had to wait in long lines in our commune square with our sleeves rolled up. The nurse used the same needle to inject everybody, and small pieces of alcohol-soaked cottonwool to clean the needle heads and skin. Mothers held screaming babies in their arms, but children aged five or over were expected to be brave enough to go up the line by themselves. Crying wasn't an option, no matter how much it scared us or how much it hurt. When I cut myself I was told by my parents to swipe my fingers on the windowsill to gather some dust to put on the cut and stop the bleeding. This was our Band-Aid and antiseptic all in one.

Our niang's remedy for severe coughs, however, involved a snakeskin collected in the fields during autumn when snakes shed their skin. She would wrap the snakeskin around a piece of green onion and make me eat it in front of her. All of it. The snakeskin was like tasteless plastic and it looked disgusting. It always made me want to vomit, but it was the most effective treatment for sore throats and coughs we had.

One day my face and neck swelled up for several days because of infected glands. Niang took me to a neighbor and he brought out a calligraphy set. He ground the black ink stick in an ink plate and mixed in some water. He dipped in his paintbrush. I thought he was going to write a secret recipe to cure my infection, but instead he asked me to close my eyes and he started to draw on my face. As he drew, he uttered some strange words to the god of healing. I didn't understand the words, but I enjoyed the cool sensation of the ink on my skin. I felt as though someone other than my niang was pampering me for the first time in my life. Eventually my entire face and neck were black. I looked scary, comical—like an evil Beijing Opera character.

I had to keep the ink on my face and neck for two whole days. I refused to go outside. My brothers just kept laughing at me. Luckily I hadn't started going to school yet, so I didn't have to face teachers and classmates as well. My swelling disappeared within two days, but still I wonder if the swelling would have gone away anyway, without the embarrassing made-up face.

Another childhood ordeal for us was warts, which we called "monkeys." An elderly man in our village, whom we called the "Wuho man," told my niang that the best way to eradicate monkeys was to wet them on the grain grinder on the day of rain. The Wuho man was in his late seventies. He was a funny old man with a good sense of humor. He had poor eyesight, rotten teeth and a long silver beard. He always had a palm-leaf fan in his hand and smoked an ancient pipe. His walk was rather stylish, with his hands folded behind his back, and he coughed and spat a lot.

He told our niang that for this treatment to work we had to keep our mouths shut on the way to and from the grinder.

So, just after rain one day, my niang said to me, "Take Jing Tring to the grinder and wet your monkeys with the water from it."

"But you promised me that I could play with Sien Yu after the rain stopped!" I replied. I didn't want to go. I thought it would be a waste of time. And I hated always having to look after Jing Tring.

"You can't go and play with Sien Yu unless you take Jing Tring to the grinder first," she threatened.

I so eagerly wanted to play with my friend that reluctantly I agreed.

Before we left for our five-minute walk to the grain grinder, our niang reminded us, "Remember, don't talk to anyone! This treatment won't work if you utter a single word on the way there and back."

I was very annoyed. I felt it would be an easy task for me not to speak, but it would be hard for Jing Tring. He was still so little. "I'll kill you if you open your mouth, do you understand?" I said to him just before we stepped out our gate. He just nodded. I took his hand and embarked on this special mission.

The first couple of minutes we managed to keep our mouths shut because we didn't meet anyone. But once we'd gone about halfway, we saw Sien Yu's mother coming toward us. "*Ni hao, liu su. Ni hao, qi su,*" she said politely, acknowledging us as sixth and seventh uncles. "Sien Yu is waiting for you at home. Are you on your way there?" she asked.

"*Ni hao, zhi xi fu.*" I returned her acknowledgement, greeting her as my nephew's wife. "I'll be coming soon!"

I couldn't believe it. I couldn't believe *I* was the stupid one, not Jing Tring. We had to go back and start our journey all over again.

Jing Tring was very unhappy and didn't want to cooperate. He kept saying, "I'm tired! I'm tired! I'm too tired to walk!"

"If you don't go," I threatened him, "your monkeys will spread all over your arms, your body, your face and maybe even in your eyes!"

"I don't want to go again! I can't!" he said.

I was desperate by this time. I didn't want to miss out on playing with Sien Yu. "Tell you what, I'll take you with me to Sien Yu's house if you finish this task with me." Jing Tring always wanted to do exactly what I did.

"You promise?" he asked excitedly.

"Yes, I promise," I replied.

"You dare to spit on it?" he asked again.

Annoyed, I spat on the ground and stamped my foot on it so that if the promise wasn't kept it would bring me unthinkable bad luck.

We went back home and started our journey again. Just as I thought things were going smoothly, we saw Sien Yu coming toward us, excitedly shouting, "What's taken you so long? I was on my way to your house to get you."

Just as I put my finger to my mouth to tell him to keep quiet, Jing Tring shouted happily, "My sixth brother promised me that I can play with you after our secret mission!" We had failed on our second try, and the old Wuho man had said that we were only allowed to try this journey three times in a single day. It was just like Jing Tring to ruin everything, I thought.

This time my little brother adamantly refused to walk. Even my promise of taking him to Sien Yu's house didn't work. "I want to stay home, I want to stay home!" he screamed.

"You children, the only thing you know how to do well is eat!" our niang said to us when we arrived back home for the second time. "Don't tell me you can't even keep your mouths shut for a few minutes."

This time, out of desperation, I carried my little brother on my back. "Shut your eyes. Close your mouth. If I hear a single sound from you, I will throw you into the well and you can spend the rest of your life with the frogs!" That scared him so much that he did as he was told. This time we completed our task, and a month later our warts had completely disappeared.

Despite our hardships, however, there were occasional joys too in our childhood. The one time of the year that we all looked forward to, the one time when we would be guaranteed wonderful food, was the Chinese New Year.

Our niang had to make and steam many bread rolls for the Chinese New Year, as gifts for our relatives. She made them in the shape of fish and peaches, representing peace and prosperity, and gold bars representing wealth. Making the bread was time-consuming. The bread rolls would split if the dough had not been kneaded perfectly. She would be too embarrassed to take the split ones to our relatives, so we would keep those for ourselves. I always wished for more split ones, but she was such a perfectionist there would be very few of those and she rarely had sufficient flour to make enough bread for the gifts, let alone for us. During the holiday season we often had corn bread, second best to wheat bread, and it was such a treat.

Before dark on New Year's Eve, my dia and my fourth uncle would take me and my brothers to my ancestors' graveyard. We took bottles of water, representing food and wine, and stacks of yellowish rice paper stamped with the shape of old gold coins, which symbolized spending money. We took many bunches of incense, representing gold bars, and carried paper lanterns. All the children had pocketsful of firecrackers. We spread the rice papers and stuck the incense on top of each grave. After we lit the paper money and the incense, we would kneel in front of each tomb and kowtow three times, calling out each ancestor's name, following a strict order, starting with the eldest of us and ending with the youngest.

"Dia, how can the dead people hear us if they are dead?" I asked.

"They know," he replied with his usual brevity.

Just before we left the graveyard to go home for our special dinner, we asked each of our ancestors to follow us home for the New Year's holiday. Our dia and our fourth uncle poured the bottles of water in front of each grave. On the way home we made sure our lanterns were brightly lit, so our ancestors' spirits could see clearly the road ahead. The children lit the firecrackers to wake the ancestors up. *"Xing gan wo men hui jia. Lu bu ping. Man man zou."* Our dia and our uncle would ask our ancestors to walk slowly and not trip on the uneven road. They talked to our ancestors as though they were still alive. My brothers and I thought this was funny, but we had to take this occasion very seriously. Our ancestors' spirits lived on, like gods in a better world, because they had been kind people before they died. They had the power to help us, influence our well-being and our fate.

The meal that night was Niang's favorite to cook, because this was the only time she had enough good ingredients. She had saved all year long for this. Cold dishes came first: marinated jellyfish with soy sauce and a touch of sesame oil; seaweed jelly with smashed up garlic and soy sauce; marinated salty peanuts and pig-trotter jelly. Then hot dishes: fried whole flounder, and we always pushed the head to our dia's side of the plate. It was the most precious part of the fish to have. But our dia didn't touch it until our niang came to sit down, and then he would push it to her side of the plate. Then there was a steaming egg dish with green chives and rice noodles. There would have been at least ten eggs in it! It was so delicious that it just melted in my mouth. There were several vegetable dishes too and they all had small pieces of meat in them. The aroma of all this delicious food, mixed with the Chinese rice wine, the incense and the pipe smoke, was unforgettable. It was so distinctively the Li family smell. And it only occurred once a year, on that special Chinese New Year's Eve.

I always volunteered to help Niang push the wind box on those nights. I dearly wanted to stay on the kang to feast on her delicious food with the rest of the family, but even more I wanted to be with my niang on this special night. I didn't want her to be cooking alone. She would bubble with happiness while she cooked. *"Da kai huo tao. Rang ta tiao wu."* Let the flame dance now, she would say. Or, *"Rang huo tao man xia lai."* Slow down the fire, let it simmer. Even pushing the wind box was fun. That night we would use black coal, not half-burned coal, and the flame would flare immediately with each push and pull of the wind box. I often wondered if the god of fire, if there was one, was happy that particular night. I wished he would be happy all the time.

Everything was special and magical that night. Each dish tasted better than the previous one served. Everyone chatted enthusiastically, but the one who talked the most that night was our dia. Happiness filled up everyone's hearts. We would forget hardship. We felt privileged. There were always too many dishes to fit on the wooden tray and many would end up on the kang. I wondered why we didn't spread these delicious dishes through-out the year. How much could we eat in one night?

The meal always ended with steaming pork-and-cabbage dumplings, all handmade by our niang. They looked precious and smelled exquisite! I always saved plenty of room for them. They truly were a labor of love. Our niang would put a one-fen coin into a dumpling, and whoever found it was destined to have luck throughout the year. One year nobody found that fen, even though our niang swore she'd put it in. Did someone eat it with-out even noticing? we asked. Nobody was surprised. We swallowed those dumplings as if we were wolves.

The very first bowl of dumplings to be served was lucky food, for the gods of the kitchen, of harvest, prosperity, long life and happiness. The second bowl of dumplings was for our ancestors. Before our niang placed each bowl of dumplings at the center of the table, with incense on either side, she would pour some broth onto the ground in four directions. "Gods, my kind gods," she would murmur, "please eat our humble food. We are blessed by your generosity." The square table was always placed in the middle of the room, against the northern wall. Before Chairman Mao and the Cultural Revolution we would have displayed a family tree and a picture of the god of fortune too, on the wall just above the table. But this was an old tradition now, a threat to communist beliefs. Any family doing this would be regarded as counter-revolutionary and there were heavy penalties, including jail.

Nobody was to touch those dumplings my niang left at the center of the table, but they always mysteriously disappeared overnight. "The gods and our ancestors have eaten them," our niang would say. I thought this was incredible, and believed her wholeheartedly.

After the meal we would go from house to house to pay our respects and wish everyone a happy and prosperous New Year. Every gate in the village was wide open. Nobody was supposed to sleep. We would play tricks on our friends if we caught any of them sleeping. Once we tied a firecracker to a friend's ankles and when he moved his legs in his sleep the firecracker went off and gave him a dreadful fright.

After midnight, firecrackers could be heard everywhere and would last throughout the night. Thousands of small red-and-white pieces of firecracker paper splattered around the streets. Many of the firecrackers we made ourselves. My favorite was the "double kicker." It was as long as an adult's finger, and once we lit it the first explosion happened in our hand and it would shoot off for about ten or fifteen yards, when the second explosion would go off.

On New Year's Day we would sleep until midmorning. Everyone was exhausted, but nobody cared. The holiday spirit lived on.

On alternate years, we went to one of our aunties' houses on New Year's Day. I loved my aunts, but my youngest auntie's house had more action, and the meals in her house would sometimes last for three or four hours. She was a beautiful lady and a good cook, with three girls and a boy, and a husband who would sing and tell us stories. He was one of the best furniture painters in Qingdao. Often he would tell us about the knowledge and tradition behind painting a piece of wood. He was very funny. He

47

loved drinking rice wine and once he'd had one small glass his voice would rise an octave and he would begin to sing tunes from some of the old Beijing Operas. He also had many photos of himself taken in different cities around China. I loved looking at them. It was unusual for a person to travel so much in China then. Most people never left the city they were born in, but because of my uncle's painting skills he was invited to attend painting seminars throughout China. I was fascinated by these beautiful photos, by the places he'd been to. We only had a few photos in our house, and I asked my parents why. "You will lose a layer of skin with each photo taken," our dia replied, "and you only have so many layers of skin to lose before you die."

"Then why did my uncle have so many pictures taken? He is still alive and well," I asked.

"Just wait," our dia would say ominously.

Our niang always sighed upon hearing our dia's explanation. She knew we were simply too poor to afford them.

The second day of the New Year was the day we farewelled our ancestors. We would light lanterns and incense and show our ancestors the way back to their graves. We would shower them with more symbolic food, drink and money, and wish them a year of good fortune and peace.

On the third day of the New Year, married daughters would visit their families. Our niang would take two or three sons with her, dressed up in our best clothes, and she would make a huge fuss about how we should behave. She took two basketfuls of bread rolls for her father and eldest brother. This was an important day for her. It was as though she had to show her family how well she'd done being married to the Li family.

We left our house before half past seven in the morning to catch the eight o'clock bus to the city. The rickety old bus was always crowded with people squeezed tightly in. We often sat on each other's laps for the one-hour trip because the elderly always

48

had first preference for seats, and the old bus clucked and chuckled along so slowly that it seemed as if the wheels would fall off or the engine would stop any minute. The bus door had to be pulled hard to open and shut it. At each stop, people pushed their way on or off, but many people couldn't get on at all because there was no room and many missed their stops altogether. One time we all had to walk because the bus really did break down halfway there. When the next bus arrived an hour later, it was as full as the bus we'd just been on.

After our niang's mother passed away, her father married a country girl the same age as our niang and moved his family to Qingdao City. Better times had come for him. He was a carpenter. The city people could afford to pay more than the country peasants for his carpentry work.

My grandfather's place was on the top floor of a very old three-story concrete building that looked as though it would crumble any time. The stairs were badly chipped, and it probably hadn't been painted since the day it was built. His apartment had two small rooms. My grandparents' room was the slightly larger room, and our niang's stepbrother and stepsister slept in another room on a tiny double bed made by my grandfather. There was no storage space. Clothes and other things had to go under their beds or hang from the ceiling or be kept under a piece of plastic outside.

About twenty families on their floor shared one bathroom for men and one for women. Both bathrooms had two toilets—concrete holes in the ground—and they always smelled dreadful, even from my grandparents' apartment, and theirs was the farthest away! I couldn't imagine how much worse the smell would be in summer. We only visited during the Chinese New Year when the weather was cold. One of the toilet holes at least, sometimes both, was blocked and occasionally all the overflowing shitty stuff even froze to the footsteps. I would always find an excuse to disappear onto the streets when I was desperate for a wee.

49

But the toilet smell wasn't the only smell we had to contend with at their place. My grandparents both chain-smoked pipes, and their two tiny rooms were constantly filled with smoke. Luckily we never stayed inside long. In fact we always made sure we didn't by making lots of noise while the adults were talking. Sometimes our grandfather would tell our niang to control her "undisciplined brats." But we never really got into trouble. Niang was just as relieved as we were to leave that stinking, miserable place.

Our second stop on that trip was at our niang's eldest brother's house, Big Uncle's. He was three years younger than she and they were very close. Big Uncle was the most educated man in our niang's family. He was politically astute, and the head of the propaganda department for the Building Materials Bureau in Qingdao. He had a son and two daughters. Their living standard was much higher than ours: we considered their three-room apartment very luxurious.

Big Uncle loved card games and also enjoyed playing a word-guessing game between the adults. The loser had to keep drinking rice wine, and the more they drank the more likely they were to lose. All the children would form a circle, cheering the adult they wanted to succeed.

"I won! Drink! Drink!" Big Uncle would declare.

"Shui shuo ni ying le? Zailai, zailai!" The opponent wouldn't agree with Big Uncle's declaration, and they would get into heated arguments. Often they were shouting so loud the women had to ask them to quiet down. Afterwards I would ask Big Uncle what story each word represented, and sometimes he would tell me a famous fable. He was an animated storyteller, humorous and witty. I thought maybe that was why he was head of the propaganda department.

The fifteenth day of the New Year was always dreaded. It marked the end of the Chinese New Year and the beginning of our harsh life once again. We were told this night was traditionally enjoyed by the emperor's family as the "Night of Lights." Beijing and other big cities would display magical lights and set off many fireworks. But the best we could do was to make torches from candlewax. We would walk around the house and shine the torches into every corner to keep the evil spirits away. Our fourth uncle always took huge pleasure in making the torches for us. We gathered wooden sticks and he would wrap pieces of white cotton tightly around the tip and dip them into a big pot of melted candlewax. Sometimes he even let us do some dipping if we behaved ourselves. I loved watching the wax harden on the tip of the sticks, and even more I enjoyed running and twisting the torch around, making different shapes in the dark. My favorite shape to make was a dragon, and I pretended my torch was a magical Kung Fu weapon as I twirled it around.

Our parents always warned us to keep the torches away from the piles of dried grass or hay that were used to ignite the coal and that every family stored in their front yard. Once I remember a neighbor's house nearly caught fire because a five-year-old boy hid in their haystack with a lit incense in his hand. The boy barely escaped from the burning haystack alive.

Chinese New Year was our dia's only holiday. Since the weather was normally very cold and the fields frozen at that time of the year, there was not much work to do on our little piece of land. Our main outdoor activity during these days was kite flying. I often sat myself apart from the other kite-flying boys. For them this was just another game, but for me this time was special. My kite wasn't ordinary. It was my messenger to the gods, my secret communication channel.

Our dia was an expert kite maker. He made very simply shaped kites: a square, a six-pointed star and a butterfly. He used an ancient Chinese cutting knife, the size of a Swiss army knife, to thinly slice the bamboo sticks. Then he'd tie the corners with thread and glue rice paper over the frame. To counter the weight we would hang long strips of cloth on the tail. The kite string was pieced together from anything we could find.

I adored making kites with our dia. This was one of the few playful times I could have with him. He would take us up to the fields on the Northern Hill and he'd sit next to me and tell me stories from his childhood. I never wanted these special moments to end.

At this time of the year there was always thick snow in the fields. The freezing, howling wind felt like small sharp knives cutting into my skin. The fields smelled, as always, of human manure. My dia would help my kite into the sky, then stand up, ready to leave. "Are you all right now? I'm going home. I've got work to do."

"Dia, can you tell me a story before you go?"

"I've told you all the stories I have."

"Please tell me 'The Frog in the Well' story again," I begged. He sat next to me, put his arm around my shoulder, and began:

There was a frog that lived in a small, deep well. He knew nothing but the world he lived in. His well and the sky he could see above it were his entire universe.

One day he met a frog who lived in the world above. "Why don't you come down and play with me? It's fun down here," the frog in the deep well asked.

"What's down there?" the frog above asked.

"We have everything down here. You name it. The streams, the undercurrent, the stars, the occasional moon, and we even get flying objects coming down from the sky sometimes," the frog in the well answered.

The frog on the land sighed. "My friend, you live in a confined world. You haven't seen what's out here in the bigger world." The frog below was very annoyed. "Don't you tell me that you have a bigger world than ours! My world is big. We see and experience everything the world has to offer," the well frog said.

"No, my friend. You can only see the world above you through the size of the well. The world up here is enormous. I wish I could show you how big it is," the frog above replied.

The frog in the well was angry now. "I don't believe you! You are telling me lies! I'm going to ask my dia." He told his dia about his conversation with the frog on the land. "My son," he said with a saddened heart, "your friend is right. I heard there is a much bigger world up there, with many more stars than we can see from here."

"Why didn't you tell me about it earlier?" the little frog asked.

"What's the use? Your destiny is down here in the well. There is no way you can get out of here," the father frog replied.

The little frog said, "I can, I can get out of here. Let me show you!" He jumped and hopped, but the well was too deep and the land was too far above.

"No use, my son. I've tried all my life and so did your fore-fathers. Forget the world above. Be satisfied with what you have, or it will cause you such misery in life."

"I want to get out, I want to see the big world above!" the little frog cried determinedly.

"No, my son. Accept fate. Learn to live with what is given," his dia replied.

So the poor little frog spent his life trying to escape the dark, cold well. But he couldn't. The big world above remained only a dream.

"Dia, are we in a well?" I asked.

He thought for a while. "Depends on how you look at it. If you look at where we are from heaven above, yes, we're in a well. If you look at us from below, we're not in a well. Will you call where we are heaven? No, definitely not," he replied.

I thought about that poor frog in the well many times. I felt sad and frustrated. We were all trapped in a well too, and there was no way out.

So I would use my kite to send messages to the gods. I found refuge from the freezing wind in a ditch and I carried a pocketful of small paper strips. I wet both ends of the paper with my tongue and looped it around the string of the kite. The strong wind pushed my paper loop up toward the kite.

The wish I sent up with my first paper loop was for my niang's happiness and long life. I told the gods that she was the kindest, most hardworking niang, but she was so poor and deserved better. I challenged the gods and said that if they really existed and were as powerful as people were telling me they were, then they should change my niang's situation and grant her a happy life. Suddenly I would get angry with the gods for not being fair to my niang. Then I would become frightened, and beg them for forgiveness. After that, I would send a second wish, for my dia's good health.

But my last wish was my most important of all. I looped a third piece of paper around the kite string, and wished to get out of the deep, dark well. I confessed to the gods all my inner feelings. I made my secret wish. I daydreamed about all the beautiful things in life that were not mine. I begged them for more food for my family. I begged the gods to get me out of the well so I could help my family. My imagination traveled far beyond the faraway kite into my own special land.

My messages to the gods often got stuck at the knots in the string along the way. I had to shake and jerk the string to get my messages past the knots. Sometimes I would have many messages stuck at different knots on the kite string, and often I was the last one to leave the freezing-cold fields on the Northern Hill. But the cold always gave in to my imagination. It was my imagination that kept my heart warm and my hopes alive.

四

4

THE SEVEN OF US

My brothers and I were like all other boys, fighting at times and getting on each other's nerves. But the bond between us was strong: we were expected to love and care for each other, to be happy for each other's achievements. The older brothers were expected to look after the younger ones and the younger ones to respect the older.

Our dia and his fourth brother grew up very close too, although my dia was nearly eight years younger. My fourth uncle and aunt could not have children, so out of love and compassion my parents agreed to let them adopt their third son. So, before he was two years old, my third brother, Cunmao, was given to my uncle and auntie a couple of houses away, and we always thought we were cousins.

It wasn't until years later, when he was a teenager, that he found out the truth.

I was feeding our hens that day with what little grain we could spare, when Cunmao stormed into our house. "Where is my seventh niang?" he shouted, which was what he called our niang.

"She is sewing on the kang," I told him. He looked so strangely emotional that I quietly followed him, and listened.

"Why did you give me away? Why not one of the others?" I heard Cunmao demand angrily.

"This was decided even before you were born," our niang replied gently. "You were not singled out. I love you just like my other sons."

"I want to come back!" he said.

There was silence. "No, you can't," our niang said at last, her voice quivering.

"You're my niang and I'm your third son. I want to come back!" I could hear his shaking voice. He was close to tears.

Our niang let out a long sigh. "I beg you to forget that I'm your real mother! Do you think this is easy for me to see you around every day? Go back and love your parents. Be good to them until they die. They love you like their real son. You're luckier than your brothers. At least you have enough food to eat. Just look at how poor we are!"

"I'd rather be starving with you than living apart from you!" Cunmao said.

"What has been done is done. Your parents would be destroyed if I took you back now! I'll always love you as one of my sons whether you're living with us or not. But you must first love them and bear a son's responsibilities toward them. You may then love us too if you desire."

There was silence again. After a brief moment she said, "Come here." And through the window I could see them hug each other, sobbing uncontrollably.

I ran away then, and hid in a cornfield. I couldn't believe my third cousin was really one of my own brothers. My heart felt wretched. My eyes filled with tears, and from that moment on I regarded Cunmao as one of my real brothers. I stayed in that cornfield for the rest of the afternoon.

Cunmao's pursuit of returning to his real family broke my parents' hearts, as well as my uncle's and aunt's. But in the end Cunmao respected my parents' position, and he remained a faithful son to my uncle and aunt. I could not imagine what emotional trauma he went through, though, especially as we lived so close.

My eldest brother, Cuncia, we called Big Brother. He was thirteen years older than I. I didn't really know him when I was growing up, because I was only four years old when, in August 1965, he left for Tibet. The central government called for hundreds of thousands of young people to go to Tibet to help advance the government's political agenda: they wanted people like my brother to influence Tibetan culture in the dominant Mandarin way. His journey to Tibet, riding buses, trains and horses, would have taken him more than a week. In his absence, my second brother, Cunyuan, took on the responsibilities of the eldest son. But Cunyuan wanted to be free and different. He too wanted to go to Tibet, but my parents refused. They needed his salary, and they were desperate for a daughter-in-law to help our niang with the domestic duties. So they arranged his marriage to a girl from our first auntie's village. Our aunt told our parents that this girl was hardworking and could cook, and would be a perfect match for Cunyuan. And now, under Chairman Mao, they could even meet each other before their wedding day to "talk about love."

But Cunyuan was in love with a classmate instead. Her father was a county official. When she found out about the arranged marriage she immediately came to our house. "Uncle, Aunt," she said to my parents, "I've known Cunyuan for nearly four years now. I love him and he loves me too! I beg you not to force him into marrying someone he doesn't love."

"Young girl," my niang replied, "you're too young to understand what love is or what is required. You don't understand him. He is not worthy of you. There is no future working in the commune."

"Aunt, I *do* know what love is! I will follow him to the end of the earth. I'm willing to eat only grass for food as long as I can be with him."

"You don't know our son's temperament. You wouldn't suit each other," my dia replied.

"Please give us a chance! I know we'll make each other happy."

"You come from a different background to Cunyuan's," my dia added. "You won't like our poor commune life."

"Yes, I will! I'll get used to it. I promise you I'll be a faithful wife and a good daughter-in-law!"

But my parents felt strongly that this girl came from a family that was too good for us. Cunyuan needed someone who was sturdier, to rein him in. "You're a beautiful girl and you will find a nice husband in the city one day. That's where you belong. We hope you will understand our decision and leave our son alone," my niang said.

By this point the girl was in tears. "Is there any chance for me to marry Cunyuan?" she asked weakly.

"No. He is engaged to someone else," my dia said.

The girl covered her face with a handkerchief and flew out of our house. I can recall it vividly: I'd felt my heart throbbing. I'd wished my parents had given in. I never saw that girl again.

Cunyuan had many emotional fights with my parents over this girl. He resented our parents for arranging his marriage and his relationship with my parents suffered terribly.

I remember my fourth brother, Cunsang, could carry heavy grain sacks on his shoulder and could balance and push a heavily loaded cart with ease. He wasn't the cleverest among us, but our niang always had a tender spot for him. She often blamed the accident he'd had as a baby, when the chairs crashed down on his head, for his poor school results. I loved my fourth brother: he was kind, honest and loving. He always smiled, and he was the only older brother of mine who didn't mind me sitting beside him while he played his card games.

It was my fifth brother, Cunfar, who was the closest to me, however. We were two and a half years apart—and we fought over everything. I was notorious in the family for loving food, and if any food was missing they would always blame me first. Cunfar seized upon this and sometimes pilfered food and blamed me for it. But I loved him. He was my protector against the bullies, my partner in games and my rival in races.

Cunfar always won our wrestling matches because he was stronger than I. No matter how hard I tried, I'd still lose. But I was a faster runner. I'd make him mad by running away from him, calling him Cunfar instead of the more respectable "Wuga," or Fifth Brother, which I was meant to use. He'd stop chasing me because he had asthma, and by the time he caught his breath I would be miles away. Then I'd make him even angrier by copying his coughs and his strange running style. He'd pick up stones to throw at me and swear to kill me ten times over if he ever caught me. "You'll have a silver beard all the way to the floor by the time you catch me!" I'd call back.

Cunfar would often have severe coughs and asthma when we were growing up. My parents tried everything to cure him. Once we had to find a young rooster and feed it a mixture of millet and cooked toad. Twenty-four hours later my niang cooked the rooster and Cunfar had to eat *everything*, including the bones. I wanted to eat his rooster so badly that I stole some from him. I don't know whether it was the toad or the rooster that worked, but a month later his asthma had gone.

So I grew up with my brothers, playing outside, under the sun, in the rain and even in the freezing winter—a wild street boy. Summer was my favorite time because I could play and run in the village and the countryside with nothing much on. Except in winter, I hardly ever wore any shoes for the first nine years of my life.

One day, late in the afternoon, the sun was setting and we were playing hide-and-seek. I was climbing on people's walls and roofs, trying to find a good place to hide. I climbed over our six-foot-high stone wall, over our toilet, trying to get behind the three-foot clay pots where the pigs' food was stored. One of the pots stored fermented millet waste and the other contained wheat shells from the soy sauce factory. But this day my foot slipped on the loose stones of the wall and I lost my balance. I fell headfirst, right into the pot of fermented millet waste. It was thick, gooey stuff and I was only about seven or eight years old and only just about a foot taller than the pot.

Our niang was busy cooking dinner, and my fourth brother was her wind-box pusher. By chance, Cunsang looked out and noticed the shadow of a pair of feet struggling upside down on the toilet wall. He immediately rushed to the pots and pulled me out. "What are you *doing*? You could have found a better place to die than the millet waste pot!" he said.

I was gasping for air, covered with the thick, gooey millet waste, seconds away from losing my life.

But nothing would stop our outdoor activities. The streets, the riverbank, the dam and the hilly fields were our playgrounds. We made our own spinning tops with carved wood and played games with marbles. Of course, we often had to help our dia too, working the small piece of land that the commune allocated to us. Sometimes we worked on it in the rain, trying to capture as much rainwater as possible. We used all the buckets and pots we had. In winter though, we didn't have to help our dia on the land, because it was always frozen hard, and the fields were covered with snow. I loved playing in the snow. We built snowmen and had snowball fights, chasing each other wildly around in the thick, thick snow. Often we would fall on the uneven roads or fields. We would roam wild, for hours, in this white world, in the vast open space of the fields, with the snow still falling around us. We would return home covered with snow, sometimes with our clothes torn, our ears, noses, hands and feet bright red from the cold, and our bodies steaming with sweat under our quilted cotton clothes. More washing and mending for our niang.

One game I especially liked was "fighting on the one-legged horse." We'd divide into two groups. Everybody had to hop on one leg and try to knock their opponent off balance with the other bent knee. If you were knocked down you were out. We usually played it on hills to make it more difficult. Another game we played used an empty can or half of a used corncob as the "object." Every player had a bamboo stick. The middle player had to use his stick to push the object back into a hole, but any player could strike the object and hit it away. Sometimes both the object and the bamboo sticks would be flying frantically at each other and the game would become dangerous. We liked using an empty can as the object much more than the corncob because of the noise the metal made, but we didn't often have that luxury.

One Sunday, in the middle of a summer drought, my brothers and I had just finished helping our dia carry buckets of water to the yam crops. The earth was dry and the ground was cracked. We were sweating and the hot sun burned our skin, so our dia allowed us to go to the dam nearby to cool down. I was the fastest runner, and when I got there some of the older boys of the village were already swimming and splashing in the middle of the dam. The water level was low. The other boys were treading water, so it looked like they were standing and, without thinking, I dived in. I had never learned to swim, and I panicked when I couldn't touch the bottom. Every time I tried to yell for help, I would swallow some water, my head going up and down, up and down. Luckily, one of my cousins was with the group of older boys and he noticed me struggling and quickly swam to me and pulled me out of the water. A minute later I would have drowned.

On another hot day that summer, a popsicle seller rode his bicycle into our village. This was a rare treat! Several of my friends had money to buy popsicles, so I ran to my niang and asked her for three fen.

"I don't have a single fen," she replied.

I knew it was true. She never had any money.

I ran to my grandmother's house. Na-na, our dia's mother, was eighty-four years old by then. We loved our na-na. She often shared treats with us. She had no teeth left, so she could only eat soft food and she often asked us to peel her apples or pears so she could scrape them with a spoon, and she would let us eat the skin and the leftovers. Her eyesight was bad and she was hard of hearing: many times she got us all mixed up, calling us the wrong name. *Zhang guan li dai,* we called it: putting Zhang's hat on Li. She often complained that things were not as good as in her era. She disliked the chaos and change caused by Mao's Cultural Revolution. She used to save her falling hair, twirl it into a little ball, and exchange it for money or sometimes sewing needles. She just might have a few spare fen, I thought.

"Na-na, would you like a popsicle?" I didn't want to ask her for the three fen too bluntly.

"No, they are too cold for me. I haven't had a popsicle for years," she replied.

"Niang doesn't have three fen for me to buy a popsicle," I said. "My dia has the money. Can you lend me three fen?" I asked, and quickly added, "All my friends have bought popsicles!"

Na-na searched around, but had no change, only a one-yuan note.

"I would be happy to take a yuan if you could spare it. I'll pay you back later! I promise!"

She thought this was very funny, me having the audacity to

borrow one whole yuan, and saying I could possibly pay her back. "Ah, one yuan!" She laughed and laughed. I was sure that if she'd had any teeth she would have laughed them off. But she ended up giving me the yuan anyway and I kept my promise. Of course I only used three fen, which I repaid a few days later. I picked up as much scrap metal and gathered as much hair as I could and sold it to the commune scrap-shop for a few fen a time. When I had saved ten fen, I would change them into a note and hide them between different pages of my copy of Chairman Mao's Red Book. After I'd paid Na-na back, I surprised my niang by producing the rest of my savings to buy some bean curd, which she loved. She questioned me at first—she thought I had stolen the money from my dia.

During those summers, some of the nights were unbearably hot. We had no fans in our house, and the breezes were too slight to blow away the swarming mosquitoes. To keep us out of mischief during these hot summer nights, the adults always told us stories. The most popular storyteller was the Wuho man, who had given my niang the cure for our warts. We loved him. He told good Kung Fu stories and countless fascinating fables. When he died a few years later, I went to see his body lying in a simple coffin. It seemed as though his body had shrunk. He had no children, so his coffin was donated by the neighbors and his burial ceremony was simple. I missed him and his enticing stories—they had a profound effect on my life.

One of my favorite activities on those summer days was catching dragonflies. They would rest on the water in the dams and I would sit by the edge and wait for them, a bamboo broom at the ready. I would tiptoe up to them, sweep them with my broom into the water, and then lift them out. Then I would tie the females to a wooden stick and circle the dragonfly aloft, so she would attract male dragonflies. I would pull down the mating pair, slowly, in circles, and catch the male when it was within

63

reach. I caught flies or worms to feed my dragonflies, and I would let them go at night.

I also liked to catch crickets, but only male crickets, which we used in cricket fighting competitions. I loved the sound the crickets made—it was just like music or singing. Night or day I would follow the crickets' singing until I caught one, but we had to take care because we often looked in dangerous areas where there might also be snakes. The crickets were smart little creatures: they concealed their homes well, and would stop their singing long before I got close. A lot of patience was needed.

I was kind to my crickets and tried to provide them with the best food and housing I could. I kept them in glass bottles with rocks, dirt and even grass, along with their water and food, but often my brave cricket fighters would become big and lazy on the good food I fed them. I would reward my top fighter with a female for company. It is not surprising then, that one of my favorite fables the Wuho man used to tell us was about a cricket. We would sit around the Wuho man in a huge circle, mostly with no clothes on because it was so hot, and he would begin, one hand smoothing his long silver beard, his ancient pipe in the other:

Once there was a Chinese emperor who loved cricket fighting. Each year the emperor required the governors in each province to donate their best crickets. To win the emperor's favor, each governor ordered his people to search for the best crickets all over the land.

Under a mountain in a small village lived a poor family, with one ten-year-old son. They named him Brave Hero. His father was a courageous hunter and his mother was kind. They loved their boy. He was the sunshine in their eyes. One day the father came home from the mountains with his biggest catch, a beautiful cricket. He named the cricket Brave Hero, after his boy. The father was relieved—he would have been fined heavily if he hadn't found a cricket within twenty-four hours. The young boy was beside himself with this cricket. He begged his father to allow him to look at it. At first his father said no, but the boy kept begging and he eventually relented. Just as the boy opened the bamboo tube in which the cricket was kept, the cricket jumped out and hopped away. Their rooster nearby ate the cricket up. The boy's father was in such a rage over the loss of the cricket that he ordered his son to find another cricket or else never return. The poor boy went into the mountains. They found him next day lying on a big rock, almost dead. The father cried his heart out. As he picked up his son's limp body, a small and ugly cricket jumped on the boy's pale face. The father brushed the cricket off and carried the boy home.

The parents wept over their dying boy. They placed him in a coffin in the middle of their living room waiting for the last breath to leave him. As they prayed in front of the coffin, they heard the faint sound of a cricket. It was the same ugly cricket that the father had brushed away from the boy's face before. The father was very annoyed and threw it outside. Moments later the governor came to collect the cricket and the father told him that he had none. Just as the angry governor was ordering his guards to burn down the house, they heard a cricket singing from the house. Its sound was strong and loud. They followed the sound to the bamboo tube and found the same little cricket inside. The governor thought the hunter was playing a joke with him when he saw this ugly little cricket and he threw the cricket toward the rooster. Just as the rooster was about to eat the cricket, the cricket jumped onto the rooster's crown and after a brief struggle the rooster dropped dead. The governor was very impressed. He asked the hunter if he had a name for the cricket. The hunter told him that he called it Brave Hero. Brave Hero quickly became the number one fighter in the kingdom. He never lost a fight. He even beat the emperor's fighting roosters. The emperor treasured him.

Back in the mountain village, the boy was still breathing. As long as their son breathed the couple would keep him lying in their living room. As the cricket-fighting season drew to a close, the emperor ordered the governor to reward the original finder of the cricket with some gold and silver because the cricket had given him such pleasure. But the parents' sorrow was too deep. Material things could not bring their son back. One day, Brave Hero mysteriously disappeared from his royal cage in the palace. On that same day the boy became alive again. The little cricket was Brave Hero's spirit. He had turned himself into the cricket to save his family.

I loved this tale. I loved the boy's bravery and I wished that I too could turn myself into a cricket and save my family from poverty. What a shame Chairman Mao didn't like cricket fights.

Our childhood in the Li Commune could never be just games and fables of course. It was around this time that the Cultural Revolution reached its most chaotic period, from about the middle of 1966. Jing Tring and I were too young to participate— six, seven, eight years old. But my three eldest brothers did. They would go out in the evenings and return late at night. They would tell me horror stories about the young Red Guards, how they burned and destroyed anything that had a Western flavor: books, paintings, artwork—anything. They tore down temples and shrines: Mao wanted communism to have no competition from other religions. Communism was to be our only faith. The young Guards would travel to other regions and investigate possible counterrevolutionary suspects. They only had to mention Chairman Mao's name and the Red Guards would not have to pay for a thing. For a brief period, those young Guards nearly bankrupted China, and the country teetered on the edge of civil war as different factions of the military supported different government leaders. But back in the New Village, we knew little of that wider picture.

My parents tried their hardest to persuade my brothers to stay home on those evenings. They even threatened to lock them out if they returned too late. But in reality there was nothing they could do—there was an unstoppable political heat wave sweeping through China. Emotions ran high and wild, especially among young people and especially in the major cities.

Then, one day, the well-respected head of our village was accused of being a counterrevolutionary. My brothers and I watched as a group of counterrevolutionaries were paraded through our village, with heavy blackboards around their necks and tall, pointed white paper hats on their heads. Their crimes were written in chalk on the boards around their necks and their names were written on their hats. They had to stand on a temporary platform in the center of the commune square and confess their crimes to the massive crowd. We went along to watch. The officials and Red Guards handed out propaganda papers. The noise from the crowd was horrendous. One man kept shouting propaganda slogans with a handheld speaker. People were shouting and jeering. During their confessions the accused had to lower their heads to avoid the objects that were thrown at them. If anyone looked up, he would be regarded as arrogant or too stubborn to change and too deeply influenced by capitalist filth. They could do nothing right: if they spoke softly they were smacked and accused of hiding something, and if they spoke loudly they were kicked and accused of having an "evil landlord-like attitude." Their confessions were often disrupted by the man with the handheld speaker, who shouted revolutionary slogans such as "Knock down and kill the capitalists!" or "Never allow Chiang Kaishek and the landlords to return!" or "Never forget the cruel life of the old China and always remember the sweet life of the new China!" And of course there were the endless "Long live Chairman Mao! Long, long live Chairman Mao!" slogans. The revolutionaries constantly pulled the counterrevolutionaries' heads back up to humiliate them even more. Often their hats would come off—almost all of them had shaved their heads to avoid their hair being ripped out.

My parents told us that the head of our village was a good man. I was confused. I couldn't understand what crime he could have committed. A few days later, however, the communist revolutionary leader led a big crowd to the head villager's house. Only then did I realize that he'd been missing from the group of accused during the parade and rally.

The door of his house was locked when we got there and the leader banged on it, screaming, "Open the door, open the door! Otherwise your crime will be increased tenfold!"

Eventually the door opened. His wife stood there, begging mercy for her husband. She told the communist leader that her husband was so sick he couldn't even get off the bed. The leader didn't believe her. He demanded to see him, but when he did he became convinced that the head villager was indeed very sick. A few years later, I remember seeing our head villager sitting by his gate on a little chair. He looked pale and motionless. He'd lost all his hair. Even his eyebrows were gone. I felt desperately sorry for him, but by that time I was one of Mao's young Guards too, and I felt guilty for even thinking that way.

I witnessed many rallies and parades during the Cultural Revolution. The Red Guards said they were killing the class enemies, which included the landlords, factory owners, successful businessmen, Guomindang Party members and army officers, intellectuals and anyone who might pose a threat to the communist government. But there was one particular rally that still, to this day, makes my heart bleed. It was a huge rally. My friends and I went along as usual. We heard the communist leader read out the sentences for about fifteen landlords, factory owners and counterrevolutionaries. Then they were loaded onto a truck. We could see their pointed white hats, with their names written on them in black ink and with a huge red cross struck through each name. They were taken to a nearby field. Despite the adults' warnings, my friends and I followed as fast as we could. By the time we got there, an excited crowd had formed a semicircle around the accused. There were so many people that nobody noticed us peeking through the cracks between the crowd's legs.

I saw the men standing against a mud wall. Someone started counting. Two of the men crumbled onto their knees. One started to scream, "I'm innocent, I'm innocent! I didn't do anything wrong! Please let me live!" Another screamed, "I have young children! They'll starve to death without me! Have mercy for my family!" Then I heard someone shouting, *"Yi, er, san!"* One, two, three . . . Guns fired. The sound ripped through my heart. I saw blood splatter everywhere. The bodies fell down. I screamed, and ran home as fast as I could.

I wished I had listened to the adults. I wished I'd never witnessed this. It haunted me in many of my dreams.

五

5

NA-NA

Chairman Mao's regime not only changed the way we lived; it also changed the way we died. Even the treatment of the dead changed under Mao's rule. Everything changed under Mao.

One day when I was still about eight, I wanted to impress my niang by cooking lunch for the family myself, when she was late coming back from working in the fields. So I placed some of the leftover food on a bamboo steamer and tried to be creative by adding a couple of my niang's precious eggs in a seafood sauce. The fire was hard to make that day, and the room soon filled with smoke. To see if the food was properly cooked, I lifted the big, heavy wok cover. I was so short that I had to stand on a little stool, and the wok cover was engulfed in steam. As I lifted the cover the stool fell from under my feet. Steam from the wok gushed out at my face. I crashed forward onto the scalding edge of the wok, burning my skin, and my niang's six precious newly purchased plates were knocked to the floor, smashed.

I was terrified! I knew it had taken my parents all year to save

70

enough money to buy those plates. And now, there they were, in a thousand pieces on the floor at my feet.

I ran to Na-na's house next door. If we were ever in trouble, we'd go to Na-na's. My parents would never yell at us in front of her. Was I ever in trouble now!

"What's wrong?" she asked when she saw my frightened face.

"I've broken Niang's new plates!" I sobbed.

"How many did you break?" she asked.

"Six."

"How many?!" she shouted. I wasn't sure if she hadn't quite heard me or if she couldn't believe I had broken all six. My niang had proudly shown the plates to Na-na only the day before.

I repeated the number louder, and stuck out my thumb and my little finger on my right hand to indicate the number six.

"Oh! Wo de tian na!" My god! she exclaimed, with an expression of disbelief. "How did you manage to break that many?"

I quickly told her what had happened. Niang would be so upset when she found out.

"Don't worry. I'll take care of it. You can have lunch with me." Na-na looked at me reassuringly. "You broke those plates by trying to help your niang. You're a *good* boy. You shouldn't be punished for this." Then she murmured to herself, "What a world we're living in now. A mother of seven has to work in the fields! I've never heard of such a thing!"

She had already cooked her lunch and was placing some food on her wooden tray as she spoke. When I saw the amount of food on the tray, I knew she only had enough for herself.

"You go ahead and finish the food," she said. "I'll wait to eat with your niang later."

I hesitated. Na-na's food was provided by my parents and my uncles and aunties. Her food was always better than ours.

"Your niang will be home any minute if you don't hurry. I wouldn't be around when she gets back if I were you!" she said.

I gobbled up her delicious bread roll quickly and ran out. When I returned home late that afternoon I found my niang very upset. I heard her sigh to my dia, "Our niang was trying to help cook our lunch. She accidentally slipped off the stool and broke all our six new plates! She *is* getting on in age."

"Is she all right?" Dia asked, concerned.

"Yes, miraculously she didn't hurt herself at all," my niang replied.

I was eternally thankful to my na-na for saving my skin. I quietly slipped into her house that evening and whispered in her ear, "Thank you, Na-na!"

"What?!" she shouted.

I was so afraid others might find out the truth if I said it any louder, so I just gave her a big kiss on her bony cheek and went back home.

My na-na's health became progressively worse for the next half year. My fourth brother, Cunsang, who always had a special bond with her, began to sleep in the same bed to watch over her. But still she worsened—she couldn't walk, she became unable to eat, lost her bowel control and gradually slipped away from us. She died about a year after I broke the plates.

As was the local custom, her body was laid in a coffin, in her living room, for three days. The smell of incense filled our houses.

"Why does Na-na's body have to stay here for three days?" I asked my third brother, Cunmao.

"In case she comes alive again."

"How can a dead person come back to life?"

He told me a story then, which he'd heard from a friend: "A couple were looked after in their old age by their only son and daughter-in-law," he began. "They were not well cared for. Most of the time they were given leftovers to eat."

"Shouldn't they have been kind to their mother and father?" I interrupted.

"Not all people are kind to their elderly as we are in our family," he continued. "One day, a distant relative of the old couple took pity on them and quietly slipped two hard-boiled eggs into their hands. They were so excited that they quickly peeled the shells off and just as they were going to eat them they heard their daughter-in-law coming toward their room. The wife told her husband to hurry up and eat his egg. Fearing their daughter-in-law would accuse them of stealing the eggs, the old man quickly put the egg in his mouth and swallowed it whole."

"Why didn't he chew it?" I asked Cunmao.

"He didn't have any teeth left," he replied. He knew by that stage I was gripped by his story. "Let's stop here," he said. "It may be too scary for you."

"Please, please! I promise I won't get scared!" I begged.

"Only if you promise me that you won't tell our parents I've told you this story if you can't sleep at night because of it!" he said.

"I promise, I promise with all my heart!" I pounded my fist on my chest.

"You swear?" he asked.

I spat on the ground and stamped on it with my foot.

"All right," he continued. "The old man choked on the egg and instantly stopped breathing."

"Was he dead?" I gasped.

"Of course he was dead!" Cunmao replied. "So they bought him a cheap coffin and had a cheap burial. In the meantime, the old lady didn't want to remain in this world without her husband and begged her son to bury her as well."

"*Did* they bury her?" I asked.

"No! It's illegal to bury a live person," he replied.

I could tell the best part of the story was still to come.

"The old lady's only treasure was a pearl necklace her husband had given her, and she wrapped it around his neck. She begged his soul to find a peaceful resting place and then come back to get her. The old man's son didn't wait for the three-day period. He buried his father on the first night after his death. The word spread wide about the buried treasure around the old man's neck. At midnight, a robber dug up the grave and opened the coffin. He could see the pearls reflected in the moonlight. The robber made sure the old man was truly dead before he took the necklace by punching hard on the old man's chest three times. Just as he reached for the necklace . . ." Cunmao stopped. "Guess what happened?"

"The old man's son showed up?" I guessed.

"Ha-ha!" Cunmao laughed heartily. "Are you sure you won't be scared?"

"I already promised you, hurry up!" I urged him.

"The old man suddenly opened his eyes wide and said in a loud voice, 'What do you think you're doing, young man?' The robber, as if he had seen a ghost, jumped out of the grave and bolted away witless."

I sat there petrified to the spot. This was the last outcome I'd expected. Cunmao opened his eyes big and wide, just like the old man's.

"Why did he become alive again?" I asked, terrified, gasping for air.

"I knew you wouldn't get it!" Cunmao scoffed. "The egg got stuck in the old man's throat and when the robber punched him, the egg was knocked loose so he got his breath back. And that's why we have to leave Na-na's body here for three days in case *she* comes alive again too."

"Then why didn't anyone punch our na-na three times?"

"Do you think our elders would do it in front of us? Okay, go and play now."

I still had a lot of questions I wanted to ask, but I could see Cunmao had had enough of me. When I asked my second brother, Cunyuan, about the reason for our na-na's three-day staying, he told me it was just to allow relatives who lived far away to see her before she was buried. But I thought Cunmao's story was much more satisfying.

I was stricken with grief at Na-na's death. At the beginning I didn't mind seeing her pale, motionless face in the coffin, but as time wore on, her face turned strange and very scary. I had nightmares for several nights.

Na-na didn't want to be buried near my grandfather because his first wife was also buried there and she didn't want any fights. She said the first wife always had priority. But she did say to my parents, a few days before her death, "If there is one thing I want you to do for me when I'm dead, it is to bury me properly." She firmly believed that her spirit would live on in a different world. So my dia and uncles asked a good carpenter to make a special coffin, carved with birds, flowers, trees and water. Our youngest aunt's husband painted it, the one who was the furniture painter and had lots of photographs.

It wasn't easy to obtain permission for Na-na's traditional burial, however, since this was now considered an old, unhealthy tradition. The government had just started forcing people to cremate the dead. Our elders had to do a lot of lobbying, at different levels of the commune leadership, but none of the leaders wanted to take responsibility. Nobody officially gave us permission to bury our na-na. But nobody said we couldn't either, so she was buried as she had wished. "This shows how important it is to be honest and kind," my dia said to us. "If it wasn't for the Li family's reputation, we couldn't do this." Na-na's burial was to be the last one allowed in our village.

The village leaders let us select the edge of a ditch for Na-na's burial site. It was a water escape channel from the fields. Any place with water was a lucky place. It lay north of our house, halfway up the Northern Hill.

Before she died, Na-na had personally chosen her funeral clothes, shoes and other essential burial items. She'd made her own clothes and shoes so she'd feel comfortable in the other world. After she died, she was washed with a warm cloth to represent "cleansing her of the filth of this world" so she'd have a clean start in the new world. Na-na's own daughters then dressed her in her burial clothes, a dark greenish-blue cotton jacket, and black shoes with flowers stitched on the soles. The man with the best writing in the village was fetched to write Na-na's name on a large piece of white paper, the same shape as the stone nameplate on the graves. Once a person died, his or her spirit would linger, looking for the place where they belonged. This temporary nameplate would show her that this was her place. If we didn't have Na-na's nameplate put up quickly, her soul might wander away and become lost forever. The man with the good writing also wrote Na-na's name and her date of birth and death on a piece of white silk, large enough to drape over the coffin. At least one person would stay by the coffin at all times during those three days, to "keep the beloved company." Any person related to Na-na or our family had to cry loudly as soon as they walked into the room, regardless of their age. The person who was "keeping the beloved company" had to cry as well and as they cried they would call out the visitor's name so Na-na would know who was paying her their respects.

On the first night after Na-na's death, we used sorghum stems and blue rice paper to make some figures of a cow and a horse, and several child-size figures. A painter would then paint some faces onto these, not human faces, but half-human faces. The models represented food and servants for Na-na to use in her new world. Na-na was so poor in *our* world, I thought to myself, and yet she is meant to die so rich. In reality, when she died, her only possession was a chest of drawers.

As soon as the sun went down on the first day after her death, the entire family formed a procession. Everyone cried loudly all the way to a temporary miniature temple, about ten minutes away from our house. The Red Guards had destroyed all the real temples, so my dia and uncles had to make this one themselves. It was only about a yard or so high—it looked like a toy temple to me, but here the local god would determine if our na-na was worthy of a happy life. If there were a god and he were fair, he would definitely look after my na-na. She was the best na-na in the world. I couldn't imagine anyone kinder.

This procession was repeated again on the second night after sunset, and very early on the third day, the funeral day, just before sunrise. Skilled diggers then went to the burial site to prepare for the coffin.

The funeral itself was expensive. Some families would spend up to a third of their savings on it. Our family hired many people, even though it cost us dearly: coffin carriers, dancers on stilts, musicians, blanket-and-quilt carriers, even people to carry mirrors, combs, cups, food, drinks and, most important, a lot of fake paper money.

On the day of the funeral, the procession began from Na-na's house, with my eldest uncle carrying a big clay pot on his head. At one point he had to drop the pot on the ground. The pot broke into pieces, the signal for everyone to begin crying, one of the only occasions when crying in public was acceptable. Only men were permitted to go to the burial site. The women were left to cry in the house and cook the feast.

The Li funeral entourage was very impressive. Many distant relatives appeared, some we didn't even know existed! The procession moved very slowly behind the coffin, all the way to the grave site. It seemed to take forever. I had never heard or seen my dia cry before, and haven't since, but there was more crying to come at the grave site. We had to kneel in front of Na-na's coffin and kowtow three times before she was lowered into her grave. I remember seeing the little windowlike holes in the grave to hold her mirror, her cups and other possessions.

The closing of the grave was the worst moment, though. My heart throbbed. I tried so hard to drive away that last frightening image of her dead face lying in the coffin. My fourth brother was the worst affected. Cunsang cried for days. He slept on Na-na's old bed for many months afterwards.

We had to wear something white for a whole year after Na-na's death. Our parents wore white shirts, but for us children the only things our niang could afford were white strips of cloth, which were sewn onto our shoes. We often went to visit Na-na's graveyard with our dia and fourth uncle, so she wouldn't be lonely in her new world. Each time, we brought her lots of symbolic money, gold and food. I loved going back to her grave to wish her a happy life, but it always saddened me too.

Within a month of Na-na's death my niang suddenly fell ill with vomiting and a high fever. Despite seeing a few local healers, her sickness persisted and on the second night she had a strange dream: Na-na accused her and my dia of not looking after her. She complained that her house was shabby and that the roof leaked. My niang tried to reason with her. "We looked after you to our best ability while you were alive and gave you a lot of money for your new world. What else can we do?"

"Who told you I'm dead?" my na-na snapped, and turned her back on my niang.

The next morning my niang told one of her sewing friends about her strange dream. "Maybe she needs help," her friend whispered in her ear. "Why don't you do a test to see if I am right?"

"I'll do a test, but why do you have to whisper?"

"There are too many loose spirits! If they overhear our conversation they might play tricks on you!"

After her friend left, my niang took out a pair of chopsticks and a raw egg and placed the chopsticks pointing north on her kang. She lit two sticks of incense, closed her eyes and called out, "Niang, mother of Li Tingfang, if it was you who showed your spirit last night and if you are in need, please show your spirit again now." Then she placed the egg between the chopsticks with the pointed end down. The superstition held that if it was Na-na's spirit calling for help, the egg should stand up on the pointed end all by itself.

My niang opened her eyes and was stunned. The egg was still standing up! Even for a deeply superstitious person like my niang, it seemed a little scary.

For a few moments she didn't know what to do, until the egg fell and started to roll toward her. She grabbed it in her hand, as though it were Na-na's spirit, and immediately kowtowed three times in the direction of Na-na's burial place. "Niang! We will come to see you soon and bring you food and money! Please forgive us for our sins!" she murmured.

When my second brother arrived home from school that day she asked him to take two of his younger brothers to check on Na-na's grave straightaway. Three of us raced each other to the burial site and found a large round hole there, dug by an animal. We were not aware of our niang's dream then, so we simply filled the hole with the loose dirt and told Niang what we'd found. As soon as our dia came home from work, she said to him urgently, "Go to our niang's grave with some food and money, and make sure the hole is properly secured and patched up."

My dia was about to ask what this was all about, but my niang stopped him. "Just go now and I will explain later!"

At first my dia was reluctant to go because all of us were waiting for dinner, but after he saw how serious and determined she was, he went back to the grave, carrying a lantern, a shovel, a bottle of water and some incense and paper money.

Later that night our niang finally told us of her dream and

her experiment with the egg. All of us children laughed and thought she was just being superstitious, but our dia was more thoughtful. "One cannot fully believe it and yet one shouldn't disbelieve it." That's what Confucius would have said, I thought. But even so, our niang's fever receded the very next day.

My parents discussed this incident often. So did our niang's group of friends, whose superstitious beliefs gave them hope beyond the harsh reality of daily life.

But one question that bothered my parents for many days after this incident was why Na-na didn't send her message about her leaking grave to my dia instead. Perhaps, my parents considered, Na-na wouldn't have thought he would take this dream too seriously, or perhaps she thought he would have been too tired to even dream. But most important, they believed that Na-na wouldn't have had the heart to strike down the main breadwinner of our family with sickness, her youngest and most favorite son.

The death of Na-na was the first time in my life that I had lost someone I loved dearly. Every time I entered or passed her house, tears would stream down my face. I kept hearing her sweet voice. I dreamed about her often. I missed her for many, many years.

六

6

CHAIRMAN MAO'S CLASSROOM

The year my na-na died was the year I was supposed to start school. The compulsory age was eight, but there was no room for my group that year, so I didn't start until later.

It was February 1970. I had just turned nine. For my first day at school, my niang dressed me up in my best clothes, a new black cotton, quilted winter jacket and hand-me-down cotton pants with patches on the knees and the bottom, and a hat for winter of cotton and synthetic fur. She also made me a simple schoolbag from dark blue cloth. My dia bought me two note-books, one with pages full of squares for practicing Chinese characters, and another one for math. He made me a wooden pencil box containing one pencil, a small knife and a round rub-ber eraser. Of course, one of the most important requirements was Mao's Little Red Book.

"This is a special day for the Li family!" my niang jokingly declared at breakfast.

"Why?" our dia asked.

"The Li family has one more scholar today." She tilted her chin at me. "I hope you'll study hard. We're not sending you to school to play. I hope you'll learn more than your dia and your brothers have learned from school."

"Mmm," our dia said. "It wouldn't be too hard to do better than your dia."

"Listen to your teachers, follow their instructions, be a good student. Don't lose face for the Li family. Make us proud," said my niang.

I felt apprehensive throughout breakfast. School meant the end of my carefree days. It meant that I had to wear clothes and shoes and conform to rules. School would teach me how to read and write, but deep down, like my dia and my brothers, I wondered what use an education would be to a peasant boy who was destined to work in the fields. How would school help my family's food shortages? I didn't need an education to be a good peasant.

The school we were supposed to go to was about a mile from our village, but there wasn't a spare classroom there at first, so our village donated an abandoned, run-down house as a temporary classroom. I knew this house. It was always vacant. I was told that a childless couple had lived there, and had mysteriously disappeared when they went to another province to visit their relatives. Our commune officials made repeated inquiries to the police but all investigations had failed. Rumors spread that the couple were spies and had secretly escaped to Taiwan. We used to throw stones at the house, and the older boys told us it was haunted. I always wanted to peek through the window and see what was inside, but I chickened out each time. And now this mysterious house was going to be our temporary school.

So, on this first day, a small group of us, around twelve neighborhood friends, walked to our school, excitedly chatting about the house and guessing what would be inside. Halfway there, we met some older students. "Here come the new scholars!" one teased. "Aren't they in for a treat?" another remarked, and they all laughed at us.

Forty-five new kids from four villages were enrolled that year. When we arrived at our school, all forty-five of us gathered outside. One teacher introduced the man beside her as our sports teacher and introduced herself as our Chinese and math teacher. Her name was Song Ciayang.

"Students, this is an important day for you all, a new beginning in your lives! I hope you will treasure this opportunity Chairman Mao gives you. I hope you will study hard, and not let our great leader down. But before we can start our lessons we must clean this place and set up your workbenches." To my disappointment, the contents of the old house had already been cleared out, so we never did discover what had been inside.

Nearly the entire house was made of mud bricks, with German-style roof tiles. There were two small wood-framed windows, but the thin rice paper pasted onto them had long ago been broken by our stone throwing. The ceiling was low and the room was depressingly dark and damp. It smelled of ancient dust, mildew and animal shit. It was revolting. We spent that entire first morning cleaning the floor, scrubbing the walls, and pasting new rice papers onto the window frames. Teacher Song brought pictures of Chairman Mao and Vice Chairman Lin Biao, and we pasted them onto the middle of the front wall. Under these we hung a makeshift blackboard. There were no chairs or desks so we were asked to bring our own foldable stools, which our fathers had made for us. We also had to make workbenches from used wooden boards which were full of splinters.

We didn't learn anything that first morning. We were divided into several small groups, and Teacher Song selected two captains. The girl captain was taller than nearly all of us who lived in our area. The boy captain, Yang Ping, lived in the east part of our village. He was considered privileged because his grandfather had been in Mao's Red Army and had died in the civil war. I never played with him because of the strong territorial pride within our village. And besides, my eldest brother had once been kicked by Yang Ping's father from behind during a fight, and even though Yang Ping's grandmother had apologized profusely and had shown kindness toward my brother, I was determined not to make friends with Yang Ping. And anyway, by the time we had selected our own spot and placed our stools next to whomever we wanted to sit with, our first day of school was over.

Next morning we started at eight o'clock. Teacher Song called out our names one by one from her roll book and we all obediently answered, *"Ze!"* Then she picked out the boys and mixed us in with the girls, which I thought was cruel, because I had chosen a spot at the back with two of my best friends. Now I was sandwiched between two girls I didn't even know.

Teacher Song handed out our textbooks. "Students. Welcome to your first official lesson." She paused. "Do you know who this person is?" She pointed to Mao's picture on the wall.

"Chairman Mao, Chairman Mao!" we all shouted excitedly.

"Yes, our beloved Chairman Mao. Before we start our first class each day, we will bow to Chairman Mao in all sincerity. We should wish him a long long life, because we wouldn't be here if it wasn't for him. He is our savior, our sun, our moon. Without him we'd still be in a dark world of suffering. We will also wish his successor, our second most important leader, our Vice Chairman Lin Biao, good health, forever good health. Now, let's all get up and bow to Chairman Mao with your heart full of love and appreciation!"

We all stood up, took our hats off, bowed to Mao's picture and shouted, "Long, long live Chairman Mao! Vice Chairman Lin, good health, forever good health!"

"Before you sit down," Teacher Song continued, "we need to perform one more school rule: I'll say, 'Good morning, students,' to you and you will say, 'Good morning, Teacher,' in reply. Now, let's have a practice. Good morning, students!"

"Good morning, Teacher!" we replied in unison.

"Good! Now sit down." She smiled. "Raise your hand if you have Chairman Mao's Red Book."

Most of us raised our hands.

"Those who don't have one, please ask your parents to buy you one from town. I want you to have them tomorrow. This is very important. We should follow Vice Chairman Lin's example and never go anywhere without Chairman Mao's Red Book. The Red Book will give us guidance in our lives. Without it we will be lost souls." We placed our Red Books on the left-hand side of our workbenches, as instructed.

"I'll be your teacher for both Chinese and math," Teacher Song continued. "You will learn how to read and write. Raise your hand if you can already read or write."

I looked around. Very few students raised their hands: mostly girls, and I was relieved. I, for one, couldn't recognize a single word in my textbook.

"Good, we have a few smart kids here. Now, please open the first page of your textbook," Teacher Song instructed.

A big colored picture of Chairman Mao stared out at me, occupying half the page, with shooting stars surrounding his face, as though Mao's round head was the sun. The bottom half of the page had words on it, which just looked like a field of messy grass to me. Whoever invented them must have been a peasant, I thought.

"Can anyone read the words on this page?" the teacher asked. The same girls raised their hands again.

"What does the first line mean?" Teacher Song asked the girl sitting to my right.

"Long, long live Chairman Mao!" replied the girl in a proud voice.

"Good, very good!" Teacher Song paused. She glanced over the class. "Yes, we want to wish Chairman Mao a long long life, because our great leader saved us. I'm sure your parents have told you many stories about the cruel life they lived under Chiang Kaishek's Guomindang regime. They were cold, dark days indeed. That government only cared for the rich. Children like you couldn't even dream of sitting here, but Chairman Mao made it possible for everyone in China to have this privilege. Today, I'll teach you how to write 'Long, long live Chairman Mao, I love Chairman Mao, you love Chairman Mao, we all love Chairman Mao.' I'll now write them on the blackboard. Pay special attention to the sequence of the strokes." She turned to the blackboard and wrote several lines with furious pace.

I was stunned. I didn't get the sequence of strokes at all! I turned to look at one of my friends. He just drew a circle around his neck with his right hand and pulled upwards, his eyes rolling and tongue hanging out, as though he were being hanged.

"Okay, now I want you to repeat each phrase after me." The teacher pointed to the first line of words with her yard-long stick. "Long, long live Chairman Mao," she read.

"Long, long live Chairman Mao!" we repeated.

"I love Chairman Mao!" she read.

"I love Chairman Mao!" we replied.

We repeated the phrases again and again until we had memorized them for life.

The next hour, Teacher Song explained in detail how to write each stroke of the words and the sequence we had to use. I picked up my pencil and realized that I didn't even know how to hold it. I looked to my right and copied the girl next to me, but I pressed too hard and broke the tip. I quickly took out my dia's knife, but as I tried to sharpen the tip, it broke again.

"Here, you can use mine," the girl next to me said.

"No. Thank you," I said, embarrassed. "I'm all right."

"I have three. You can use it for this class and return it to me later," she said in a soft voice.

Three? She must have come from an official's family to have so many pencils!

"What's the matter?" Teacher Song suddenly appeared in front of us.

"He broke his pencil," my desk-mate answered.

"Oh dear, and you haven't written a single stroke yet," she said.

My face swelled up like a red balloon. I reluctantly took the girl's pencil. Under Teacher Song's gaze I carefully placed the tip on the paper and to my horror the strokes popped out of my uncontrollable pencil like popcorn, ugly and messy, in all directions. They looked nothing like what was written on the blackboard.

"I can't do it," I conceded hopelessly.

"Let me help you," Teacher Song said patiently. She placed her hand over mine and we finished "Long, long live Chairman Mao" together.

"Good. Now you know how, repeat these words five more times and you'll be fine," she said, and went to help some others. I quickly looked at my friend behind me. He shook his head in disgust at the words he was supposed to write, and made funny faces. Another friend in front of me kept grunting and kicking his workbench. Others gave him dirty looks. It was as though he was a trapped tiger, but my friends' reactions made me feel better. At least they felt the same as me.

It might have been cold outside, but all through class that day I felt agitated and hot, beside myself with frustration. It felt like I was sitting on thousands of needles. My whole body itched. I wasn't sure if it was paranoia or lice. All of the students scratched, even our teacher scratched herself occasionally. Itchiness became a permanent feature of our class for the first few years of my schooling. That day I itched so much I couldn't sit still, and before I knew it a huge splinter from the bench stuck right into my thumbnail. Nobody could pull it out and blood gushed everywhere. I cried all the way home with my bloodied hand. My fourth uncle was there, home from his nightshift, and he managed to pull only half of the splinter out with a pair of pliers. The other half was left in there until the nail fell off a few weeks later. My niang smacked a thick layer of dust on the wound and, with throbbing pain, I was sent back to school.

The class was only halfway through the third hour of Chinese when I returned. The rest of the day went by excruciatingly slowly, and we only had a ten-minute break between each hour. Teacher Song's sweet voice went in one ear and out the other. The lessons were far beyond my comprehension. My thoughts were instead out on the streets and in the fields. I felt trapped and bewildered. I couldn't wait for each ten-minute break to arrive.

During the final hour of our lessons that day, as I continued to try and write with my bloodied finger, I heard a bird chirping outside. My heart immediately flew out and joined it.

I was always fascinated with birds when I was a child. I would watch them and daydream. I admired their gracefulness and envied their freedom. I wished for wings so I too could fly out of this harsh life. I wished to speak their language, to ask them what it felt like, flying so high. I wondered which god to ask or indeed if there *was* such a god who had the power to transform humans into animals. But then I also thought of the constant danger of being shot down by humans or eaten by larger animals. And the birds never seemed to have enough food to eat either, because they were constantly nibbling human feces. Without food, life as a bird might not be much better than life as a human. And if I became a bird, I would not see my family again. This would surely break my niang's heart. Sometimes I thought I might be able to help them more as a bird, flying high in the air and spotting food for my family. I sat at my desk that day and remembered a tale my dia once told me:

Once upon a time, a hunter shot down a bird, his arrow injuring one of its wings. The hunter could speak the bird's language and when the bird begged him not to kill her, to her surprise, the hunter said, in her own language, "I don't want to kill you, but I have no other food to eat." The bird promised him that she would return his leniency by finding food for him once she could fly again. The bird had only one condition: the hunter had to share any findings with her. The hunter agreed.

True to her word, the bird passed on information to the hunter. "There is a dead squirrel up the mountain by the big rock." The hunter was ecstatic. He followed the bird's guidance and found the squirrel. He happily shared it with the bird. The bird went on to provide the hunter with other food, and their sharing arrangement continued.

But gradually the hunter became greedy and stopped sharing with the bird. The bird wanted revenge. One day the bird told him about a dead mountain goat. The hunter followed the bird's instructions and rushed to the location. From the distance he could see a white object lying on the ground, surrounded by a small group of people. He was worried that those people who had arrived before him would take the goat. He rushed toward the goat. "That's mine, that's mine! I killed him!" But the white object was not a goat. It was a man wearing a white shirt. The hunter was charged with the man's murder and was sentenced to death by a hundred cuts. The hunter told his story about the bird, and appealed to a higher court.

The higher court judge didn't believe that this hunter could speak the bird's language, so on the day of his execution, the judge asked the hunter, "What are those two birds saying up in the tree?" The hunter replied, "The birds are angry about their missing children and said, 'Judge, judge. There is no animosity between us. Why did you hide our babies?'" The judge found the hunter innocent and released him, for the judge had secretly removed the young birds from the nest, to test the hunter's innocence.

I liked this tale and its moral: that it's important to keep one's promises. I also liked the fact that the little bird had out-witted the powerful hunter.

That day at school I continued to daydream about my birds while others practiced their writing. I scribbled mindlessly on my practice pad, my thoughts interrupted only by Teacher Song's voice. "All right, that's enough for today. I want you to practice what you've learned at home. It is called 'homework.' Tomorrow, I expect you to remember what we've done today. Do you understand?"

"Yes!" we replied.

"Good. Now I'm going to teach you a song. You would have heard it before. It is called 'I Love Beijing Tiananmen.'"

We'd heard this song many times over our village's loud-speakers. So Teacher Song led and we sang:

> I love Beijing Tiananmen,
> The sun rises above Tiananmen.
> Our great leader Chairman Mao,
> Lead and guide us forward.

The singing became my favorite part of our day.

On the way home we exchanged our feelings about that first day of school.

"What a boring day!" one of my friends said.

"Boring? It's horrible!" said another.

"I hate sitting next to girls."

"What about the bird?" I asked.

"What bird?"

"Didn't you hear it? On the windowsill during the last hour," I said.

"I was struggling so much trying to write 'Long, long live Chairman Mao,' why would I hear a bird?" another friend replied.

We stopped at a sandy bank by the little stream south of our village and were surprised to discover that Yang Ping's group of friends had beaten us there and were playing "horse fight" already. This was one of our favorite games, and I soon joined in with my friends. One person would sit on another's shoulders, and opposing groups would try hard to unseat their opponents. Both Yang Ping and I were physically similar and were the "anchor horses" at the bottom. That day we were the last two standing on each team. We fought one another tooth and nail until we dragged each other down in a draw, totally exhausted, muddy and with our clothes torn. Yang Ping and I immediately struck up a good friendship after that, and our after-school gatherings became frequent. My niang cursed me for my irresponsible behavior, though, because my clothes were always either torn or dirty or both. One afternoon, after our usual "horse fight," Yang Ping and I went on wrestling, tripping and pushing each other to the ground. Yang Ping went down hard on one of his arms and broke it. I felt so bad and afraid that his family might make my family pay his hospital costs, so I kept the accident a secret. When my parents did find out, from one of my other friends, they were livid. "Why didn't you tell us?" my niang demanded.

"I was afraid his parents would ask us to pay for his medical bills."

She sighed. "What a silly boy you are! Yes, we are poor! But we can't lose our dignity over this, even if it means we have to borrow money from our relatives." But when my parents offered them our assistance, Yang Ping's family politely refused.

The only real pet I ever had was a bird that I caught myself during that first week of school. In the springtime of each year, groups of beautiful birds would arrive at the small stream south of our house. Sometimes my niang would do her washing there, and my friends and I would splash or skip stones over the surface of the water.

On this particular day, I'd taken an old pot with a lot of holes in the bottom and a piece of my kite string. I tied the string onto a wooden stick, placed the pot on the sandbank by the stream and supported it with the stick on a forty-five-degree angle. I left a few dead worms under the pot and hid in a ditch about twenty yards away, holding the other end of the string.

Some birds flew near my pot a few minutes later. One hopped under and began to eat the worms. I pulled the string excitedly, trapping the bird inside. I could not believe how beautiful this bird was. I was convinced it was female because its feathers were too colorful for a male. I named her Beautiful River Treasure. My second brother, Cunyuan, made me a simple wire cage for her. I didn't want to leave my Beautiful River Treasure. I was obsessed with her. I collected worms for her on the way home from school. I showed her off to my friends. I even promised them a baby bird each, if I could catch a male bird and get her to mate. I thought she was the most beautiful bird in the world. One day she might teach me her language, I thought, or she might learn ours. I imagined her flying above me and landing on my shoulder whenever she wanted to, spotting food, just like the bird in my dia's story.

I told everyone that she was such a happy bird, because she chattered and sang all day and all night. She drove my whole family crazy, though. "She isn't singing, she is crying, 'Let me out, let me out!'" Cunfar said, acting as though he was the poor bird.

"Don't be silly, she loves me. I'm her savior. Look at all the food she gets."

But in reality she ate very little. After school one day that week, I rushed home with some worms in my hands and found my Beautiful River Treasure dead in her cage. I sobbed my heart out. I blamed every member of my family for her death. I thought they'd killed her because of her singing. I had lost my first and only pet. My heart was broken. Deep inside I knew I was responsible for her death. Instead of helping her, I had taken her freedom away, and I hated myself for it.

I made a beautiful box as her coffin and took her back to the bank of the stream where I had caught her. I buried her under a large tree where there was good Feng Shui. I knelt in front of her little tomb and apologized for my stupidity and told her that she was the only pet I'd ever owned and loved. I never tried to catch another bird to keep as a pet again.

We spent our first two weeks of school in that stinking temporary classroom until a room became available at the proper school. This consisted of single-story brick-and-stone classrooms joined to each other just like commune housing. I knew the local school well because sometimes I had secretly climbed over the walls and played there with some of my friends on Sundays.

But today was different. At eight that morning, the head of the school welcomed us, and we were led by Teacher Song to our official classroom. It was a square room with two rice-papered windows on the outside wall, and a window and a door on the inside. There was slightly more natural light here than in the temporary classroom, and the ceiling was high and the air fresh. Pictures of Marx, Engels, Lenin and Stalin were glued on the back wall. On the front wall were large pictures of Chairman Mao and Vice Chairman Lin Biao, smiling warmly to us from above the blackboard. The blackboard was already filled with the words we were to learn that day. Under the blackboard was a foot-high concrete platform, and we had desks and small benches to sit on. This was luxurious compared to the temporary classroom!

My fourth and fifth brothers were also at the school, and this gave me comfort. It was my fourth brother's sixth and final year before he moved to the middle school, and my fifth brother was in his third year.

After the first two weeks of school, I still had no idea what I'd learned or why I should study. Listening to Teacher Song babbling on just made me sleepy, especially if we had afternoon classes, which went from two until six. The only thing that kept me awake was the thought of playing with my friends during those ten-minute breaks.

After our second class one day, we were told to go out onto the school ground to have our first fifteen-minute physical education class, with all two hundred and fifty students. The sports teacher stood in front of everyone with a loudspeaker in hand and shouted out the eight exercise routines accompanied by recorded music. They were simple arm and leg stretching exercises that took no more than five minutes. The new students were placed in the last line, and we simply followed the older students in front of us.

I found my fourth brother, Cunsang, as soon as we'd finished. "How is it going?" he asked.

"It's boring! I hate it!" I replied.

"Join the tribe. Why did you think I wanted you to make chaos when my teacher came to our house that time?" He was reminding me of the time we received the broomstick beating from our dia.

"How can you understand the writing? It all looks like grass to me," I said.

He burst into laughter. "That's what I thought the first few weeks. It will get better, I promise."

I didn't believe him. "What's the use of learning words anyway?" I asked.

"I don't know," he replied honestly.

I followed him to my fifth brother's classroom on the opposite side of the school ground and found Cunfar in the middle of a pile of bodies, wrestling each other onto the ground.

"How was your first lesson, scholar?" he teased breathlessly, as he dusted off the dirt.

"All agony, no fun," I replied.

"The math is even more fun!" Cunsang gave a wicked smile.

"Can't be worse than Chinese," I said.

"Just wait!" he replied, as the bell rang for the next class.

I had prepared myself for the worst in our math class, but to my surprise the numbers were more bearable than the grasslike Chinese writing. But even so, numbers represented nothing to me, and I still preferred to dream of running wild outside and playing games with my friends.

The journey to and from school was much more interesting than the study itself. Besides stopping at the sandy bank to wrestle and play horse fights, we occasionally detoured to a local butcher shop that only killed pigs. The heart-piercing screams of the pigs were horrible. We would watch as our own pigs, with their legs tied, were carried away to be killed for meat. The pigs always seemed to know what was about to happen to them: they would refuse to eat, even if given better food. I would hear their desperate screams and would press my hands hard against my ears and run away to hide rather than witness this unbearable scene. The thought of our own happy pigs being sliced up by the butcher always made my stomach churn.

I wasn't the best student in my year, but I did earn enough votes among my classmates to become one of the first Little Red Scarf Guards in our class. We wore a triangular red scarf around our necks, and for this honor we had to qualify in Mao's "Three Goods": good study, good work and good health.

I didn't learn much academic stuff at all during my time at school, except the many propaganda phrases and songs, and many of those I didn't even understand. I learned how to write simplified versions of the Chinese characters and some basic math equations, but I really only lived for the two weekly sports classes. I was good at the sporting stuff. We had rope hopping, and track-and-field which was mainly running, and by the second half of our second year Teacher Song had selected Yang Ping as the captain of our class and me as the vice captain.

By this time I was ten years old and the campaign to "Learn Lei Feng" had started in all the local schools. Our textbooks were full of Lei Feng's inspiring stories. He was a humble soldier who did many kind deeds. He helped the disadvantaged and especially the elderly, not for personal glory but because he wanted to be a faithful and humble soldier of Mao's. Lei Feng's diary showed how devoted he was to Mao's ideals. Extracts from his diary were published and included in our textbooks. Every-one of all ages in China was encouraged to learn from him. Everyone wanted to be a "Living Lei Feng." We learned a song that encouraged us to "pick up the screw by the roadside and give it to the police," to contribute to our great country in any way, from the smallest contribution, such as the little screw, to the great sacrifices of one's life, like Lei Feng himself.

One day a student from our school found a coin on the road and gave it to his teacher. He was instantly praised by the head-master as a model student. His action was what Lei Feng would have done. From then on, much money was found by students by the roadside and the headmaster's money jar quickly filled up, until one day a parent complained that his child had taken all their savings and given them to her teacher.

For a brief period some students stopped attending school or were late for classes because they said they were helping the elderly and the needy just like Lei Feng. But they were just being lazy, and the teachers soon found out. A moral, a "tonic story," for these students was told in our classes:

> One day, Lei Feng was late for his military activity because he was carrying home an elderly lady with bound feet. The head of his army unit criticized him without knowing the real reason behind his tardiness. Lei Feng apologized and wrote in his diary that he should be able to do kind things for the needy as well as carrying out the normal required activities.

After this, the school demanded that all kind deeds should be conducted *outside* school hours.

I, like many of my classmates, wanted to be a hero like Lei Feng. The things he did deeply moved me. His spirit of "forgetting himself to help others" was my living motto. Some classmates and I often went to veterans' homes to help them sweep their yards or carry water from the wells. We even picked up horse droppings from the street and took them to the fields as fertilizer. We needed to do at least one kind deed each day and write it down in our diaries. I thought maybe someone would read my diary after I'd died and realize I'd done even more kind things than Lei Feng. Then I would be a hero too! But I was only ten years old. I didn't think of it as another propaganda campaign to secure our loyalty to Mao and his communist state.

During those school years of mine, the central government released Mao's newest propaganda campaigns one after another. Our regular classes were constantly disrupted and we were ordered to study Mao's latest magical words by heart. Often our school organized rallies when we would march around the villages playing drums, cymbals and other instruments, carrying gigantic pictures of Chairman Mao and waving red flags. Everyone carried

Mao's Red Book, and we marched with pride and honor. I felt so happy to be one of Mao's Little Red Scarf Guards. Once I was chosen to lead the shouting of the political slogans. When we passed our village, I glanced around and saw my niang and my fourth aunt standing in the middle of the crowd. I shouted at the top of my voice then. "Long, long live Chairman Mao!" Other leaders shouted at the same time. Different sections of our class followed different leaders. It was completely chaotic, but we all wanted our mothers to see and hear us.

"Niang, did you hear me?!" I asked her when I came home that day.

"How could I hear you? It was like a zoo out there!" she replied.

One day at school, during lunchtime, some shocking news about Mao's chosen successor came through our village's loudspeakers. Vice Chairman Lin Biao's plane had been shot down over Mongolia. It was October 1971. Lin Biao had been trying to flee to the Soviet Union when his evil motives were discovered. There was speculation that the plane he was on contained many top-secret documents. The most nerve-racking speculation was that there were factions of the military loyal to Lin Biao who could be attempting a coup to topple Mao's government.

As young boys we were told how close Lin Biao was to Chairman Mao, how devoted and trustworthy he was to Mao's political cause. After all, he had written the foreword in Mao's Red Book. Lin Biao was said to have always had the Red Book in his hand.

When we returned to our school that afternoon, all scheduled classes were suspended. We were summoned to the school ground. Two speakers were set up by the headmaster's office. With microphone in hand, the headmaster read out a document from the central government. Lin Biao had been planning a major coup for a number of years, and Chairman Mao had narrowly escaped several assassination attempts. How fortunate it was that our great leader was safe and that we would still be able to enjoy our sun, our rain and our daily oxygen! We must study harder to strengthen our resolve so we, the next generation of communist young guards, could carry the communist red flag forward.

After this speech, he ordered us back to our classes to study Mao's Red Book for the rest of the afternoon. I, like all my classmates, was truly scared that if Lin Biao had succeeded, we would all live in the dark ages once more. This only made me more determined to be a good young guard of Chairman Mao's. At dinner that night, all of my brothers talked excitedly about Lin Biao's demise. But our parents' reactions were different.

"Who cares about Lin Biao!" our niang said. "All I'm concerned about is food on the table."

"Your niang is right," our dia chipped in. "Who has time to worry about the government? What we need is enough food so we can survive."

Our parents were not alone in taking little notice of Lin Biao's fate. But at school in the following days we had many discussion sessions about the Lin Biao incident. When there was no more information from the central government, the school eventually resumed its normal schedule.

During my second year at school, we learned how to write "We love Chairman Mao" and "Kill, crush Liu Shaoqi, Deng Xiaoping and the class enemies." I still wondered how useful all this talk about Liu Shaoqi, the Chinese president, and his right-hand man, Deng Xiaoping, was meant to be. Sometimes we'd write these things in chalk on the walls of people's houses. Over time, with people scribbling over each other's writing, all the words became muddled. Some of the older boys often wrote rude remarks about people they didn't like, and common family names such as Zhang, Li, Wang and Zhou often got mixed up in the scribble.

One day, an education official from the Qingdao government passed through our village and noticed some of the writing: "Kill, crush, Mao, Zhou and Lai," it read. The official charged into the village office and demanded a thorough investigation. Many people were questioned by the police. And for the first time I could remember, mass hysteria began in our commune.

The next day, in the middle of our math class, our headmaster and two policemen came in and asked all the students who lived in the New Village to stand up. We didn't know what was happening. The headmaster told us to follow him to his office. The door was shut behind us and we were divided into two groups. The police questioned us, one by one, for a whole morning. To my great surprise, the topic was about the writing on our village wall. I thought it was going to be about something much more important! Did you write on the wall? What did you write? Did you see anyone else write on that wall? Have you seen any strangers in your village lately? Do you know anyone who may dislike Chairman Mao or Premier Zhou? I was so puzzled. I couldn't imagine anyone not loving our great leaders, and anyway, anyone who was a counterrevolutionary would surely have been shot already.

Without any success, the officials eventually let the matter go. But the police appeared in our village quite frequently after that, and none of the children ever dared write anything on the walls again.

It wasn't long after this, on the way home from school, that I found something that was to become my secret treasure. It was a book. Only about forty pages, lying on the street near the garbage dump. I picked it up with the intention of taking it home so our family could use it as toilet paper, but somehow I started to read the first page and couldn't stop. It was a foreign story translated into Chinese. I couldn't understand all the words but I could make out that the story was about a rich steel baron, in some place called Chicago, who fell in love with a young girl. I'd just got to the bit where he used his money to build a new theater when the pages ran out. How I wished I'd had the rest of the book! It was such delicious reading! Love stories were hard to find. I would have given anything to read the whole thing. But the Red Guards destroyed any books that contained even a hint of romance or Western flavor. You would be jailed if such books were found in your house.

I kept those forty pages for a long time, locking them like a treasure in my personal drawer, never realizing the danger I'd put my family in. I read it many times. I pored over the words. I wondered how the people in the story could have such freedom. It sounded too good to be true. But even after hearing years of fearful propaganda about America and the West, the book was enough to plant a seed of curiosity in my heart. I asked some of my brothers if any of them had read such a book and hoped that one of them could tell me the rest of the story. But none of them did. My fifth brother even accused me of making it all up, but still I was not going to divulge my sacred find.

To satisfy our need for stories, some friends and I turned to the opera and ballet storybooks which our older siblings were given at school. We would act out different characters, and especially loved the scenes with guns, swords or fighting. Acting out the dying scene was always a delight! Everyone wanted the hero's role but we had to share that over different days. We play-acted like this even before we started school in the mornings. We couldn't read many of the words in the books, so we based the plot on fables we'd been told or we made up stories and dialogue as we went along.

More stimulus for our hungry imaginations came from the touring movies. Once or, if we were lucky, twice a year, a small group of people from the Qingdao Propaganda Bureau would come to our village to entertain us with a movie about things like

101

Mao's Red Army triumphing against the Japanese army, or Chiang Kaishek's Guomindang regime, or the struggle against the class enemies, or touching stories about Mao's revolutionary heroes. There were also popular opera and ballet movies such as *The Red Lantern* and a ballet called *The Red Detachment of Women,* but the first half hour of every showing always screened documentaries about Mao's faithful followers—unbelievable but inspiring stories for us youngsters to absorb.

The day before the movie was to be shown, our village had to put up a temporary wooden frame to hang the movie screen from. We set our little stools or bamboo mats in front of it as soon as the frame was up, to secure our places and, to prevent anyone from stealing our belongings, at least two of my older brothers would sleep there overnight. Arguments often flared up about whose place was whose, but as soon as a date was set and the names of the movies were known, we would discuss nothing but the coming event. I could hardly contain my excitement! I was such an emotional mess at the movies. *Everything* would make me sob. My emotions would linger for many days afterwards as I went endlessly over the details of each movie in my mind. My devotion to Mao and his ideology was greatly intensified. I wanted to be a revolutionary hero! Another child of Mao! But I loved the Beijing Opera singers as well, their singing, dancing, fighting and acrobatic skills. They were as close to a Kung Fu movie as we would ever get. The Kung Fu masters were the heroes of my imagination, but the Kung Fu books and movies were banned in China then. We had only the folktales told by some of the elderly people in our village to keep that passion alive.

I liked the stories and the fighting in the Chinese ballet movies too, but I really thought the people looked funny standing on their toes, and they didn't speak any words, so opera always won over ballet when it came to choosing a play for us to act out. Secretly I held a dream—one day I would be able to sing and do the Kung Fu steps that the opera singers did. But I knew deep in my heart that this dream would never come true. It was the commune fields for me.

七

7

LEAVING HOME

I was nearly eleven years old when, one day at school, while we were busy as usual memorizing some of Chairman Mao's sayings, the headmaster came into our freezing classroom with four dignified-looking people, all wearing Mao's jackets and coats with synthetic fur collars.

I immediately thought of the incident about the writing on the wall. Not again. What's wrong this time? But to my surprise, the headmaster introduced them as Madame Mao's representatives from Beijing. They were here to select talented students to study ballet and to serve in Chairman Mao's revolution. He asked us all to stand up and sing "We Love Chairman Mao":

> The east is red, the sun is rising.
> China's Mao Zedong is born.
> Here to give us happiness.
> *Hu lu hai ya.*
> Our lucky star who saved us all.

As we sang, the four representatives came down the aisles and selected a girl with big eyes, straight teeth and a pretty face. They passed me without taking any notice, but just as they were walking out of our classroom, Teacher Song hesitated. She tapped the last gentleman from Beijing on the shoulder and pointed at me. "What about that one?" she said.

The gentleman from Beijing glanced in my direction. "Okay, he can come too," he said in an off-hand manner, in perfect Mandarin dialect.

The girl with the big eyes and I followed Madame Mao's people into the headmaster's office. It was the only room with a coal-burning heater, a handmade contraption cobbled together from a bucket, with pipes attached in all directions like spider legs. Despite this luxury, though, the room was still extremely cold.

There were other children already in the room when we arrived—ten children had been chosen altogether, and we all wore our thick-quilted homemade coats and pants and looked like little round snowballs as we stood together in the freezing room.

"Take all your clothes off except your underwear! Step forward one by one! We are going to measure your body and test your flexibility," a man with glasses ordered.

Everyone stood there nervously. Nobody moved.

"What's your problem? Didn't you hear? Take your clothes off!" our headmaster barked.

"I'm sorry," one of the boys answered timidly, "but I don't have any underwear."

To my surprise, I was the only child who had underwear, hand-me-downs from several older brothers, multi-layered and patchworked with mending by my niang. All ten of us during that audition had to share my one set of underwear.

The officials measured our proportions: our upper body and

105

our legs, our neck length, even our toes. I watched a few of the students being tested before me, and they cried out and winced. One of the officials came over to me and bent both of my legs outward. Another official held my shoulders to stabilize me and a third pushed his knee against my lower back, at the same time pulling both of my knees backward with great force to test the turnout of my hip joints. It was so painful it felt like everything would break at once. I wanted to scream as well, but for some reason I didn't. I had a stubborn thought: I didn't want to lose my dignity, I didn't want to lose my pride. And I clenched my teeth.

By the time they'd finished testing everyone, only one boy and one girl were selected to go to the next level. I was that boy. I was excited but frightened. I didn't know what was going to happen. The officials mentioned ballet, but all I knew about ballet was what I'd seen in the movie *The Red Detachment of Women*. I had no idea what ballet was all about.

The audition was a hot discussion topic both at school and in our village over the next few days. At first my parents didn't pay much attention. There was no way in the world anyone in our family could have any artistic talent. Several of my brothers and my classmates teased me. "Show us a ballet step! Show us a ballet step!" But they knew I had no idea. For me, the most exciting aspect of it all was not the ballet but the possibility of going to Beijing to be near our beloved Chairman Mao; the possibility, however unlikely, of getting out of my deep well.

I went to the commune office a few weeks later to go through the next level of audition. This time they sent notices to parents beforehand, asking candidates to come dressed with underwear.

This audition was much harder. The girl with the big eyes from my class didn't pass this round: she screamed when they bent her body backward and was disqualified for inadequate flexibility of her back. Then it was my turn. One teacher lifted

106

one of my legs upward, two others held my other leg steady and straight. They kept asking me if it hurt. Of course it hurt: it was excruciating! But I was determined to be chosen, so I kept smiling and replied, "No, it doesn't hurt," as they lifted my leg higher and higher. Be strong! Be strong! You can bear the pain! I kept telling myself. I did bear the pain, but the hardest thing was pretending to walk normally afterwards. They had torn both my hamstrings.

After the audition at commune level we went through to county, city and provincial levels. Each time there were more children who auditioned and each time more were eliminated. During the physical examination at the county level, the scar on my arm from the burn I received as a baby nearly disqualified me. One of the teachers from Beijing noticed it and referred me to a medical examiner.

"How did you get this scar?" the doctor asked.

I didn't want anyone to think of my niang as irresponsible, so I told him I'd cut my arm on a piece of broken glass and that the cut had got infected.

"Do you have any funny sensations, like itching on rainy days?"

"No, never." I looked straight into the doctor's eyes. I prayed he wouldn't eliminate me. I prayed for my niang's sake. She would be so sad, feel so guilty, if I was disqualified because of this scar. She didn't need to suffer any more.

After the examination, as I was putting my clothes back on, I overheard the doctor talking to a tall teacher from the Beijing Dance Academy. The teacher's name was Chen Lueng. He was the same gentleman from Beijing that Teacher Song had tapped on the shoulder that day at my school. "That boy's scar will definitely get larger as he grows," the doctor said. My heart sank. My only chance of getting out of my deep well was gone. I would be disqualified. I made up my mind never to tell my niang it was the scar

107

that did it. The scar was from an accident. My niang was the best mother with the most loving heart. No one should take that reputation away.

When the physical tests were completed, we were tested for other abilities: our response to music, our understanding of Chairman Mao's ideology. They also checked our family background three generations back. Chairman Mao's communist theory about the so-called "three classes of people" was crucial when selecting us. All three classes had to be represented—peasants, workers and soldiers. Children whose families were associated with wealth and education anywhere in the past three generations were classified as class enemies and were disqualified. Madame Mao wanted to train us to be faithful young guards, so our backgrounds had to be pure, safe and reliable.

The final hurdle in the selection process was for the officials to meet my family. They wanted to meet everyone: parents, brothers and grandparents, to check out their physical proportions. I was nervous that they might have a problem with my niang because she was short, but her larger-than-life personality, and my dia's good figure, saved the day.

Days passed, weeks passed. No news from Beijing. The hope in my heart gradually dimmed with each passing day. I felt disappointed, then devastated. I became quiet. I shrank into my own cocoon. I kept looking at my scar, convinced it was the sole reason that I'd missed out. I wanted to cut my arm off to rid myself of the scar. But still, I didn't blame my niang. It wasn't her fault. It was just my unfortunate fate.

Everyone in my family had also given up hope by now. I could tell they felt sorry for me, because they all went out of their way to be nice. This only left me feeling sadder.

Then one day, just as my dia was going back to work after lunch, a group of village, commune, county *and* city officials suddenly came into our small courtyard, for our door was always open. They had broad smiles on their faces. My parents offered them some tea. Some sat down on our crowded kang, others just stood around. Eventually one of the officials asked my niang, "Which of your sons is Li Cunxin?"

My niang pointed at me.

The city official turned back to my niang. "Your lucky son has been chosen for Madame Mao's Beijing Dance Academy."

I was stunned. We were all stunned. A whole month had gone by! How could this be? My mother was speechless, but her face smiled like a full-bloomed flower. "Thank you! Thank you!" was all she could say.

My dia poured more tea for the officials, and then more, and then still more. His face was filled with pride.

When all the officials had left our house, all my dia said was, "I'd better get to work. I'll see you tonight." But he looked at me in a strange way, as though he was seeing something new.

After everyone had gone, my niang and I were left to ourselves. She looked at me for a long time, lost for words for the first time in her life. Finally she said, "My lucky boy, I'm so happy for you. This is the happiest day of my life!"

"I don't want to leave you," I said.

She looked at me with a slight frown. "Do you want to stay here and eat dried yams for the rest of your life? My dear son, this is your lucky chance to escape from this cruel world. Go, go and do something special with your life! Become someone other than a peasant boy. Don't look back! What is here? A leaking roof, your brothers' smelly feet and an empty stomach?"

"Stop it!" I said. I put my hand over her mouth. Happy tears welled in her eyes. She pulled me close and hugged me tight. I heard the loud beat of her heart, as though any minute it would jump out with joy.

She hugged me for a long time. I was too afraid to move.

I wanted us to stay like that forever. My entire body melted under her warmth.

"What about you?" I eventually asked. "Can you come to Beijing with me?"

"Do you want me to come and wipe your bottom, silly boy?" she replied with a chuckle. "You are the lucky one. Don't you think your brothers would love to have a chance like this? No, I can't go with you, but my love will. I will always love you, with all my heart. I know you have your secret dreams. Follow them. Make them come true. Now, go and play with your friends." She gave me a gentle push, but just as I was disappearing into the streets, she called out. "Don't forget to come back and help me push the wind box!"

A few days after this, we received a letter notifying me that I had been awarded a full scholarship and that I was to leave for Beijing in four weeks, just after the Chinese New Year. For the reopening of Madame Mao's new Beijing Dance Academy, fifteen students had been selected from Shandong Province. Fifteen from over seventy million people. Twenty-five students from Shanghai, three students from Beijing and one student from Inner Mongolia were also selected. It was February 1972 and I had just turned eleven.

The whole village came to congratulate my parents. There would be one less mouth to feed and now at least their sixth son had some hope of escaping from the poor living conditions and of making a decent life for himself.

Several of my niang's lady friends gathered on our kang one day, shortly after this, to sew, gossip and drink tea as usual. One of the ladies said to me when I walked into the room, "Jing Hao, take off your shoes, let me see your feet."

I was puzzled, and hesitated to take off my smelly shoes.

"Ah ya, come on, don't be shy," my niang urged me. "You can't be a dancer if you're shy!"

I reluctantly took off my shoes. The lady took my feet in her hands, like a doctor examining a seriously sick patient. Suddenly she shouted with excitement, "Look at this, I was right! Look, just look at his three long toes! I knew his feet would be different. *This* is the reason he was chosen! These three long toes will help him to stand steadily on his pointe shoes."

All the ladies, including my niang, nodded their heads and praised her wisdom. As I was putting my shoes back on, another lady added, in a more serious tone, "I heard it is very painful to stand on your toes. You must have a high pain threshold."

"Yes," a third lady said. "I heard dancers often get bloody toes from standing in their pointe shoes all day long. It must be like binding your feet and standing on top of them!"

I couldn't imagine my toes growing together and walking on my heels like Na-na used to. I began to worry. Eventually I had to tell myself not to think about it until I had at least tried on the pointe shoes. Then I'd know.

News of my selection spread quickly throughout our commune. Our usually quiet village sprang to life. People began to talk about me. "A smart kid." "That boy was born with a lucky look." I was embarrassed by all of these comments. I especially felt uncomfortable with my niang's friends' constant examinations. Besides my three long toes, they were convinced that my double-folded eyelids, which made my eyes appear larger, were a factor too. It was true that many of my friends in the village had eyes that looked smaller than mine, but now people would stop me in front of my friends and examine my eyelids. One of my niang's friends even believed that the teachers of the Beijing Dance Academy had specific roles in mind for a dancer with a scar on his arm.

Our Chinese New Year was extra special that year. My eldest brother was home from Tibet. Everyone gave me firecrackers as gifts. It was a joyous time.

A few days before New Year's Eve, however, one of my "double kicker" firecrackers went wrong and exploded in my hand. It nearly tore off my whole thumbnail, and blood gushed out from under it. My parents immediately worried that this could jeopardize my chances of going to Beijing, so as an extra precaution they took me to the hospital to get my first tetanus shot, an expensive luxury. If it wasn't for Beijing, nobody would have bothered. "Put some dust on it," my niang would have said.

My last dinner at home. Nine of us sit around the food tray. My niang has cooked a delicious meal. She's made an egg dish with bits of dried shrimp, and Chinese cabbage with a few pieces of pork. We also have a cold dish—marinated jellyfish—and she has used her precious flour to make some mantos. My dia and my older brothers drink rice wine while everyone talks enthusiastically about my bright future.

I am quiet. I can't eat much, despite the good food. My stomach is too full with anxiety and dread. I am too afraid to look into my niang's eyes because if I do I know my tears will flood out.

As soon as dinner is finished I announce that I am going to my friends' houses to say good-bye.

"Why don't you do it tomorrow?" my fifth brother, Cunfar, says.

"I won't have enough time tomorrow," I lie.

"Stay! We can play your favorite card game," Cunfar persists.

"Why didn't you show Jing Hao this kind of passion before?" my fourth brother, Cunsang, says, which makes everyone laugh.

"Speedy return if you want to go tonight," my niang says. "You should get some good sleep in your own familiar bed. Who knows if you can stomach the luxurious life in Beijing."

I quickly slip off the kang and go outside.

"Who *couldn't* stomach a luxurious life!" I hear my second brother say as I hurry into the darkness. I have no intention of going to my friends' houses. I just want to be alone. I walk through the usually scary, dark narrow lanes between the houses and I pass my friends' places but don't go in. You should be happy, I keep telling myself. And I am, deep inside, happy about this God-given opportunity, but I am overwhelmed by the sadness in my heart as well. I don't want to leave my niang, my dia, my brothers and my friends. Already I feel so alone. I can't imagine how alone I will feel in Beijing. I look up at the stars, and even they are few and distant tonight.

Eventually I wander home. All my older brothers have gone out. My parents have already spread the quilts on the bed and are waiting for me.

"How are your friends?" my niang asks.

"Fine," I reply. I look at her eyes for the first time that night. They are moist.

"Sixth Brother, can I sleep on your side tonight?" my little brother, Jing Tring, asks.

"Yes," I reply. For the first time I am happy about that. I wish I could put him and the rest of my family in my pocket and take them to Beijing with me.

Tonight, as Jing Tring is sleeping, I look at his content and peaceful face. Suddenly I feel a rush of brotherly affection for him. I wish I'd been kinder to him. I wish I'd taken time to enjoy his company more.

My niang has made me a black corduroy jacket to take to Beijing, but I know my youngest brother loves that jacket. I know my parents don't have enough money to make him one too, so in the middle of the night, I pretend to get up for a wee, and quietly take my new jacket out of my bag and tuck it inside one of the papier-mâché clothes boxes—Jing Tring will find it there after I'm gone.

113

The morning finally arrives. I've had a restless night and I wake with the first sound of the rooster's call. My dia rose earlier, to pack my belongings in two string bags. They are net bags, loosely woven, so you can see clearly what is inside. Many of my relatives, friends and neighbors have given me presents: souvenirs or some local specialty food such as dried shrimp. The shrimp has a strong "dead fish" sort of smell and it makes the bags stink.

Some of my classmates and friends have chipped in to pay for us to have our photos taken together. They also give me a beautiful diary with many pictures of Chairman Mao in it. The photo means a lot to me because my parents can't afford to waste money on such a luxury. We have very few photos, and only one family photo—a black-and-white one of my niang and all her seven boys. There is also my niang's handmade quilt, a thin futonlike mattress, two small hand towels, a metal washing basin, a metal mug, some clothes, apples, pears, and a Qingdao specialty called "sorghum sweet," a soft candy made from the grain. My niang has also packed some dried snakeskin. No one has noticed that I have taken out the new corduroy jacket.

After he finishes packing my bags, my dia quietly hands me five yuan. "I wish I could give you more, but this is all we have. Be good. Don't let the Li name down." He leaves for work, saying he'll try to make it back for lunch so he can see me one more time before I leave.

My niang is busy making dumplings this morning, as a special treat to send me on my way. I want to stay with her for every remaining minute, but I can't. I know if we look at each other we will not be able to control our tears. So I walk around the village, bidding farewell to my friends. I ask several of my niang's friends to come to our house after lunch to keep her company. I don't want her to be sad and on her own. I go to my na-na's grave and to our ancestors' burial place and kowtow. I want to smell the earth, the air, to remember the surroundings and take everything in. This village has been my life for my whole eleven years. Even the things I hate about it are suddenly not so bad. My heart feels as though it is hanging in midair. I return home for lunch.

My niang has made many dumplings for my last lunch and although they are my favorite, I can't eat even one. A hot ball of emotion is plugged in my throat. All six of my brothers are at the table. Everyone pushes their bowl of dumplings in front of me, but still I eat nothing. I want to say something special to each of my brothers, but few words are spoken. Time seems to run so fast and before we know it, it is time for me to go. Now I have to say good-bye to my niang and my brothers.

My brothers take my bags outside. My dia did not make it back for lunch. I look at my niang for the first time today and we both burst into tears. We can say nothing. We just hold each other. Then some of her friends come into our house, as I had asked them to, and I go quickly into the street.

My oldest brother, Cuncia, is to come with me as far as Qingdao City, and as a special honor our village has provided us with their only tractor to take us there. The admission letter from the Beijing Dance Academy said that all fifteen students chosen from Shandong Province are required to meet at a dormitory where we will spend the next eighteen hours before we embark on our train journey to Beijing. As the tractor pulls away from our house, three of my brothers run after us in the dust, crying and shouting good-bye. I can no longer hide my emotions; I sob and sob, all the way to the city.

The tractor journey takes us over an hour. The ride is bumpy, but I don't really notice. Finally we reach our gathering place, a kind of dormitory divided into six rooms. Everything smells moldy and dusty, and the rooms are dark with only small windows. It feels foreign and unwelcoming. Nothing feels right. I am shy. I already miss my parents and brothers.

The time at the dormitory allows us to meet the other students. Four are from the countryside and others are from the city. There is something different about the city students. They seem more worldly than us country kids. There is also a man wearing a military uniform. He is called "the political head." And there's one of the teachers who auditioned us. They have come to Qingdao to collect us and will accompany us on our train trip to Beijing. We are briefed by the political head about certain rules and expectations the academy has for us. I have trouble understanding some of the terminology because they all speak in the Mandarin dialect.

By the time night comes, I still have not eaten since breakfast, so my brother peels me an apple. It's the first time I've ever had a whole apple to myself. I feel so lucky and so special. We settle down for the night. My only real comfort is my big brother, sleeping on a small bed next to mine.

Early next morning, we take a bus to the train station, an old building crammed with hundreds of people. I have never been to a train station before. I've only seen trains from a distance. Our train is a steam train, puffing out volumes of smoke and making an enormous noise. Our teachers push their way through the crowds and onto the train, and we pass our luggage through the windows because everyone is fighting their way on at the same time.

I leave my brother standing on the platform and find my seat on the train. Then, five minutes before departure, the loudspeakers announce that all family members and friends are to leave the platform. This is my last chance to say good-bye to my brother. He extends his hand through the window. As I grasp it I feel him give me something. It is a two-yuan note, his cigarette money. He will have to go without his beloved cigarettes for the next few months. I know how precious his cigarettes are to him. But he quickly runs into the crowd before I can say anything.

116

I hold the money in my hand, tears streaming down my face, and watch Cuncia disappear into the crowd.

I listen to the sound of the train. With a sudden jolt, a massive puff of steam swallows our carriage and Qingdao Station slowly slips away. With the click-clack sound of each passing section of the track I know I am moving farther and farther away from my parents. My heart races along with the gathering speed of the train. I don't know how I am going to survive the next twelve months before seeing my niang again. I long to sleep next to my parents. Even my brother's smelly feet don't seem too bad now.

We have reserved seats on the train, but being Chairman Mao's good children, we give our seats to some elderly people who can only afford to buy standing-room tickets. Five people are squeezed on a bench for three. The overhead rack is overflowing with luggage. A couple of times the train makes a sudden jolt and some bags crash down onto unfortunate passengers below.

At first, the trees and fields flashing by are familiar sights, but then the landscape changes and the trees, crops, even the smell of the air, become different and unfamiliar. Even though it is winter, the windows are open to allow the fresh air in.

At almost the halfway point in the journey, the train stops at Jinan, the capital of Shandong Province. Here the station is grander than Qingdao's, and well lit. Our teachers tell us that we can go and stretch our legs. There are peasants selling smoked chicken, steamed bread, roasted peanuts, sunflower seeds and sweets. Most of the students from the city buy something, but the country students like me just watch.

Later, back on the train, the political head and the teacher lead us to the dining car. Not many people are allowed in this car. In fact, only government officials are allowed, but we are Madame Mao's students, so we are invited to go along. We occupy nearly half the car. There are two cold dishes on each table, a plate of pickled peanuts and some thinly sliced marinated beef. The beef is tough but delicious—this is heavenly food! We quickly demolish the cold dishes and then three steaming hot courses arrive: a whole fish, stir-fried pork with green chives and a mixed vegetable dish. We each have a bowl of rice too. The rich and delicious smells take my breath away. Every dish is shining with oil! Even the sauce for the vegetable dish is full of flavor. I have never seen so much meat in my whole life! We devour the food like hungry tigers. I wish for more, but I am too embarrassed to ask.

I hardly sleep for the entire twenty-four hours of the train journey. Just before we pull into Beijing Station, our teachers warn us that it will be very crowded. Stay very close, or we will get lost.

I am stunned when I see the sea of people at the station. There is no way our teachers could have prepared us for such a scene. Instead of hundreds of people, I see hundreds of thousands, all pushing and shoving in a huge open space. The ceiling is so high and bright, almost blinding me with its many fluorescent lights. It is so grand. Even the passageways are chock-a-block with people, sleeping on the floor while they wait for their next train. The sound is deafening—hundreds of thousands of people all talking at the same time. The smell too is indescribably strange— virtually everyone carries some kind of hometown delicacy: I have my apples, pears, sorghum sweets, snakeskin and dried shrimps, but who knows what others are carrying. The smell makes me want to escape this place as quickly as I can, but my bags are too heavy and I can only move slowly. I try so hard to keep up with my group. I enter a tunnel, but when I come out the other end, the familiar faces of my fellow students are nowhere in sight. My two bags are pushed and pulled by the crowd, and several times I nearly lose my balance. I look around. I don't know which direction to take. I am exhausted and desperate, so I move to the side, out of the way of the fast-moving people. I sit down against a wall, lost.

I am frightened. I want to go home to my niang. I start to sob. A soldier comes up to me and asks me why I am alone. I tell him I have become separated from my group and don't know which way to go. He kindly takes one of my bags and leads me to the exit. I am so grateful to him, this Lei Feng–like soldier, and as I step out of the crowded train station I am relieved to see one of our teachers from the Beijing Dance Academy.

It is Chen Lueng, the tall teacher who auditioned us, and he is with a couple more teachers from the academy who are at the station to greet us. A bus is waiting, too, and I am the last person to climb on. The students from Shanghai had arrived an hour before and are already impatiently waiting on the bus.

I hear one of the teachers tell the driver to close the door. I want to be helpful, so I start to pull the door closed, but the driver has pushed the control button and the door closes automatically in front of me. It takes me by total surprise. The buses at home don't have doors like this. I stumble back and fall. Everyone laughs. I have made a fool of myself within the first few minutes of being in Beijing. I feel desperately alone. At this moment I realize I have entered a completely new world.

Throughout the eleven years of my childhood in Qingdao, I'd always lived with the harsh reality of not having enough food to fill our stomachs, of seeing my parents struggle, of witnessing people dying of starvation, of constantly being trapped in that same hopeless, vicious cycle as my forefathers. I had been determined to get out of that deep, dark well. I cannot remember how many times I'd wanted to let go of my life and relieve some of my parents' financial burden. I would have sacrificed my own life to help my family, but would it have made much difference? Whom did my life belong to anyway?

But somewhere deep in my heart there is a buried seed, a seed of hope. It isn't even a light. I can't see any light to guide me out of this cruel and unfair world. But that seed of hope has always existed, and it implants itself in my mind. Its power is strong. It makes me feel that one day everything will be all right. It is my escape, and my secret dream.

Beijing is my chance. I am scared to leave my parents, yet I know this will be my only chance of helping them. I am afraid of what is waiting for me, yet I know I have to take that first step forward. I can't let my parents down. I can't let my brothers down. I am carrying their dreams as well as my own. My niang said never look back.

I pick myself up off the floor of the bus, and walk down the aisle toward my seat.

PART TWO

BEIJING

8

FEATHER IN A WHIRLWIND

At first, despite missing home, the thrill of being in Beijing near our great and beloved leader Chairman Mao completely overwhelmed me. Here I was, part of the Beijing Dance Academy, with Madame Mao our honorary artistic director. My family, my relatives, the people in our village and commune, even the Shandong Province officials themselves, would all have enormous expectations of me: from this moment onward, I would have an "iron rice bowl"—a good job and enough food for life.

On the way to our academy on the bus that day we detoured to Zhongnanhai, where Chairman Mao, Madame Mao and all the top government officials lived. It was a huge complex, right next to the Forbidden City, with barbed wire and high, faded red-gold walls. Security guards stood beside huge red wooden doors, their hands firmly grasping their semiautomatic guns. Guards seemed to be everywhere, spread evenly along the walls, ready to pull the trigger on anyone who might pose a threat.

I simply couldn't *believe* I was here! Here, where our godlike leader slept, worked and made all his important political decisions. What was it like in there? I wondered. I could see many tall trees inside, and I'd heard that there was a fishing pond there, called Daiyutai. I imagined it had lots of different fish in it, and it must surely be round, like the image of Mao, our sun.

I was stunned with the sheer scale of Beijing: enormous buildings, endless street-lighting, wide smooth streets, nothing like the muddy dirt roads we had in Laoshan County. And the men and women—their Mao-style jackets looked so smart! I could see very few patches on their clothes. And the number of cars, buses, jeeps, bicycles—it simply shocked me. How could there be so many bicycles in one city! Officers in army uniforms directed the flow of traffic, but nobody seemed to pay much attention to the traffic lights themselves. I was completely fascinated. I'd never seen traffic lights before.

As the bus pulled into Tiananmen Square, my heart leaped. I could see long rows of gigantic light poles. I could see an ocean of people. I immediately noticed the Gate of Heavenly Peace on our left and the grand building of the People's Congress on the right. They were so familiar—I had seen them in so many pictures: even in my collection of Mao's buttons at home there was one with Chairman Mao smiling and waving at me from the top of the Gate of Heavenly Peace. It made my spine shiver. Tiananmen Square was our great symbol of communism. It was here, on the Gate of Heavenly Peace, facing millions of jubilant people, that Chairman Mao declared the birth of the People's Republic of China on 1 October 1949. It was a date that all the children of China had etched into their minds.

For our first day in Beijing it was sunny, and the combination of body heat from the crowd, the sunshine and the smog made the square warm. Our bus wasn't allowed to drive too close to the center, so we got out and our political heads and teachers herded us toward the Gate of Heavenly Peace. People swarmed everywhere, many stopping to take pictures, so it took some time before we could get close. Then one of our political heads told a security guard that we were from Madame Mao's school. That mention alone was enough, and he happily let us into the security area surrounding the Gate of Heavenly Peace, so we could pose for several group photos.

It was only once I settled back onto our bus that a sense of insecurity began to overwhelm me. I sank down into my seat and looked out the window. The buildings around the square seemed to stare at me. Why are *you*, peasant boy, here in this magnificent city? Throughout my childhood I had always dreamed of coming here. I had always believed I never would. Yet now I was here, among fifteen million people. I felt like a feather swept up in a whirlwind. I was only eleven years old. Nothing could have prepared me for this.

Our bus traveled through the city streets and gradually the tall buildings of Beijing were left far behind. We drove on and on, heading, we were told, toward a village called Zhuxingzhuang, about one hundred and twenty miles away. The name meant Zhu's New Village, and it was to be our new home.

The wide, open fields of the countryside seemed to invigorate me. The fields here were flat compared to the layered fields surrounding my hometown, but there were enough similarities in the countryside to relieve my anxiety just a little. It was a long drive, and one of the teachers suggested we sing propaganda songs as we went along, and this too temporarily kept my attention.

Eventually, just as our bus turned into a drive, the political head proudly announced, "We are here! Our school is on the left."

I could see tall, bare trees on each side of a driveway (it was February and still bitterly cold) and within a couple of minutes our bus turned toward a metal-barred gate that had bright red letters over the top of it: Central 5-7 Performing and Arts University. The numbers, our political heads explained, referred to 7 May 1970, when Madame Mao delivered a famous speech to the arts and education communities, using Chairman Mao's philosophies to encourage all intellectuals to engage, both physically and mentally, with the three classes: peasants, workers and soldiers. They were golden words to the Ministry of Culture, so they proposed that Madame Mao should be the artistic director of this new university, and that it should be located in the heart of the communes, where future artists could learn and work among the peasants every day. In such an isolated site, surrounded by communes and fields, students would be protected from any negative influences from the city. Madame Mao supported this idea, and the project quickly received the central government's backing.

Our bus came to a stop inside a compound, and we all filed out. A small group of officials and teachers helped the girls with their luggage before we were all taken inside a new three-story building. I smelled fresh paint as we entered, an overpowering, unfamiliar smell, but the teachers didn't seem to notice. Before we climbed upstairs to the second floor, one teacher read out our names and divided us into groups according to our age and gender. I was put in the younger boys' class.

There were three stairways: we went up the center one, and I noticed next to the other stairs there were two bathrooms, one for each sex. The teachers explained things as we went. The boys' bathroom was divided into two sections: the outer section was for washing, and there was only cold water there. We were told that we had to collect our hot water from the boiler room near our canteen. Water coming through pipes, instead of having to carry buckets from the well! I thought it was amazing!

Next we were shown our bedrooms. There were four rooms, two for boys and two for girls, and about ten or eleven

126

of us to a room. The beds were crammed in so close together. It would be a luxury to have a bed all to myself, but I knew I'd still miss my brother's smelly feet and long for the security of my parents.

We were allowed a few moments to put our personal belongings away, so I put my snakeskin and the smelly dried shrimp and my other items in a little bedside chest of drawers next to the bed I was allocated. Then I got out my niang's precious handmade quilt and carefully folded it on top of the bed. Then all of us, all forty-four students, were taken to the sports ground near the canteen by our three political heads. They organized us into four straight lines according to height, the smaller ones at the front and the tallest at the back. I was the second smallest boy in my line.

Once everyone was standing quietly, the head of our academy, a broad, strong man in a green army uniform, started his lecture. "Students, I am your director and you can call me Director Wang," he said in a rusty, deep voice with a distinct southern accent. He looked around. I could see his scary little eyes. There was complete silence. "On behalf of our beloved Madame Mao, I welcome you to the Central 5-7 Performing and Arts University. You are privileged to be chosen to be part of Madame Mao's new school. Do you know what your chances of being chosen were?" He paused. "One in a billion! That's right, one in a *billion!* You are the lucky and proud children of the workers, peasants and soldiers of China! You will carry Chairman Mao's artistic flag into the bright future. Not only will you receive six years of ballet training, but you will also study Chinese folk dance, Beijing Opera Movement, martial arts, acrobatics, politics, Chinese and international history, Chinese and international geography, poetry, mathematics and Madame Mao's Art Philosophy. What's Art Philosophy you may ask?" He paused again and looked around once more with his scary little eyes. "Art Philosophy is the relationship between politics and the arts. It is Madame Mao's wish that you don't just grow up being a dancer, but a revolutionary guard, a dedicated and faithful servant of Chairman Mao's great crusade! Your weapon is your art. Madame Mao and over a billion pairs of eyes will be watching your progress. The expectation is enormous. The hurdle is high. The task is difficult. But what you are assigned to do is *glorious!*

"Your parents helped Chairman Mao win his first war. You can help him win his future battles. You will need skills and mental strength. They don't come easily. You will need to work hard every day of the year. Your daily schedules will be posted on the bulletin board on your floor and they will be strictly followed and reinforced." Another pause. "Any who are not up to this important task, raise your hand now!" His head did not move, but those scary little eyes moved from left to right, and right to left. Nobody raised a hand. He smiled, which made his already tiny eyes look even smaller. "Good!" he continued. "There are five people working full-time to support each of you here. I hope you don't let them, and over a billion other people, down. Now, you can go to your supper."

Director Wang's lecture left me confused and lost. I vaguely understood that we had been assigned an important job, that I was to devote my life to Chairman Mao's revolutionary causes. But this was nothing new. From the first day of school we were told to love, follow and even die for our great leader, Chairman Mao. Director Wang's words were clear and authoritative about that, but I couldn't grasp the rest of what he said about art and politics. I wondered whether Chairman Mao's artistic flag was going to be a different color from the flag of China. I didn't know what to think. All I could think of was standing on my toes in a pair of pointe shoes all day.

Next we were led, in line, to the canteen, a large square room with many tables and chairs in it. By the time we arrived, there were over a hundred students from the opera and music academies already sitting at their tables. It was unbelievably noisy.

We were told we were to have slightly better food than other academy students, because of the physical demands of our training. I saw two big bowls full of steaming food on each table, and on each side of the canteen were several larger tables for bread rolls, rice and soup. We were each given two metal rice bowls plus a small soup bowl, a pair of chopsticks and a soup spoon. Everyone had exactly the same bowls. Easy to get them mixed up, I thought.

We sat down, eight of us to a table, and divided the food evenly among us. On my table, only one girl and one boy looked familiar: I'd seen them on our train trip to Beijing. The others were all from Shanghai and although they talked a lot I didn't understand a thing they said because they only spoke Shanghai dialect. The boy next to me, who was as small as I was, turned and said something to me—I looked at the two Shandong students to see if they'd understood, but they just shook their heads and when I tried to tell him, in my Qingdao accent, that I couldn't understand, he just smiled.

The food looked inviting and it smelled delicious, but I had no appetite. My stomach felt like a twisted knot. I looked out the windows. I could see that it was already dark outside, and the darkness cast a sadness in my heart. The sadness began to creep up and overwhelm me. I forced myself to eat a few mouthfuls of rice but it was tasteless, so I quickly rinsed my bowls, chopsticks and spoon and quietly left the canteen before anyone noticed.

It was cold outside. The grounds were deserted. I could see only a few dim lights between the canteen and our dormitory. I looked up at the distant moon, and a few faraway stars in the night sky. I was afraid to go back to the dormitory alone in this unfamiliar darkness. I looked at the steamed-up windows of the canteen and knew that I couldn't go back there either: they would surely laugh at me. I had to keep going. I thought of my

129

parents and all my brothers back home, and with each step toward our dormitory building, I fought my fear and growing loneliness.

The building was pitch-black. All the lights were turned off. With shaking hands I searched for the light switches, but I couldn't find any. Slowly I felt my way up the stairs and eventually found a switch at the top. I got to my room, but I had no desire to turn on the lights there. Instead I groped my way to my bed, dived onto it and grabbed the precious quilt my niang had made for me. I plunged my face into it and wept.

I remember that first night alone so well. I was adrift. My niang's quilt was like a life-saving rope in the middle of an ocean of sadness. I couldn't stop the tears from welling in my eyes and I couldn't stop thinking of my family back home. It would be their evening playtime now: my dia's simple stories, my niang's sewing and my brothers' game of finding words in the wallpaper. I tried to tell myself to stop thinking like this, but I couldn't. I couldn't stop feeling the quilt and smelling its familiar smell. I couldn't stop this unbearable homesickness, like a merciless dark ocean, and me, left in the middle of it, without a lifeline. The rope I was clutching onto wasn't enough. I was drowning, deeper and deeper, and it would be for many nights in those first few months that I would cry myself to sleep.

That was the first night I had ever slept on my own, yet all I wanted to do was transform myself into a bird and fly home to sleep with my family again, in my parents' bed, next to my younger brother's smelly feet, even for just one night. My misery was so intense that I was only vaguely aware of my classmates returning from their supper. To hide my tears, I pretended to be asleep and buried my head under my niang's quilt.

The next morning, I was jolted back to reality. The familiar smell of the smoke as my niang cooked breakfast and her loving voice were not there. Instead there was the harsh sound of the wake-up bell. I was not back home, I was here, alone, somewhere foreign. I looked around the room and remembered every detail of the night before.

There seemed to be loud bells for everything that morning. Speed and efficiency were all important. Strict orders, schedules and rules had to be rigidly observed. And it was still so early—we'd been woken at half-past five. We rolled our blankets military style, and brushed our teeth (a completely new, strangely uncomfortable experience—I had to watch the others to see how they did it). Then we washed our faces and the bell rang again within five minutes to call us outside onto the still-dark sports ground.

We soon discovered that every morning would be the same. Each class captain would report that all students were accounted for and we'd jog for half an hour around the open fields, half asleep, every day of the year. I loved the fresh air in the mornings, but at first I found it hard to wake up so early. Breakfast was at seven-fifteen: rice porridge, steamed bread and salty pickled turnips. Never dried yams. Sometimes we even had eggs if we were lucky.

That first morning after breakfast we went to try on our ballet and Chinese folk dance shoes, our white vests, dark blue shorts and royal blue cotton tracksuits. These were all we would need for the next six years, we were told. The ballet shoes had small strips of leather wrapped around the toes and the heels, so only the worn-out leather strips would need to be replaced and the whole shoe would last a long time. The dark blue shorts had elastic on the waist and around each leg. They felt very strange. Then we were introduced to Chiu Ho, the head ballet mistress, who took us to the shoe workshop for our ballet shoe fittings. It was the moment I had been dreading.

Chiu Ho, we soon learned, was considered one of the most knowledgeable ballet teachers in China. She had been trained

131

by the visiting Russian teachers in the 1950s, and despite her diminutive size, she was the teacher we would learn to fear most.

In the shoe workshop, Chiu Ho told us to choose the tightest ballet shoes possible because, she said, they would eventually stretch. We were then greeted by a short hunchbacked man who looked so strange that he terrified us, but he was supposed to be the best maker of ballet shoes in China. His workshop wasn't big, but it had racks and racks of ballet shoes, including pointe shoes. There were stacks of leather and cotton fabrics too, and buckets full of shoe glue, which had splattered everywhere. A few old sewing machines sat on the workbenches against the walls. It was very crowded, and my eyes immediately fixed on the rows of pointe shoes, for I feared these the most: the time would come when I would have to squeeze my feet into these tiny, tiny shoes.

"Boys first!" Chiu Ho barked. One by one we tried on the ballet shoes. They were so small they cramped my long toes. I couldn't imagine how uncomfortable the hard pointe shoes would be.

"Okay, boys are done! You can all get out of here!" Chiu Ho bellowed.

"What about the pointe shoes?" I asked.

"What about them?" She frowned.

"Don't we have to try them on?" I asked.

She looked at me, then she and the shoemaker roared with laughter. "No, only girls wear pointe shoes!" Chiu Ho chuckled.

I felt like collapsing with relief! I wouldn't have to walk like my na-na after all! But I didn't realize that even the small flat shoes Chiu Ho had given me to wear would be enough to cause permanent damage to my toes.

We spent the rest of that day preparing for the official start of our training the following day. The Beijing Dance Academy, due to Madame Mao's involvement, was, we were told, regarded as the most prestigious dance school in the whole of China and the only one to offer full scholarships which would pay for our food, our board, our tuition and our training clothes. Our parents would have to provide our everyday clothes, blankets and spending money, and a tiny little shop within the academy grounds sold other essentials such as soap, toothbrushes, toothpaste and sweets. Madame Mao's military officers would head key departments of the university. These were the "political heads" we had already encountered, and we soon learned to be terrified of them too. Even our teachers seemed to show them an unusual amount of respect. They had absolute power and would become our political and ideological mentors.

We checked our timetable for our classes the following morning. Our first would be ballet, followed by Chinese folk dance and Beijing Opera Movement. We would do ballet every morning; other classes alternated on different days. Lunch was at noon. Between 12.30 p.m. and 2 p.m. we would have our midday sleep, a Chinese tradition, and from 2 p.m. to 5.30 p.m. we'd have normal school subjects such as mathematics, Chinese, history, geography, politics and Madame Mao's Art Philosophy. From 5.30 p.m. to 6 p.m. was dinner time, and then for two hours after that we were expected to either study politics or practice ballet. We didn't know, then, that political studies would fill most of our evenings for the next five years.

Next day arrived. My first ever ballet class was at eight o'clock, taken by Teacher Chen Lueng, the tall man from Beijing who'd auditioned us at school in Qingdao. His familiar face was my only comfort.

The studio we were taken to seemed huge and empty with only ten boys and a pianist in it. It was snowing outside and the windows were frosty. There were some heaters along the walls, but they were so inefficient they might as well have not been there. We wore our little shorts and vests, and shivered with cold.

Chen Lueng gathered us in a semicircle. "Can anyone tell me what ballet is?"

We all just looked at each other.

He smiled gently. "Ballet is an art form that originated from dancing in the French imperial courts. It is a universal art form now," he explained. He then told us that our syllabus would be based on the famous Vaganova method from Russia, which had produced some of the world's finest dancers, including Nureyev and Vasiliev.

Everything he said went in one ear and straight out the other. These names didn't mean anything to me at all.

"The first two years, we call them the foundation years, are considered crucial. I'll be your teacher for this period. To start with, I'll teach you some basic positions and exercises. Over the course of this first year, I'll teach you some ballet terminologies. They are in French. The French gave all the steps and movements names. Internationally everyone uses these French terminologies. However, it is Madame Mao's wish that we should give the steps Chinese names as well. Therefore, not only will you learn the French terminology, you'll also learn the Chinese names. I expect you to remember them."

I couldn't believe what I'd heard. *French?* I had such problems understanding Chen Lueng's Mandarin, let alone French! I had to think of some way to remember the ballet terms, though, so when Chen Lueng started talking about the French word *tendu,* I tried to remember the sound and immediately thought of the Chinese sounds *Ton Jiu,* which means "nine pieces of candy"—backward. For *penché,* I thought of *Pong Xie,* which means "crab." Some words I couldn't find any Chinese equivalent for. *Arabesque* was simply not worth the effort. By the time I finally worked out *Ar La Bai S Ker,* I had to remember five different Chinese words and that sounded even more ridiculous. Eventually I tried to write the words down in a diary I'd been given, but my Chinese vocabulary was completely inadequate. So I drew little pictures instead. It was the only thing I could do. I was too embarrassed to ask for help. I was so afraid they would laugh at me, this uneducated peasant boy.

During that first ballet class I couldn't feel my toes at all in those tight, tiny shoes and in the freezing-cold weather. Chen Lueng told us to stand with our feet turned out in all sorts of funny ways—he called them first, second, third, fourth and fifth positions. It felt ridiculous. I couldn't imagine anyone in their right minds wanting to watch us do these ugly positions. Surely even Madame Mao would fall asleep if we performed like wad-dling ducks! I had such difficulty getting my feet to cooperate. They kept rolling inward.

The studio was very damp and dusty. There was everywhere the smell of sweat and mildew. Through the beams of light I could see millions of tiny dust motes floating in the air. The wooden floor was so old that it splintered, and for our feet to get some grip Chen Lueng showed us how to sprinkle water on the floor using a metal pot, which looked almost exactly like a water-ing can with many holes in its large, round showerhead. We twisted the head to spin the water out onto the floor while walk-ing backwards. To qualify as a student of the Beijing Dance Academy, one had to be able to do this quickly and efficiently.

Everything felt weird in that very first class. We had to extend our arms to the side, palms facing forward, just below shoulder height, while Chen Lueng walked among us, pushing our arms down and asking us to resist him with all our strength. We held this position for several minutes until he told us to relax. He said this was to develop our arm strength, so our arms would look soft, never strained. This was not dancing, I said to myself. Where were the leaps and skips? How could I possibly suffer this agony for six years? My feet felt so cramped. I couldn't imagine how bad it must be for the girls standing on their toes in pointe shoes.

That first class lasted nearly two hours, but it seemed like forever. I couldn't wait for the bell to ring so I could take those horrible shoes off and let my cramped toes stretch out. I thought about running in the streets as I did in my commune, or wrestling with my friends. I didn't want to dance. I wanted to go outside and make a snowman and throw snowballs.

Our second class that morning was Beijing Opera Movement. Our teacher was Gao Dakun. "Hurry up, you're late!" Gao shouted. "Spread out around the barre!" he barked. "Beijing Opera movements are all about flexibility and suppleness. If you don't have suppleness, you can't be good in my class. Do you understand?"

We all nodded, terrified.

"Good, let's start with your legs up on the barre," he said.

I looked at the barre in front of me. It was as high as my chest.

"What are you waiting for? Didn't you hear me? Your leg on the barre!"

I was one of the three smallest boys in our class. I tried to put my leg up but the barre was just too high.

Without another word Gao walked over to me and lifted my leg. I felt a tinge of pain in my hamstring and automatically bent my knee.

"Keep your knee straight!" He pushed my knee down on the barre. "Now I want you to bend your body forward and try to touch your toes with your head. Stay down there! Don't get up until I tell you so!" Gao ordered.

The pain was excruciating and was increasing at an alarming rate.

"Didn't you hear me, keep your knees straight!" Gao shouted at Zhu Yaoping, the small boy from Shanghai who'd spoken to me at dinner the night before. "Keep your head down!" he told Fu Xijun, another boy from Qingdao. "Okay! Now, let's change legs!"

My right leg was now in such pain that I had trouble even lifting it off the barre. I quickly glanced at the other students. I wasn't the only one suffering.

When I lifted my other leg onto the barre, I knew what to expect this time. So I started to count. I was prepared to count up to fifty. I wondered if I was the only one counting as a way of coping with such agony, until I heard the boy next to me counting too.

Each time, from that first class on, I prepared myself for the worst. I decided I needed to be mentally strong enough to last through at least a hundred slow counts. But if Gao left the classroom to get himself some water or have a cigarette, then the hundred counts would increase to who knew how many. The pain made me want to scream. Often Gao would lean on our bodies and force us down lower. We would be in terrible trouble if we bent our knees. My hamstrings would often tear, but we were not allowed to stop. We were not allowed to scream or cry.

I hated Gao Dakun and his class. I feared confronting him. I dreaded looking at him. Just the thought of his class made my stomach churn. He always seemed angry and he constantly screamed at us. He called us names too. He called me "the boy with the brainless big head," and I hated him even more.

Before our midday sleep on that first day, as we were heading back to our room, Zhu Yaoping, the small boy from Shanghai, slid down the stair rail at our dormitory. It looked fun, so I copied him. We ran up the stairs and slid down the rail, chasing each other, until one of the political heads appeared from nowhere. "What do you think you're doing?" he growled.

We stood there, hearts thumping.

"You are *never* to do this again! Do you understand? You could break your legs if you fall. This is not allowed in Madame Mao's school!"

There was no fun in this place, I thought. Only rules.

We had other classes that day, but they were just a blur. I

couldn't understand the teachers' Mandarin accents, but at least we were to have an early dinner because, we were told, we were going to see the Central Ballet of China perform.

We went by bus to the Heaven's Gate Theater close to the center of Beijing. The ballet was one of Madame Mao's model ballets, with the familiar title *The Red Detachment of Women*. Zhu Yaoping and I sat next to each other. I managed to stay awake for the first act, but during the second I could no longer fight off my sleepiness. My eyelids got heavier and heavier and I eventually fell into a deep sleep. I was woken only by the applause at the end of the act.

I was frightened when I looked around. I didn't know where I was or what I was doing. The trip to Beijing, the whole of the last twenty-four hours, all seemed like a dream. When I recovered from the initial shock, I realized that Zhu Yaoping and all my classmates had already left. Suddenly I had to go to the toilet but by the time I found it there was already a long queue, and then the bell rang and the ushers were urging people back to their seats. I hurriedly followed some people into the theater but couldn't find my classmates. I panicked. I went back to the lobby again. "I've lost my group, I can't find my seat," I told an usher.

"May I see your ticket?"

"I don't have my ticket, our political head has all of our tickets," I replied.

By this time the lights were fading. The usher grabbed my arm. "Follow me, I'll help you find your group after the performance," and he pulled me into the theater and found an empty seat in the back row. I was nervous being separated from my friends, but soon tiredness overcame me again and I slept through the rest of the performance. Then, just as the lights came on, the usher pulled me out of the theater and we waited for the familiar faces of my friends. They eventually emerged two doors away. I was so happy and relieved when Zhu Yaoping

138

rushed up and said something to me in Shanghai dialect. I didn't even care that I couldn't understand a word of it.

On the bus trip back to our university, I began to feel terribly sick. It was as though the whole world was spinning. I wanted to vomit. I told the teacher, who asked the driver to stop the bus, and I hopped off just in time. They put me in the front seat after that, just behind the driver. One of the teachers assured me that I only had motion sickness and I would feel better sitting there. But I'd never been sick when I went on the bus with my niang to visit our grandparents. I felt traumatized, embarrassed, trapped in my own emotionally torrid world.

It was midnight by the time we went to bed that night, way past my bedtime in Qingdao. I thought of my niang, my dia and my brothers, all sleeping together in their own beds, and I felt my homesickness begin to return. After the lights were turned off, I clutched onto my niang's precious quilt once again, covered my head with it, and sobbed myself to sleep.

九

9

THE CAGED BIRD

Every morning was the same. It seemed that I had only just
closed my eyes when I heard the ear-piercing scream of the five-
thirty bell. I would drag myself to the washing room and pour
freezing-cold water on my face to drive away my sleepiness. The
jogging, the early-morning exercises and breakfast all happened
while I was still half asleep. Only my cold cramped feet, the awkward ballet positions and the French names in Chen Lueng's
class would wake me up.

Later that week we had our first Chinese folk dance lesson,
with Teacher Chen Yuen. He was younger than the other teachers we'd had so far and wore a pair of spectacles. He seemed
friendly, with a funny sense of humor, and he even told us jokes.

In Chen Yuen's class we got to dance much more freely. I particularly loved a Mongolian horse riders' dance we began to
learn. But the best part of this class was the four musicians who
sat at the front of the studio and played their traditional Chinese
instruments. I thought they were beautiful. One played a "piba,"

which looked like a guitar but sounded hollow and sad. There was also an ancient-looking horn and an "erhu"—a two-string instrument which produced the most heart-wrenching sounds, and the "yanqin," a string instrument so beautiful and powerful that I thought there were twenty different instruments playing at once! I loved it. I loved the passion of their music. I had never heard anything like it. Their music made me *want* to dance: I could hear the clip-clop sound of the approaching horses; I could hear those Mongolian riders roaming the deserts, and I longed to be free like them.

That same day we had our first politics class too, and I was surprised to find that the campaign to denounce Lin Biao was still in full swing. The Gang of Four's theory was that shit attracts flies, and that Confucius was the shit and Lin Biao was the fly. So a "criticize Confucius" campaign was organized. We were to discuss why Lin Biao was attracted to Confucius and how dangerous this had been to Mao's political cause. Our teacher started our first lesson by telling us all about Confucius. He had already written down one of Confucius' sayings on the blackboard by the time we'd all sat down at our little wooden desks:

When the perfect order prevails, the world is like a home shared by all. Courageous, worthy and capable men are elected to public office and hold posts of gainful employment in society; peace and trust among all men are the maxims of living. All men love and respect their parents and children, as well as the parents and children of others. There is caring for the old and there are jobs for everyone. There is also nourishment and education for the children and a means of support for the widows or widowers, disabled and all that find themselves alone in the world. Everyone has an appropriate role to play in the family and society. A sense of sharing displaces the effects of selfishness and materialism, and a devotion to public duty leaves no room for idleness. Dishonesty and conniving for ill gain are unknown. Villains such as thieves and robbers do not exist. The door to everyone's home never needs to be locked or bolted, day or night. These are the characteristics of this ideal world, the world everyone shares equally.

"Now," our teacher began, "can any of you tell me the hidden *evilness* in this Confucius saying?"

No one spoke. I was puzzled by the teacher's question. I didn't understand all the words on the board, but there seemed nothing wrong with it to me. Confucius' society sounded beautiful, just like the ideal communist society.

Our teacher continued. "There are several key words that you must be able to detect. For example, 'the perfect order.' *Whose* definition of the perfect order? The rulers'? The emperors'? This is a trap! Confucius wants the poor ordinary people to behave and follow the rules, which were set for them *by* the rulers, for the benefit *of* the rulers. Do you see this point?" the political leader asked.

We all nodded obediently.

"My second point: have you realized that Confucius only mentions men. Where are the women? In his mind women are not even worth mentioning! But Chairman Mao says, 'Women are half of the sky!' And finally Confucius talks of villains, thieves and robbers. Whom did he mean? Could he possibly mean the rulers and the emperors?"

We all shook our heads.

"No! He means the poor peasants and workers who cannot get enough to eat or clothes to wear. They have no choice but to steal. *Now* do you see these hidden, poisoned agendas?"

We nodded again wholeheartedly. I was amazed. I knew our teacher was right. Why hadn't *I* seen these hidden, poisoned agendas?

"Now can you see why this little fly, Lin Biao, was attracted to the Confucius pile of shit?"

"Yes!" we all shouted, and our politics teacher smiled triumphantly.

During that class, I heard some baby birds screeching loudly on the rooftop outside, so after the class was over I told Zhu Yaoping, who was fast becoming my best friend at the academy, and we climbed out a small window onto the steep rooftop four stories high. There we found ten hungry little birds in a nest under a roof tile. They opened their mouths wide and screamed at us for food. Zhu Yaoping wasn't overly interested in them—he just wanted to get out onto the rooftop. But my heart poured out to the little birds and I gently put all of them in my pockets. I'd feed them some of my lunch and play with them for a while before I put them back.

Our next class was math, the last class before lunch, so I put the birds in my desk. But in the middle of our lesson the birds started to screech—loudly. Very loudly. The teacher was furious when she saw the birds, and told me to get out of her class and report to the political head's office right away. I was terrified. I thought they would expel me for sure.

Director Wang looked at me with a stern expression when I arrived at his office. "Cunxin, *what* do you think you were doing? Do you want to kill yourself, to embarrass Madame Mao? This behavior of yours will not be tolerated here. This is not your commune! You will study the relevant sections of Chairman Mao's Red Book and write a thorough self-criticism to read to your class."

"I have never written a self-criticism," I replied. "I don't know how."

He looked at me with a tinge of sympathy then. "You must write why you are wrong for climbing on the roof and promise you will never do it again. Make sure you use some of Chairman

Mao's sayings as the basis for your reasoning. Say that you regret your actions and that this will never happen again."

I wasn't allowed to go back to my class, so Director Wang let me use his desk while he went to a meeting.

After many tries and some agonizing soul-searching, I finally completed my first ever self-criticism:

> My dear and respected teacher and classmates,
>
> I'm very sorry I climbed on the roof, and even more sorry for taking the poor baby birds out of their comfortable home. The reasons for my action were: One. I heard their screams and saw their widely opened hungry mouths, I felt sorry for them and afraid that their parents wouldn't come back and these baby birds might die. Two. I love birds and always have.
>
> *But*, after speaking to Director Wang, I realize that this is wrong and I should never do it again! *Why?* Because of the following reasons: One. I may slip and die and this would cause embarrassment for Madame Mao, because I'm her student. Two. Our great leader Chairman Mao said in his Red Book: "Study hard and improve upward every day." By thinking about and playing with the birds, I won't be able to concentrate on my studies like Chairman Mao wanted me to. Three. If I died because of trying to save the birds, I won't be able to serve in Chairman Mao's revolution anymore. Four. Also my parents won't be able to ever see me again and my niang will die of sadness.
>
> Because of these four important reasons, I promise that I'll never do it again. If you ever catch me doing it again, I'm willing to let the thunder kill me!
>
> Chairman Mao's Faithful Student
>
> Li Cunxin

I was pleased I'd thought of that last line: "Let the thunder kill me" was a swear word from our commune. But in truth I didn't really believe that playing with the birds would have caused any harm to Chairman Mao's revolution at all. In truth I felt humiliated. I'd never had to do this in my old school.

My self-criticism passed the test easily, and my teacher and classmates burst into laughter when I read that last line. I also had to stand outside our classroom for a whole hour afterwards. "Cunxin, have you fed the poor birds yet?" the boys teased as they walked past, and my face burned with humiliation.

I hadn't meant what I'd written. I hadn't learned anything about serving Chairman Mao. All it made me realize was just how much freedom I was being denied. I would never be able to play with my beloved birds again. Now *I* was a bird trapped in a cage where even my feet had to conform to the rules.

There were so many different classes to get used to in that first week. Despite the bird incident, I liked the math class to begin with and I was quick to understand the new equations, but progress was slow and I lost interest quickly. I didn't understand the importance of math to a ballet dancer, and to cope with my boredom I began to daydream. I could hear the Beijing Opera students' voices coming from their studios and my heart wanted to leap out and join them instead. I thought about the Beijing Opera films I'd seen back in our commune, and I dreamed constantly about being a singer. I was often in trouble for not paying enough attention, especially in the ballet classes. My despair and lack of attention dominated my work. My teachers thought I was hopeless.

We also had our first acrobatics classes and Chinese classes in that first week. Acrobatics training was very strenuous. We had to do handstands against the wall, and exercises like bending backwards and lowering our hands to the floor, the ultimate aim being to grasp our ankles. Sometimes the teachers would order us to stay in this position until they allowed us to slowly bend back

145

up to standing position. But the pain made our backs numb and we didn't know which muscles to use to help us get up again. The teachers also made us do a lot of quick back bends to the floor, ten or twenty at a time, nonstop. It's surprising that we were not permanently injured. But our teachers continued, relentlessly. "What you're doing now is merely the foundation work," they would say. "Eventually we'll teach you back flips, front and back somersaults, when your back muscles are stronger."

Chinese class was run by Teacher Shu Wing. He was calm most of the time, but occasionally he would burst into a rage because of our laziness or tardiness. He had elegant handwriting, and I often lost myself just watching him write on the blackboard. Words leaped out of his white chalk in beautiful dancing movements. He also taught us poetry, his favorite subject. He would teach us some of Mao's simple poetry, but his real passion was for classical poetry. He would discuss each word in tremendous depth. Sometimes a single word represented a whole fable or event. His talent and knowledge were immense, and his class was one of my favorites. In his class we were told we had to learn Mandarin quickly, or we would be sent home.

Gradually, over the first few days, I began to make friends at the academy. Zhu Yaoping, Jiao Lishang and I were often in the same group of activities. We were the three smallest boys, and although we couldn't communicate well because of our different dialects, we managed in the end. Zhu Yaoping was the liveliest and naughtiest. I liked him. He made me laugh. At nights he slept on the bed next to mine, and he would often get up to tricks. In our first week there, one of the other boys ground his teeth so loudly in his sleep that it kept us awake and drove us all mad. Finally we were so fed up that we tied strings to his wrists and ankles and when we heard him grinding his teeth we'd pull the strings all at the same time. The poor boy. And another

146

night, after we'd had beans for dinner, one of the boys from the older class started to fart. He said he could fart on demand, yes, truly, as many times as he was asked! We were rolling on the floor from laughter. Even one of the normally stern-faced political heads couldn't help laughing.

The first week at the academy slowly came to an end and for our first Sunday a trip to the famous Ming Tombs had been organized. The trip north to Shisan Ling took over two hours by bus and again I suffered from dreadful motion sickness. They had to stop the bus twice. I felt guilty and embarrassed creating such inconvenience.

I still enjoyed the Ming Tombs though. I had never seen so many pieces of jewelery! Colorful rare gemstones, gold and silver, the emperor's and empress's drinking goblets, swords, costumes and crowns. How rich Chinese history was! I was enormously impressed and extremely proud of China's glorious past. China truly was the happiest and richest nation on the planet.

But even then I began to wonder. If China *was* such a rich country, why didn't my family have enough food to eat or enough money to buy clothes? I couldn't imagine what it would be like living in a poorer country like America. But of course I didn't blame Chairman Mao. It was Chinese imperial corruption, foreign invasion or Chiang Kaishek's Guomindang regime that were to blame. I was thankful to Chairman Mao, eternally thankful, that he had saved us. Only he would lead us to greater prosperity and happiness.

A week later another trip was organized, this time to the Summer Palace in northwest Beijing, but just the thought of the bus trip there and back was enough to make me feel sick, so I told one of the political heads that I didn't feel well and he gave me permission to stay behind.

I went exploring around the university grounds as soon as

147

the buses had left. There was a small orchard on the southeast corner near the gate—mainly apple and peach trees. They were bare at this time of year, but I could just see some new shoots popping out of the branches: spring wasn't far away. Right next to the orchard was our four-story studio building, and along the east side were the dormitories. To the northeast, I could see the low, flat-roofed single-story buildings that were used by the two music academies. They looked just like tiny matchboxes.

To the north, however, there was an empty stretch of land. I was immediately drawn to it and as a curious peasant boy I soon found myself digging my fingers down into the still half-frozen soil to see if there was anything planted, but the soil seemed completely barren. The land was surrounded by a chest-high barbed-wire fence and I could see a row of young weeping willow trees just this side of it. On the other side was an irrigation channel.

I ran over to the willows and began to climb one. These trees triggered such sadness in me. I saw the long drippy leaves and thought of my own sad tears. I wondered if the trees suffered hardship and sadness too. I climbed up and sat quietly inside the long leaves. I thought of all the events that had taken place since I had left my family only two weeks ago.

I leaned my head against the trunk and whispered my homesickness and loneliness into the trees. My tears flooded out. They fell down my face just like the leaves of the weeping willows. I sobbed freely. Nobody was there to see.

I felt better after my secret confession to the trees, and I knew I would hide in them many times during my first year. I had found my refuge, and I would treasure my time there. It became my own secret hiding place.

After a while I climbed down from the willows and wandered to the northwest part of the university grounds. There was a large pigsty there and a vegetable patch beside it. There was also a swimming pool, but it was empty at that time of year. I thought of the time I nearly drowned in the dam back home, and the hairs on my neck stood on end. I prayed that the teachers wouldn't make us use this pool in summertime.

I wandered back to the canteen just in time for lunch. I didn't expect to see anyone there, but to my surprise I noticed a boy sitting by himself at one of the music academy's tables. He was a bit younger than I and looked lonely and sad, so I collected my food and walked over to him. "Do you mind if I sit with you?" I asked.

He shyly shook his head.

I sat down opposite him. "My name is Li Cunxin. I'm from Qingdao. I'm a student in the dance academy. What's your name?"

"My name is Zhang Xiaojia," he replied timidly.

"Where are you from?"

"Henan province."

"Why didn't you go with the others to the Summer Palace?"

"I felt sick. What about you?" he asked.

"I didn't feel well either," I replied. "What musical instrument do you play?"

"I'm not playing anything yet."

"Why?" I became curious.

"No one has been assigned one yet. We were told our teachers will test us and then they will decide what instrument we'll learn," he said.

"Did you play anything before you came?"

He shook his head. "They only chose me because of my long fingers—and my parents are peasants. What about you? Did you dance before?" he asked.

"No, I've never danced before. I didn't even know what ballet was. I still don't. I just had long toes and a bit of flexibility. And my parents are peasants too."

"Do you play badminton?" he said all of a sudden.

"What's that?"

"I will show you, just follow me!"

So after lunch I followed him to his dormitory, where he took out two racquets and a feathery flyer from under his bed. We ran outside and played badminton in the space between the two dormitory buildings for hours. We drew a line in the dirt with a stick in lieu of a net. We didn't keep any score, the flying feathery thing just bounced back and forth, up and down, back and forth, and those were the happiest few hours I'd spent since leaving my family. For once we weren't being judged or criticized. We just enjoyed each other's company. Zhang and I became good friends, and that more than anything helped ease the intense loneliness and homesickness we both experienced. I only wished he was in my class.

Before the students left for the Summer Palace that day, the political head of our group had asked me to wash his white shirt while he was out and I happily accepted this job. I wanted to do it well for him—I wanted him to like me. "Use your toothpaste to wash it," he'd said. "Make sure you wash the armpits thoroughly." But the armpits were badly stained by sweat. I used so much of my toothpaste and washed the shirt so many times, but the stains still remained.

When the political head returned I proudly handed him the pressed and folded shirt. But he was not impressed. "I told you to use toothpaste! Just look at the stains!" He shook his head as he walked away.

I was angry. I had used nearly half my tube of toothpaste, which I could hardly afford to buy. I ended up having to cut the toothpaste tube and turn it inside out, so I could use every last bit of toothpaste—all because he'd wanted a clean shirt.

From the minute we arrived at the academy, we were expected to wash and sew our own clothes. At home, my niang had done all our sewing and washing. Having to do this myself only compounded my loneliness. I missed my niang terribly. I so dearly wanted to hear her voice, but I never telephoned the village to speak to my parents. I didn't have the money. Instead I wrote letters, but not too often because that cost money too. My parents wouldn't be able to read my letters themselves, but I knew one of my brothers would do that for them.

The first letter I sent home was so hard to write. I desperately wanted to tell them how much I missed them and how homesick I was, but I knew this would only make my niang sad. Instead I told them about the train trip to Beijing and how exciting everything was. I wrote about seeing Chairman Mao's compound, about Tiananmen Square and the Ming Tombs, about the beautiful jewelery I'd seen and how I wished I could take just one piece home to give to my niang. I told them I had plenty of good food: I could find oil and meat in every dish! How I wished I could share it with them. I told them I had to wash and sew my own clothes, and that I'd left my corduroy jacket in one of the papier-mâché clothes boxes for Jing Tring to have instead.

I didn't think this letter would cause my niang sadness, but I was wrong. My second brother Cunyuan replied soon after and said that when he'd read the letter, my niang had sobbed.

One of my favorite places I'd discovered in the academy was the library. It was only a small room, with just a few shelves of books. There were no foreign books and almost all of the books were picture books—stories about foreign children written by Chinese authors, and the stories were always sad and tragic. Most of them were about struggling colored children in America and how the whites mistreated them, or they were about the struggle between good and evil. The good characters were always beautiful and handsome. The evil characters always had big crooked noses and fat ugly faces. They were Chiang Kaishek's Guomindang officers

151

and spies, or the foreign enemies. I hated the evil guys and felt so sad for these impoverished colored children. I often shed sympathetic tears and I felt even more grateful for the heavenly life that Chairman Mao had given us. If *our* life was heavenly, then these poor children's lives in America must be hell indeed.

There were several different newspapers delivered to our academy too, for the political heads and teachers to read. The *People's Daily* was the official paper of the government, but there were also the *Workers' Daily*, the *Soldiers' Daily* and some other industry papers. All were full of propaganda and all were controlled by the Gang of Four. We could only read them after the adults had finished with them, and by then they were a day or two old, sometimes up to a week old. But still we read the editorial comments—the Cultural Revolutionary ideas and themes, pages upon pages of domestic news, unbelievable human achievement stories that denounced the old filthy ideas of the rightists and antirevolutionaries. There would perhaps be a couple of pages of sports and less than a page of international news—the information pitifully thin. There was also the *Reference Paper*, but this was only available to a certain level of Communist Party member, and it included slightly more international news and slightly less propaganda. Occasionally, though, someone would find an old copy and pass it around.

We'd only been at the academy about two weeks when one day all of us were called out into the grounds, just before lunch. We waited in our usual four lines. All three political heads were looking very stern indeed as they stood on the stairs in front of us.

Director Wang began. "We have discovered a serious misconduct by one of our students," he said. "According to this student, there were others involved in the same misconduct. I want this matter thoroughly investigated!" We all looked at each other. No one knew what he could possibly be talking about.

Director Wang continued. "We have told you before that *no*

one is to touch the *Reference Paper*. Today, we have discovered a student reading it! I want to know who took the paper from our offices, who read it, and how long this has been going on. This is a most serious matter. The first class this afternoon has been canceled. You will instead discuss why this is a serious matter and how you should prevent it from happening again. I want the students who have read the *Reference Paper* to write a self-criticism and to search deep into their souls!"

During lunch, the guilty students went to the three political heads and confessed. I was one of them. I spent my entire nap time trying to work out what crime I had committed just by reading a newspaper. There was nothing in it that could shake my faith in Chairman Mao.

When the bell rang to signal the end of nap time, I was still scratching my head for answers. At least I hadn't actually stolen the paper, I thought. Someone had passed it to me. Thankfully he'd also confessed so at least I didn't have to tell on him. That was something I never wanted to do.

Our afternoon discussions about the matter went by very quickly. Under the guidance of our political heads we discovered several major issues we hadn't even thought of before: we were too young to digest the contents of this newspaper so we could get the wrong impression and our communist faith could be affected; stealing was a serious crime; reading something that was restricted only to Communist Party members and knowingly passing it around to others was dishonest; and finally, we had broken the academy rules.

I wrote my self-criticism based on these four findings, and it passed the first time. But deep down I didn't feel good about it at all. I still couldn't think of *anything* that would affect my belief in communism. Certainly not a newspaper. After all, I'd only read some sports and international news.

153

✝

10

THAT FIRST LONELY YEAR

Those first few weeks at the Beijing Dance Academy were an agony of loneliness. Nights were the worst. I couldn't wait to get to bed so I could clutch onto my niang's quilt, my only security. I hated myself for it, but the quilt was like morphine, soothing my pain, and in those first months at the academy I became introverted and spoke very little.

I knew I had no choice but to stay in Beijing. My parents, my brothers, my relatives, my friends, my old schoolteachers and classmates, my village and commune, all of their wishes and expectations made it impossible for me to go back. The loss of face would be unbearable. It would damage my family's reputation forever. My success was my parents' only hope of breaking that vicious cycle of poverty. I couldn't let my parents down, even if I did feel trapped in a cage of rules, routines and frustration. Every day I couldn't wait for classes to end. Every day I couldn't wait for the year to end so I could return home to see my family and roam the streets and fields once more.

I wasn't alone in missing home. I witnessed many teary eyes among my fellow classmates. The girls sobbed more than the boys. Our political heads and teachers showed more tenderness toward the girls, though. The boys would be laughed at if they were discovered sobbing. The boys were told, time after time, that crying was a sign of weakness.

The city kids seemed to cope better than the country ones. They were more confident and adjusted to the routine faster. The Shanghai kids coped well—they were generally fairer skinned too, but us country kids were darker. I was probably one of the darkest, but fair skin was considered beautiful in China so even there I felt inadequate compared to the others, and I stuck with the students from the countryside.

Our first weeks at the academy weren't made any easier when a vicious virus swept through the school. I was among those who had the severe cough, the sore throat and high fever. Naturally I did what my niang would have done—I took out a few pieces of my precious dried snakeskin and wrapped a green onion in them. I tried to be polite and offered to share it with some of my classmates, but it was as though I'd offered them poison. They thought I was evil. So to prove my sincerity I ate one in front of them, but my teachers and classmates were so repulsed they moved quickly away. I lost a few friends over that, but I did notice that their symptoms lasted much longer than mine, despite their expensive pills.

The academy's toilets were another challenge. I appreciated the idea of being able to flush away the poos to who knows where, but the reality that always confronted us was blocked toilets. We had no choice but to poo on top of a hole that was already full of shit, and the smell was revolting. It penetrated through the walls. It lingered in the building. Often I had to run to other floors to use the toilets there and most of the time other students would already be waiting. Toilet rush hours were the worst—in the mornings after waking up, after breakfast, after lunch, after nap time, and the worst time of all was after dinner before the "go to sleep" bell. I would wait until I was absolutely desperate. I would close my eyes, hold my breath and charge into the toilet, trying to breathe as few times as possible.

One day as I joined the queue for the toilet, I saw a classmate of mine standing outside meditating. A dreadful smell pushed through my nose and I knew immediately that at least one or possibly both toilets were blocked.

"How many?" I asked.

"Both of them!" he replied desperately. I backed out of the bathroom, took a deep breath from the open window by the stairs, and charged onto the wee stand.

On my way out, my classmate was still outside taking deep breaths. "Still working up your courage?" I asked.

"I'm sure the smell will damage my health!" He shook his head in disgust, but he too took a deep breath and charged in.

The toilet might have been one of the worst things about the Beijing Dance Academy, but the showers were one of the best. We were assigned to take showers on different days, usually three times a week. We had to get in early, though, because the hot water would run out and latecomers were always left with cold showers.

My very first shower was like magic. One of our teachers led ten of us to the changing room, which had wooden benches along the walls for us to put our clothes on. It was very damp, with a pleasant soapy smell. We had to bring along a facecloth, a washing basin and soap. We had no shampoo. Massive amounts of steam pushed out into the changing room as the class of students before us came out. I hesitantly followed the other boys into the shower. I was a little afraid, but I'd heard some adults in our village talking about this thing called a shower, so I tentatively popped my head under the jets of water. It was wonderful! Warm water streamed down my hair and over every part of my body. I opened my mouth to breathe. Warm water filled it up and it felt so good that I kept my mouth open and let the water glide over me.

I was surprised to see my classmates show no particular reaction one way or another to the shower. Maybe they'd had one before, I thought. But all I wanted to do was stay under all day. Compared with the filthy, cold water in the washing-basin back home, this was a thrilling experience. I wished my family could have the same privilege. I had never felt cleaner. But we didn't know, then, that in winter we would be encouraged to take cold showers, to make our hearts and minds grow stronger.

The food at the academy was also good. Beyond good. We had rice nearly every day and it tasted so glorious because I rarely had it at home at all. And, luxury of luxuries, we had fresh fruit twice a week! Apples, pears and occasionally even bananas. We would get one piece each, or if we were lucky, sometimes even two. I savoured every bite. With enough food to eat for the first time in my life, I was in ninth heaven. I wished I could share the food with my family too: my niang and my dia deserved to have this.

One of the treats we soon experienced at the academy was, once a month, watching documentaries and occasionally a movie. All of the foreign films were from other communist countries. A North Korean movie that I remember particularly well was about a young man who had lost his ambitions for the communist cause, and a beautiful girl, a Communist Youth Party member, who helped him and fell in love with him. What I enjoyed most about this movie was not the politics but the love story. For the next couple of weeks I started to behave differently toward the captain of the girls' class. She was a pretty Qingdao girl with big, bright eyes. I imagined that if I performed badly enough in class, the political head might send this girl to help me, or more excitingly, perhaps she might even volunteer. But all I got was criticism and dirty looks. The longed-for love and attention never materialized.

Within the first month of our arrival in Beijing, we heard that the president of America, Richard Nixon, was to pay a historic visit to China. It was February 1972. People in Beijing were jubilant. The government's propaganda machine went into full swing and the Chinese media boasted of nothing else. This visit by Nixon was confirmation that Mao's communism had won the final battle against capitalism.

I didn't share this euphoria. I didn't care about Nixon. I was too homesick. But I did notice that the attacks on America's evil capitalist values by the Chinese propaganda machines eased considerably while President Nixon was there.

The first few weeks and months of our dance training I found impossibly hard. I had no idea what I was doing. Nothing made sense, I couldn't do the exercises no matter how hard I tried, and I doubted myself constantly. My torn hamstrings from Teacher Gao's exercises were continually painful and I'd injured my back during the acrobatics classes too. I knew I was destined to fail—it was just a matter of time before they sent me home.

One day we were given some exciting news: Madame Mao was coming to our university in person, in just a few weeks' time. Our academy was to prepare some dance exercises, and a small group of students would be selected to perform for her.

I wasn't included. I was heartbroken. I had been so excited at the thought of performing for Madame Mao, and now it wouldn't be.

After Madame Mao watched the specially prepared performance, she said to the officials, "The dancing looked all right, but where are the guns? Where are the grenades? Where are the political meanings?" She wanted us to combine traditional ballet steps with some Peking Opera movements, so from that point on our teachers made major changes to our training syllabus. In the middle of a classical plié we had to stiffen our hands into Kung

Fu gestures while we were doing port de bras, and we had to finish off with a deathlike stare we called "brightening the presence." Our teachers took it all very seriously. We had to prepare these "model" ballets, a combination of Western and Chinese styles that were a monument to Madame Mao's obsession. In reality, it was political ideology gone mad. But our university strictly followed her instructions and policies. We became nothing more than Chairman Mao's political puppets.

I knew that some of our teachers were incensed by this approach, but they had to bury their integrity and their love for Western ballet in their hearts. If they didn't, they would risk being labeled counterrevolutionaries, and be sent to jail or the pig farms. It could cost them their lives.

They knew Madame Mao's approach could never work. In classical ballet training we had to turn our joints out, but with Beijing Opera movements we were required to do the opposite. Ballet steps needed fluidity and softness. Beijing Opera required sharp, strong gestures. But propaganda ensured we believed that the Chinese model ballets were the world's best. They were groundbreaking. They were "uniquely Chinese." Nobody dared to question this, and we continued to do what we were told.

We spent a lot of time at the academy studying Mao's theories. We were expected to memorize every word in his Red Book and relate them to our daily activities. In fact, we spent more time on Mao than we did on ballet and all other subjects combined. Often we were divided into small groups to discuss Chairman Mao's most recent ideas. We were taught to focus on the meaning of each word. Once a student even suggested that if we really understood the meaning of Mao's words, then we wouldn't need to eat. His golden words would replace our daily food. That student received high praise for his remarks from our political head. I just thought he was crazy—he'd never known starvation, that was clear.

159

We were encouraged to tell everyone about our impure thoughts. We were rewarded for reporting when a fellow student's behavior wasn't in keeping with Chairman Mao's great political vision. We were even told once, by one of the political heads, that a brave and faithful young Red Guard loved Chairman Mao so much that he informed the police that his parents had Taiwan connections. Both parents were arrested, and their son was upheld as a national hero, Mao's model guard.

I too would have done anything for Chairman Mao. Anything, except tell on my parents. I loved my niang and my dia too much to betray them for my belief in Chairman Mao's revolution.

Madame Mao also wanted us to spend three weeks each year with the farmers, the workers or the soldiers. These were called the "Learning Three Classes" sessions. We had to live and work among the peasants or workers or soldiers and at the same time keep up our dance training. At the end of each "learning session" we had to put on a performance.

Our first three-week summer holiday was spent in one of these learning sessions, with the peasants in a nearby commune. How I welcomed the wheat and the cornfields, the smell of manure, the sound of the crickets! Even the raw earth was wonderful to see, but it all made me homesick too. I wanted to go back to my village and catch my beloved crickets and dragonflies again. I wanted both worlds: the good food of the academy and the freedom of my home.

I worked well in the fields, and I was surprised that my classmates from the city had little idea about how to work on the land. I truly believed Chairman Mao was right: if these kids didn't come to the commune and work with the peasants, they would have no idea where their food came from.

We continued to practice our ballet, acrobatics and Beijing Opera Movement every day while we were living with the peasants. We used wire poles and walls for our barre. The dirt ground was uneven and uncomfortable and the scratching sounds of our feet brushing through each movement were unbearable—like fingernails scraping down a piece of glass. Our ballet shoes wore out so quickly, and they were always filthy with mud. We even had to do cartwheels and back flips in the fields. Sprained ankles were not uncommon.

We slept and ate at different peasants' homes during our stay, but by the third day so many students suffered stomach cramps and diarrhea that the school officials had to quickly call in our own academy chef to cook for us. The male students, including me, were assigned to guard our kitchen supplies so nobody would steal them.

"Why would anyone steal our food?" I asked one of our political heads. "Aren't the peasants our role models?"

He thought for a moment. "We are not guarding against the peasants' stealing," he said. "We're guarding against the enemy's evil motives. They might try to poison us. It's the hidden things we must watch for. Do you understand?"

I didn't understand, but I nodded anyway. I saw his expression and knew this was the end of the discussion. I thought that surely by now all our enemies would have been wiped out in all of Mao's campaigns and revolutions.

The weather was still hot when we returned to our university. And shortly after, the dreaded visit to the swimming pool occurred.

"Students who can't swim, raise your hands!" the same political head who'd asked me to wash his sweat-stained shirt instructed. A few hands went up—mine was one of them. Almost all of the kids who couldn't swim came from Shanghai or Beijing. I was the only one from Qingdao who couldn't swim.

"A boy who comes from a city by the sea and can't swim?" the political head sniggered.

I felt the blood rush to my face. I wanted to go back to my dormitory. But I knew I couldn't, so I followed instructions and hesitantly took off my clothes.

"Where is your swimming suit?" the political head asked me. Everyone looked at my practice shorts.

"I don't have a swimming suit."

"Didn't I tell everyone to buy one yesterday?"

I didn't answer. I didn't want to tell him that I couldn't afford one.

He gave me an annoyed look and shook his head. "Okay, everyone. Students who can swim can go now. Students who can't, follow me."

He took us to the shallow end of the pool and demonstrated the so-called "frog style," or breaststroke. Following his instructions, I tried to swim but my body sank as soon as I started to circle my arms. I kept swallowing water. I looked across and saw my classmates swimming and diving like fish and wished I could be like them. The political leader spent all his time helping the girls. He never looked in the boys' direction once. I dipped my head under a couple of times and my nose filled with water. I wondered if I would ever learn to swim.

But by the end of that summer I did learn, even though I was still constantly afraid of the water. It was a couple of my classmates who eventually taught me.

That summer in Beijing was hot. We had no air-conditioning or fans, and when the heat became unbearable, we slept on the floor in the dance studio. Over twenty of us slept in there, and even with the studio's many windows, the body heat made it difficult to sleep. Mosquitoes would come out in the thousands and zoom around like little vampires. We slapped about frantically, trying to chase them away, and the slapping sounds could be heard throughout the night.

During the second half of our first year, the school added several new classes. One of them was Art Philosophy, Madame Mao's brainchild, the one we'd been told about on that first day, and surprisingly I liked it. It was designed to help us understand the relationship between the arts and politics. Chairman Mao's idea was that the arts should be important political tools.

Our teacher for Art Philosophy was a tall, talkative man. During class one day, he went into one of his little detours, talking about Mao as a brilliant political strategist. "The one political strategist I think was the best ever was Adolf Hitler! Like Chairman Mao, he seized on the psychological needs of an entire nation. He rallied millions of people to go to war for him. He made them *believe* it was all for their own good. Both Chairman Mao and he are master politicians, brilliant at understanding the people's psyche."

I, like most of my classmates, didn't have a clue who Hitler was. I thought he must have been a great communist, just like Chairman Mao.

Our teacher was brave to draw parallels like this, and often his true interests seemed to lie in areas other than the subject he was ordered to teach. He tried to show us how to look at a subject beyond the surface, beyond the obvious. One day he brought a plaster model of a man's head into our classroom. The surface of the model was as smooth as porcelain. He sat the model on his lecture table. "Raise your hand if you think the surface of the model is rough?"

What a stupid question, we all thought. It was obvious the surface was smooth. Nobody raised a hand.

"Now, raise your hand if you think the model has a smooth surface."

Everyone raised their hands.

"I think you are all wrong or at best, you are only *half* right. I want you to look at it more closely and then tell me your answers."

This time there was a magnifying glass beside the model. We looked through it and were surprised to discover millions of tiny holes on the smooth surface of the head.

That class lasted only one and a half years. It was mysteriously dropped after that, and I never saw Madame Mao's Art Philosophy teacher again. I once asked one of the political heads about him. "He is no longer needed at our academy," he answered bluntly. "He has been assigned a different job."

Throughout that first year at the Beijing Dance Academy, I was considered a laggard by most of my teachers. I labored through the days with no aim, no self-confidence, and I couldn't keep up with the pace. It was too much for an eleven-year-old peasant boy. I felt that not a single teacher liked me. I wanted to shrink and run for cover. I longed for my parents' comfort and love, but here there was no one to go to for help. So I pulled myself further inwards, desperately trying to stay afloat, but constantly sinking.

We'd been at the academy for about nine months when our teachers organized another day trip for us, this time to the Great Wall. Again, fear of motion sickness terrified me, but I wasn't going to miss this opportunity for anything.

It was a windy autumn day. We were given three hours to climb the wall. Its bulk and beauty stunned me. The size of the stones, its breathtaking height into the misty mountains, its endless snakelike meandering—it all made me gasp. I had seen pictures of the Great Wall before, but to actually stand on it, to look upon this incredible human miracle . . . I shook my head in disbelief. A fable that my niang had once told me immediately came to mind. It was about a poor young man, Wang Shileong, and his bride. Wang Shileong's name meant "ten thousand humans." It was said there was a section of the Great Wall that could never be built unless ten thousand bodies were buried as its foundation. Rumor had it that Wang Shileong's body alone could support that section. When the imperial soldiers buried him under the wall, his new bride stuck a knife through her heart and was buried there with him. I remembered my niang had said that this story portrayed a Chinese woman's determination to remain faithful to her man. "But this principle of faith also applies to a man," she'd said. "You are expected to be faithful to your woman with all your might until death eventually separates you. A girl's heart is pure and sincere. If you treasure her, she will love you unconditionally until the end. But you must never take a girl's love for granted."

I was touched by my niang's story and I admired the bride's strong will and faithfulness. "Wouldn't it be nice to see the Great Wall one day?" my second brother, Cunyuan, had said. Now, here I was, climbing on the ancient stone steps and wishing that my family could see it too.

The end of our first year at the academy was approaching, and the end-of-year exams were coming up. Our possible grades were: excellent, very good, good, below good, above average, average, below average and . . . bad. Tension was high among the teachers as well as the students. It was judgment day for the teachers as well.

I wasn't worried about my academic classes because I knew I wasn't the worst there, but my dancing classes were another matter.

There were four dance-related exams that year: ballet, acrobatics, Chinese folk dance and Beijing Opera Movement. Acrobatics and Chinese folk dance were less of a worry, because the teachers were kinder and those classes were fun. But for my ballet and Beijing Opera Movement classes I was scared to death. We had to perform in front of academy officials, students from other classes, Chiu Ho and a panel of teachers who had pen and pad in hand.

There were over fifty students, teachers and officials already sitting by the mirrors in the front of the studio on the day of the

165

Beijing Opera Movement exam. The sunlight shone through the windows, and I could see the dust entwined in the beams of sunlight. We walked into the room in a line—and upon seeing the many pairs of eyes, I froze completely. My mouth went dry and my tongue felt swollen. It was as though all those eyes were focused on me, and me alone. I even heard the sound of my own breathing and felt the hairs rise on the back of my neck.

We were placed on the barre first and before the pianist struck the first note, I was already dripping with sweat. I panicked. I couldn't remember the dance combinations even though we'd been preparing them for four weeks. It wasn't so bad on the barre, because everyone did the same exercises at the same time and I could follow the others, but once we moved into the center of the floor, the ten of us were broken up into three groups.

I was trembling all over. My legs felt weak, and I couldn't remember a single thing. I was in front now, and I had no one to follow. I peeked at the mirror, and I could see that others were following my mistakes. Teacher Gao Dakun looked at us with such anger, but he couldn't call names out because of all the people watching. As the exam went on I performed worse and worse as the dancing steps increased in difficulty. The agony lasted for over an hour. I wondered what other names Gao Dakun would call me after this!

I knew that exam had been disastrous. I was so distressed that I missed lunch and ran to my weeping willow trees. It was over two hours later that I went back to our dormitory. My confidence was shattered.

When I entered the roomful of eyes again the following morning, I noticed our ballet teacher, Chen Lueng, was already standing by the piano looking very tense. My heart pumped faster. This exam was to be judged mainly on barre work—we spent over three-quarters of our class time on it—and with our thin vest and shorts, I felt every muscle, every technical fault would be exposed and magnified, even the scar on my arm. Each exercise seemed slower and more excruciating than in class. I didn't hear a single note of the music and before I'd even lifted my legs, I could already feel them cramping. Chen Lueng had screamed at us all year for holding on to the barre too tightly, and here I was, gripping onto it for dear life.

Finally the torture of those end-of-year exams was over. We waited for our grades, and I knew in my heart this was not something I should be looking forward to.

I was right. My highest grade was "below good" for math and Chinese. The rest of my grades were "average," even for ballet, and my worst grade was "below average" for Teacher Gao's Beijing Opera Movement exam, which was no surprise to me at all. Nothing I did would ever please him.

I wasn't the worst student in my class, but with my poor results I was definitely near the bottom and I still felt wretched. We all knew each other's scores because our teachers read them out, loudly, in front of the entire class. My face flushed with each announcement of my low grades. Twenty-two pairs of eyes pierced me like needles. It summed up my miserable first year. I was convinced that soon Director Wang would call me into his office, tell me I was no good, and ask me to go home and never return.

11

THE PEN

Our first year was finished. Soon I would see my family again. My beloved niang. The Chinese New Year holiday was coming up and the school gave us our food allowance for the month to buy our train tickets home.

Everyone was excited. The school bus even took us on a shopping trip to Beijing to buy presents for our families. I only bought one yuan worth of sweets, though, and kept the rest, three whole yuan, to take back to my family. I knew three yuan would make an enormous difference to my dia and my niang, more difference than any number of gifts I could buy.

The last two days before going home seemed excruciatingly long. I counted every minute. I was terrified the whole time that I'd be called up by Director Wang about my poor grades, so I avoided our political heads at all times. But on the final day, just after lunch, I accidentally bumped right into the very person I'd been trying to avoid.

"*Ni hao*, Director Wang." My faced blushed. My heart thumped.

"*Ni hao*, Cunxin. Are you looking forward to seeing your family?"

I nodded, petrified. Here it comes, I thought.

"Have a safe trip!" He smiled at me and walked on.

What about my poor grades? What about expelling me? I was so relieved. I became excited beyond description. Now I could think only of seeing my parents and brothers and it made the final hours seem even longer.

On the way to the Beijing train station, my heart raced faster than the wheels of the bus. A political head and two teachers escorted us and again, the grandness of the station and the number of people rushing about amazed me.

We fought our way onto the train and settled in our seats. A siren sounded. The train slowly moved off. My heart was already in Qingdao with my family, and the anticipation was unbearable. Thoughts of my parents, brothers, relatives and friends, memories of making firecrackers, images of New Year's Eve, the scent of incense, the flame of candles, the delicious taste of my niang's dumplings, the drinking games and my second uncle's singing—all rushed to my mind. Images lingered—fond memories, wonderful thoughts. Then suddenly I remembered my report card. I imagined the gossip, how humiliating it would be for my family. It would be the most reputation-damaging, face-losing event in the Li family's entire history! How could I explain such low grades? How could I tell my parents that I hated dancing? It was all too confusing, and I told myself to worry about it later. I was tired from the exams anyway, and I fell into a deep sleep and didn't wake up until three stops before Qingdao Station.

It was still dark outside when we arrived, but dawn wasn't far off. My second brother was going to meet me at Cangkou Station, one stop before Qingdao, because it was closer to our commune. I looked at the familiar countryside gradually emerging in the dawn light, and my heart raced faster and faster.

As the train pulled into Cangkou Station I saw my second brother, Cunyuan, standing among a crowd of people under the dim light. I shot my head out of the train window. "*Erga! Erga!*" I called excitedly. "Second brother! Second brother!"

He saw me then, and started to run alongside the train. "It's *so* nice to see you! I waited for half an hour!" he shouted as he ran.

That image of Cunyuan running by the train was so joyful an image that it would remain with me, always.

My dia had walked to work that morning so Cunyuan could pick me up on Dia's bike. Our ride home together took nearly an hour. I sat on the back seat with my legs dangling on either side, my bag hanging over one shoulder, the early morning mist cold on my face.

"How are you?" Cunyuan asked as he pedaled.

"Fine, I'm happy to be home!" I replied.

"Tell me, what is Beijing like?" he asked anxiously.

I told him about the wide, paved streets and the grand buildings. I told him of the Great Wall, the Ming Tombs, the Forbidden City and of course glorious Tiananmen Square.

Cunyuan was utterly enthralled. He would occasionally interrupt with a question and ask for more details, so I told him about the polluted air, the vast number of vehicles, bikes and people, hundreds of thousands of people. When I told him about the food we had, he said, "You're making my mouth water! You are truly fortunate!" Then he was silent for a few minutes as though he needed time to imagine what eating such good food would be like.

"Did you meet Chairman and Madame Mao?" he asked eventually.

"Not Chairman Mao, but Madame Mao came to our school and spoke to us!" I replied.

"Oh, you are lucky, indeed, indeed!" he murmured.

I knew he was envious of the lifestyle I had in Beijing and would have loved to have had the same opportunities. So, trying to make him feel better, I told him about the blocked toilets, my dislike of some of the teachers and my dreadful homesickness.

He laughed at me for making such an issue about the toilets. "Surely they are better than our hole in the ground at home. That doesn't even have a roof over it!"

"I like our hole in the ground much better," I argued. "At least the foul smell can escape. Remember our grandfather's toilets in the city?" I asked.

"Not *that* bad?" he asked.

"Worse, much worse! More people pooing!" I replied, and he laughed. Then he asked, more seriously, "Why do you hate your teachers?"

"They are mean, and some shout at us all the time," I replied.

"Have you ever heard of a saying that says bitter medicine isn't necessarily bad and sweet medicine isn't always good for you? Surely if you were good, they would have no reason to shout at you," he said.

"But I'm no good at dancing. I can't concentrate when they shout at me. I just want to come home," I confessed.

He was shocked by this. "Cunxin, just look at the color of my skin and then look at yours. Within a year your skin has become whiter and mine darker. You don't want my life and my destiny. A peasant's job is the lowest job one can have. This is my first year working in the fields, and I hate it already. It is brainless work. My whole body is always covered with mud and sweat, and what is my reward? Not enough money to feed myself for a single day! Is this the kind of life you desire? Please, don't tell our parents about your homesickness. Especially our niang—she already misses you so much. She cried every time I read your letter. This last week, she hasn't stopped smiling and laughing, and she hasn't slept a single night. Please, only tell her the good things about Beijing."

By this time I could just see our village in the distance.

"Niang started cooking early this morning," Cunyuan continued. "So you could have a bowl of dumplings waiting when you arrived home!"

I knew Cunyuan was right about what I should say to my parents. I made up my mind to keep my sadness to myself.

As we turned into our street, we passed some neighbors. "Welcome home!" they called. Down the street I could see my fifth brother, Cunfar, and my little brother, Jing Tring, waving and jumping up and down by our house. They rushed in to tell our niang I was back, and within minutes a small crowd had gathered by our gate. As we came closer, I saw my niang come out and my heart pounded with excitement. She wore the same dark blue cotton jacket with patches on the elbows, an apron, and the same patched trousers as always, but she looked older than I remembered. The past year had taken its toll.

I jumped off the bike, and tears filled my eyes as we rushed to each other and she hugged me tightly in her arms. "How I missed you!" she cried. "How I missed you! I nearly died missing you!" she kept repeating.

I was in ninth heaven again. This was what I had been dreaming of ever since I left her a year ago.

My fourth aunt rushed out of her house then, hobbling on her tiny bound feet as fast as she could. "Where is my sixth son?"

"*Si niang.* How are you?" I asked.

"You are whiter and a little fatter than when you left us!" she said proudly.

We all went into our house then. Nothing had changed. I could smell the ginger, garlic and green onion dumplings. I was so happy. All my brothers sat around, and everyone talked and

172

talked. It was as though we were trying to tell all our stories of the past year, all at once.

Niang didn't say much, but from the way she looked at me I knew she had missed me terribly. Throughout the day I simply hung around her—I felt safe. I felt loved. I was a little child of hers once again.

"Can I help you wash those shirts?" I asked as my niang was preparing her laundry.

"I'm fine," she said. "Don't you want to see your friends?"

"I'll go later," I replied.

"Did you miss home?"

I hesitated, remembering what my second brother had said. "No, not too much, only a little!"

"That's good. There isn't much to miss back here. Only a hard life!" She sighed.

Just then a couple of my niang's friends walked in. "Aya! Look at him, he has grown!" one said.

"He has become so white," said the other. "Look at his beautiful skin! This would only come from nutritious food. What a lucky boy you are!"

I dutifully answered their questions about Beijing and life at the academy and then escaped to pay my respects to my relatives, neighbors and friends, and to spend the rest of the morning roaming the streets, playing some of the old games with my brothers and friends. I had missed them so much and I felt so relieved to be back.

After lunch, my fifth brother, Cunfar, suddenly dragged me outside into our front courtyard. "I nearly forgot!" he said excitedly. "I have a present for you. Just wait." He went into our little shed and pulled out a small glass jar. "I've kept my prized cricket champion for you since summer! He has beaten all the crickets in our village and now he is yours!" Proudly he handed me the jar.

"Really?" I held the jar as though it was a priceless treasure. "What did you name him?" I asked.

"The King," Cunfar replied. "He is so handsome, just wait until you see the size of his teeth!"

I carefully opened the lid. "Come on, King," I called and tilted the jar sideways. Nothing happened.

"He won't recognize your voice. Let me try," he said. "Come on, King! You can come out now!"

Still no cricket came out. "I'll kill you if you don't come out!" he shouted impatiently.

"Let me see." I gave the jar a gentle shake and tipped it upside down. The cricket dropped out, dead.

"Oh, my King!" My brother was devastated.

"Don't worry, Fifth Brother. I'm sure you'll find another champion next summer."

"You would have been so proud of him. He fought like a true warrior. His teeth were as sharp as knives. I'm sorry you didn't get to play with him."

I too was sad that the King was dead. From the look of him he'd been a strong cricket.

Later that afternoon, my second brother, Cunyuan, rode on the bike again to collect our dia from work. Jing Tring and I ran to the intersection at the edge of our village. I was excited to see my dia again, but I was anxious about my grades too and worried about his reaction. I saw them ride up, and my dia hopped off in front of us. "You're back!" He smiled one of his rare smiles.

I nodded. That was all he said to me and all I had to reply. I loved my dia dearly, and I knew he loved me as well.

My niang had already prepared a special dinner as a welcome treat by the time we arrived home. There was so much excitement! We all sat around the kang and again I explained what my life was like in Beijing and I tried hard to mention only the positive elements of the experience. "We can't match the food you had in Beijing, but I hope you still like my dumplings," my niang said as she set a bowl of steaming hot dumplings in front of me.

"This was all I'd dream about, but we did have dumplings all the time at the academy," I lied. I pushed the bowl in front of my dia, because I knew there wouldn't be enough for everyone.

"*Liuga*, can you count how many times you ate meat there?" Jing Tring asked.

"Nearly every day!" I replied.

Cunsang was wide-eyed with disbelief.

I nodded. There was silence.

"Madame Mao wouldn't let her students starve, would she?" Niang said finally.

A few weeks before I arrived home Cunsang had been accepted by the Chinese navy, and he was going to be a sailor on one of the battleships stationed in the Shandong Province area, so we talked about this as well. After dinner I took out the sweets that I had bought in Beijing, and everyone tasted a piece. Our dia would keep the rest as gifts. Then I suggested playing our word-finding game, looking for words from the newspapers that covered our walls, and my brothers happily agreed. We had so much fun. It was just like old times.

Before bed, when I was alone with my parents and Jing Tring, I handed my dia the three yuan that I had saved.

"Why didn't you buy something for yourself in Beijing?" my dia asked.

"I thought this would help the family," I replied.

"*Zhi zhi zhi!*" My niang just sighed. She was sad that I'd felt the need to give back whatever I had to my family.

With my second brother now working in the commune, I could tell that my family's living conditions had improved, even if only slightly. They still ate the same kind of food, but now there was a little more for my niang to cook with: limited rations of meat, fish, oil, soy sauce and coal, plenty of dried yams and, once a week, corn bread. And besides the New Year's special food, my niang had cooked me dumplings not once but a couple of times, because she knew they were my favorite. Even so, there was never enough for everyone, and the dumplings traveled from my bowl to my niang's, my niang's back to mine, and then I would pass one to my dia. But he'd move his bowl away and the dumpling would slip onto the wooden tray. Niang would sigh yet again. "Silly boy, just eat them! I know you have good food to eat in Beijing, but you won't be able to have my dumplings again for a whole year!"

I attracted attention wherever I went in my village now. I was a celebrity.

"Did you *really* see Madame Mao?" one peasant man asked me.

I nodded.

He suddenly grabbed my hands and shook them violently. "It's a privilege! Such a privilege!" he shouted ecstatically.

Many people stopped me like that and asked me about Beijing and university life. I knew they were expecting to hear about glorious, heartwarming experiences, so I found myself telling everyone only the best aspects of Beijing. Everyone wanted to know about the food. I had to glorify everything. They longed to hear something that would give them hope. Hope was all they had, and I couldn't let them down.

One day, four of my old friends and I were playing our "hopping on one leg" game when one of them asked me to give them a dance lesson. "Teach us something we can perform in our school show!" he begged excitedly.

I hesitated. What could I possibly teach them?

"Please, please! Help your old friends!" they all persisted.

I knew they would be disappointed if I said no, so after

dinner that night we gathered together in the same room where my na-na's dead body had once rested for three days. It was mid-February and still very cold. My friends wore their thick cotton jackets and pants and, under the low-wattage light, they looked just like four enormous cottonwool balls.

"I want to teach you a Beijing Opera Movement exercise," I began. "It will get your legs warmed up first. Otherwise you'll injure yourselves. Let's put your legs on the windowsills." This was the only place I could think of that was roughly the height of a barre.

My friends just looked at me with peculiar expressions.

"All right, let me show you." I put my right leg up on the windowsill.

"See. It's not too hard," I encouraged, and I helped them to put their legs onto the sill as well. But as soon as I'd helped the last friend's leg up the others had already lowered theirs.

"It's too high!" one of them complained.

"Can't we use the edge of the kang?" another suggested.

So we moved to the bedroom and used the hip-high edge of the kang, which was much easier.

"Okay, now straighten your legs and your hips," I told them as I pushed one of their legs straight.

"Ow!" they screamed.

"Now, let's change legs," I instructed.

They lifted their other legs up to the edge of the kang, but all they did was scream and groan. "Can't you teach us something less painful and more fun?"

I could see this was going to be a challenge. I couldn't think of anything that was fun, exciting and painless as well. Out of desperation, I showed them some relatively easy ballet positions.

"I don't know whether you can use them in your show or not, but they're not painful." I demonstrated first, second and fifth foot positions. "You can hold on to the edge of the kang," I told them. They all tried, but their feet caved in every time they straightened their knees.

"Is this all you have learned in the past year?" one of my friends asked.

I nodded.

"Surely it was more fun than this! Come on, teach us something easy so we can impress everyone at the show."

I didn't know how to answer him. Fun? I thought of Gao Dakun pushing our bodies onto our legs, putting the full force of his weight on us.

My friends didn't ask me to teach them any dance movements after that.

My month at home went by as fast as the blink of an eye. I dreaded going back to the rigid routine of the university.

On my last night home, after dinner, when everyone except me and my parents had gone to bed, my dia handed me eight yuan.

"It's too much," I protested.

"Take it. Things are more expensive now. Our lives are looking up with your second brother working." Then, completely unexpectedly, he handed me a sealed envelope. "I was going to get you some sorghum sweets, but I bought you this instead. I'm sorry I didn't have enough money to have it wrapped."

Inside the envelope I found the most beautiful fountain pen. It was deep royal blue, my favorite color. I could tell it was an expensive one. It would have cost my dia at least two yuan.

"I hope you will use it every day," my dia said, "and every time you use it, you will remember your parents and our expectations of you. I don't know what grades your classmates have received, but I hope you will come home with better grades next year. Don't let us down. Let us be proud."

I had expected my parents to talk to me about my poor

178

grades. I had expected harsher words. But that pen, and the few words my dia said then, caused bigger waves inside me than any accusations could ever bring. He didn't blame me. He didn't accuse me, but I felt I had let him and my whole family down. I couldn't bear to look at him. Instead, I looked at my niang, but she had buried her head in her sewing. I knew that every time I used my dia's pen, his words would echo in my mind.

十二

12

MY OWN VOICE

The train trip back to Beijing this time was a happier experience. Even the settling-in period at the academy was easier because by now all of us could communicate with each other in Mandarin. I couldn't stop thinking about my dia's pen, though, and his pride-provoking words. I knew that every time I used that pen, I would feel guilty, because my attitude toward my dancing hadn't changed. I still hated it.

In May that year, Madame Mao visited our university for the second time. This time I did get to perform for her, and afterward we all gathered at the sports ground where, with indomitable authority, she told us to study hard and be good students of Chairman Mao's. Her entourage of cultural officials stood beside her with expressions of the utmost admiration and respect. She told the university officials that the dance students were technically weak. So additional classes were added, including martial arts.

Madame Mao also ordered two young champions from the Beijing Martial Arts School and the Beijing Acrobatics School to join us as model students. They were awesome. I was especially impressed with Wang Lujun. He could master ten back flips in a row with ease. He could do "double flying legs" with incredible height, but his "butterfly" was the most difficult and exciting step to watch. You had to swing your body from right to left, with head and body at chest height, at the same time pushing both legs up in the air in a fanning motion. When the movement was done properly it looked just like a butterfly flying in the air. Wang Lujun could do thirty-two of them in a row! He was legendary.

Although Lujun was good at acrobatics, martial arts and Beijing Opera Movement, he struggled hard at ballet. Because he had come in the middle of that second year, he'd missed learning the basics, and the way the muscles were used in ballet was so different from the way they were used in martial arts. He told me many times that he wished he could go back to martial arts again but, for the same reason as me, he felt trapped. He had a duty to perform and there was no way back.

Lujun was honest, and he had a strong sense of fairness. Later he was nicknamed the Bandit, and he liked it so much that the name stuck.

One day, later in that same term, I remember the Bandit bought ten fen worth of sweets: his father often sent him spending money, and he would occasionally slip a sweet or two into my hand. But this time his class captain found out and told the head teacher. The Bandit was ordered to write three self-criticisms. He dug deep, but he genuinely couldn't think of a single reason why he *shouldn't* buy sweets. So I gave him some ideas—the ten fen he'd spent on sweets could have saved someone from starvation. Or his selfish action could corrupt his mind. I didn't really believe this, but I had to convince him that it was the only way to get him out of trouble. He had to learn how to survive this psychological brainwashing too. Fortunately, it worked and his self-criticism passed the test.

After that incident, the Bandit and I became good friends, and a few weeks later, to my great surprise, he asked me to become his blood brother, a tradition from the Kung Fu masters' era and a bond that would last a lifetime. But in many ways the forming of this bond often rivaled real brotherly love, so at first I said no. I had six brothers already. I didn't need another. The Bandit was very disappointed, but he wasn't deterred and the following Sunday, he invited me to go for an outing. We got permission to leave the university (without this we were never allowed beyond the gate), and the Bandit took me to a small eatery at the base of a mountain on the outskirts of Beijing. He ordered a small bottle of rice wine and a small plate of pig's head meat—a wonderful delicacy. It was white and full of lard. Delicious! What my niang would give for such a treat! I didn't like the rice wine, though, because it was so strong, nearly 100 percent proof.

After we'd finished, the Bandit took out a small knife, a piece of paper and a pen. He asked me once again if I wanted to be his blood brother. He had tears in his eyes as he prepared himself for my rejection.

I thought carefully for a while, then told him my real fear, the fear that I couldn't live up to his expectations. I took my six brothers for granted. I had never considered how best to be a good brother.

He laughed at that, and said he loved me for who I was.

I relented. We cut our fingers and dropped some blood into a cup of rice wine and shared the same drink together. We then made up a poem. The rhythm and the sounds of the Chinese words were beautiful, and we worked on it for over an hour. We knew our friendship would be special—life at the academy was so lonely and so tough, the only thing we had was friendship. When the Bandit and I became blood brothers, we knew we were establishing a bond that would ensure our emotional survival for the next few years.

That year, the different academies in our university selected even more students, and our complex in the countryside just wasn't big enough to accommodate them all. So Madame Mao ordered each academy to go back to its old location in the city. We were told to pack our few belongings, because we would be moving out when we returned from our next three-week summer holiday, which would be spent with the workers at a garment factory outside Beijing.

Unlike our academy in the countryside, our new city site was much smaller and very cramped. Boys and girls occupied different sections on the second floor of a three-story building, with eight students sleeping in each small room. We slept in four-bed bunks with one tiny drawer for our personal belongings. Anything that didn't fit there would have to be stored under our bed. We would share those poky little rooms until we graduated.

We had a new director now too. And there were more new teachers. On the first day in our new academy, we were told we would have a new ballet teacher, Xiao Shuhua.

Teacher Xiao was a small boyish-looking man. Other teachers called him by his nickname, Woa Woa, which meant baby. "I'm excited to work with you," he said to us in the first class. "Although I'm your teacher, I'm also your friend. We will work together and learn together, and make our classes fun. Not only will I teach you ballet steps, I'll also try to teach you the appreciation of ballet. Ballet is the most beautiful art form in the world. I hope, by the time I'm finished with you, you'll have the same appreciation. We should know each other's strengths and also our weaknesses. For a start, I want all of you to know that your new ballet teacher can't turn. I have the worst pirouettes in the world!"

Teacher Xiao was a happy man with a quick temperament. His happiness and emotions fluctuated depending on how his students performed. He encouraged us to write down our achievements, mistakes, new discoveries, even the combination of dance steps, every day, in our diaries. He was intolerant of laziness and lack of commitment. He would fume with anger if we didn't remember the dance combinations or his individual corrections. But he was also quick to praise and to demonstrate. He had a breathtakingly enormous jump, and he was very lean and fit. He always carried a notebook to his classes, with every step and every combination written down in detail.

Although Teacher Xiao's own turning ability was poor, he was determined to help his students perfect their turns, so he embarked on months of turning classes. We would complete our barre work within fifteen minutes and the rest of the two hours would be all pirouettes. The first thing he wanted to tackle was our fear of turning. Sometimes I felt the whole universe spinning around me when I walked out of these classes. Many nights I dreamed about doing multiple pirouettes and the feeling was incredibly exhilarating. It was like a "millet dream," I thought. There was a well-cited fable in China, which Teacher Xiao repeated to us many times:

A poor Chinese scholar, on his way to the capital to attend the emperor's annual scholars' competition, suddenly ran out of money. He was still far from Beijing, and now he had no money to hire a horse. He was hungry and tired and as he passed a small, run-down home he smelled a wonderful fragrance coming from within. He knocked on the door and an old lady stood in front of him. He begged her for some food, but she was so poor she only had millet soup to offer him. He thanked her and sat in a corner to rest while the soup cooked. He immediately fell asleep and dreamed that he had won the competition and that he would live a wealthy and happy life with many wives, concubines and children. When he woke up from his dream he

184

believed this was his fate, until he glanced at the millet soup cooking in the wok, and realized that he was in truth just an ordinary man and the things he had dreamed were too good to be true.

"Great things don't come easily!" Teacher Xiao insisted, and I thought of his unattainable pirouettes. We worked on three consecutive turns for over a year. It seemed impossible to master. The perfect balance on a high demi-pointe, the shape of the hands, the crisp spotting with our heads, the turn-out of both legs, straight back, pressed-down shoulders—the coordination of all these elements together. So many things to remember! For a long time, it seemed that we would never achieve more than three pirouettes but still Teacher Xiao worked us tirelessly, day in and day out.

Teacher Xiao didn't seem to notice me much in the first two classes. I was shy and physically underdeveloped. He seemed to think I was the one with the least interesting face and couldn't understand why I had been chosen in the first place. But during our third class he apparently noticed something unusual about my eyes. He began to try to find out what kind of boy I was. The more he found out, the more interested he became. He discovered that I remembered every word he said, as long as I was interested. So he *made* me interested in ballet, and quickly realized that I didn't cope well with forceful shouting, which was common practice among the teachers at the Beijing Dance Academy. Instead I responded well to gentle encouragement. He noticed every subtle improvement I made. He made sure that I knew he'd noticed. He gently and gradually led me into the intricacies of ballet, nurtured me, dealt with my self-doubt and inadequacies with encouragement, and slowly moved me from the back of the class to the front.

Apart from more and more ballet, we also started geography and history classes that year. We spent very little time on international geography. Our teacher tried hard to mention America as little as possible and no one took his class seriously, but I wanted to know about the other countries, even though I had to hide my interest. Our history class also dwelled mainly on China, but here I found the rise and fall of the different Chinese dynasties fascinating, especially the Tang and Ming dynasties with their great art, crafts, porcelain, medicine and splendid poetry.

We had a new teacher for our politics class too that term, Chen Shulian, but we really only studied communist history and Mao's political ideas. We were starved for knowledge from anywhere outside of China. We learned a little about Marx, Engels, Lenin and Stalin, but only as a backdrop to Mao's great political achievements. "Our Chairman Mao is the one who has brought Marx's communist philosophy to life!" Chen Shulian told us one day. "He is leading us to the first stage of communism."

"Are we in the first stage of communism now?" a student asked.

"Yes, but this is a long road. We have to work hard at it."

Another hand was raised. "What is the final stage of communism like?"

"Oh, it is the ultimate wonderland! There is no starvation, no class distinction, no need to work long hours. There will be total equality. Everyone will work willingly and share equally. There will be no greed or laziness, no cheating or unfairness. We will have the best of everything! It will be total happiness!"

Chen Shulian's vision was like morphine for the sick. It gave us a reason to bear our present harsh conditions. She portrayed Chairman Mao as the greatest political strategist ever, a man who could outmaneuver all his political enemies. She rigidly followed the textbooks. It was uninspiring to me, but I felt this was an important class all the same if I wanted to become a true communist of tomorrow. Chen Shulian must have impressed her superiors, though, because she became the head teacher of our group the following year.

Our Chinese folk dance class became my favorite class that year. I liked Teacher Chen Yuen's jokes. Sometimes he took students to catch frogs in the rice fields, or cicadas at night with our flashlights. On weekends, we would fry the frogs' legs and cicadas in his room on a small electric burner. His hobby was photography, and he often invited some of the students to help him.

But during the first half of that year, Chen Yuen's personality suddenly changed. He joked less. He stopped organizing out-of-school activities. He stopped his photography and became withdrawn and sad. I didn't understand and asked if there was anything wrong. His answer was always the same. "Nothing is wrong." Then one day, suddenly, he disappeared. Later we heard that he had been discovered engaging in homosexual activities. He was sent to a pig farm in the countryside to cleanse his filthy mind. Homosexuality in Mao's China was a serious criminal offense.

A year later, just as suddenly, Chen Yuen returned to the school as a carpenter. He had lost his reputation, his teaching job, his wife and his position in society. Most significantly, he had lost face. His association with dance had come to an end. He was now in the lowest class of people in China, and his every move was monitored. He had to write a weekly self-criticism and progress report to the Communist Party Monitoring Committee in our academy. I never saw him smile again.

But Chen Yuen's misfortunes went from bad to worse. One Sunday he was using the big machine saw and lost three of his fingers. There was no compensation, and he had to pay all his medical expenses. He couldn't use a saw after that, and he ended up cleaning the toilets. His loss of dignity was unbearable to watch, even for a young boy like me.

Chen Yuen's replacement was his former teacher, Ma Lixie. Small, thin and animated, he had an unusually loud voice and a habit of rubbing his palms together at furious speed before demonstrating an exercise, as though this gave him courage or inspiration. I learned so much from Ma Lixie. His demonstrations were of perfection. He taught us a Korean crane dance, encouraged us to learn the essence of the dance, every subtle eye and even hair movement to feel like the bird's feathers. He dared us to think the unthinkable and explore the unexplorable. He dared us to be better than he. "*Qing chu yu lan er sheng yu lan*," he would say: the color green comes from the color blue, but it is the stronger of the two. He challenged us to be the color green.

That year I also met a new student, Chong Xiongjun, a tall boy with a pimply face, from one of the outer suburbs of Beijing. He was two years older than I. After lunch one day, he asked me if I'd like to spend one Sunday with his family.

"I would love to, but I don't know if my teacher will let me," I replied.

That afternoon I went to one of our political heads to ask permission to go to Chong Xiongjun's home. He said that my parents would have to write a letter to the academy. The academy couldn't take responsibility if something should happen to me, and even if my parents did give their permission, I would only be allowed to go once a month.

A reply from my parents would probably take at least three weeks by the slow Chinese post.

In the following weeks, I received my parents' reply, written by my second brother, Cunyuan. They were excited about me going to the Chongs' home, especially my niang, who was happy that I would have a family close by to go to.

Xiongjun and I set off at eight o'clock the following Sunday morning. It took three different buses to get to Chaoyang district, and it was nearly ten o'clock by the time we arrived at their house. Xiongjun's grandmother was outside waiting for us. She gave him a big hug and told him she missed him so much. Xiongjun called her Lau-Lau. She reminded me of my na-na—she was old, small, with bound feet, poor eyesight and very few teeth. She looked at me and smiled broadly. "You can call me Lau-Lau too!"

The Chongs lived in a row of single-story concrete apartments, very much like the commune layout in Li Commune, except that the space was wider between each row and the apartments were built with concrete blocks. Even the floor inside was concrete.

The Chongs' apartment had three rooms. The entrance room was used as the kitchen, dining room and living room, and the rooms on each side of the entrance room were the bedrooms. There were no doors between each room; instead they had black cotton curtains. There was no toilet, only one outside the building that was shared by about twenty families.

I soon learned that both of Xiongjun's parents worked at a local glass factory. His father reminded me of my dia, a hard worker and a man of few words. His mother seemed a little younger than her husband and, like my own niang, she was the personality of their family.

We played cards after our tea, a game called "Protecting the Emperor," which at first concerned me a little. I thought it sounded very antirevolutionary. Then I helped to make dumplings. Xiongjun's mother was surprised. "Look at Cunxin's dumplings. They are so pretty, and I bet they will taste good too."

"Ma, if you keep embarrassing my friend, he won't come again!" Xiongjun said.

That day was also the very first time I'd tasted beer. It was room temperature because there was no refrigeration, and my first mouthful was all foam.

"Do you like it?" Xiongjun asked, laughing at me because the beer made me cough.

"Yes, I like it a lot," I replied, but I felt very light-headed after my second glass.

Besides the dumplings and the beer, we also had a dish of freshly caught fish, stewed with soy sauce, vinegar and different spices, cooked until the bones were soft enough to eat. It was delicious. Xiongjun's mother was a good cook, and I could tell they had spent a lot of money on this meal. They were clearly in a much better financial position than my family. Here there were two full salaries feeding five people, and plenty of food.

After lunch, his father took us all to the glass factory where he worked. There I saw hundreds of thousands of crystal-clear marbles in huge piles, and special machines that heated the glass up and pulled it into thin threads. I loved playing marbles at home and they were expensive to buy, so I asked Xiongjun's father if I could keep one as a souvenir and take it home to show my brothers. Without a word, he went over to talk to the gate-keeper and when he came back I couldn't believe my ears. "You can have a pocketful of them," he told me.

"Really?"

He nodded. I was so excited when I put my hands into the huge pile of glass marbles. My brothers and my friends would be amazed. There would be enough to give one each to my brothers, cousins and even a few to my best friends. I held the shiny balls in my hands and looked at Xiongjun's father again. "Are you sure?"

He nodded once more and smiled. I was beside myself with excitement. It was as though they were balls of gold.

That Sunday with them was the best Sunday I'd had since leaving home. They made me feel like I was a member of their own family. Before I left that day, Xiongjun's mother handed me a small bag of dates. "I hope you like our family. You will come back again, won't you?" she asked sincerely, holding my hand tight.

I nodded excitedly. I only wished I could go home to see my *own* family on Sundays too.

The next Sunday visit was a whole month away, and I longed for it to come sooner. But after my second visit the bus fare had nearly eaten up all my spending money, and I knew that I couldn't ask my parents for more. The third time Xiongjun invited me to his home I had to make an excuse. "I don't feel well, I can't go."

He was very disappointed and went without me.

The next month I tried to make another excuse.

"Are you still my friend?" he asked.

"Yes, of course."

"Don't you like my family?"

"Don't be silly, of course I like your family." I felt dreadful not telling him the truth.

"Are you embarrassed by my mother's praises of you?" he persisted.

"No, you have a wonderful mother!"

"Then why don't you come? When you don't come, they think we've had a fight and that you don't like me anymore. I had to defend myself! Please come, everyone is looking forward to seeing you again."

Tears welled in my eyes. I looked away. "I can't afford the bus fare. I only have eight yuan for the entire year. I can't ask my family for any more."

"Why didn't you tell me earlier! I have enough money for both of our bus fares. My family will kill me if they find out that you couldn't come because I had the money and didn't pay for you! Come on, the bus will be full if we don't hurry."

We left around nine o'clock and the lines at the bus stop

were so long that by the time we arrived at Xiongjun's home it was nearly noon. But, as before, my day with the Chongs was filled with happiness and affection. "The dumplings aren't the same without Cunxin's involvement," Xiongjun's mother said at lunchtime.

Before we left that day, Xiongjun's mother handed me two yuan. "For your next bus fare. Make sure you leave earlier next time or I'll have no one to help me make the dumplings," she said.

At first I refused to take the money, but she insisted. "This is the best two yuan I have ever spent. Take it!"

Along with the Bandit, Xiongjun became one of my closest friends. I formed a strong relationship with each and every one of the Chong family. Everything the Chongs made for Xiongjun, I also received a share of, and I continued to visit them regularly throughout the next few years. They unofficially became my adopted family.

I went home to my own family in Qingdao for the Chinese New Year holiday that year, and this time I went with much improved grades. Chinese New Year had always been my favorite time of the year, but now it was even more special because it was my one chance to see my family and friends once more. My family could never visit me in Beijing. Just one return train ticket was equal to half my dia's salary for a whole month.

I brought back some Beijing sweets and a bag of jasmine tea from the Chongs as gifts to my family, and the marbles were an enormous hit among my brothers and friends. "They are the most beautiful marbles I've ever seen!" Jing Tring cried with excitement. He flew outside and proudly showed them to all his friends. He even placed them under his pillow that night.

My family shared the sweets and tea with some of their relatives and friends, and they were deeply touched by the Chongs' generosity. In the end they had only enough tea left for one pot to have themselves, on the eve of Chinese New Year. My niang declared that this was the best tea they had ever had.

My holiday month at home went by too fast. My parents and brothers showered me with love and affection. Their lives hadn't changed much from the year before, but I did notice some friction between my second brother, Cunyuan, and my parents. A few days before I was to leave for Beijing, my parents made Cunyuan write a thank-you letter to the Chongs to express their appreciation for looking after me. Cunyuan had to rewrite it several times because my parents weren't satisfied with the words he used. Two nights before my departure, just as our niang sat on the kang after dinner, Cunyuan read his latest version.

"And if you don't like it, write it yourself!" he said, annoyed.

"It's better than the last one," my niang said, "but it's still not *deep* enough. Can't you say something like, 'We are so touched by your generosity that we could have kowtowed for you if you were here,' but without actually saying that?"

"Why don't you cut your heart out and send it with Cunxin to show them?" Cunyuan was growing angry.

"I would if someone else could wipe your bottoms for you when I'm not here anymore!" she replied.

"If you really want to show the Chongs your heart, why don't you give Cunxin to *them*, like you did Cunmao?"

"Watch your tongue!" Our niang gave him a stern look.

"You would give us all away before Cunxin. He is our family's crown jewel," Cunyuan continued.

"You are *all* my treasures," our niang said. "I love each one of you. I would rather die than give any of you away!"

"*Hnnng!*" Cunyuan was sounding bitter, disgruntled.

"*Hnnng* what? Have I done any less for you?" our niang asked him.

"Yes! You let your other sons go and pursue their futures! Except me! I can't even marry the person I love!" Cunyuan was shouting now. "Why should I be kept at home? Why can't you let *me* go to Tibet?"

"Haven't we explained to you before? We need you here," our dia waded into the conversation.

Cunyuan looked at our dia and hesitated. Our dia's words were indisputable in our family. They represented a certain kind of finality.

But Cunyuan was too emotional and wouldn't let it go. "So, *I'm* the one being sacrificed! Why don't you just say that I'm the least important of all your sons!"

"Can you repeat what you've just said?" my dia asked calmly. I could tell he was trying hard to contain his rage.

"I said . . ."

Whack! Dia reached over and slapped Cunyuan on his face with such enormous force that I feared his jaw might break.

"I dare you to repeat such ungrateful things about your niang!" Our dia then leaped off the kang and charged at my second brother.

"Stop it! Stop it!" Our niang stood between them. Cunyuan was holding his face, stunned. A moment later he came to his senses and fled.

Our dia was still raging with anger. "I can't believe we have such an ungrateful son!" Niang was sobbing by this point. "What have I done wrong with him? *What* have I done wrong?"

We sat there in shock, soaked with sadness. I was deeply upset by Cunyuan's accusations against our niang. I couldn't believe he was so angry. I couldn't understand why. But I did feel sorry for him. I had heard about the central government wanting more young men to go to Tibet, and Big Brother Cuncia had suggested to our parents that Cunyuan should go. I'd thought the whole issue had been resolved by now.

My niang was upset and teary all through the next day.

"How long has this been going on?" I asked her when the two of us were left alone.

"Ever since your big brother wrote from Tibet a few months ago," she replied.

"Why don't you let him go?" I asked again.

"He has just started working. We need his income for us all to survive. How can we lose him so soon after we have lost your big brother to Tibet? We just can't afford to! The best thing for him would be to marry that nice, steady girl your big aunt introduced him to." She sighed.

"Couldn't he send money back from Tibet?" I asked.

"Have we seen a single fen from your big brother in Tibet? He can't even feed himself from what the government gives him!"

We both fell into silence. Now I understood.

"You are the luckiest person with enough food to fill your stomach," my niang continued, "and now the Chong family likes you!" Then she became more serious. "Never forget where you come from," she said. "Work hard and make a life of your own. Don't look back! There is nothing here except starvation and struggle!"

Cunyuan didn't come home for the next two days. I was worried. I knew our parents were worried too. He came back on the morning I was to leave for Beijing. He looked terrible, as if he had not slept for the two days since he'd run away.

Everyone was quiet at breakfast that day. "Take care, be good. Listen to your teachers. See you next year," my dia said to me before he left for work. Soon after, Cunyuan rode off on Dia's bike and told me he would be back in time to take me to the train station.

Nearly two hours later he finally arrived home and handed me a small brown paper package. "You can open it when you're on the train," he said.

I recognized the wrapping paper from the only county department store and I knew he would have ridden all this time to get there and back.

When it was time for me to leave, my niang walked outside to the gate with us. "Write as soon as you arrive or I'll be worried sick!" she said. She turned to Cunyuan. "Be careful, especially on the narrow roads. Just stop if you see a truck coming."

"Why do you care?" Cunyuan muttered under his breath.

"Niang, I'm going now," I said to her, trying to defuse the tension.

She didn't say anything. Tears welled in her eyes. I hesitated. Maybe I should have asked her sewing friends to come.

Cunyuan wanted to leave earlier than was needed, so I sat on the backseat of my dia's bike and waved at my niang, at my brothers, relatives and neighbors. I tried hard to fight back my tears. Maybe it was the distraction of Cunyuan's situation, but I felt slightly easier leaving home this time. Cunyuan rode away as fast as he could as though this would release his anger and frustration.

Once we were on the main road, I asked him how he was. He didn't reply. He just pedaled harder. About halfway to the station he hopped off the bike and said, "Let's talk."

Now I understood why he wanted to leave home so much earlier.

"I'm sorry you had to witness this unpleasantness," he said as he pushed the bike off the road. It had been a crisply cold morning when our dia had left for work, but now it was midmorning and the sun had made it warmer. The train wasn't scheduled to arrive for at least another two hours, and we were about half an hour away. Cunyuan took out a small bag of tobacco, rolled a cigarette and sat crouching against a concrete power pole.

"Are you all right?" I asked, trying to find something to say.

No answer. He puffed his cigarette furiously. I could tell from the movement of his chest that his emotions were like a rough

196

sea. All of a sudden he dropped his cigarette, hid his face in his hands and sobbed. I didn't know how to comfort him, so I just rushed up to him and held his shoulders.

"Why me?" he said. "I should never have been born!"

I felt helpless. There was nothing I could say.

Eventually he lifted his head. "Why won't our parents listen to me and let me go to Tibet? Why won't they let me marry the person I love? What have I done to deserve such treatment? What is my future here? Should I be satisfied to work in the fields for the rest of my life? Tibet is the only opportunity I have to do something with my life. At least I could get a government-sponsored job and see what's out there! Look at our big brother, look at *you*, and then look at the rest of us!"

"I wish I could give you what you want. Can't you talk to them again?"

He shook his head. "I've tried so hard to convince them both about Tibet and my marriage. They don't want to lose another laborer in our family." He rolled another cigarette, then continued, as though he was talking to himself. "I dived into the dam on the Northern Hill one day last summer. I thought of staying under the water and never coming up. Maybe I will have a better life in another world." He sighed. "*Why* do we have to live in this world? There is no color in this life! I wake up early every morning before the sun is up, I go and work in the fields. Under the burning sun, in the pouring rain, in the freezing snow and with an empty stomach, seven days a week, fifty-two weeks of the year, no Sundays off, no free days. I only come home to sleep. My dreams are the only comfort I have, and most of those are nightmares. Often I am too tired even to remember my dreams. I'm twenty-four years old! There is no end to this suffering!"

I crouched beside him and listened in shock and with an ever more saddened heart. I wished I'd had a magic cure for all his problems, but I knew there was none. Millions of young people were going through the same agony and despair all over China.

"Let's not talk about my situation anymore," he said at last. "How are you coping at the academy? Are you happier there this past year?"

"It's getting better. But I still miss home. I even miss the harsh part of life sometimes," I replied.

"But surely there is nothing here you would miss! I'd give anything to be in your position."

"Why don't we swap?" I teased, trying to cheer him up.

"The Beijing Dance Academy would laugh their teeth off if they saw my bowed legs! But to see Beijing would be a great privilege. Go back and work hard. You have the opportunity of a lifetime. Your brothers can only dream of it." After a brief pause, he asked, "Do you still like cricket fights?"

I nodded. Why, suddenly, would he ask me about cricket fights?

"Remember how great you feel when your cricket is victorious. Have you ever put yourself in the shoes of the losing cricket?"

I shook my head.

"Sometimes I feel like *I* am the losing cricket and I cannot escape. Life is the victorious cricket, chasing me around until it hunts me down and slowly chews me up. Did you ever have this feeling?"

Again I shook my head.

"I always imagined that as long as I could fight, I would be able to find a way out, but I'm not sure anymore. I'm fighting against life, the life I was given, but not the life I desire."

I was speechless, silenced by his despair.

We arrived at the station, and soon the rattling train slowly rolled toward our platform. A couple of my friends popped their heads out of the windows looking for me, and my brother passed my bag in to them.

It was time to part. We just stood there and looked at each other. There was still much that I wanted to say. I wanted to hug him but I couldn't possibly—it wasn't the thing to do for the opposite sex in China, let alone the same sex. "I'm going now" was all I said as we stiffly shook hands.

As the train moved away I could see him wiping tears from his face. I stuck my head out the window and waved. He just stood there, like a statue, until we moved out of sight.

I squeezed onto the bench seat beside my friends. I answered my friends' questions about my holidays, but my brother's aching voice kept echoing in my ears. Suddenly I remembered the parcel he'd given me. I took it out and untied the brownish strings. It was a box of sorghum sweets with a note attached, roughly written. "These are for your friend Chong Xiongjun's family," Cunyuan had written. "They represent your six brothers' mountain-weight of gratitude and our sincere thanks for their kindness in looking after you . . . Please forgive me for the last two days. What I want in life can only remain a distant dream. I beg you to forget it . . ."

I lost control then. I tried to stop the tears but the harder I tried the more they welled up and I covered my face with my handkerchief.

"What's wrong?" Several of my classmates became very concerned.

I didn't know what to tell them. "I just want to be left alone," I said.

I found myself trying to answer Cunyuan's unanswerable questions. I thought of the dying cricket trying to escape from his tormentor with neither the will nor the physical condition to do so. I felt sick. I felt an enormous swell of compassion for my poor, trapped brother.

My grief for Cunyuan continued to overwhelm me all through my journey back to Beijing. "There has to be a solution!

199

There has to be a solution!" I kept telling myself. But I knew there was none. Poverty itself was his problem, and I began to realize how enormously privileged I was to have gotten out of Qingdao. For my brothers it wouldn't matter how hard they worked or how long they persisted, little would change in the end. They would most likely be in the same situation, twenty, thirty or fifty years from now.

When the sun set and the stars began to appear I felt exhaustion overwhelm me. I asked my friend Fu Xijun to swap seats with me so I could sit against the window.

I knew now, with sudden shock, that I could never go back to the life I used to have. I would always miss my parents' love and my brothers' company, but I knew deep in my heart that my future now lay ahead, not behind. This trip home had once and for all stripped off the fantasy of the ideal countryside life I'd always thought was possible. What my second brother was going through in his mind was far worse than the lack of food, the starvation. His soul was dying. If I hadn't gotten out I too would have faced the same fate.

I fell in and out of sleep throughout that trip back to Beijing. We kept swapping seats so each of us could have a turn leaning against the window, but for the last three hours of the trip I was wide awake. I thought about the year ahead. I was looking forward to facing the challenges. A mysterious voice sounded in my ears: "Cunxin, you are privileged. You are lucky. Go forward. Don't be afraid and don't look back. There is nothing back there, only your family's unconditional love and that will always propel you forward."

But now, for the first time, this voice wasn't my brother's voice. It wasn't my dia's. It wasn't even my beloved niang's. This voice was my own.

十三

13

TEACHER XIAO'S WORDS

In the spring of 1974, when I was thirteen, the Beijing Dance Academy was invited to go to Tiananmen Square to hear our beloved Chairman Mao speak.

This was an opportunity beyond my wildest dreams! I was so excited I didn't sleep at all the night before. I'd only ever heard Chairman Mao's voice over a loudspeaker in our commune or on a radio at the academy. I had memorized so many of his sayings from his Red Book and I had four large volumes of his communist theories by my bedside, the guiding principles of my life. I was so lucky to be born in the time of Chairman Mao, our living god, and now I was going to see and hear him in person!

Suddenly a sense of shame overwhelmed me. I hadn't been good enough to deserve this honor! I twisted and turned all night. I kept repeating in my head the first words I had ever learned at school. "Long, long live Chairman Mao." When I was a little boy I truly believed he would have goddesses accompanying him and there would be clouds surrounding him, just like a real god.

I woke up very early on the morning of the rally. I had extra energy. I was dressed in my best Mao jacket and ready to leave by six o'clock.

The bus journey to Tiananmen Square took us nearly an hour. No motion sickness for me that day. We could hear an extraordinary noise as we got close—loud drums, cymbals, trumpets, instruments of all kinds mixed in with the exuberant, feverish shouting of propaganda slogans. We were led by security guards, wading through a sea of red banners, an ocean of people. It was like an enormous carnival. A joyous celebration.

The organization must have been meticulous. There were police everywhere, and they strictly controlled our every movement. Clearly no mishaps would mar this nationally publicized demonstration, a demonstration of a people united in their devotion to Chairman Mao. Everyone was assigned a location—there was no seating, but packing millions of people into Tiananmen Square took time, so various groups were there to play music and entertain us. The excitement was contagious. Emotions were at fever pitch. I had never been in a crowd where people were so open and friendly. This was the happiest moment in all of our lives. And, reinforcing our sense of Mao's godliness, it was a brilliant, sunny day.

After a few hours of almost unbearable anticipation, the moment arrived: Chairman Mao, Madame Mao and the rest of the Gang of Four, the premier of China, Zhou Enlai, and many other central government leaders, appeared on the podium of the Gate of Heavenly Peace. Rippling to the distant boundaries of the square, the crowd cheered, clapped and jumped like a crazed animal. The ground vibrated under my feet. The entire world would hear this! Millions of people shouted, "Long, long live Chairman Mao!" Everyone wore red armbands and red scarves. There were thousands of red banners and flags with "Long, long live Chairman Mao" written on them. People sang and danced, eagerly clutching their Red Books in their hands.

I experienced an extraordinary sense of belonging, a sense of being in the presence of some divine being. I was so proud to be a young Guard of Chairman Mao. Tears rolled uncontrollably down my cheeks. I looked around. I saw others too, weeping with joy and pride. It seemed like hours before Chairman Mao gestured for us to sit down and, following the ripple through the crowd, we immediately obeyed.

Mao spoke for no more than half an hour, his familiar voice seducing us through the many loudspeakers placed around the Square. His speech was constantly interrupted by thunderous applause. We went up and down, down and up, like yo-yos, our ovations many times longer than his speeches. He spoke with the heavy accent of Hunan, which made it difficult for me to understand him, but I didn't mind: I knew, as everyone else in China knew, that we would study his speech in its entirety for at least the next few months.

Many hours after his speech we were still in the square, singing and dancing for pure joy.

Soon after that momentous visit to Tiananmen Square, we went on another trip, this time to an area on the outskirts of Beijing called Pingu. We were told it had similar terrain to Dajai, a model area where peasants cultivated fruit trees and crops in rocky mountainous conditions. We were told that the most precious gift one could take to Dajai was a bucketful of soil.

Learning from the peasants was reaching fever pitch at around this time. Besides taking small trees, and *two* bucketfuls of soil, every student was asked to fill a pocket with soil as well, as a symbol of this most precious gift.

I was so excited about going to Pingu. I imagined green

wheat and cornfields spreading over the mountainsides, luscious fruits hanging down from the branches of the trees. No one could have prepared me for the disappointment to come.

I suffered through dreadful motion sickness on the uneven and winding mountainous roads for over five hours on the trip to Pingu. But when we arrived I was shocked to see nothing but brown, bare hills and a few sprinkled patches of green. Many tourists were there too, paying homage to the great miracles of this Dajai-like place. But there were more visitors than plants. A local guide showed us some pictures of the abundant wheat and corn at harvest time and told us we'd come in the off-season, but I wasn't convinced. I was a country boy. I knew nothing would grow on those rocks, not even weeds. Even if they put our soil over the rocks, one heavy rainfall would have washed it straight down the mountain. Of course I didn't dare question Mao's directive, but I did wonder if Mao had ever come to see places like this for himself.

In the second half of that year the head of the Communist Youth Party at our academy asked me to apply for membership. This was indeed a privilege. Only the most politically devoted students could join. I was flattered and surprised.

I handed in my application and then had to have private heart-to-heart discussions with three different party leaders. I also had to read a thick party manual, full of communist ideals, which were already familiar to me from the Red Book. When the committee felt comfortable with me they assigned two members to sponsor me. My friend Fu Xijun was one of them.

After the final vote of all the Communist Party members, five new members, including me, found ourselves standing under the flag of China with Mao's Red Book raised by our faces, pledging our allegiance to the Communist Youth Party: "I willingly and proudly join the Communist Youth Party. I swear to love Chairman

Mao, love the Communist Party, love my country, love my people and love my fellow colleagues. I will respond to the party's calling and strictly observe all party rules. The party's interests come before mine. I'm ready to give my all, including my life, to its glorious cause. We are dedicated to the principle of bearing hardship and letting others enjoy the fruit of our work . . ."

From that moment on I officially became a Communist Youth Party member. My life now had true purpose—to serve glorious communism. Once again I felt a powerful sense of belonging, of being closer to our beloved Chairman and Madame Mao, of being wholeheartedly embraced by the Communist Youth Party and of feeling a new beginning from that day forward.

I took my role as a Communist Youth Party member very seriously. This had been my political destiny from birth. I was one step closer to becoming a full Communist Party member, my ultimate political dream. Now I could contribute to Mao's political cause more effectively, enthusiastically participate in all of the party's agendas and try my hardest to make a difference whenever I could.

But politics was constantly changing around us—Mao knew the Gang of Four was incapable of managing China's economic affairs and by 1974 Mao felt increasingly threatened by Deng Xiaoping's popularity. Deng Xiaoping's reputation was spreading fast. Within the walls of our academy, however, the influence of Madame Mao was still paramount and she alone controlled our political education.

Madame Mao might have been pleased with our political development but she still wasn't happy, apparently, with the standard of our dancing. The vice Minister of Culture, an ex–principal dancer with the Central Ballet of China and famous for dancing the leading role in Madame Mao's model ballet, *The Red Detachment of Women*, was asked to do something about it. So he sent another retired principal dancer from the Central Ballet, Zhang

Ce, to be the new vice director of our academy in charge of technical standards. Zhang Ce brought back one of his former teachers, Zhang Shu, to be head of the ballet department.

Zhang Shu was one of the founders of Chinese ballet, along with Chiu Ho and Chen Lueng, and was widely considered one of the most knowledgeable ballet experts in China. He was a small man with an even temperament, and he often watched our classes and occasionally taught us. From the very beginning he seemed to notice me, and I found out that he'd even told Teacher Xiao that I was one to watch.

One day, soon after Zhang Shu's arrival, I lay on my bed reading the Monkey King story, a Chinese classic and one of only a few stories we were still allowed to read. As I lay down I felt something hard under my thin cotton mat. When I put my hand under it I found a thin book. It looked very old, and when I flipped through it I saw that it was all in a foreign language. I couldn't understand any of the words of course, but there were quite a few pictures in it too—all of different ballet poses. It seemed to be a schoolbook of some kind. The young teenagers' ballet positions were beautiful and their figures were exceptional. I was especially impressed by a boy posing in arabesques. He was wearing a light cotton vest which looked like ours, with black tights, white socks and shoes. His lines were clean and extended. His placement was perfect. He seemed no older than I. I wished that one day I would be good enough to demonstrate in a book just like this, for the next generation of dancers.

I didn't know for certain who had put that book under my mat, but I had a rough idea and I knew it would be far too dangerous to show the book around. Whoever put it there would have wanted me to keep it to myself.

Zhang Ce's and Zhang Shu's arrival at the academy marked the beginning of our new focus on technique. Extra time was devoted to dancing, and some of our academic classes were dropped. Like Zhang Shu, other experienced teachers who had previously been accused of being rightists were now rehabilitated and allowed to return. One was a Russian ballet expert who spoke very good English and who had also translated several Russian ballet books into Chinese before he was labeled a rightist. He'd had to do the lowest and filthiest jobs while he was in the countryside, but his only crime had been his knowledge of Western arts.

Around the same time another "antirevolutionary" also came back to our academy from the brain-cleansing camps. He was a piano tuner, about fifty years old, with large ears that curved forward. He'd been recalled because all the pianists had complained so profusely about the out-of-tune pianos and because there simply wasn't anyone else the academy officials could hire who wasn't classified either as a rightist or an antirevolutionary. That piano tuner tuned and banged on the piano keyboards all day long. He took his time and always walked with his head lowered, constantly afraid that if he ran out of pianos to tune, he would be assigned cleaning, washing or any number of other lowly jobs.

The Russian ballet expert was not as lucky. He had to sweep, clean and scrub floors, walls and toilets. One day he was assigned to push a heavy two-wheeled cart while some of us loaded it with soil mixed with horse manure. Some of my classmates began calling him "the filthy rightist" and accused him of being too slow and lazy. I couldn't stand it—I didn't know what crime he had really committed, but after a few trips of pushing the heavy cart I could tell he was exhausted and I volunteered to help.

"Thank you, young man," he said quietly.

"You're welcome," I replied.

"What is your name?"

"Li Cunxin."

"I will *always* remember it!" he said, profoundly grateful.

The next day, during one of our political meetings, I was accused of being weak because I'd felt sorry for the rightist.

"I wasn't feeling sorry for him," I lied. "I wanted to make the process faster so we could contribute more to the peasants."

In the second half of that same year, our academy auditioned some music students. They'd already had some music training and had come from all over China. I never understood why they didn't go to the music academy instead, but they didn't and they lived in a couple of small crowded rooms in our own studio building. One of the violinists in that group, Liu Fengtian, was also a good hairdresser. I often asked him to cut my hair because I couldn't afford to go to a professional hairdresser. He was the first person ever to use a pair of scissors on me. Before that we roommates cut each other's hair with a pair of blunt hair clippers, and our hair often got caught in the middle of the clippers. The only way to get it loose was to pull the hair out. Needless to say it wasn't a very good look, but we were thankful all the same. A haircut was always a painful experience before Liu Fengtian's arrival. He was a good violinist who played with real passion. I loved watching him practice on the sports ground. He became one of my closest friends.

It was in this third year that my attitude toward dancing finally changed. For the first time since I had come to the academy I felt confident in my ballet class. I began to do well with our two new, technically difficult steps for the year: the single tour en l'air and the triple pirouette. With Teacher Xiao's gentle nurturing I made noticeable progress. I worked hard and listened to every word he said. I tried to understand the essence of his corrections and wrote down my new discoveries in my diary every day. I practiced on the side or behind the first group, even if it was not my turn, and my rapid improvement surprised many of my teachers and classmates.

My progress in ballet also helped me in other classes, especially in acrobatics. Now I was making good progress with backward somersaults, which I had been terrified of the year before. But one day, as I was doing one, I thought the teachers were waiting and ready to support me. I was wrong. They had turned their attention to another student. I took off, then suddenly panicked because I couldn't feel their hands supporting me. I crashed down from shoulder height, my back and head landing on the hard wooden floor, which was covered only by a thin threadbare carpet. I was knocked unconscious.

When I recovered I looked up to see my teachers and my classmates leaning over me with anxious, panicky looks. My head and neck throbbed with pain.

They carried me to my bed and told me to have a good sleep. At lunchtime, the Bandit and Fu Xijun brought me a bowl of noodle soup with an egg in it—a special treat if you were ill. We had to have the academy doctor's written report to be allowed such special food.

No official assistance, no medical care, no X ray was offered. I was told to go back to my normal routine that afternoon. But my neck pain was intense and persistent.

By the next Sunday I was no better and the Chongs took me to a seventy-five-year-old lady, a local healer, who massaged my neck and cracked it with amazing force. A few days later the pain disappeared, but my neck was never the same after that accident and it often gave me problems. Regardless of injuries, however, the teachers in our acrobatics classes believed in working under harsh conditions. Once they even made us do our class, including somersaults and backflips, in the snow. Luckily for us, Teacher Xiao complained to the academy director and lessons in the snow never happened again.

A few weeks before our midyear exams, Teacher Xiao finished our class late one day, and I was desperate to go to the bathroom before our next class. I only had ten minutes, and as usual there was a long queue. I was a couple of minutes late for Gao's Beijing Opera Movement class.

He stopped the music. "Here comes my prized student with the brainless big head! Why are you late?" he shouted.

I had intended to apologize sincerely to him and explain why I was late, but to my great surprise, entirely different words came out. "I'm not a brainless big head! I do have a brain!" I was so angry and short of breath that I stuttered badly.

"Get out of my class! Get out! *Never* come to my class again!" He pointed at the door, and his face was red with fury.

I ran to our dormitory and sat on my bed. There were no tears. I was in such a rage that I simply felt like killing him. He had treated me unfairly. He had called me names. He hadn't even noticed my improved attitude over the last few months—he probably never would.

I couldn't just stay in my room, though—I feared he might report me. I had to do something, and I had to act fast.

I ran to Teacher Xiao's office and found him alone, reading. I stuttered my way through my story, telling him what had happened with Teacher Gao, and he listened attentively.

"Sit down," he said when I'd finished. "Cunxin, I understand your anger and I think Teacher Gao was wrong. He shouldn't have called you names. I will go to Director Xiao and tell her what you have told me. If Teacher Gao goes to her, she will at least have both sides of the story and I will carry a little more weight than you. However, before I go to Director Xiao, I would like you to do a difficult task for me," he said.

"What?" I asked, puzzled.

"I want you to go to Teacher Gao and talk to him."

"I don't want to go near him! He hates me!" I jumped up from my seat.

"I know how difficult this will be, but I want you to give it a

210

try. Have you ever told Teacher Gao how you feel about him calling you names? Are you the only boy he has singled out?"

Teacher Xiao's questions made me think. I wasn't the only student Teacher Gao shouted at and called names.

"Sit down, Cunxin," Teacher Xiao said again. "I want to tell you a story . . ."

One of the guards in an emperor's palace went to his teacher and wanted him to make him the best bow shooter in the land. The teacher told him to go away. The guard returned every day and begged his teacher to teach him. Day after day, week after week, month after month the guard came. He came in the rain and he came in the snow. After one whole year, the teacher was moved by the guard's perseverance and determination and finally accepted him as his student. The teacher asked him to pick up a heavy bow and hold it up. After a few minutes the guard's arms started shaking with tiredness. The teacher made him carry very heavy loads in each hand every day. After a while when he picked up the heavy bow again it felt like a feather in his hands. One day he asked his teacher, when would he teach him how to shoot an arrow? The teacher told him that he wasn't ready yet and instead asked him if he could see anything far into the sky. He looked up and looked as hard and as far as he could but couldn't see anything. His teacher told him to look at a tiny little spider in a faraway tree that he could hardly see. He kept focusing on it with one eye at a time. Gradually he began to see the spider clearly and eventually when he used both of his eyes the little spider seemed as large as his shield. His teacher said that he was now ready to teach him how to shoot an arrow. Soon the guard became the best bow shooter in the land.

"Remember, Cunxin, nothing is impossible," Teacher Xiao said. I left Teacher Xiao's office full of hope. I ran to Teacher

Gao's office as soon as our next class was finished. He was just coming out of the door, with bowls and chopsticks in hand, going to the canteen for lunch.

"Teacher Gao, may I talk to you for one minute?"

He looked at me angrily. "Better be brief! Come in!"

Once I closed the door he said, "Why were you late for class today?"

"I was waiting to use the toilet," I replied.

"Why wasn't anybody else late? Are you the only person needing to go to the toilet?" he asked.

"I tried to hurry but there wasn't any toilet available. I'm sorry."

"If you showed as much enthusiasm for your dancing as for the toilets, you wouldn't be where you are with the standard of your dancing," he fumed. "Okay, I accept your apology. Now, go to lunch!" He rose, ready to go, but I didn't move.

"Teacher Gao, could I tell you something?" I said.

"What?" he asked impatiently.

"I don't like you calling me the boy with the brainless big head. What if I had called you the teacher with the brainless big head?"

His face turned from red to green and back to red. He sat back down.

"I know I haven't been good at your classes and my dancing standard is poor," I continued, "but I was very homesick then. Now my attitude has changed. I want to be a good dancer. I hope you'll give me a chance and judge me by my future work."

He was speechless.

After what seemed a very long time he said, "I'm sorry that I called you something I shouldn't have. I won't in the future as long as you work hard. Any other issues?" he asked.

"No." I stood up and just as I was walking out he asked, "Cunxin, are you going to be able to do your split jumps in the exam?"

"I will," I replied.

I ran down the stairs three at a time. I felt light. I wanted to fly into the air and sing happily like a river bird. I ran to the teachers' section of the canteen and saw Teacher Xiao waiting in line to collect his lunch. I gently tapped him on his shoulder. I smiled at him and he smiled back. We both knew what we meant.

My confrontation with Teacher Gao was the first time in my life that I had really faced a problem and tried to solve it. The problem was like a real tiger before I confronted it and a paper tiger once it was solved. My confidence began to grow.

By the beginning of June, every class was preparing for our midyear exams. Academy officials would attend these exams— and there was intense competition among teachers, especially in the ballet department. The third and fourth years were especially crucial because teachers would select students as their "talents" to spend most of their time and attention on. The exams were always nerve-racking, with twenty or thirty teachers and school officials, plus thirty or forty students, all sitting in front of us. In this third year, however, and for the first time in my ballet exam, some teachers began to notice me, especially Zhang Shu, the head of the ballet department. I felt good about myself in that exam too, and Teacher Xiao came to me afterwards and said, "Cunxin, well done, I'm proud of you. Your diligent work for the past six months has paid off. I hope you'll keep it up."

After lunch that afternoon, after I had confronted Teacher Gao, while everyone was taking their naps, I quietly slipped into one of the studios and started to practice my split jumps for our Beijing Opera Movement exam. I had such problems with this step. Even the Bandit couldn't figure out what was wrong. We had to jump into a split on the floor and bounce right back up again, without using our hands. Half of the class could do it and the other half couldn't. I couldn't. But I had to. I'd given Teacher Gao my word.

213

I limbered my legs on the barre and started to practice. After a number of fruitless tries I suddenly discovered something. Even before I started jumping into the split, my hands were already subconsciously preparing to protect me. My lack of self-confidence didn't give my body a chance. So I tried putting my hands behind my head when jumping into the split. My body kept falling to the side, so I turned my front leg out and my balance was corrected. Next I turned my attention to bouncing up from the split position without using my hands. This was far more difficult to overcome. Every time I did it I would feel nothing but pain in my hamstrings and I couldn't find the right leg muscles to get me up again. I simply had to use my hands.

After many tries I still hadn't made any progress. But I kept telling myself, "I've given Teacher Gao my word! I've given him my word!"

The pain in my hamstrings increased and so did my frustration. I was angry with myself. I nearly gave up several times. Out of total desperation, I hit my thighs with my fists. "Stupid you! Why aren't you smarter?" I screamed at myself. "Why can't you figure this out?"

Just hitting my thighs didn't seem to be enough, so I went to the barre and banged my hand on it. The barre shook and vibrated in protest. "Yes, you might be able to help," I said to the barre. I held onto the barre with both hands and did my split jumps underneath. At first, I used my arms to pull me up from the split position. Gradually I relied on my arm strength less and less. Eventually, muscle by muscle, I discovered which muscles in my legs were useful and when my hands were finally off the barre I had made my breakthrough.

I was overjoyed. I ran to the center of the studio and jumped into the split and bounced up again, into the split and up. I jumped and bounced and jumped and bounced like a madman. Even the hamstring pain was bearable now. I couldn't believe I had done it.

In my soaking-wet practice clothes, I flew down the stairs and quietly slipped back into our dormitory without anyone noticing.

In the exam that afternoon, after I successfully completed the split jumps, Gao Dakun's face showed utter disbelief, and I smiled to myself in triumph.

My improvements and small achievements over the next few months were like winning battles in a war. I worked harder not only in Teacher Gao's class but in all my classes. Teacher Gao treated me with respect and he never called me "the boy with the brainless big head" again.

From then on my confidence grew and grew. My exam grades improved remarkably. Teacher Xiao gave me a "good" grade and even Gao gave me a much-improved "above average." But I knew there was still much more to do. I wanted to be among the top students in my class. I wasn't sure how long this would take, but I knew I would get there eventually. I had the bow-shooter's image from Teacher Xiao's fable stored firmly in my mind, and I was determined.

That year we experienced one of the worst autumns in Beijing since our arrival in 1972. Because of massive fuel shortages over the years, virtually every tree in and around Beijing had been cut down and the strong winds blew up the treeless soil on the outskirts of the city, covering the ancient capital in dust. We called it Beijing Dust and once the strong winds started to whirl we would avoid the streets as much as possible. If we had to go out, we wore small white face masks to shield us from the dirt. Some people wore sunglasses too, but I could never afford a pair of those. When Xiongjun and I returned from his family on Sundays, our face masks were always covered with dust and pollution. But we had to wear them, or by the end of the day we would be coughing up thick black mucus.

The next Chinese New Year holiday, on my trip home, I visited my fourth brother, Cunsang, on his battleship. It was February 1975. He had been in the navy for a year and was well liked by his superiors and his fellow sailors. He was stationed in Qingdao that year, and the commander of the ship asked the chefs to cook me a delicious meal. I had to earn it, though, by performing for them on the big metal deck. They applauded everything I did, but I could tell they were bored with my pliés and arabesques: the back flips and the martial arts movements were much more interesting, and they were so impressed when I told them I had seen Chairman Mao and even met Madame Mao in person.

After lunch Cunsang and I sat on the edge of the ship's deck with our legs dangling over the side. It was a beautiful winter day, with the sun warm on our heads. I asked him if he enjoyed the sailor's life.

"No, I hate it," he said simply. He missed home, especially his girlfriend, Zhen Hua, and couldn't stand being apart from her for much longer. He was now only two years into his standard four-year service. He told me that his political mentors in the navy wanted him to apply for Communist Party membership. They'd said promotions would follow but that he'd have to stay longer than the four years before he would be considered for such enhanced privileges.

Cunsang told me he would not serve beyond his four-year term. He wanted to marry Zhen Hua as soon as he retired from the navy. Then, all of sudden, to my great surprise, he leaned forward and dived gracefully into the sea. The deck was far, far above the surface of the water. He called out for me to dive down too, but when I looked over the edge I froze with fear. Eventually one of Cunsang's sailor friends brought me a pair of shorts and a white cotton vest for me to change into, then lowered me down to the freezing water with a rope. Within minutes my teeth started to chatter uncontrollably, and my lips had turned purple.

Cunsang had to ask his colleagues to pull me up, but he swam on for another half an hour. I sat on the deck, shivering, wrapped in towels—and Cunsang never mentioned his unhappiness again.

Teacher Xiao went to Qingdao too for a few days that New Year's holiday, and paid a surprise visit to my family, driven by the desire to know his students' families better. Our third year was now completed and Teacher Xiao had been teaching me for one and a half years.

He arrived at our house one day just as we were about to have lunch. The special New Year food had virtually been depleted, and there was no time or money for us to go shopping. Our dia was home for lunch that day, and our parents were embarrassed to serve what was left to my teacher. "Can you wait for about half an hour, so I can prepare you a better meal?" my niang begged.

"Please, Auntie, this is not what I'm here for, and I'm so hungry." Teacher Xiao hopped onto the kang and sat between Cunfar and me, legs folded like us in the lotus position. "The reason I came unannounced was so that you wouldn't have to prepare a special meal just for me. I want to eat what *you* normally eat. This way I can truly experience what your life is like."

That meant experiencing dried yams, a few pieces of leftover corn bread, pickled turnips and sorghum soup. Teacher Xiao started with a piece of corn bread.

"Tastes good!" he said, out of politeness, but my niang took this to heart and immediately started to pile pieces of corn bread in front of him.

"No, no! I can't eat this much! Besides, I want to taste *this*— what do you call this?" he said enthusiastically.

Oh no, I thought. Not those.

"Dried yams," my niang replied.

Sure enough, he gagged on the first piece and had to drink

217

a great deal of sorghum soup to wash it down. But the sorghum soup didn't taste too good either. I couldn't help thinking it was funny, but I didn't dare laugh out loud.

I showed Teacher Xiao around the village after lunch—he was shocked at our poor living conditions. "Cunxin, you must be thinking about your family constantly while you are in Beijing?"

"Yes. I think about them when I'm eating—meat, fish, rice or fruit. I wish I could help them," I replied.

"You can," Teacher Xiao said.

"How?"

"By working hard and becoming the best dancer you can! I have watched you over the past year and a half, Cunxin. I have no doubt that you have the inner strength to become a special dancer. Now I understand where that inner strength comes from. The strength of your parents' character is in you. It is the most valuable quality anyone can possess. If you are ever in doubt about your own abilities, all you need to do is think of your parents and what they have gone through. Your desire to help them is your incentive to work hard." He paused, with passion in his eyes. "Cunxin, I would dearly love to make you see ballet through my eyes. The subtleties of each step! The elegance of each movement! Ballet is one of the most refined art forms in the world!"

"But I can't do the high jumps or turns," I said. "Actually, I have nothing special to make me a good dancer."

"Cunxin, nothing is impossible for a determined human being. Physical imperfections are easier to overcome than mental deficiencies. Remember the bow-shooter fable?" he said. "Nothing is impossible if you put your heart and soul into it! Let's make your family proud! Become a good dancer, the greatest dancer you can be. Starting next year, I expect to see nothing less than the best from you."

It was true that Teacher Xiao's fable of the bow shooter had left a deep impression on me. But from that day on it became an inspirational driving force. Whenever I met difficulties or challenges in my dancing, like the split jumps, I always went back to this fable for my basic inspiration: hard work, determination and perseverance. That day, Teacher Xiao's words had touched me deeply, and I knew that he cared.

十四

14

TURNING POINTS

I returned to start my fourth year at the Beijing Dance Academy later that February of 1975.

Before class one morning, Teacher Xiao called me to his office. "Cunxin, you have had a great last year. I'm very happy with your work and the progress you have made. I hope you can keep it up. Don't let any outside influences pull you off track." He hesitated for a moment and I wondered why he was saying all this.

Then he continued. "I may not always be your teacher, Cunxin. There are people out there who feel that I am not good enough. Some of them have the power to replace me. There's not much I can do." He paused again and I could see he was holding back tears. "All I want you to know is that even if I'm no longer here to teach you, you should continue to work in the same way. I have no doubt you will have a bright future."

My heart sank with shock. I couldn't bear to lose Teacher Xiao! He had been my mentor, my only mentor, the only teacher in whom I could confide. He was like a parent to me.

"Is there anything I can do?" I asked.

He shook his head. "I've tried to convince them. But it's up to the academy officials. Now, go to your class. You'll be late," he said.

I felt tears form in my eyes. I had been looking forward to this year's work with Teacher Xiao. He was the teacher who had taught me to love dance. He was the one who could make me succeed.

"Cunxin," he added, just as I opened the door to leave, "I would like you to concentrate on your jumps this year, whether I'm your teacher or not. I'm not talking about average jumps. I mean brilliant jumps, gigantic jumps. Your turns can wait until next year."

I nodded, with a stomachful of sadness, and ran quickly to my next class. But I kept hearing Teacher Xiao's voice. I couldn't get it out of my mind. I didn't know what I would do if I lost Teacher Xiao. I can't lose him! I kept telling myself.

After lunch I went to Zhang Shu, the head of the ballet department. He liked me, and I felt sure he would listen. "Teacher Zhang, Teacher Xiao is a good teacher. He's the best I've ever had," I said.

He frowned. "What are you talking about, Cunxin?"

I didn't want to say that Teacher Xiao had told me about his possible dismissal, so instead I made something up as quickly as I could. "I heard rumors from some students that Teacher Xiao may no longer be teaching us."

Zhang Shu smiled gently. "Don't worry, no decisions have been made at this point. Every teacher likes to teach talented students. Don't be concerned. Just concentrate on your studies," he said.

"But Teacher Xiao is everything to me! Without him, I'd be back in the commune already. He made me *like* ballet! He showed me how beautiful it is. I'll be lost without him!" I tried hard to control my tears.

221

"What do your classmates think of him? Do they all agree?"

"Yes, one hundred percent!" I replied without hesitation.

"All right, I will take your feelings into consideration."

I left Zhang Shu without knowing if my words would make any difference at all, but I was determined to try anything in my power to keep Teacher Xiao. And, as the weeks and months went by, Teacher Xiao remained as our ballet teacher, and I was happy.

With Teacher Xiao's encouragement I worked on my jumps daily. I worked hard in class but I knew my progress was still too slow. I would never have big jumps with my flat feet, I was told by some teachers. But Teacher Xiao never lost faith and I never lost my will.

During that year, Teacher Xiao again worked us hard on our pirouettes and I finally overcame my difficulties. I felt good about myself—now I could complete three consecutive pirouettes consistently. Then, after class one day, Teacher Xiao said, "Cunxin, I want to see you do five pirouettes from now on. No more three pirouettes!"

I thought I hadn't heard him properly. "Teacher Xiao, you mean *four* pirouettes."

"No, I mean five," he replied, challenging me. "Don't think, just do it. I would like to see you do ten pirouettes one day."

My mouth dropped open. I wasn't sure whether to laugh at his madness or cry. He must be kidding, I thought. I only just felt comfortable doing three pirouettes without fear of falling. Ten pirouettes was completely crazy.

"Cunxin," he said, as though reading my mind, "to be the best, first you have to dare to *try!* Nothing is impossible as long as you're not afraid to achieve it. I don't want you to be the best in your class. I want you to be the best in the world."

Teacher Xiao's words echoed in my ears for days. He was talking about a standard of dancing that was far, far above me. These were things I could only dream about. No, ten was too many pirouettes even to dream about! How could a fourteen-year-old peasant boy think about being the best in the world? But Teacher Xiao's challenge was like a new seed that implanted itself in my mind. From that day onward, I had an aim and a vision. I wanted to be the best dancer I could possibly be.

That year, our academy was chosen to participate in an important public performance, the first for Madame Mao. We were to dance an excerpt from China's most famous ballet, *The Red Detachment of Women*. I thought this ballet was brilliant—all about Chairman Mao's army and their bravery, with the dancers doing leaps and turns with guns and flags and grenades: I loved it.

The whole academy was ecstatic about the coming performance. Everyone was vying for a part. The role of the hero, Chang Qing, a captain of the Red Army, was given to the Bandit. I was among five boys chosen to play the peasant boy, the "little fat boy." The name had nothing to do with his appearance, and eventually I was selected to be second cast to a slightly older boy. But still, I was just so happy to be one of the final two.

Chen Lueng, my first ballet teacher, was the rehearsal master for this performance. One day during rehearsal he suddenly switched me and the older boy around and I became the first cast. Both of us were shocked. The Bandit was very happy for me, but I clearly saw the disappointment in the other boy's eyes. I felt terrible. I had taken something precious away from him. I went to Chen Lueng after the rehearsal and told him that I would be happy to remain as second cast.

"Cunxin," he said, "life is not meant to be fair. As an artist you have to remain honest to your art form. You are better than he and deserve to be seen. If I didn't do what I felt was best for our art form then I would have failed as a teacher. You should stop dancing now if you don't want to be the best."

Deep inside I knew Chen Lueng was right, and his words affected me. I knew ballet was an art form based on honesty. The audience could see a good dancer from miles away.

I went to the other boy and told him I was very sorry for taking his place.

That was my first career break and I worked very hard on that role. Teachers started to notice me more. The role didn't just give me a rare opportunity to perform in front of Madame Mao: it also gave me confidence.

The role of the little fat boy didn't require any technically difficult dancing. The most challenging thing was a number of deathlike "brighten the presence" stares. The scene we were to perform for Madame Mao was called *"Chang Qing Zhi Lu,"* or "Chang Qing Showing the Road." For our entrance the Bandit and I walked on with furiously fast heel-toe Beijing Opera walks. I lunged in front of him dramatically with a gun in my hand and both of us looked right into the audience with our deathlike stares. No movement was allowed, not even a breath or the blink of an eye. Then I had to play this embarrassed gesture, to scratch my head because my gun was exposed, which always triggered whispers of laughter from the audience. I was told that Madame Mao laughed too when I scratched my head. I was happy that Madame Mao laughed, and I practiced the scratching head bit so many times to make it as convincing as possible.

This was also the year I started to do better in other classes, especially Chinese. I grew to love Chinese class and our teacher Shu Wen very much. He was a true intellect. He taught us with passion.

One day in his class we were studying a fable that was half a page long. It took Shu Wen a whole week to help us unravel the meaning and intricacies of the story. It was about a young farmer who had wasted his precious planting season because he'd waited and waited for a blind rabbit to run into a tree and kill itself after another had done so on the edge of his land. "I have discovered the secret of getting food without physical work!" the farmer assured his wife. "I'll bring home a rabbit every day, and we'll have meat to eat forever." But no blind rabbits came. By the time he realized his stupidity, it was too late. The crucial planting season was over, and his family's savings were gone.

Again the essence of this fable left its mark on me. Nothing comes easily. There are no shortcuts. Things only come when one works for them. Time should be treasured.

After our midyear exams that year, we all sat in a circle on the floor and Teacher Xiao read out his report on the progress of each student. Then we were allowed to grade Teacher Xiao's performance. A couple of students criticized Teacher Xiao for raising his voice and shouting at them. Teacher Xiao gracefully apologized. But when the bully Li Ming accused Teacher Xiao of favoritism toward Fu Xijun and me, he lost his temper. "I am proud to have the integrity to be fair to the diligent students. Anyone who has achieved something deserves praise and encouragement. Xijun and Cunxin have made huge progress. Learn from them."

Li Ming's face turned from white to red, then from red to a funny shade of ash. I didn't know whether he was embarrassed, angry or ashamed. Maybe he was all of those things. *I* was certainly embarrassed by Teacher Xiao's praise in front of the class, but still, his acknowledgment meant a lot to me and his words continued to encourage me.

We started our pas de deux classes in the second half of that year. I liked this class—it was my only chance to touch the girls. At first, the girls and the boys were on different sides of the studio. Then we were paired by our teacher according to size and strength. I secretly wished to be paired with the girls I liked, of course, but that was as close to the girls as we got. As soon as the music ended we would go back to opposite sides of the studio.

In the second half of that year, some ballet films were shown to us. They were Russian and had previously been banned. We weren't supposed to learn anything technical or artistic from them: we were just supposed to criticize the story. *Giselle*, for example, was clearly a story from a rotten capitalist society. We endlessly criticized the pathetic peasant girl, Giselle, who did nothing with her life other than desire the jewelry and lifestyle of the wealthy. We analyzed her pursuit of filthy material values. We laughed at her naïve love for the deceitful Prince Albrecht. How stupid and disgusting she was to turn her back on the peasant who truly loved her. "You can tell this ballet was designed by a capitalist," our political head said. "He has glorified the rich and portrayed the peasants as whores. What a contrast to *our* model ballets! Our three classes of people are our heroes!"

We were all Mao's faithful children, and we all wholeheartedly agreed with our political head, but I couldn't help quietly admiring Albrecht's brilliant dancing. The dancer was Vladimir Vasiliev from the Bolshoi, and the images of his dancing left me gasping for air.

During the Cultural Revolution almost every new creation in art was a joint project. Many new works had to have a Communist Party leader as one of the main creators or it would never get off the ground. There would normally be more than one choreographer, set designer, lighting designer and composer for any Chinese ballet, and the final product always looked as if the various parts didn't quite fit together. Individualism was firmly discouraged. *The Red Detachment of Women*, which we'd performed for Madame Mao, was one of these ballets and it took eight years to complete. But once I'd seen the beautiful *Giselle* I began to doubt *The Red Detachment of Women* was quite so artistically brilliant.

It was during our busy end-of-year exam preparation time, in January 1976, that the premier of China, Zhou Enlai, died. Several long remembrance and reflection sessions were organized

226

at the academy to commemorate Zhou's great contributions to China. I was surprised to see so many of my teachers sobbing.

Right after Zhou's death, Deng Xiaoping was arrested. Mao appointed Hua Guofeng to succeed Zhou Enlai, but it soon became clear that Hua Guofeng was an ineffective leader. He was a follower, a puppet of Mao and the Gang of Four. The Gang of Four immediately organized a "Denounce Deng Xiaoping" campaign. He was labeled an old rightist whose motive was to corrupt the communist system and eventually overthrow it. Some of his speeches were published, and I learned one of Deng Xiaoping's most famous sayings: *Bu guan shi bai mao hai shi hei mao, zhuo dao lao shu jiu shi hao mao.* "It doesn't matter whether the cat is white or black, it's a good cat as long as it catches mice." But many people only halfheartedly participated in the "denounce Deng Xiaoping" campaign. In fact, it almost backfired. Rumors began circulating about Madame Mao's male concubines. She was frequently accompanied by a handsome retired dancer, or a retired opera singer, a movie actor or a Ping-Pong champion. People started to notice. I could sense a huge tide of resentment developing against the Gang of Four.

Around the same time we started to rehearse another model ballet, and this time I was chosen to be the main character. The ballet was called *The Children of the Meadow*, a Lei Feng type of story about the new generation of children under Mao and their devotion to his cause. Some dancers from the Central Ballet of China came to teach us the steps and I was awestruck by the dancers' technical abilities. Even the "little bouncing ball" himself was there, a dancer from the Central Ballet of China known for his incredibly fast turns and jumps. He was such an inspiration—I vowed to reach his standard one day too.

We rehearsed one act of this ballet for several months and then performed it initially in our academy theater. I received some encouraging comments about my performance—my biggest fan was one of the chefs from our canteen! I had no idea about different aspects of performing and no stage fear at all. But this changed quickly when, a week later, we were bussed to an industrial city near Beijing called Tangjing to perform for the public. During the opening night performance my brain went completely blank. I couldn't think. I didn't know what I was doing on stage. I couldn't even remember what happened afterwards. All I could remember was that I had forgotten the steps. My partner looked at me, and I realized I was just standing on stage doing absolutely nothing. That was my first stage fright, at age fourteen, and I would never forget it.

After that performance the head of our ballet department Zhang Shu spearheaded an important project which we began in 1976. We were to create a full-length ballet, our academy's first such project, and everyone was excited about the auditions. The story was about a teenage brother and sister whose parents were captured by the Guomindang army and hanged on an old symbolic tree called *Hai Luo Sha*. The ballet was named after the tree. After the parents' death the two brave young children were separated and joined different factions of the Red Army. At the end of the ballet they came back with Mao's armies, reunited, and killed the murderers of their parents.

I was overwhelmed and utterly surprised to be chosen as first cast for the lead role. All of a sudden I was the envy of the entire academy. The pressure was immense but the opportunity for me to dance in a new creation was beyond my wildest dreams.

The choreography took over six months. We rehearsed every afternoon. Day in and day out we repeated many new steps and sweated over many movements, only to find out it wasn't what the choreographers had in mind. I changed three to four soaking-wet T-shirts every day. My legs started to cramp. Out of compassion one of the choreographers brought me cups of warm sugared water to replenish my lost energy. Sugar was such a rarity in China—an immense treat.

There was no doubt this role was technically very demanding. I worked hard, but different choreographers had choreographed different sections of the ballet and I had to listen to three different people's instructions at once! It was so confusing. The ballet underwent changes right up to the last minute and on the opening night, in front of thousands of eyes, my nerves turned my muscles numb. My whole body trembled. My legs felt weak. I was exhausted even before the curtain went up. On my grand entrance I was supposed to perform this explosive series of giant leaps, but my legs felt like noodles dangling in the air. The second half of the ballet went better but the difficult dancing parts were mostly in the first half and, naturally, the person who played Chairman Mao received most of the applause.

I was disappointed with myself beyond description. I had let the whole academy down. I had let Chairman Mao and Madame Mao down. I went to all three choreographers and apologized. I went to Zhang Shu the next day and asked him what I could do for my nerves. "Experience, only experience will help you," he said.

The end of this year was the first and only time that we went to see the army stationed outside Beijing: there were several elite divisions, and about ten of us were assigned a soldier each as our mentor to accompany and instruct us every day. Their daily schedule was strict, and we had to keep up with them. At five o'clock we were dressed, washed and outside in line on the parade ground within five minutes. Our Beijing Dance Academy's strict schedule meant that we had met that kind of efficiency before, but still, waking up at five was hard. We jogged and practiced our morning routine before breakfast and practiced our dancing on any flat surface we could find. Then we

229

joined some of the soldiers' training activities for the rest of the day. We learned how to walk, turn, stop and run the military way. We even learned how to fall and crawl under imaginary tanks and enemy gunfire. Many of us had bruises all over after those first few days. We learned how to hold guns too—important for our political ballets, we were told. We spent days at target practice and my eyes became so tired, but again I thought of the bow shooter that Teacher Xiao had told me about and I was determined to practice hard.

Grenade throwing was one activity I wasn't good at, no matter how hard I tried. We practiced with fake grenades at first, but after a few days my shoulder joints were swollen with nagging pain. On the day we were scheduled to throw the real grenades we first had to throw a fake one so our throw could be measured. I pumped myself up with courage. I imagined a group of enemies standing in front of me. This was a life-and-death situation. I gathered all my strength and threw the fake grenade out with all my might.

It fell way short of the target, embarrassingly short. It didn't even carry over twenty yards. But I wasn't the only one—many of my classmates also failed to reach the required distance. The academy officials wisely canceled our real grenade-throwing event, just in case.

Apart from the gun shooting I didn't really enjoy my military experience at all. I spent the whole time longing to return to our academy routine. I wanted to get back to my leaps and pirouettes.

This was the same year that I was elected as one of the three Communist Youth Party committee members and vice captain of my class. Then one day a Communist Party official at the academy called me into his office. "Cunxin, you have done a good job at the Communist Youth Party. You have set a wonderful example for all the students. Although you are still too young to join the party, we would like you to start thinking about it now.

230

Communist Party members are the purest and strongest communist believers. We believe you have that mental strength. The party would like to educate you to become a true Communist Party member, to carry the party's torch, to raise the country's flag every day, every hour, every minute. The responsibilities are enormous, but Communist Party members are a glorious breed of human being."

I nodded dutifully and left his office confused. To join the Communist Party was every young person's dream. But when I heard his words about a glorious breed of human being I began to wonder. I thought of the Communist Party members I knew: some were special people like Teacher Xiao and Zhang Shu. But there were also some I didn't want to be in the same company with, such as some of the political heads. And besides, with my increased interest in ballet I had little time for long meetings. Lately I'd even started speeding up the meetings I chaired at the Communist Youth Party, and I'd even been considering relinquishing some of my responsibilities. When I asked Teacher Xiao and Zhang Shu about this conflict between the endless meetings and my dance practice, both of them advised me not to give up my political position. It was important for my artistic future, they said. Later, much later, I was to discover their advice had been right.

Soon after Zhou Enlai's death, there was a massive earthquake in the coal-mining city of Tangshan, about a hundred miles east of Beijing. Officially, over two hundred thousand people were killed and over a hundred and fifty thousand injured. There were rumors that this earthquake was an unlucky sign, a sign of hard times and unrest ahead. It happened in the middle of a long, hot summer, while we were preparing for our midterm exams. Millions of victims were homeless, and all the hospitals in many cities were filled. Several older buildings fell down in Beijing too. Our academy was considered an old building, so we had to vacate it and live temporarily in tents in Taoranting Park. Tremors went on for two whole days. Torrential rain poured down relentlessly. Shops in Beijing ran out of plastic covering for people to use as temporary shelters. We left our building in such a hurry that many students didn't even bring their clothes. It was wet and freezing at night and we had very little food: biscuits and dried bread for two days.

My second brother, Cunyuan, was a volunteer at the local hospital in Qingdao looking after some of the earthquake victims, who came in by the trainload. Those victims were so shocked that any loud noise at all would terrify them, Cunyuan told me. One knocked a hot-water bottle onto the floor in the middle of the night. It exploded and sent the earthquake victims into immediate panic—they started to scream and tried to run for cover, and that in turn caused the whole building to shake. One of the nurses tried to calm them down by blowing a whistle, but that made the situation even worse. Panic turned to utter terror. People became desperate. A few poor injured victims jumped out of the building and killed themselves in an attempt to escape.

Then, later that year, the unthinkable event . . .

Our beloved Chairman Mao died.

China paused. The whole nation mourned. It was early September, and I remember gathering in front of a loudspeaker on the sports ground and hearing the announcement of his death by his successor, Hua Guofeng. We cried our hearts out. I thought of my na-na's death. But this time, crying for Chairman Mao, it was like a religious experience mixed with a certain fear. I had worshiped Chairman Mao. His name was the first word I had learned in school. The words from his famous Red Book were embedded in my brain. I would have died for him. And now he was gone.

The day after we heard about Mao's death, the Bandit and I

232

gathered at a quiet corner of our academy grounds and sat on a concrete Ping-Pong table to talk about this shocking news. China's future was now uncertain. Mao's death could only mean immense insecurity. As a young Red Guard, I was plunged into grief. I felt lost. There hadn't been much color in China before, but now things would be bleak indeed.

"There will be total chaos in China soon," the Bandit said despondently. "There will be civil war, maybe even the old chieftain warfare will return again. We should be prepared!" he said, becoming emotionally charged.

"Where would you go to fight a guerilla war!" I said, amused.

"Back to the mountains of Shandong Province of course!"

"I'm not sure I want to leave ballet and live in the mountains for the rest of my life," I replied.

"Where is your courage? Didn't Chairman Mao fight many years of guerilla warfare?"

"Yes, but you don't have to be a guerilla to serve the communist cause. Our best weapon is ballet," I argued.

But the Bandit wasn't convinced. "Only guns will determine the final outcome!" he said.

We went on, arguing philosophically for a while about wars and communism and politics. "All right," he said, "who do you think will be our next leader?"

"I don't know. Who do you think?" I asked.

"Hua Guofeng, Chairman Mao's chosen successor, who else?" he replied.

I laughed. "I think someone with stronger military backing will be China's next leader!"

"You don't think Hua Guofeng has military backing? Don't you think Chairman Mao would have secured military backing for him before he died?"

"I don't know. Hua Guofeng came from nowhere. He doesn't have a military history."

We talked about which leader in the central government did have a military history. We thought of three. Suddenly I shouted, "What about Deng Xiaoping?"

"Shh!" The Bandit looked around and made sure there was no one close who could have heard. "Are you *crazy*? He has just been disgraced! His reputation is damaged forever. Besides, if Chairman Mao didn't like him, we shouldn't either."

Both of us sank into our own thoughts. I knew what he said made some sense, but I didn't agree with him entirely. "Deng Xiaoping did very well with the economy while he was managing it, and he has a military history," I said.

"How do you know he did well with the economy?" he asked.

"The standard of living improved in my hometown."

This was true. My family's living standard had gradually improved under Deng's leadership, and some of the seasonal planning decisions had been handed back to the peasants.

"Do you think Madame Mao will become our next leader?" the Bandit asked.

I shook my head. "Haven't you heard the rumors about her male concubines?"

"Do you believe them?"

"No, but if there are rumors like this in Madame Mao's own academy, just think what people are hearing all over China."

A month after Mao's death, on 6 October 1976, our academy received another enormous shock. The news came casually. Madame Mao was arrested along with the other members of the Gang of Four. I felt like an abandoned child.

The Gang of Four were removed quickly and easily. Neither the military nor the police backed them. At our academy we carried on our normal routines, except when the political heads were removed, which meant no more political studies and more time to practice our dancing.

Hua Guofeng made no attempts to change the direction that Chairman Mao had set for the country. For the first six months of his government, it was business as usual. But everyone could feel that change was inevitable. The military may have adopted a low profile but few people knew what was really going on.

In the meantime, my dancing had caught Vice Director Zhang Ce's attention. All of a sudden, not only was I Teacher Xiao and Zhang Shu's targeted student, but now Zhang Ce's favorite. The end-of-year exam was so enjoyable that I could have done it again and again, even with all the future uncertainties in China. I had found my confidence at last.

十五

15

THE MANGO

I was nearly sixteen by now. It was the time when our academy doctor told me that I had to have my tonsils removed. I'd had repeated infections over the years, so I was placed on a three-month waiting list.

On the day I went to hospital I was not allowed to eat or drink anything. The scheduled time for the operation was 9 a.m., but the doctor didn't see me until noon. Then a nurse poked some acupuncture needles into my body—the Chinese anesthetic. I had no idea what to expect.

During the hourlong operation I could feel the pain, the cutting sensation, and I lay there as the blood gushed down my throat. It felt as though the doctor was using a very dull knife. I thought of the poor pigs in my hometown and how I used to watch them being slaughtered on my way to and from school.

I was exhausted when I was wheeled out of the operating room. I could not talk, and my throat was so swollen that it felt as if there was a big hot ball stuffed down it.

The nurse took me back to my room where the Bandit, Fu Xijun and Xiongjun were waiting for me. They'd sneaked out of the academy to visit me, and they'd brought me two thermoses full of popsicles. I loved popsicles, but I didn't feel like eating them that day. My throat throbbed relentlessly. Still, the Bandit insisted I eat at least two to keep the swelling down. He'd had his tonsils out the year before, and he said I should be thankful—both medical technology and doctors' skills had improved significantly since last year, he said.

What significantly improved technologies? The useless needles? The dull knife? I couldn't imagine anything worse than what I'd just been through. But I didn't say anything—it was too painful to talk.

That night I couldn't sleep. The pain was excruciating, and there weren't any painkillers. How I wished my niang was there to comfort me.

July 1977: our sixth year at the Beijing Dance Academy. We were allowed to go home for our three-week midterm summer holiday this year, but we had a choice: we could stay back and practice if we wanted to.

I wrote to my parents and told them I had decided to stay. Of course I dearly wanted to see my family, and I missed them: the thought of the cricket sounds, catching dragonflies, eating my niang's dumplings all seemed so tempting, but this was the first time I felt happy staying on.

During these three weeks a campaign to apprehend the followers of the Gang of Four started. The vice minister for Culture along with all other key cultural ministers were arrested. Our vice director, Zhang Ce, and Director Xiao of our academy were also apprehended. I will never forget Zhang Ce's desperate face as he walked out of the academy gate. He had done nothing wrong except be appointed by one of Madame Mao's followers. Now he was disgraced. Tension and uncertainty floated in the air.

I was determined, however, not to let these events distract me from my practice. I had to concentrate. Zhang Shu and several other teachers stayed back at the academy, too, and I asked them to coach me.

One day Teacher Xiao suddenly appeared in the studio when I was practicing my turns. "How are you, Cunxin?" he asked.

"Fine. I thought you wouldn't be here this holiday."

"I just thought of something that might help you with your pirouettes," he said. I was still working on five consecutive pirouettes and was having tremendous problems breaking this crucial barrier. Teacher Xiao knew I was going to work on it throughout the holidays, but after less than half an hour of practice, my pirouettes were getting worse and I was getting increasingly frustrated.

"Why am I so stupid! Why can't I do five?" I slumped onto the floor.

"If five pirouettes were that easy to achieve, wouldn't every dancer in the world be doing it? Cunxin, have you ever tasted a mango?"

"No." I wondered what he was talking about this time.

"Mango is the most wonderful fruit with the most unique taste! One can only get it in certain parts of the world and only for a short season. I want you to treat pirouettes like a mango. If I gave you a mango now, what would you do with it?" he asked.

"Eat it," I replied.

He laughed. "You deprived boy!"

"Why? Wouldn't you?" I asked.

"Why so impatient? I can understand that you want to taste the mango eagerly, but the fun is in the *process*. First I would admire the unique shape, notice the color, enjoy the smell. I would feel the weight, cut the skin and savor the fragrance.

Perhaps I would taste the skin and even the nut if I were daring. *Now* comes the ultimate satisfaction, the pulp. Yes, you need to enjoy every step of the process, taste the many layers of the fruit and enjoy it for its full value. I want you to treat pirouettes in the same way. Be daring! Discover the secret and essence of pirouettes. If you don't go all the way and taste the pulp, someone else will. I dare you!"

Teacher Xiao and his mango triggered my imagination, and I challenged myself to go a step further, to experiment with new feelings. I poured my passion into it, and I started to enjoy each step of the process.

This was the first time I had three weeks to myself at the academy. I spent most of my time practicing, slept late some mornings, skipped breakfast often; I went to Taoranting Park, ran around the lake and watched people practicing tai chi. I played Chinese chess and card games with a few other remaining students, and I visited the Chongs. I even had the shower room all to myself for a whole half an hour one day.

The three weeks allowed me time to think about the future and to reflect on the past. Now I laughed at the image of that sad, introverted little boy who'd been so afraid to stand on his toes all day in a pair of pointe shoes. I couldn't believe that now, less than six years later, I was the vice captain of our class and one of the heads of the Communist Youth Party. Now I pursued excellence in my dancing. I took pride in my own challenges.

The three weeks passed quickly. I enjoyed every minute. I couldn't wait for the second half of the year because I had set myself even higher hurdles now, and I was desperate for the chance to try to overcome them.

The rest of the students returned from the holidays, and our study resumed as normal. Later that term a former graduate of the Beijing Dance Academy and a close friend of Teacher Xiao's,

Yu Fangmei, returned from Japan and brought back a television, a video player (something so new that we'd never even heard of one before) and some videotapes as gifts to the ballet department. There were videos of Baryshnikov, Nureyev, Margot Fonteyn, even two American-trained dancers including Gelsey Kirkland. At first these videotapes were shown to the academy officials and teachers as "reference" only. Students were not allowed to be exposed to such bad Western influences.

I passed Teacher Xiao in the hallway one day shortly after Yu Fangmei's visit. "I wish you could see Baryshnikov dancing one day!" said Teacher Xiao eagerly.

I had heard a little about this Russian ballet star. He was the ballet world's new phenomenon. "Is he better than Vasiliev?" I asked.

"Yes! Yes, from the technical point of view. I have never witnessed a more spectacular dancer!" Teacher Xiao said, and he shook his head with amazement.

"Is there any way I can get to see those videos?" I asked hopefully.

"We've discussed this already," Teacher Xiao replied. "The officials are worried about capitalist influences. Let me speak to Teacher Zhang again."

A couple of days later, during an afternoon rehearsal, all the senior students were called to a studio on the third floor. I immediately noticed the television and video player sitting on a bench in front of the mirrors.

Zhang Shu waited for the excitement to calm down.

"Baryshnikov is probably the most outstanding ballet dancer in the world today. The sole purpose of watching these tapes is for you to learn from him, to make you understand what today's world dancing standard is. This is *not*, I repeat, *this is not* for you to learn about the Western world's lifestyle! By watching Baryshnikov, you will realize how hard you have to work to reach this same standard

240

of dancing. Today, we'll show you Baryshnikov's own production of *Nutcracker* and *The Turning Point*.

I was captivated with Baryshnikov. I had never seen anything like *Nutcracker* before. I couldn't believe how beautiful the music was. Baryshnikov and his partner, Gelsey Kirkland, danced to a standard far beyond what I thought any dancer was capable of. During the five-minute break between videos, not one of us left the room: everyone was afraid of losing his spot. How could anything rival *Nutcracker*? I thought. But I was wrong. The video of *The Turning Point* totally blew me away. I was mesmerized. I couldn't take my eyes off Baryshnikov. My heart leaped with each one of his astonishing jumps and accelerating turns. His movement was graceful, his execution brilliant. For the first time in my life I saw how truly exquisite ballet could be.

From that moment on I loved ballet with a passion. I dared to believe that if Baryshnikov could dance like that, then so could I. I was sixteen years old, but I was impatient. I felt a new sense of urgency. I scrapped my previous standards and set new ones. This was how I could make not only my parents but also the whole of China proud.

Now I raced through my meals so I could get back to the studio to practice my jumps. I woke at five every morning. I strapped sandbags to my ankles and hopped up and down the four flights of stairs in our studio building. I practiced my leaps, covering every inch of whichever studio was vacant. I was obsessed. I wanted to fly like the beautiful birds and dragonflies, so I wrote the word "fly" on my ballet shoes to remind myself of my goals. I embarked on endless sit-ups and exercises everywhere I could find a flat surface and a few minutes to spare. People thought I had gone mad, but I didn't care. I had only one desire now—to dance like Baryshnikov.

By the end of 1977, my sixth year, after all of my exercises, practice and determination, my jumping ability had improved, but I still wasn't the best. I knew there was a long way to go. It was then that Teacher Xiao started to challenge me with my turns.

I couldn't turn naturally, but my newfound inspiration with my jumps made me work harder and harder. I set impossible goals for myself. One night I had an idea. When everybody was asleep I went to the studio, with a candle and a box of matches. I put the lighted candle at one end of the studio and started to practice my turns. The candle threw only a faint light in front of me. It was hard, but I thought if I could turn in the dark, then turning in the light would be easy. I couldn't take the risk of turning the light on, of my teachers catching me staying up so late, but I continued, night after night, relentlessly. By the end of the term I had left shallow indentations in the studio floor where I had endlessly, repeatedly, turned.

Many people were very surprised to see my rapid improvement, but not Teacher Xiao. One night, he *did* catch me practicing my turns. It was way past lights-out time and I thought he would be very angry, but instead he said he wasn't surprised and he kept my nighttime practice sessions a secret between us.

I realized too, around the same time, that I couldn't do a perfect split either and knowing the importance of being able to have that flexibility I worked hard on my hamstrings. I once fell asleep in bed in the split position and when I woke I had to be helped up by my classmates because I couldn't feel my legs at all. One of the teachers told me then that I had big thighs and that I would never do principal roles with thighs like mine. I was depressed for so long about this. I even wrapped plastic around my thighs so they would sweat and become thinner.

By now I was practicing in those studios five times a day compared to the usual once-a-day routine of the other students. I practiced when I first got up. I practiced before class, at nap time, at afternoon rehearsals and after dinner just before bedtime.

When I ran out of dry T-shirts, I would practice bare chested. Even my ballet shoes would be soaking with sweat. "I thought *I* worked hard as a student—I practiced three times a day, but five times is unheard of!" Teacher Xiao said, amazed. Then, more seriously: "Please look after your health. I want to see you last the distance."

By this time, Mao's chosen successor, Hua Guofeng, was under house arrest, and Deng Xiaoping became the leader of China. I felt a dramatic change of attitude within the Beijing Dance Academy. Previously, Deng Xiaoping had been denounced for his slogan about the cat: but now this idea came back in full force. He didn't care which system China used as long as it worked for China.

We had a new academy director too, Chen Jingqing, who decided that our six-year course of study would be extended for another year. We wouldn't graduate now until February of 1979. We'd wasted too much time, she said, studying politics instead of dance. Director Chen believed that another year was needed to concentrate on the pursuit of technical excellence alone.

So even by the beginning of 1978 I could feel the real impact of Deng Xiaoping's reforms. He was the first person who had dared to say that to follow Mao's every word was wrong and that the political campaigns and studies must be stopped. Some Communist Party members were skeptical and so were many others. The Cultural Revolution had left such horrifying memories. Why should they believe new policies now? China was unsure, and too numb to act quickly.

It was during our last year at the academy that we began to openly practice our art form without being accused of being an unbalanced student. Political pressure waned. Selected Western books, films and performing groups began to appear in China. Getting hold of a foreign book or watching a foreign "colored film" soon became an obsession. We were desperate for Western knowledge. If we came across a book with sex scenes in it we'd secretly copy it, every word by hand, under our blankets, in flashlight, and pass the copies around. How thirsty we were for foreign literature and how fascinated we had become about the Western world!

Deng Xiaoping's new policy created a breath of fresh air within our academy, but it was strangely foreign at first. The required biweekly Communist Youth Party meetings were reduced to once a month, and no one questioned it. My conflict between attending meetings and practicing ballet was resolved. The Communist Party's pursuit of new membership slowed, and political party leaders no longer had the same influence. The pursuit of material things, that capitalist tumor, began to take on a different meaning. Maybe it was because the Beijing Dance Academy was one of Madame Mao's strongholds and her influence was so deep for so long, but it took awhile before we started to embrace Deng's new policies wholeheartedly. For me, however, this extra year of study turned out to be my best yet. We started to watch some old Russian ballet films such as *The Stone Flower*, *Swan Lake* and *Spartacus*. We saw famous ballet stars like Galina Ulanova, Maya Plisetskaya and of course Vladimir Vasiliev. We were even allowed to watch that famous Russian defector Rudolf Nureyev dancing with one of the Western world's most respected ballerinas, Margot Fonteyn. Images of these extraordinary, inspiring dancers stayed in my mind for many, many weeks.

It was around this time, when reading Western ballet books was no longer a crime, that I asked Teacher Xiao if he had been the person who had left that ballet book under my mat in the third year.

"Did you like it?" He smiled enthusiastically.

"Thank you." I nodded and I meant it from the bottom of my heart.

十六

16

CHANGE

Late 1978. Just months away from graduation. On a Saturday night in the biggest dance studio on the fourth floor our teachers organized a party, and all the senior students were invited.

It was no ordinary party. It was a waltz party. There were colorful clothes, long dresses, people there I'd never met before, even a few officials from the Ministry of Culture. And there was a strange round silver thing that looked like a land mine, a ball turning slowly from the ceiling and spinning out hundreds of different colors and shapes from the lights. It was wonderful! We were totally entranced. Dancers led their partners elegantly across the floor. Teacher Xiao was the star, and many ladies were immediately taken with his style.

After watching the dancing for a while I gathered enough courage to ask a teacher to show me how to waltz. She explained the basic foot movements, and that male dancers should lead, but it was impossible to avoid stepping on her feet! I kept treading on her toes and apologizing profusely.

I might have been hopeless in my first waltz, but I enjoyed it enormously. It was the first time I had heard such beautiful, romantic music. This never would have been possible under Madame Mao's directorship, I thought. Under Madame Mao any kind of waltz would have been considered a corrupt influence and would have been banned along with every other form of Western filth. But now things were different. Such freedom was refreshing, unique.

Other things changed too. We began to watch more and more foreign films. We would find any possible way to get into the heavily guarded theaters where these "colored films" were shown. Fake theater tickets were made. Wigs and mustaches were stolen from the costume shops of the academy. Once we got into the theater we would find every possible way of staying there for the next screening. We would hide behind the window curtains, behind the doors, behind the screen on the stage, even in the toilets. Anything to get to see those films. Years of isolation from Western culture and suppressed sexual freedom had found their outlet.

One day the Bandit meticulously glued the torn halves of some used theater tickets together. We whitened our hair and slipped into the theater with our fake tickets without being detected. The place was packed with people, crammed to both sides, and it was dingy and dark. The Bandit and I sneaked to the center and sat in the aisle. We didn't have rehearsal until three, plenty of time to finish the movie and get back. But neither of us had a watch. "Lujun," I whispered. "How will we know when it's time to go?"

"Don't worry, I have an internal clock," he said confidently.

I was going to say more, but the movie had started. It was an American movie about a love triangle. The translated Chinese title was *Hurt Too Much to Say Good-bye.* Two inept translators, a man and a woman, provided mediocre translation over a pair of microphones, but they often forgot to translate and we, the frustrated audience, were left to guess for ourselves most of the time.

I couldn't believe the colorful clothes the women wore in these movies. So different from how Chinese women dressed. I did wonder if the high-heeled shoes were comfortable, though. They looked just as bad as the pointe shoes.

Some of the actresses were breathtakingly beautiful, but they all looked so much alike. It was in this movie that I witnessed a kiss for the very first time. My heart raced, my blood boiled when I saw that kiss. I wondered what it would be like—really kissing someone.

The Bandit's internal clock didn't work. By the time the movie had finished we were late for our rehearsal, and we ran as fast as we could back to the academy and quickly changed our clothes.

As we approached the studio I heard Teacher Xiao's voice. My heart immediately sank. Teacher Xiao was the last person I wanted to offend.

Teacher Xiao turned and looked at us and, without changing his expression, went on coaching the other students. I was embarrassed beyond description. I glanced furiously at the Bandit: I wanted to pull his internal clock out and smash it to pieces.

"Cunxin, come to my office after your next break," Teacher Xiao said at the end of the rehearsal.

I spent the whole of the next rehearsal thinking about what I should say to Teacher Xiao. If I told him the truth he would be thoroughly disappointed with my lack of discipline. I still hadn't decided what to say when I knocked on his office door.

Teacher Xiao got straight to the point. "Why were you late?"

"I went to a movie," I stuttered. I had to tell him the truth.

"I had a feeling you had gone to a movie, but although you have told me the truth it doesn't take any of my disappointment away."

"I'm sorry, Teacher Xiao. I thought I would be able to make

it back in time for the rehearsal but I didn't realize it was so late. I promise it won't happen again."

He looked at me intently for a few moments. "Cunxin, this wouldn't have surprised me if it had been any other student. But I am extremely surprised and disappointed that it was you! I don't question your dedication, but I do question your judgment. I don't care if you watch a hundred movies in your spare time, but classes and rehearsals are your learning opportunities."

I nodded. I knew I was unquestionably in the wrong.

Then in a different tone Teacher Xiao asked, "What was the movie?"

"A colored film."

"What's the name?" he asked.

"Something like *Hurt Too Much to Say Good-bye*," I replied and lowered my head.

"Any scenes without clothes?" he asked seriously.

"No, only kisses," I replied.

"Okay, off you go." He shook his head as he spoke, but I could see a subtle smile. I was glad I was honest with him. I could never have lied to him. Not to Teacher Xiao.

"Colored" movies weren't the only distraction in those last few months. I was besotted with a girl from Shanghai called Her Junfang as well. We would often pass secret adoring looks to each other and when she acknowledged my gaze my heart would race at a thousand miles an hour.

One night we secretly met in a dark studio. I could sense her unease. I felt my face burning. The air seemed so thick that I found it hard to breathe. We would be expelled if the teachers discovered us.

"How was your holiday?" I whispered.

"Fine, how was yours?"

"Good. I brought you some sorghum sweets," I replied.

"Thank you, I like them. I brought you some Shanghai cakes."

We edged closer to each other. Suddenly we heard the door of Zhang Shu's office open and we froze. My heart was suspended in the air.

To our great relief his footsteps went in the opposite direction. We only had a few minutes to get away, so we nervously exchanged our gifts and quickly tiptoed out of the studio.

When I finally sat on the edge of my bed in the dark with Her Junfang's gift in my hands, my heart was still pitching like a rough sea. I hated myself for being such a coward, for not holding her when I had the chance. I couldn't believe that I had forgotten all the passionate words I had rehearsed in my mind before our meeting. And we never had the opportunity to get close to each other again.

About the same time the Bandit confided in me about his own passionate love for a classmate of his, Zhou Xiaoying. But in his efforts to pursue her he had somehow paid more attention to her girlfriend instead, and she had fallen for him. We tried to guess each girl's feelings, but after more than an hour of heated debate we got nowhere.

"I think a face-to-face talk would be better. That way she can see and feel your emotions and sincerity," I said.

"She would never agree to meet with me alone! She's too shy!" He shook his head hopelessly. "I love her with all my heart. My love for her is the purest thing on earth. I wish I could cut open my heart to show her how sincere and pure it is!"

I had no idea the Bandit loved Zhou Xiaoying that much.

"Can you speak to her for me?" he asked suddenly.

"Are you crazy?"

"Please, I beg you! If I lose her I will kill myself!" he said.

I saw tears in his eyes. "Okay, I will speak to her," I heard myself saying.

But by the next day the Bandit had changed his mind. "She

will think that I am gutless having you represent me. And your political career would be in trouble if anyone found out. No, I can't let this happen," he said. Instead he'd decided to write a blood letter.

A couple of days later he rushed up to me, and I immediately noticed one of his fingers wrapped in a white bandage. "You *did* write her a blood letter, didn't you?" I asked.

"I did!" he replied with excitement. "I think it will show my heart and passion better. It's all up to fate now."

But Zhou Xiaoying never replied to that blood letter. Both Zhou Xiaoying and her friend threw hateful looks at the Bandit whenever they met, as though he had betrayed both of them. He was devastated. I knew how much he loved her, but there was nothing I could do to help. He continued to pursue her for several more years, to no avail.

By now, with the exception of the Sundays I spent with the Chongs, I used almost every spare moment to practice. My diaries were full of notes about dancing, which I wrote after every practice class. I learned more in that one year than in the previous six years combined.

Around the time when we were preparing for our graduation the London Festival Ballet came to perform in China, one of the first professional companies allowed to perform under Deng Xiaoping's "open-door policy." They came to perform with us at our academy theater and everyone talked about the "big-nosed people," the foreigners.

I had such problems trying to distinguish one big-nosed person from another. They all looked alike, whether they were in the movies or in dance videotapes or there in person. I had to remember what clothes they wore to differentiate them. If they suddenly changed costume between scenes I would be totally lost. And they seemed to speak so fast, without any commas or stops. One of the foreigners who came was an eighteen-year-old dancer called Mary McKendry, and she watched me dance the "Three Little Boys Dance."

The Festival Ballet performed *Giselle,* and two mixed programs, including Harald Lander's famed *Etude.* I loved *Giselle,* and by now we didn't have to analyze its political content. I wished I could watch this kind of dancing every day: it was astonishingly expansive, and the big-nosed dancers' artistic interpretations and discipline quickly gained our respect. *Etude* too was one of the most technically challenging ballets I had seen—I longed to perform it, to learn more about Western culture, to work with these great choreographers.

Our graduation exam preparations went on for over three months, and everyone worked very hard. Our final average grades would determine which dance company we'd get into. The Central Ballet of China would select only the top graduates. Others would be sent to cities far away or to provincial song-and-dance troupes.

A month before our final exam Teacher Xiao came to me and said, "Some teachers say I have allowed you to do too many solos in your exam. Most students will do one or two, only one student is doing three. I think six might be too much for you. I don't want to burn you out," he said.

"No, I want to do all six!"

"Are you sure? Because once I hand my submission to Zhang Shu it will be very hard to change."

"Yes, I'm sure I can do it," I replied confidently.

He thought for a moment. "All right, but just remember, try to find the secret of doing every step as easily and effortlessly as possible. That is what dancing is all about."

To prepare six solos for my graduation exam was difficult, but I thought of what Teacher Xiao had said and I went into every detail of every step, trying to taste the pulp of the mango. Each solo required a different technical and artistic approach. The first was from one of Madame Mao's model ballets, *The White-Haired Girl*, and I was to dance with an imaginary grenade in my hand, ducking enemy bullets with fast, crisp movements. I worked hard on my two political solos, but my real passion and love was for the Western classical solos. In those, however, I had such problems with a double tour en l'air and to achieve good height as well as complete the two turns down to kneeling position in the flash of an eye was an enormous challenge. My right knee was grazed and bleeding from constant landings, and often I would pull splinters from my skin. I also developed painful shinsplints from trying to perfect the double cabriole in *Giselle*. Images of Baryshnikov, Nureyev and Vasiliev continually inspired me. But with this double cabriole all my previous approaches failed. I wasn't even tasting the skin of the mango. You have to work smarter, you have to get to the delicious pulp, I kept telling myself.

A few days before the exam I made the breakthrough. I had to dramatically change my weight distribution in the air and bend my body backwards as far as my flexibility allowed. When I finally got it right the feeling was sensational.

In the end I did perform all six of my solos, and I enjoyed every step I danced. After seven years at the academy I even mastered eight consecutive pirouettes, occasionally ten. And now here I was, one among the last generation of Mao's dancers about to graduate.

For our graduation performance our academy wanted to revive *Swan Lake* for the first time since the Cultural Revolution. It was a difficult task—all the records on Western ballets, including *Swan Lake*, had been destroyed during the Cultural Revolution. It was one thing to put together just one solo from a ballet like *Giselle* but quite another to reproduce a full-length ballet. Teachers had to recollect details from past performances of many years ago, but miraculously this collaboration worked and resulted in the complete ballet being produced. I was thrilled to be chosen as third cast for Prince Siegfried. I concentrated on nothing but my rehearsals. I worked on my weaknesses and focused on my goals and, by the time the teacher in charge of the rehearsals finally decided who was to dance the leading role on the opening night, I had been chosen as first cast.

As I rehearsed my role as Siegfried I asked my friend Liu Fengtian what he thought of my portrayal of the prince. He said my dancing was good, but I didn't look Western enough. I looked like a peasant boy pretending to be a prince. I knew what he said was true. Deep down I knew I had no idea how I should portray him. I had no problem with the dance steps, but I knew nothing of European royalty. Even my teachers didn't know how a prince would carry himself. We knew only about our comrades and our political causes, but what a prince represented was in direct conflict with the values of communism.

In desperation I watched a few old Russian films so I could study a prince's walk, the way he held his arms and hands and how he looked at people. I even permed my straight hair (the costume department took care of that) so I could make myself look and feel more like a prince. But how could a Chinese peasant boy understand a Western prince's arrogance, his passion and his love? Our culture had always taught us to hide our emotions.

I danced that opening night of *Swan Lake* at the Beijing Exhibition Hall. The performance went well. But I couldn't get rid of the peasant prince image, and I was not satisfied. My aim was to eventually be as good a prince as even the Western dancers. But I knew that would have to come from within. I knew that only experience and maturity would determine whether I could *be* that handsome prince and not just a poor peasant boy acting out a role.

Then, soon after that performance, an event occurred that would change my life forever.

Officials from the Ministry of Culture informed us that a fine choreographer and brilliant teacher, the artistic director of the Houston Ballet, was to teach two master classes at our academy. He was part of the first cultural delegation from America ever to visit communist China. The choreographer's name was Ben Stevenson.

十七

17

ON THE WAY TO THE WEST

Twenty students, including me, were selected to attend Ben Stevenson's classes. Ben seemed to enjoy teaching at our academy, and I was exhilarated with his approach. Compared to our restrictive training, his seemed so much easier and freer. He approached dance mainly from the artistic aspect, emphasizing relaxation and fluidity of movement rather than strict technique. I found him fascinating and inspiring, and my body felt good while I performed in his classes.

After the second class, Ben offered our academy two scholarships for his annual summer school at the Houston Ballet Academy in Texas. It was incredible, unbelievable news! The chance to leave China, to see the West! Nobody believed that this could be true. But Ben was told that he couldn't choose the students himself. The academy would nominate who would go: we would have to wait and see.

Ben gave the invitation letter to the academy officials in March, and he expected the students to be in Houston by July.

Then the two students were chosen. One was a boy called Zhang Weiqiang. The other was me.

We were ecstatic. So was the whole school. It was too impossible to be true! How could I be going to America? How could I?

The academy officials thought it would be difficult for us to obtain our passports and visas that quickly, so they didn't pursue the matter seriously until they received a phone call from the Ministry of Culture a few weeks later. None of them knew then that Ben Stevenson had powerful friends in America. One was George Bush, who had just finished serving as the first U.S. envoy to China after President Richard Nixon's visit in 1972. And his wife, Barbara Bush, was a trustee of the Houston Ballet. Both were serious balletomanes and both were well respected by the Chinese government. George Bush had formed a good relationship with Deng Xiaoping: his political connections would no doubt ensure the acceptance of this scholarship invitation. And it did. Zhang Weiqiang and I were granted permission from the Ministry of Culture to go to Houston very quickly indeed.

Zhang Weiqiang and I went to the Beijing Passport Bureau as soon as we possibly could. The police handed us two application forms, and we were told to write down both our Chinese and English names. Zhang and I looked at each other. We didn't have any English names.

"Write your name in pinyin then," the policeman said.

Pinyin was invented by the Chinese government to help foreigners pronounce Chinese words. But it was based on Latin pronunciation, not English, and I didn't have a clue how to write my name that way. So I just put my family name first, as usual in China, and wrote "Li Cunxin" on my application form.

"Is this your real birth date?" the police officer asked when he read my completed forms.

I had written 10 January 1961. "Yes. What do you mean 'real'?" I asked.

"Is it your Chinese calendar birthday or the official calendar birthday?" he asked.

My family had always used the Chinese calendar, never the official calendar. It had never occurred to me that government agencies used the same calendar as the rest of the world.

"No good," the police officer said when I told him. "We need the official calendar. You'll have to go and find out before we can issue you a passport."

But that date was the only birthday I knew. My parents wouldn't know either, because most babies in the countryside were delivered at home and local records would state the Chinese calendar date only. Peasants never used the official calendar for anything. It wasn't until much later that I discovered my official birthday was set as 26 January.

Zhang knew his official birth date, though. His application was fine.

I began to panic. I was nearly in tears. I *had* to get my passport and visa in time for the summer school in Houston. I couldn't miss this opportunity! I begged the police officer, "Please, Comrade. Who would care *when* my exact birthday is? I don't have enough time to find out. I will miss this opportunity to serve our country!"

He hesitated then. "All right," he said eventually, and I sank with relief.

Our visas were approved by the American consulate in Beijing in a matter of days. We were overwhelmed with excitement. But once the euphoria faded away, panic struck. Zhang and I could speak no English. How would we ever understand the Americans?

An English tutor gave us a crash course for a few days, starting with the English alphabet and ending with simple phrases such as yes, no, good morning, hello and good-bye. I used Chinese words to help me pronounce the English words, as I'd done to learn the French ballet terms, but they sounded ridiculously Chinglish and I really had no idea how I would make myself understood.

We also had to go into the Ministry of Culture to be briefed by the officials. The head of the Educational Bureau, Wang Zicheng, met us briefly. He spoke with a gentle, persuasive voice. "Work hard while you're there, show your American hosts how hard Chinese people work. Don't forget that you're representing China and the Chinese people. Treasure this opportunity. Bring back knowledge. Resist capitalist influences and make sure you exercise your communist judgment." He shook our hands and left, but his assistant continued to lecture us. "Be polite at all times. If you don't understand what people are saying, just say 'yes' and smile. Never say 'no.' Never. 'No' is a negative word. People might be offended." She too told us not to let filthy Western influences into our pure communist minds. Everything we did or said would represent China and the Chinese people.

She then took us into a room which contained a few racks of used Western-style suits and ties. She said they had a small supply mainly used for government delegations going to foreign countries. We had never worn a suit before, only Mao's jackets, but we were told to borrow a suit each from the ministry. We tried quite a few on but all were too big for our skinny bodies. We ended up choosing the smallest suits, but the shoulders still came halfway down our arms and we had to fold the sleeves up. We also borrowed two ties and a suitcase each.

Zhang and I, to our utter astonishment, soon became a news item in China. We were the first official exchange artists between China and America since Chairman Mao took over power in 1949.

I telephoned my parents for the first time since leaving home all those years ago. I rang from Director Chen's office. My second brother, Cunyuan, came to the commune phone first. "*Ni hao, Erga!*" I screamed excitedly into the phone.

"*Ni hao*, Cunxin! What's wrong?" he asked, sounding concerned. Something dreadful must surely have happened for me to use a telephone.

"Nothing! I am going to America for six weeks!" I replied.

There was silence. "Really? You're joking," he said.

"No! I'm not joking. I am going to America with another student," I replied.

"My brother is going to America!" he screamed loudly to the people in the commune office. I could hear a roar of cheers.

"I can't believe this!" he continued. "America! I heard everyone there carries guns. If they don't like you they'll just shoot you. And everyone has cars. Niang is here . . ."

"Jing Hao!" my niang called.

"Niang, how are you?" I asked. I was so happy to hear her voice.

"I'm fine. Are you really going to America?" she asked breathlessly.

"Yes, I'll be leaving in a few days."

"*Ah!* Why didn't you tell us earlier? We could send you some apples and dried shrimps to take on the road," she said.

"I am going on a plane. I was told no food is allowed on the airplanes."

"On the *airplane? Wo de tian na!* How *unthinkable!* My son is going to fly on the airplane!" I heard her say to the people in the office, and there were more cheers.

"Ask him how many hours will it take to get to America?" I heard one of the commune leaders ask.

"Tell that Uncle, I was told that I have to fly to Tokyo first, the capital of Japan, and then it will be something like twenty hours to America."

"Please be careful. Stay away from the evil people in America.

Don't they kill colored people there?" my niang asked, sounding worried.

"I'm going with another student. We'll look after each other. I've also met the American dance teacher from Houston. His name is Ben. He seems nice."

"Just be careful. These foreigners are wild! They are different from us. Don't trust them."

I wasn't surprised by my family's concerns about America. For so many years we had been told that the West, especially America, was evil. We'd heard of nothing but the mistreatment of black people, the violence on the streets, the use of firearms. Even I, who had read a few books about America since the downfall of the Gang of Four and didn't totally believe what I had learned in the past, was still suspicious and apprehensive.

I could never have imagined, however, that this conversation with my niang and Cunyuan was the last one I would have with them for many long years.

In the last few days before we were due to leave, the whole academy became excited for us. Teachers and classmates constantly congratulated us. We were called into Director Chen's office once again. She was all smiles. She gave us the familiar lecture, told us to study hard, to show the Americans our work ethic. Never to lose face for our great nation. Never to allow Western influences to penetrate our staunch communist values.

Our day of departure finally arrived. That morning, eight of my friends including the Bandit, Chong Xiongjun and my violinist friend, Liu Fengtian, went out to a nearby café and brought back some pig's head meat, some red sausages, pickled vegetables, watermelon and a few jugs of warm beer. They had to smuggle the beer into the academy: we would be in trouble if we were found out by the teachers. For two hours we would enjoy our food together, our companionship, before the academy's jeep took us

*My classmates and myself, center front, wearing Mao's Red Guard scarves.
This was taken in early 1972, in Laoshan.*

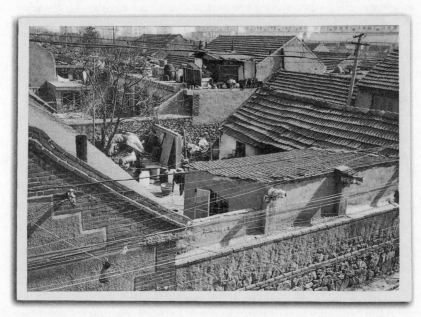

*The New Village, Li Commune—the world of my upbringing. This photo was taken
in 2002—nothing much has changed since I was born.*

Proudly wearing Mao's army uniform, in January 1974— aspiring to become a true and faithful follower of the communist ideal.

My beloved niang washing, forever washing, in the courtyard of our home. This was taken when I went back to China in 1988.

My first lonely day in Beijing, posing for one of our group photos in Tiananmen Square—I am in the front row, fourth from the right.

The Beijing Dance Academy—my world for seven long years. Here it is in 1997—again, nothing much had changed: the studio building is on the right, hot-water boiler room and teachers' rooms in the center, and the canteen to the left.

Hai Luo Sha, *one of our political ballets, with me and "Chairman Mao."*

Rehearsing Hai Luo Sha *with Teacher Zhang Shu in 1976. In the background are Mao's grand words: "Have your country in your heart and the world in your vision."*

First contact with the West—Zhang Weiqiang and I in New York in 1979.

On the steps of the Vaganova Ballet School in Leningrad—my first trip to another communist country.

Defection. April 29, 1981. Being freed from the consulate with Elizabeth Mackey and Charles Foster.

Finally at ease as the Western prince—
Sleeping Beauty *in 1984.*

With Barbara Bush at the White House in 1991. She was instrumental in bringing my parents to the U.S. and in fostering my relationship with China.

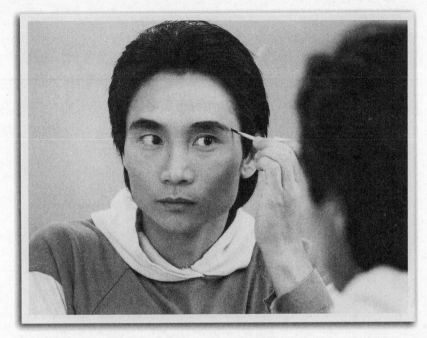

Applying my makeup for a performance with the Houston Ballet—a new identity, a transformation: what would my niang and dia think of this? I lived in another world now.

In Glen Tetley's Rite of Spring—*making the giant leaps I'd always dreamt of.*

The Esmeralda pas de deux with Mary, in 1990, in a gala performance at the Sydney Opera House.

My beloved family in Melbourne in 1997—my wife, Mary, and our children, Sophie, Thomas and Bridie.

to the airport. We speculated about what America would be like. I promised I would tell them everything when I returned. "Don't you let a big-nosed girl kidnap you over there!" said the Bandit. How he wished that he was allowed to go to the airport with me.

When it was time for Zhang and me to leave, our friends fought over carrying our luggage to the jeep, and in the commotion the Bandit quietly shuffled something into my hand. "Read it on the plane," he whispered.

I quickly slipped the paper into my pocket. Before we stepped into the jeep, our friends, teachers, everyone came forward to shake our hands. Teacher Xiao was very emotional. "*Yi lu ping an!*" He wished me a safe trip and shook both of my hands hard. "Cunxin! Cunxin! I know you will make China proud! Bring back new knowledge! I can't wait to share all your discoveries when you return!"

The last to say good-bye was the Bandit. Tears filled his eyes, and he couldn't speak a single word.

"Six weeks will disappear before you know it!" I said to him.

As the jeep pulled away from our academy buildings, the last thing I saw was the Bandit's tear-stained face.

I'd never been to an airport before, except the abandoned military airport near our village where I'd tried to dig up half-burned coal as a small boy. But this Beijing Airport was not what I had expected at all. It was strangely quiet compared to the hustle and bustle of Beijing Station. Everything was orderly.

We were hours too early and the check-in counter wasn't even open, so Zhang Shu, the head of our ballet department who was accompanying us, took us to a little canteen and bought us each a Coca-Cola. We'd heard all about Coca-Cola—the most successful invention of the Western world. We couldn't believe we were about to taste some. I took a big mouthful and swallowed it eagerly. Too eagerly. I nearly choked with all the fizz. So did Zhang Weiqiang. We looked at each other and laughed. Our first Western experience, an American icon, and I didn't like it at all.

We said good-bye to Teacher Zhang before we checked through immigration. Zhang Weiqiang and I were now on our own. We sat on the bench in the waiting room and looked at each other. We hadn't a clue what to do. We looked out the window toward the huge airplane with "China Airlines" written on it. I had never seen a plane so close. It was gigantic. It was overwhelming. How could a heavy thing like that ever get off the ground?

When the time came for us to board, several uniformed airline people escorted us downstairs to a bus, which took us out to the plane. As we moved closer the plane became bigger and bigger and bigger. I felt like a tiny insect.

We walked up the steps, and as we entered the plane a pleasant cool air seemed to cover me completely. I liked it, but I wondered where on earth it was coming from. And I couldn't believe how big the inside of the plane was! Rows and rows and rows of colorful seats.

Eventually we found our seats and waited nervously for something to happen. When it did, I nearly suffocated with excitement. I looked out the window. I saw the accelerating engines. My heart was pounding. My stomach churned—I didn't know whether to laugh or to scream. I could never have imagined this! My heartbeat raced faster and faster, my excitement flew higher than the clouds! Here I was, leaving behind our great nation of communists with its steadfast beliefs and ideology forever supporting us. I felt unbelievably proud.

Our plane leveled out, and once I was over the shock of the takeoff I began to explore and investigate everything I could. Movies to watch! Music to listen to! And a hostess to serve us beautiful meals: rice with fish, Japanese noodles. The hostess asked us what kind of drinks we would like. I chose something called Sprite this time.

We were treated like royalty. I felt bad just sitting there being waited on and letting someone else do all the work. What would my niang say? So I offered to help the hostess wash the plates. She just looked at me with a very strange expression. "No, thank you," she said.

This must be a millet dream, I thought. Too good to be true. But I pinched myself and it hurt. I was like an ant in a hot wok. I couldn't stay still for a minute. I went through the contents of the seat pocket in front of me and found a little bag that contained unbelievable luxuries: a miniature toothbrush, toothpaste, a pair of socks and eye covers for sleeping. Zhang and I even kept the safety card as a souvenir. It had a picture of the entire plane on it! What would my niang and her sewing circle think of this! How could they even begin to imagine it?

I looked around and noticed that most of the passengers on the plane seemed to be Chinese, government officials most likely. Many of them gave us rather surprised looks, no doubt wondering how two young students could be so privileged to be flying overseas. Very few government officials were allowed overseas, let alone students like us.

With all the excitement of the takeoff I had forgotten about the Bandit's note. I opened the white envelope he had given me, and a small piece of paper slipped out. It was a poem:

> As blood brothers,
> the departure of one
> will never wane the love in our hearts.
> Not fortune or money,
> but only the pursuit of innocence and honor,
> will strengthen the love in our hearts.

I thought of the past seven years and our hard and lonely life at the academy. Without the Bandit and his friendship, my life there would have been unbearable.

The three-hour flight to Tokyo went by very quickly. We were told we had to get off the plane for a couple of hours at Tokyo Airport. I couldn't believe we had traveled so far in only three short hours. But once again Zhang and I didn't know what to do. We were too afraid to leave the gate area in case we missed our flight, so we just wandered around or stood together until it was time to board. I happened to glance up at a coffee-stand's price list and noticed that a cup of coffee cost U.S. $3.00. I did a quick calculation. That was nearly half a month's salary for my dia! Perhaps I had got the numbers wrong. I did the sum again. No, that was right. I could only look at the list in total astonishment.

This time we boarded a Northwest Airlines plane and walked directly onto it through a sort of tunnel without having to walk up any steps at all. This plane was even bigger than the first. Much bigger. This was something called a jumbo jet, we were told. It was awesome. There were endless rows of seats and we were, amazingly, ushered to an upper deck. Blankets and pillows were neatly placed on the seats, and there were more gift bags and more flight safety cards for us to keep as souvenirs. There were even magazines, which we couldn't read, but we did look at the pictures. A beautiful car was splashed across two pages with $35 written below it. Perhaps this was how much it would cost the Americans to buy this magnificent car, Zhang and I pondered.

This time over half of the passengers in our cabin were foreigners. I noticed a strong smell of perfume from some of the women, and I couldn't quite get used to it. The combination of watermelon and beer at my farewell party caused me a great many trips to the toilet too. I thought the hostess must have thought something was wrong with this Chinese boy who kept going to the toilet all the time.

It was impossible for me to believe that I was actually sitting on this gigantic airplane on my way to the West. I looked down at the thick beautiful clouds and thought I was in the ninth heaven. I was so excited, but neither Zhang nor I had a clue about what was waiting for us.

十八

THE FILTHY CAPITALIST AMERICA

Our plane began to descend through thick cloud. We were about to land in Chicago. All of a sudden I remembered those few pages from the book about the steel tycoon in Chicago, the book I'd found on the street in our commune, years ago now, the one that had stirred up such curiosity in my heart and mind. I longed to see if the little knowledge I had learned from that book was true about this Paper Tiger country.

Zhang and I got off the plane and collected our luggage. Then we just stood there in our oversized suits and looked around. We didn't know anyone except Ben Stevenson. How would we recognize the person who was supposed to meet us?

People around us collected their luggage, came and went, while we became more and more nervous. What if nobody showed up?

Suddenly I saw some people standing behind some glass windows on a second floor, and there was Ben, jumping up and down like a yo-yo, trying to catch our attention, with a card with my name written on it in Chinese. Zhang and I were overjoyed. Ben came to meet us just outside Immigration.

"*Ni hao*," he said, one of the few Chinese phrases he knew. "Hello," I replied, one of the few English words I knew.

Ben asked us some questions and I tried to use the words from my dictionary to show him how ecstatic I was, but Ben was just happy to share our excitement with nods and smiles and when we couldn't understand his words we just smiled more and said yes. My dictionary became my best friend from then on, but I had at least learned some expressions already: "Oh dear me" and "Upon my soul." They'd be very useful, I thought. I also knew a few propaganda words and some communist expressions that might come in handy. And although my English was not good, Zhang's was even worse and I ended up translating for him as well.

We boarded a flight to Houston and with Ben by our sides we began to relax. As we flew over the American landscape I noticed how green it was and that it was neatly divided into squares by straight roads and streets. We saw many little square patches of blue too. Ben said they were swimming pools—he mimed swimming and drowning motions with his arms. He made us laugh but I could hardly believe there could be so many swimming pools in just one area. The contrast with the bareness of China was so amazing that I started to wonder once again about America's prosperity and the stories we'd been told.

When we arrived at Houston Airport we were met by Clare Duncan, head of the Houston Ballet Academy, and two Houston Ballet board members: Preston Frazier, a very tall man who spoke softly, and Richard Holley, a medium-sized man who spoke loudly. They handed Zhang and me a small bunch of native Texas flowers and a cowboy hat each. Zhang and I hesitated. We didn't know whether to accept these gifts or not—we were suspicious. We simply didn't trust these Americans. But I was the assigned leader of the two of us, because my political standing was higher than Zhang's, so eventually I told Zhang to accept the gifts. It was the first time anyone had ever given me fresh flowers.

The Americans' happy smiles also made us nervous. This is not what it is supposed to be like. Something is wrong here. They are our enemies. Behind their smiling faces will be a hidden agenda. I'll find out what it is soon, I said to myself.

Like the inside of the plane, the airport was surprisingly cool. I thought we had been given the wrong information about Houston's hot weather, and I was thankful we had our jackets on. But the pleasurably cool air didn't last long. As soon as we walked outside an intense and humid heat, like a hot wet blanket, overwhelmed us. I found it hard to breathe. Then one of the ballet board members, a woman Ben introduced as Betty Lou Bayless, ushered us into her car and it was cool in there too. Betty Lou was an elegant, softly spoken lady with a kind face. Her car was so comfortable, so smooth. This was the first time I had ever been in a car. Such luxury could only be enjoyed by government officials in China, and I felt incredibly privileged. I could hardly contain the excitement in my heart.

When we passed downtown Houston and saw all the modern office buildings and the spectacular skyline I thought to myself, if Houston looks this prosperous, what would New York and Chicago be like? Nothing I had seen so far matched the dark, decaying, depressing picture of America that the Chinese government had painted in my mind. Instead I saw high-rise buildings, wide clean streets, a green and orderly environment. I knew our foreign hosts could maybe fake their behavior, but they simply couldn't have built these buildings just to impress us. I was confused. Someone had lied to us about America being the poorest nation in the world and China being the richest nation. It seemed to be the opposite. But still I was confident I would eventually find many things about America that I could hate.

We arrived at a large house in a fenced complex with a security gate and guards. Zhang and I were ushered through a big sliding glass door—and my jaw dropped . . .

I saw a huge room, beautiful beyond belief, with pastel colors, sofas and matching chairs. And mirrors, giant mirrors. There was carpet too—beige, soft and bouncy. To the left I saw a kitchen—and my jaw dropped even lower. A refrigerator stood against the wall, as tall as me and four times as wide. And an electric stove and *two* sinks. And there seemed to be many other things—gadgets whose purpose I couldn't even imagine. The kitchen was simply enormous. So many wooden cabinets on the walls and under the counter. Has the Western world gone mad with all this? Did they have a robot toilet to wipe their bottoms? I couldn't help myself from being constantly shocked. Everything was new. Even the air smelled new.

Ben showed us around and led us upstairs to our bedroom, which had two single beds in it, a small walk-in closet and the same luxurious carpet as downstairs. There was a chest of drawers and small tables with lamps beside each bed. It even had its own bathroom with a human-sized bathtub! I had never used a bathtub before. Couldn't be more beautiful than a shower. Couldn't be.

That first night in America we were taken to a local Chinese restaurant called the Mandarin. A Chinese lady greeted us at the door with rather broken Chinese. She wore a long black silk gown, and she had a heavily made-up face. I thought she looked more like a Beijing Opera singer, but she smelled so strong! She must have poured a whole bottle of perfume over herself.

The restaurant was very crowded, but we were taken to our own private room. Clare Duncan and the two gentlemen we had met at the airport, the quiet Preston and the loud Richard, were there too, as well as two other friends of Ben's, Jack and Marcia. Both Ben and Richard joked throughout the night and made everyone laugh. But Zhang and I knew we were facing six possible class enemies here. We didn't know what attitude we should have toward these people. If this were China they would have been killed or jailed under Mao's regime simply because of their wealth. But here they were, relaxed, joking and laughing like they were having the time of their lives.

We had a couple of tasty Tsingtao beers from my hometown, the first time I had ever had one, and as the evening progressed we gradually let our guard down just a little and joined in the fun. Ben ordered many delicious dishes, including Peking Duck. I'd never had Peking Duck before either, and it just melted in my mouth. Here we were, having two Chinese icons right here in America. No one is going to believe me back home, I thought. I noticed too that these Westerners called Beijing "Peking" all the time—even that seemed odd.

Many courses later, Ben asked us if we were still hungry. We didn't understand what he was saying, but we remembered that we had to keep smiling and saying, "Yes, yes!" just as the Chinese officials had told us. But more and more food kept arriving. Eventually I just held my head and shouted, "Oh dear me!" and everyone burst into roars of laughter.

In desperation I went to the Chinese lady who owned the restaurant. "Can you please tell Ben to stop ordering any more food? Our stomachs will simply burst!"

"But he hasn't even ordered dessert yet," she said.

"What dessert?"

"Sweet dessert. Don't you have them after dinner in China? American people love their dessert," she replied.

I'd never heard of such a thing called dessert.

By the end of the evening we had so much leftover food on the table I asked Ben if we could take it home. I couldn't bear the waste. I thought of all the starvation in China. But everyone that night seemed to admire our slimness, and I couldn't understand why. In China being thin was a symbol of poverty, and being fat meant you had money to buy good food. Later I discovered that many people in America went to expensive diet clinics to lose weight. I could easily help them, I thought, just by sending people to China and feeding them those dried yams for a while.

When we got back to Ben's place that night I had my first bath. The water soaked my body and soothed my every nerve. I even let the water come over my face and I blew bubbles like a child. It was incredible. I couldn't decide whether I liked the shower or the bath better. The bed was a different matter, though. The soft, bouncy mattress was very uncomfortable!

When I woke up next morning I had to pinch myself to make sure that everything was real. When I heard Ben's voice down-stairs calling us for breakfast, I knew it was true. I *was* in America. For six whole weeks.

Ben had already cooked us some bacon and eggs. "Would you like some English muffins?" he asked.

Zhang and I exchanged horrified looks. "No, thank you!" we replied quickly. What a terrible thing for Ben to offer us for breakfast, I thought to myself.

This time Ben was puzzled. "What's wrong?"

With the help of my dictionary, I replied. "Muffin meaning horse shit in Chinese."

Ben roared with laughter. "First 'Oh dear me' and now 'horse shit'! We're going to have a lot of fun this summer," he said.

Next he offered us some orange juice. He sliced several oranges and by the time he had filled up three glasses he had used nearly ten! I felt like a criminal drinking that precious glass of juice. My family had never even seen an orange before. And it was the first time that we'd ever tasted bacon, toast, butter and jam too. We had *masses* of food. Ben couldn't believe where it all went. He had to cook another package of bacon and fry more eggs. It was as though we hadn't eaten for eighteen years.

After breakfast we went straight to the Houston Ballet Academy, which was within walking distance of Ben's apartment. The academy was in an old single-story brick building shared with the Houston Ballet Company. There were four medium-sized studios.

Clare Duncan, the head of the academy, took us around and introduced us to the teachers and students. It was the first day of the summer school, and it was like a zoo in there. Zhang and I were completely confused. Everyone looked alike, and their names were impossible to remember.

"Ballet class, when?" I asked Ben, with the aid of my dictionary. Seeing all the students dancing and hearing the music made me eager to begin.

"You can start today if you like," Ben replied.

The only word I understood was "today," but that was enough.

When I looked into the studios I noticed all the male students wore black tights, white T-shirts, socks and shoes. The only pair of tights I had was given to me by one of my teachers back in China. He'd gotten them from a British ballet dancer, and they were bright blue. Zhang had a white pair of tights—I wasn't sure where he'd gotten them from.

"No pants," I told Ben after I found the word "pants" in my dictionary.

"You don't need pants for class." Ben was puzzled.

"Pants, pants!" I repeated as I demonstrated a plié and pointed at my legs.

"You don't need pants, you only need ti . . . oh, *tights!*" Ben shouted excitedly.

"Yes!" I wasn't sure what the word tights meant, but it looked like Ben had understood so I smiled broadly.

Ben quickly organized for us to go to a dance-wear shop. Ben

272

had given Stephanie, the company manager, enough money to buy Zhang and me two pairs of tights, dance belts and a pair of ballet shoes, over two hundred dollars worth each. I quickly did a currency conversion: two hundred dollars was equivalent to over two years of my dia's salary. How could I justify Ben spending two years' salary on my dance wear! "Do you *realize* how *much* these tights and shoes *cost*?" I said to Zhang.

"No. How much?" he asked.

"Over a thousand yuan!"

His jawed dropped then too.

It was lunchtime when we arrived back at the academy, and a Houston Ballet board member, Louisa Sarofim, was already waiting to take us to lunch at a nearby restaurant.

From the way the restaurant owner treated Louisa, I knew we were about to have lunch with yet another class enemy. The restaurant was amazingly elegant and cool, with fresh-cut flowers everywhere.

We were handed a menu each. I couldn't read anything except the prices, and nothing was below $14.95. Since Louisa was going to pay, I thought I should be modest and not order anything too expensive. I didn't want to leave a bad impression. I told Zhang of my intentions. "I will do the same," he said.

We chose two of the cheapest items on the menu. I hadn't any idea what I'd ordered, but I was confident that in a restaurant of this stature we wouldn't be left starving.

Minutes later, the waiter placed a small plate of green salad in front of me and a small bowl of green soup in front of Zhang. I still remember the look Zhang gave me. I forced out a smile and quickly turned my eyes away.

"Are you okay?" Ben asked, concerned.

"Okay!" I replied brightly. Zhang just nodded. Louisa probably thinks we're so thin because we don't like to each much, I thought.

I poked my fork into the greens and tasted a leaf of my very first salad. "Good taste!" I said to Zhang, trying to encourage him.

"Good taste!" Zhang replied and forced himself to finish his green soup. Luckily the waiter kept circling our table with freshly baked bread.

Louisa dropped us back at the studio, and Clare Duncan showed us to the men's dressing-room. I put on the tights we had bought that morning. They felt very soft and comfortable compared to my bright blue pair from home.

The studio was packed with dancers when we arrived. On the center barre the students moved up to make room for Zhang and me. Then Ben walked in. I remember he wore a T-shirt with "London" written on it and a pair of silklike black pants. His energy and his passion for his teaching seemed to inspire everybody. During the class I kept a keen eye on other students, and to my surprise I discovered Zhang and I compared well to the others. The precision of our technique was high, and this could only have come about from the strict discipline of our Chinese training.

There were students here from England, Canada and other places, a result no doubt of Ben's international reputation as a teacher, choreographer and artistic director. Our schedule was full each day. There were many classes—ballet, character, modern ballet, pas de deux, body conditioning and choreographic workshops. I wasn't sure what to expect in the modern ballet class, but our Chinese folk dance classes and tai chi movements made it easy for us to find some common ground. The body conditioning class was different—it was based on something called Pilates, and I could see it would help me understand my own body and deal with my physical weaknesses and injuries.

Everyone in the classes seemed to be busy making new friends. Zhang and I couldn't remember their names or understand what they were saying, but we were warmly embraced by many of the students. We were even given fifty dollars per week as a living allowance. I never dreamed of having that amount of money in my entire life! Eight months of my dia's wages! I tried to save as much money as possible from that living allowance so I could help my family when I returned to China.

We soon discovered that Ben was a very good cook and he also loved entertaining, so we were surrounded by people all the time we were there. That meant a lot of nodding and smiling on our part. Zhang and I were not bad cooks either, and we were a big hit in the kitchen. We were so used to hand-washing every-thing, though, that we hardly used the dishwasher or washing machine. After breakfast one morning Ben had to rush to a board meeting, and he told us to put the dirty dishes in the dish-washer and turn it on. When I opened the cupboard to get the dishwashing detergent, there were quite a few boxes of powder for me to choose from. Naturally I chose the biggest box, filled the dishwasher with laundry powder and turned it on. A few minutes later the whole kitchen was foaming. Masses of foam covered the kitchen floor, and I was sent into a total panic.

During that second week in Houston, Ben's good friend Barbara Bush invited us to her house for lunch. I remembered she even had an indoor pool. She apologized for Mr. Bush's absence: he had to attend a presidential rally in California that day.

I felt very privileged to meet Barbara, but her husband was such a high-profile politician that I was deeply suspicious of her hidden political agendas. Would she try to corrupt our political beliefs? I mentally prepared myself. But all we received was gen-erosity and friendliness. Barbara didn't seem like a politician's wife at all. She reminded me of my niang. She was elegant and generous, and talked about China very fondly.

That day we'd been asked to bring our swimming suits. We didn't have any, so Ben had to buy them for us, like so many other things. Barbara and Ben chatted happily while Zhang and I swam in her indoor pool where the water temperature was perfect, a pool owned by one of the most powerful ladies in America. I could never have dreamed of this.

Barbara also had a little dog called Fred. She adored Fred. She'd even taken him to China with her while Mr. Bush served as the first envoy. She talked about her dog as though he were a child. She told us that Fred was a very intelligent dog. I thought that if her dog had been a dog in my hometown, someone would have eaten him for dinner.

We went to board member Louisa Sarofim's house a few times too. I couldn't believe her wealth. When I saw her garden, her pool and the surroundings I thought I had just walked into a well-maintained park. She took us inside, and I saw some of the most beautiful paintings I had ever seen. Ben told me later that most of the paintings were worth millions of dollars. A million dollars? The number was too enormous for a Chinese peasant boy to comprehend. She must have more money than a god, but she was so nice and unpretentious and she loved ballet and took immense pride in the Houston Ballet's developments. The amount of wealth surrounding ballet in America seemed amazing to me. There was money everywhere. Once I even saw a ballet board member leave a hundred-dollar bill on the table after a meal. Of course I quickly tapped him on the shoulder. Didn't he realize he'd left a hundred dollars behind? But he simply nodded his head and walked out. It blew me away. Over a year's worth of my dia's hard, hard work and it was simply left on the table. Sometimes I heard people talking of hundreds of millions of dollars, but again, such numbers didn't exist in my vocabulary. The financial and cultural gaps were simply too great to comprehend.

During the first week of the summer school, Ben arranged for us to attend an English-language course, and I began to learn ten to fifteen new words a day. I carried a piece of paper everywhere I went, with my new English words written on it. The most effective place for me to learn them was in the bathroom. My English improved quickly, and I ended up translating for Zhang. Clearly he should have spent more time in the bathroom.

I was constantly surprised by how much freedom the American people had. One day in the dressing room one of the students from New Orleans noticed my Mao button on my dance bag.

"Do you like your Chairman Mao?" he asked.

"Yes, I love Chairman Mao!" I replied with my fist over my heart.

"Well, I don't like our president, Jimmy Carter. I don't think he's a good president at all," he said.

"No good? Jimmy Carter?" I asked, amazed.

"No good." He pointed his thumb down.

"Shh . . . !" I looked around nervously. "You not scared people listen to you talk about your big leader this way?" I asked in my broken English.

"No, why? I can say anything I like about our president. This is America."

"If I say bad thing about Chairman Mao," I whispered, "I will go jail and may be killed," I sliced my finger dramatically across my neck.

"You're kidding!"

"Yes, it is true!" I replied.

"You know," the student continued, "Ronald Reagan, he's the governor of California and wants to be the next president. He was only a Hollywood actor before."

"Actor?" I didn't understand what "actor" was so I took out my dictionary. An actor who wants to become the president of America? Surely I had translated incorrectly.

Ben choreographed a dance for Zhang and me over the next few weeks using George Gershwin's music. We had such difficulties understanding what Ben wanted us to do in the rehearsals, though. Everything was *so* relaxed, and our minimal understanding of English made it intensely frustrating for Ben. Zhang and I could easily complete the difficult and challenging turns and jumps but taking an effortless walk across the studio without turning out our feet or pointing our toes was a real challenge. At one point during a rehearsal Ben grabbed my arms and shook my entire body. "Relax, relax!" he shouted. Then he rushed over to Zhang and did the same. Zhang's shoulders will pop out of their sockets any minute, I thought. When I finally got the hang of what Ben wanted, it felt like I was cheating. It was too easy and casual. It didn't feel like dancing at all. But I *could* feel the gradual progression and developments in Gershwin's music, and I could feel Ben's choreography naturally meshing into it.

By the end of our six-week stay I had started to relax. I began to make friends among the students, the dancers in the company, the balletomanes and even some board members. Each weekend we had to report to the Chinese consulate officials. One of the senior consuls was Zhang Zongshu, and his wife was a translator in the consulate. They were assigned to look after us.

It turned out that Ben had decided to ask Consul Zhang if I could come back to work with the company again.

Once more Ben's influence worked. Consul Zhang and the Chinese consulate sent a favorable report to the Ministry of Culture. I was granted permission to return for a whole year to work with the Houston Ballet, only two months after my scheduled return to China. There were also discussions about the possibility of Zhang Weiqiang's return too.

The thought of being able to come back to America made me happy, but really it sounded completely unbelievable. I was so grateful to the Chinese government. I felt that they really cared for me. For me, a peasant boy. Communism truly was great.

For our last few days in America, Ben took Zhang and me to Washington, D.C., and New York. We didn't do much in Washington except pose for photos in front of the White House and the Kennedy Center. In some ways I was disappointed. I had expected to see a massive number of security guards with machine guns around the gate and the fence, just like I'd seen in Beijing on my first day there. But there were only a few guards standing by a small gate, looking rather relaxed. They even let us stand next to the fence to have our pictures taken.

We stayed with two close friends of Ben's while we were in New York. They were involved with television, and they had two skinny, funny-looking dogs that sang while one of them played the piano. Those dogs would be eaten back in Qingdao too.

Ben rushed Zhang and me around like mad to see as many of the great sites of New York as possible—the twin towers, the Empire State Building, the Statue of Liberty, Central Park, the theater district: I was in awe of this hustling, bustling city. Everything surprised and impressed me—the gigantic buildings, the number of cars, the cleanliness compared to Beijing. But it was the little things that left deeper impressions on me. A friend of Ben's showed us a thing called an ATM. I was speechless when twenty-dollar bills began spewing out. I'd seen a lot of electrical appliances in Houston, but to see money coming out of a wall was beyond my wildest imaginings.

Just like any tourist, with our limited money we bought a few souvenirs such as "I Love New York" buttons, postcards, and mugs with big apples on them. My favorite was a T-shirt that had my face and "I Love New York" printed on it, a present from Ben. But we found New York scarily expensive. I couldn't stop comparing everything to China and thinking about my family's poor life back home.

After New York we returned to Houston for our last two days before heading back to China. People gave us farewell gifts. My heart filled with ambivalence with each good-bye. Ben had made our stay such a positive experience, and he was proud to have arranged for the first two Chinese cultural exchange students to come to America. He had been thoughtful and generous, protective and kind. He had poured special interest into our dancing. I knew I could never repay him. So by the time Zhang and I said our final good-bye to Ben at the airport, we felt sad to be leaving a special friend.

On the plane I thought of the possibility of returning to Houston in only two months' time. I thought of how I'd felt about America and its people before I came. I laughed when I remembered my initial suspicions.

But most of all I thought of those dark, scary images of capitalist society and how they had now been replaced by an entirely different picture in my mind. China's most hated enemy and the system it represented had given me something that was my heart's desire. Now I was frightened. Now I was confused. What should I believe? What communism had taught me? What I'd seen and experienced? Why had Chairman Mao, Madame Mao and the Chinese government told its people all those lies about America? Why were we so poor in China? And why was America so prosperous?

I kept resisting my doubts all the way home on the plane back to China. I tried to tell myself that my strong communist faith was still unshakeable, but I knew I was lying to myself. I knew I had to believe what the Chinese government wanted me to believe, or at least I had to pretend to. All this made me even more afraid. I was never supposed to question my communist beliefs and I never, ever thought that I would. So I kept telling myself that I was happy to return to China, because that's where my parents, brothers, friends and teachers were. That's where my roots were. I'm the fish and China is the pond. I can't exist anywhere other than China.

But still the doubts persisted. I had now tasted freedom, and I couldn't lie to myself about that.

十九

19

GOOD-BYE, CHINA

The first thing I did when I returned to the Beijing Dance Academy was to tell Teacher Xiao, Zhang Shu, the Bandit and all my friends about my new discoveries in dance: the Gershwin pas de deux, the Martha Graham technique, the body conditioning classes. I simply couldn't hide my excitement and enthusiasm. I had decided, however, that I wouldn't say anything at all about how much I liked America. I especially wouldn't mention the sense of freedom I had experienced. I desperately wanted to, but I knew it would give the authorities reason enough to deny me permission to return to America. I wouldn't take that risk. As an old Chinese saying goes, "The wind will carry the words to other people's ears."

The freedom I'd experienced in America occupied my mind constantly. In China, Chairman Mao and his government's absolute authority could never have been challenged. We didn't have individual rights. We were told what to do, how long to work each day, how much we would be paid, where we would live and how many children we were allowed to have. I struggled with my communist beliefs: memories of America were so fresh. What if *I* were to have that same freedom? What could I do with my ballet then?

Eventually I talked myself into believing that if I had stayed in America any longer, I would surely have seen so many bad things about capitalism that I wouldn't have liked America at all. Even so, I was surprised that I was wavering after spending only six weeks there. How could eighteen years of communism be so easily influenced by six short weeks of capitalism? Without Chairman Mao I was lost. He was my god. Would I still die for Chairman Mao? Now I wasn't sure.

I also started to question certain aspects of our ballet training in China. I became frustrated at the lack of freedom in my teachers' thinking. I began to feel once again like a trapped animal. I couldn't wait for the two months to pass so I could go back to America and continue my learning.

As soon as we returned, Zhang and I had to report to Director Chen of our academy and to the Ministry of Culture, who required a written report from us about our American trip.

"Would you like to meet this evening to work on the report with me?" I asked Zhang.

"Why don't you just write it yourself," replied Zhang. "I trust you."

But I told him that I needed his help because our report would require a certain degree of deception if we were to avoid any suspicion from the officials.

"Write what you have to write. I will understand," Zhang said.

I was happy that Zhang trusted me to complete this task, but I found it very difficult to write bad things about America. I simply couldn't think of any. So I made up some bad things about "rotten capitalist influences." First I described the daily routine at the Houston Ballet Academy and the new experiences in Ben's ballet classes. I emphasized the goodwill Zhang and I had generated for China. Then I put a considerable amount of time and effort into describing the diseased aspects of America. I described the restaurant owner from Taiwan as one of our class enemies, with her strong perfume smell, her thick makeup and her plastic smile. I described a black neighborhood in Houston, the decaying houses and leaking roofs. I said it was infested with flies and mosquitoes and that people slept outside on mats on a dirt floor. Only a privileged few lived in air-conditioned luxury homes. I expressed sorrow for the poor black people of America. I emphasized our superior communist system and Chairman Mao's valued principles.

"This is great! Thank you, Cunxin!" Zhang said enthusiastically after he'd read the report.

But I wasn't happy. I felt angry that I'd had to do this at all.

When we handed in our report and returned the borrowed suitcases, ties and suits to the ministry, Wang Zicheng's deputy also asked us to relinquish any living allowance we'd been given.

Zhang and I were completely shocked. "We spent most of the money on food while we were there," I replied. I didn't tell her we'd also spent some of it on gifts for our families and friends.

"I want every remaining dollar here by tomorrow," she demanded.

So being good and honest Red Guards we gave all our remaining money to the ministry the following day. But I was desperately disappointed—I had planned to give that money to my family. They needed it more than the ministry did.

Going back to America so soon meant that I wouldn't be able to see my parents until after my return the following year. I knew they'd be eager to hear from me, so I wrote them a letter. "I will miss you dreadfully," I wrote, "especially upon New Year's Eve. I will raise my glass full of Tsingtao beer in a faraway foreign land and drink to your health and happiness. I will kneel and kowtow to you. If you sneeze, you will know that it is probably because I am mentioning your names. I hope you will understand how much I want to come home and tell you all about America. There is so much to tell it would take me too long to write it all down. Please be patient and wait for another year, and before you know it I'll be back. I have brought presents back for you. I will bring them home next year. I am sending along with this letter a flight safety card so you can see the picture of the plane that I flew on. They are the most beautiful, awesome things in the world. I was flying so high above the clouds. I wish you could have the chance to fly in them one day. I'm sending with this letter all the love in my heart to all of you. I want to tell Niang that I miss her dumplings and all her delicious food. With all the expensive food I had in America, nothing tastes as good as Niang's dumplings."

On the third day after I returned, Zhang Shu, the ballet department head, asked me to teach a master class to all the ballet teachers in the academy to show them what I had learned while I was away. Teach my teachers a class? I felt nervous about that, but it went well and I continued to participate in most of our practice classes and rehearsals while I was getting ready to reapply for my passport. Our passports had been taken back by the ministry as soon as we'd arrived home.

I was happy to see my good friends at the Beijing Dance Academy again, especially the Bandit. I gave him an "I Love New York" button and some postcards from the cities I'd been to. He wasn't sure he'd be able to wear the button in public, but he loved it all the same. "How do you say 'I love New York' in English?" he asked excitedly. "I wish I could have the privilege to see New York one day!"

"You will," I replied, but I knew that was very unlikely.

"You didn't fall in love with a pretty big-nosed girl while you were there?" he asked suddenly.

I laughed. "No, don't be silly. Of course not! What about you? Over Zhou Xiaoying yet?"

He shook his head sadly.

"What did you do with the rest of your holiday?" I tried to divert the conversation away from Zhou Xiaoying.

"I went home to see my father and mother. They all asked about you! They are so proud of you going to America, and they want me to bring you to Hezi to spend a holiday with them sometime." Hezi was his hometown and reportedly where Confucius was buried. It was something the Bandit always boasted about.

"I will come after I get back from America next year," I replied.

"Tell me, what do you *really* think about America?" he asked.

I hesitated. I wasn't sure what to say. I wanted to tell him about the freedom I had tasted, but I knew this would only lead him to misery. "There were many clean and wide streets, a lot of cars, tall buildings and good living standards," I said instead. "But the best thing was Ben. He was so nice and kind, and I love his teaching." Then I told him about the White House, about New York, the ATM machine and all the electronic gadgets. He was especially surprised and excited about the ATM machine.

"Did you see anyone carrying guns on the street?"

"No," I replied, but I didn't want to talk about America any more. I told him I hoped he'd have the chance to see it all for himself one day, and quickly changed the subject.

I received my visa papers from Houston toward the end of the second week and immediately went to the Ministry of Culture to reapply for my passport. But when I arrived the deputy had some devastating news. "Cunxin," she said casually, "I've just received a directive from the minister's office. The minister has changed his mind. He has refused your request for a passport."

I couldn't believe what I was hearing.

"The minister is concerned about potential Western influences. He thinks you are too young."

"But I've been there once already, and the Western influence did nothing to me! Didn't you read our report?"

"Yes, I did. It is very good. But the minister has made up his mind."

I walked out of the building in total despair.

As soon as I arrived back at our academy, I charged into Director Chen's office. "Director Chen, did you know about this?"

"Yes, but only this morning."

"Why?" I pressed.

"The minister thinks you are too young to go to America by yourself. It is a dark and filthy world out there," she replied.

"But the minister already gave me permission before I left America!" I said, full of emotion. "I have to go back! To learn more from Ben's teaching, to serve our country better!"

"I understand your feelings. I'm disappointed too. But you must trust the decision of the party. You shouldn't question the wisdom of the minister's decision. Now, go and carry on with your normal activities. You are only a tiny part of the communist cause. Forget your personal desires. And if you don't mind, I have work to do."

I left Director Chen's office frustrated and angry. I walked right out of the academy. By this time they were more relaxed about senior students coming and going, so the security guard didn't stop me. I didn't know where I was going or what I was going to do. I just needed time to think, so I bought a five-fen entry ticket to Taoranting Park. I walked faster and faster. I broke into a run and ran without any thought or purpose, trying to drive away what was in my mind and heart. I ran like a blind, scared tiger. It was as though a beautifully sunny day had, without warning, turned dark and unfamiliar. All I could see was a never-ending road, leading nowhere, only closing into a circle, a circle that was full of misery. My heart was racing, my legs were cramping and I gasped for air. "I have to get out!" I kept telling myself.

Along the edge of the lake there were many weeping willows. I was still fond of willows, but ever since we'd moved back to the city I hadn't had the need to confess to the trees anymore. Not like when I was eleven and homesick, back in the early days. Now, seeing the willows swaying from side to side in the breeze, I longed for refuge once again. I climbed onto a small tree and in under the cover of the leaves. I spoke to the weeping willows for the first time in five and a half years. How could my opportunity to go back to America be taken away so easily, just like that? Those six memorable weeks, the things that I saw and experienced . . .

America was real. America was out there and I had seen it. The plane trips, the cars, the cowboy hats, the "bloody" steaks, the raw salad, the ballet classes and the Gershwin music. It was all so vivid and close. And now the ground I was standing on had disappeared from under me. I desperately tried to think of the real reason why the minister had suddenly changed his mind. Was it my report? Did I write too many good things about America? Perhaps Zhang got jealous and said something unfavorable to the ministry? Or was what I'd been told by the deputy true?

I had no answers, but I knew I would do everything I could to find out the truth. Calm down, Cunxin, I told myself. Think of ways to persuade the minister to change his mind.

I went back to the academy just before dinner. "Teacher Xiao is looking for you!" the Bandit shouted from a distance as soon as he spotted me. "Are you all right? You look terrible," he asked as soon as he noticed my face.

"I'm not allowed to go back to America," I replied.

"Why?" cried the Bandit.

I couldn't say. Tears choked my throat. I ran to Teacher Xiao's office and knocked on the door.

As soon as I closed the door, he rushed up to me and hugged me tight. "I heard the news, I'm sorry," he whispered.

I was stunned by his hug at first. Hugging still wasn't a

communist thing to do. "Why, why, *why* did he take it away from me?" I sobbed. "What did I do wrong?"

"Sit down," Teacher Xiao said. He pulled a chair out from under his small desk and lit a cigarette. "According to Director Chen, the minister feels that you are too young to go to the West for a whole year."

"Do you think this is the real reason?"

"It appears this is the only reasonable explanation."

"But he gave me permission to go back before I returned! What made him change his mind?"

"I don't know. Teacher Zhang and I asked the same question."

"Is there any way we can find out?" I persisted.

"You never give up, do you?" Teacher Xiao smiled.

I shook my head.

"Teacher Zhang and I have convinced Director Chen to send a petition to Minister Wang to see if he will change his mind. I don't know whether it will work. All we can do is wait," he said.

"Thank you, Teacher Xiao," I said.

"Don't thank me. You need to thank Teacher Zhang. He did most of the talking. We both felt that after only six weeks in America your dancing had already improved enormously. I can't imagine what a year would do for you. To miss this opportunity would be an unforgivable mistake. Ben Stevenson can offer you opportunities we cannot offer you here. Now, go to dinner. Otherwise there will be nothing left," he urged.

I didn't hear back from the ministry for over a week. Then, on a Tuesday, Zhang Shu called me into his office. Teacher Xiao was already there. As soon as I entered the room I knew the news was bad.

"Cunxin," Zhang Shu began, "we have just been informed by the ministry. Our petition has been turned down. I'm so sorry."

My heart was bleeding. I tried hard to hold back my tears.

"Cunxin," Teacher Xiao said, "Teacher Zhang and I have decided to give you permission to take three weeks' holiday to visit your family. You haven't seen them for nearly two years. I'm sure they are really missing you."

"Thank you," I said, and stumbled out of Teacher Zhang's office.

A door to a whole new world had shut right in front of me, and I could do nothing more about it. All I wanted to do was go to sleep. I was tired and I was devastated. Just as I'd done on that very first night at the Beijing Dance Academy seven years ago, I plunged onto my bed and pulled my niang's quilt over my head. The bright possibilities of ballet and a political career had lost their luster. My self-doubt resurfaced, and I lost all my mental strength and will.

I couldn't understand why not going back to America was affecting me so much. I became angry with myself for being so selfish. I was lucky to go to America once, and I should be satisfied and thankful. But a stronger voice kept rising above all other voices in my mind. "I *want* to go back. I want to study with Ben. I want to improve my dancing and most importantly I want to taste that precious freedom once again."

I jumped out of bed and ran to Teacher Xiao's office. "Teacher Xiao, do you know where Minister Wang lives?"

He frowned. "Yes, why?"

"I want to see him."

"I don't think he will see you even if you do go to his residence. I think you would be better to go to the ministry and make an appointment with his assistant instead."

"I don't think his office will let me make an appointment. He has already refused my case twice, and it would take too long for his office to schedule me in. I don't have that much time to waste. Besides, he is not a tiger. He won't eat me, will he?" I added, remembering what Teacher Xiao had said to me once about Teacher Gao.

"You and your memory," he said. "I will never underestimate

both your memory and your resolve." So he wrote the minister's address on a small piece of paper and handed it to me. "Good luck," he said.

The following evening I took two different buses and forty-five minutes later arrived at Minister Wang's residence.

It was an impressive compound with high walls and a tall, metal-barred security gate. There was also a guardhouse and a military guard with a semiautomatic machine gun at the ready.

"Hello, Comrade," I said to the guard as confidently as I could. "I'm Li Cunxin from the Beijing Dance Academy. I'm here to see Minister Wang."

"Do you have an appointment?" he asked.

"No, I don't," I replied honestly.

"Go home if you don't have an appointment," the guard growled.

"I only need to see him for one minute. Please, it's an urgent matter," I begged.

"No, go home. You cannot see the minister without an appointment. Move! If you don't move, I'll have you arrested."

I left, angry and humiliated. This was not how comrades should treat each other.

But I was back the following night. This time, a different guard was at the gate.

"Hello, Comrade. I'm Li Cunxin from the Beijing Dance Academy, and I've just returned from America representing China. I was told to meet Minister Wang tonight," I lied.

"What time is your appointment?" he asked.

"I'm not sure. Our academy made the appointment for me."

"Wait a minute. What did you say your name was?" he asked.

"Last name is Li," I replied, hoping he wouldn't ask for my first name. Li is a very common last name in China, so maybe someone else with the last name of Li had an appointment with the minister that night, I prayed.

"What's your first name?" the guard asked.

No such luck. "Cunxin," I said.

"I don't see any appointments made with the minister tonight," he said, checking the appointment book. "Are you sure you have come on the right night? The minister is attending a banquet. He won't be back until late."

"I'm sorry, I must have the date wrong. Thank you," I said to the guard. I walked to the end of the street and turned the corner, then sat on a stone doorstep and waited for the minister's return. I took out my list of twenty new English words and tried to memorize them. Then I went over what I was going to say to the minister, keeping an eye out for his car.

By midnight I was freezing and tired, and there was still no sign of the minister's car. I ran to the nearby bus stop to shake off the cold and caught the last scheduled bus back. I missed the last connecting bus, so I had to run for half an hour after that to get back to the academy. The security guard was already asleep, and I climbed over the gate as quietly as a cat.

The next day after our ballet class Teacher Xiao called me to his office. "Cunxin, I'm worried about you. Why don't you give yourself a break?"

I shook my head and told him what I'd done the last two nights. "I won't give up until every possible avenue has been explored," I said defiantly.

I could see tears in Teacher Xiao's eyes. "Cunxin, for all the years I've known you, I have never once doubted your determination. But here you are not dealing with internal factors. You are dealing with things beyond your control. Like a flea trying to overpower an elephant. Just give yourself a break. There will be another opportunity in the future."

"Isn't there any other way?"

Teacher Xiao shook his head. "The minister rarely reverses his decisions. Your situation is the least of his worries."

But still I would not give up. On the third night I returned to Minister Wang's residence, and this time I doubled my list of English words to forty and wore more clothes. I was prepared to wait all night for a chance to see the minister.

The same guard from the first night greeted me. "Hello, Comrade. Do you have an appointment this time?"

"Yes, one of my teachers has made an appointment with the minister's deputy, and I was to meet him tonight at seven-thirty," I said matter-of-factly.

"Wait here."

My heart thumped and my face turned red and I hated myself for lying. If it weren't for the darkness the guard would have easily detected my guilt simply by the color of my face.

A few minutes later, the guard came back. "You can't even lie properly! Go home and don't come back again until you have a proper appointment. Otherwise I'll shoot you."

I noticed the guard was in a better mood than the first night. "Comrade, I'm sorry that I have to lie to you but I *must* see Minister Wang, even just for one minute." I told him the reasons why I wanted to see the minister. I begged him to put himself in my shoes and to give me a chance. "I promise that I'll only take one minute of his time."

"Okay, but I don't know when the minister will be back, and I can't guarantee that he will see you."

This time I didn't have to hide at the end of the street. I walked back and forth, memorizing my forty English words and going over what I would say to the minister for the hundredth time.

Just before ten o'clock the guard called me over. "Xiao Li, I am going inside at midnight. If the minister is still not back by then I can't guarantee my replacement will let you hang around."

"I understand," I replied.

Then he hesitated. "What's America like? Tell me a little," he asked quietly.

"What do you want to know?" I asked.

"Anything!" he replied eagerly.

I told him about the cars, the tall buildings, the ATM machines . . .

"People can get money out of a machine in a wall?" He was very amused.

I was mindful not to show too much enthusiasm about America. When I told him about the guard at the White House with no machine guns, he was amazed. "You must be joking."

"No, it's true. Security is very lax there."

"What is the White House like? Is it really white?" he asked.

"Yes," I replied, trying to sound as though I didn't care much about the White House at all.

"I can't believe they let a Chinese ballet student get so close!" Under the dim light I could see his expression of disbelief. To leave no doubt in his mind about my commitment to communism, I told him that I despised our class enemies in America and that I was sympathic toward the American poor. But I could tell he was more interested in hearing about things like ATM machines.

About an hour later, two bright headlights appeared from one end of the street.

"Stand aside, this is him," the guard said and quickly walked to the driver's side. I couldn't hear what he said, but a couple of minutes later the minister's car drove through the entrance and the guard pulled the gate closed behind.

"Sorry, Xiao Li. The minister didn't want to see you."

"What did you tell him?" My heart was still palpitating.

"I told him why you were here and that you'd been here for several nights. But all he said was 'Drive on.' He was rather annoyed."

I walked away under the faint streetlight. My whole world had crumbled. That was my last chance, my very last chance. I would never go back to America now. I had been beaten at last. How naïve you are to think your existence would mean so much to the communist cause! I told myself. Do you think an important leader such as Minister Wang would spend a single second thinking about you, a mere peasant boy? How foolish to believe everyone was equal in China. I had believed this communist doctrine for so many years. But in the minister's eyes I was no one. He didn't even bother to glance out of his car at this eager and pathetic boy.

I thought bitterly of the minister riding away in his flashy car. I thought of a story we'd been told at school about Mao not eating pork, of him deliberately suffering hardships just like the rest of us, and I seethed with rage.

I realized then that China was like any other nation on earth. There was no equality. But I, like all the Chinese people, had given Chairman Mao and his government our unwavering support for many, many years. I never questioned them. What choice did we have? The media was totally controlled by the government. One couldn't escape their brainwashing. "Cunxin, you've been manipulated all these years. It's time to wake up. The government and Minister Wang are no longer there for you. You have to look after yourself. You only have one life to live."

I went back to the academy and lay awake until the early hours of the morning.

I don't know what time I finally fell asleep. I didn't hear the wake-up bell in the morning. I didn't wake when the Bandit shook me at lunchtime, and I slept through the morning classes and afternoon rehearsals. I felt someone putting his hand on my forehead to feel my temperature. "Cunxin has a fever," I heard them say. My throat throbbed. My bones ached. My entire body was burning. But the most painful thing was my memory of the night before. Sleep was the only thing that would cure me of my misery and my shaken beliefs. I held on to my niang's quilt for dear life.

Finally I heard the voices of Teacher Xiao and the Bandit. "Wake up, Cunxin, wake up!"

I forced myself to open my eyes and look at their kind, caring faces. Tears welled in my eyes and I began to sob. "Leave me alone. I want to go back to my dreams."

"Cunxin, just listen to me now!" Teacher Xiao said. "You have two choices. Think of this as a card game: you can simply give up and stop participating or you can play on and see what happens. You have a long life and career in front of you. There will be many triumphs as well as setbacks, but if you give up now you will never taste the mango!"

I looked first at Teacher Xiao and then at the Bandit. I burst into uncontrollable sobs. My anger, my disappointment, my injured pride and my shattered beliefs all forced their way out at once. I sobbed and sobbed and sobbed.

The next day, from Director Chen's office, I made a phone call to Ben Stevenson in Houston. "I can not come," I told him. "My big leader in government say no." Once more my heart was bleeding with pain.

He asked me some questions I didn't really understand. The only words I detected were "why," "disappointed" and "sad." I kept asking him to repeat. Eventually he screamed down the phone in sheer frustration. "You! Come! Later!"

"No. Big leader say no. I. Write. Letter. For you."

After I had spoken to Ben, I immediately phoned my village and asked for my parents. "Fifth Brother, it's Cunxin. I am coming home."

"Aren't you going back to America?" he asked, surprised.

"No, not anymore," I replied.

"Why? What's wrong?"

"Nothing wrong. I will explain when I get back. Tell our parents not to go spending money on special food for me," I said.

"Are you all right? Did you do something wrong?"

"No. I didn't do anything wrong. I'm all right. The minister for Culture thinks I'm too young to go back alone. I have to go now. I will call you once I get my train ticket." I quickly put the phone down. I didn't want him to hear me crying.

For the following two days I was very emotional. I couldn't wait for the sun to go down so I could clutch onto my niang's quilt and quietly shed my tears.

Two days later I purchased my train ticket, ready to go home for a three-week holiday. But that afternoon, as I was mindlessly scanning through the *People's Daily*, a headline caught my eye. "Minister Wang, the Minister for Culture, Will Lead a Delegation to South America for Five Weeks."

I pulled the paper to my chest as though I had found a treasure and immediately ran to Teacher Xiao's office.

"Teacher Xiao, Teacher Xiao! Read this!"

"Yes. I've read it already. The minister is going to South America for five weeks. What's strange about that?"

"Who will be in charge of the ministry while he's gone?" I asked.

Teacher Xiao suddenly understood. We walked down to level two together and knocked on Zhang Shu's door.

"There may be a way for Cunxin to go to America after all," Teacher Xiao said.

Zhang Shu was amused, but Teacher Xiao handed him the newspaper. He quickly scanned the headline and frowned.

"We can lobby the vice minister in charge to ask permission for Cunxin to leave!" Teacher Xiao shouted excitedly.

"The vice minister might be reluctant to take on the responsibility knowing Minister Wang had refused it before," Zhang Shu said thoughtfully.

"Can't we lobby *all* the vice ministers?" I suggested.

They looked at each other and laughed. "All five of them?" Zhang Shu shook his head.

"It would be extremely difficult, but not impossible," Teacher Xiao added.

They discussed who the key minister in the ministry was and they decided on Lin Muhan, a well-known intellect in China and a labeled rightist who had been through some horrifying times during the Cultural Revolution. He was now in charge of the educational area within the ministry and a strong advocate for talent. Zhang Shu felt that he would be sympathetic toward my situation.

I wrote to my family that night and told them I couldn't go back home just yet.

Our intense lobbying efforts lasted over two weeks.

Teacher Xiao told me years later that he and Zhang Shu had even gone to Lin Muhan's own residence in their final effort to get me back to America. Teacher Xiao made a promise to the minister: within five years Chinese ballet dancers would be the best in the world.

This time they succeeded. Lin Muhan lobbied the four other vice ministers and signed the permission for me to go to America for one year.

With passport in hand I went to the U.S. consulate in Beijing as soon as I could, and my visa was granted within days.

I called Ben. "I can come! Plane ticket, please!" I shouted, my heart blossoming like a flower.

Two days later I received a phone call from Northwest Airlines. My reservation was confirmed. I was to leave China in three days.

My last three days were frantically busy. All my friends wanted some special time alone with me. On my last Saturday night, Teacher Xiao invited the entire class to his apartment and cooked us a delicious meal. We all helped with the washing, cutting and cleaning. He even made an egg, apple and potato salad. We banged our glasses together and shouted, "*Gan bei!*" Teacher Xiao stood up and raised his glass. "I wish to propose two toasts. The first is to all of you for putting up with me for over five and a half years of shouting and carrying on. This may be our last gathering together. I'm proud to be your teacher and I wish you all the best of luck. You're Chairman and Madame Mao's last generation of dancers. You have studied under the most strict and disciplined rules imaginable, but this will give you an edge over the others. You'll be the last dancers of the era." Teacher Xiao stopped briefly to calm his emotions. "I'll boldly make a prediction. Your dance training will never be duplicated. Your dancing will proudly stand high in Chinese ballet history."

He paused again. "My second toast is to Cunxin's American trip. I hope you will respect your past and charge toward the future. Perfect your art form. Make all of China proud. *Gan bei!*"

This was the very last time our class would ever gather together with Teacher Xiao.

I felt so happy about going back to America, but I wished that I could go home to my family before I went. I longed to see my parents and brothers again, especially my niang, but I couldn't take the risk of going back to Qingdao. The possibility of the ministers changing their minds was very real. For the time being I had to be content with the thought of seeing my family in a year's time.

I visited my adopted family, the Chongs, that Sunday and tasted their delicious dumplings for the last time. That night at the Beijing Dance Academy, the Bandit, Liu Fengtian, Chong Xiongjun and some of my classmates organized a farewell party. The mood of the whole evening was happy and warm, but there was also a sense of sadness—no one knew if we would ever gather together like this again.

So in November 1979, a month after my original planned date, I left China for the second time. I didn't know it then, but it would be many, many years before I could return.

PART THREE
THE WEST

二十

20

RETURN TO THE LAND OF FREEDOM

I felt only total exhaustion as soon as the plane soared into the air. The past few months had worn me out, and even up to the last seconds before the plane took off I feared that the Chinese government might still change its mind and I would be dragged off the plane and back to Beijing forever.

The thought of never being allowed out of China again was terrifying. I so desperately wanted a freedom of expression and thought that I couldn't have in China. I so desperately wanted to conquer the ballet world. And here was my chance. Now I wouldn't have to dance for Mao's communist ideals. Now I could dance for myself, my parents, my teachers and my friends back in China. The communist influence was fading fast.

Janie Parker, one of the principal dancers of the Houston Ballet, picked me up from Houston Airport. I'd briefly met Janie toward the end of the summer school three months before, and I remembered her sunny personality. I was so happy to see her again.

Janie drove me back to Ben's place through perfect autumn weather. I thought of the filthy, dusty Beijing air and I opened the car window to let the fresh, clean Houston air gust against my face, my long permed hair flying wildly in the wind. For a second I thought this was not real. I wasn't meant to be back here again.

I took a deep breath. My spirit felt free.

I was to stay for twelve months, but even then I knew that America the second time around would be a totally different experience. My beliefs were now completely altered after my experience with the Ministry of Culture and after having the time to think about what I'd seen in the West. Now I knew, with absolute certainty, that I had been manipulated by Chairman Mao's communist propaganda for many years. My personal contribution to communism had never been important. I was just one of over one billion other Chinese people used as a political puppet and I felt deeply betrayed.

My first month back at the Houston Ballet Academy was a trial-and-error time—I kept discovering and experimenting with new things. Ben continued to let me stay with him, and I continued my relentless pursuit of both English and dancing. I carried my list of new English words with me everywhere. But there were also the classes and rehearsals during the day and keeping up with Ben's busy social schedule in the evenings too. So soaking in the bath or sitting on the toilet remained the best times for me to memorize new English words. I tried to record something in my diary at least every other day, first in Chinese, but then as I increased my English vocabulary, my diary became 50 percent Chinese, 30 percent English and the rest was French ballet terminology.

Ben started rehearsals for *Nutcracker* soon after I arrived back in Houston. Ben's *Nutcracker* was completely different from the Baryshnikov version I'd seen on the video back in China, but I immediately fell in love with it. It had the freedom of expression I'd been longing for. I did two solo roles, both requiring only straightforward dancing and no acting, but I was so thankful to be in it: it was my first ballet with the company dancers.

It was through *Nutcracker* that I first noticed Lori Langlinais. She was in her early twenties, a talented dancer and a beautiful girl, full of life. Her contagious laugh reminded me of my niang's. We quickly became good friends, she treating me like a little brother and I regarding her as a big sister even though we had huge difficulties communicating with each other in those early weeks. We used to call each other "Big Ballerina" and "Big Ballerino."

Within those first few weeks I made many new friends, including Keith Lelliott, another dancer who was staying at Ben's place, and principal dancer Suzanne Longley. With Christmas now approaching, one of Ben's friends who had become my friend too, Preston Frazier, bought me a children's book about Christmas. With the help of my dictionary and some of the pictures I worked out that on Christmas Eve this long silver-bearded man called Santa Claus would ride on a sled pulled by nine reindeer, all with very strange names. I remembered the one called Rudolph, because of Rudolf Nureyev, but what was even stranger was that Santa Claus went down people's chimneys and put presents in children's stockings! Sounds like a capitalist version of Lei Feng, I thought, the humble soldier Mao had promoted in China as one of his model communists. This must surely be Western propaganda. And what was even more amusing was that Jesus was born to a virgin. How bizarre!

Most of what I learned about Christmas, however, was to do with shopping. With my limited scholarship money I bought a few presents for my American friends when Ben took me to the famous Galleria shopping mall just three days before Christmas. There was a mass of people there, all gone mad over shopping.

Everyone carried enormous numbers of bags and pushed their way around the crowded mall. Christmas trees were everywhere—bells, ribbons, wreaths and all. It was incredible! But most incredible of all was the money. Ben spent nearly five thousand dollars on presents in only a couple of hours. My father's salary for sixty-five years! My father's entire lifetime of backbreaking work. My family could live on this amount for over half a century. Ben had spent it on presents in one day alone. It was incomprehensible. It was shocking. I thought of my family and felt sick. How *could* there be such disparity in the world?

The Christmas Day party at Ben's house was a mega-event as well, with over forty friends, dancers and students. Ben had at least one present for every person there. I even received presents from Santa Claus, left in my very own Christmas stocking hanging by the mirror in Ben's living room. Ben didn't have a fireplace, though, so I wondered how on earth Santa had gotten in. But secretly, deep in my heart, I wished I could exchange even just a few of those presents for cash and give the money to my family instead. So many years of my father's earnings seemed tied up in those presents.

Ben's Christmas food was a feast too. A huge sizzling turkey, a big shining ham, trays and trays of roasted potatoes, cakes and puddings. I refused to guess how much he would have spent—it was simply too agonizing. I kept telling myself to enjoy it, but all I could think of was dried yams and my family's survival.

So many things like this in America shocked me. One day as I was being driven home by Ben's friend Richard I noticed that he was wearing a sports jacket which looked very smart. But it had patched elbows—and yet he drove a Mercedes. Only the poor wear patched clothes, I said to him. He thought this was very funny. Then he asked me what I would like to do most in America. I told him I would like to be able to drive a car, so he pulled over. "Come on, you drive," he said.

"I don't know how!"

"Just push on the pedal and watch the road. Easy," he said.

I got into the driver's seat, nervously pushed on the pedal and the car immediately accelerated. The speed took me by complete surprise, so I pushed my foot down harder. I froze. Richard made a desperate grab for the steering wheel and slid one of his legs over to the brake. We were inches away from what appeared to be a very large ditch. "Oh, dear me, my heart is hot!" was all I could say.

My second driving experience was at Disneyland, this time in a golf cart. Dorio, another principal dancer, asked me to give it a try. Easier than driving a Mercedes, I thought. But I was wrong. I pressed the accelerator and the cart started to move very slowly because we were going uphill. Dorio kept telling me to push my foot all the way down, so I did, but once we got over the top of the hill we quickly gathered speed and before I knew it, this time we really were stuck in a ditch, right between two huge trees. Perhaps, said Dorio politely, he would teach me how to drive properly another time.

After Christmas, when we'd finished the *Nutcracker* performances, Ben took me and some other dancers to a beach house in LaPorte, about an hour and a half from Houston, to celebrate the new year of 1980. It was a wonderful party. Ben made a delicious roast beef. Champagne flowed all night and we wished each other *xin nian kuai le,* Happy New Year. People made New Year resolutions, such as losing weight and so on.

But after much celebration, much food, champagne and wonderful company, I just wanted to escape for a little while. So with champagne glass in hand I quietly left my American friends, slipped out of the house unnoticed and strode along the beach, thinking only of my niang, my dia, my brothers and my friends back home. I wondered what they were doing just then. I wondered if they were thinking of me. I wondered what *their* next year would bring. I hoped, for all of them, that it would at least bring more food to eat.

The summer school that year attracted even more students than the one I'd attended the previous year. My friend Zhang Weiqiang received permission from the Ministry of Culture to come back for that summer school too, plus three more students from the Beijing Dance Academy. I was so happy to see some of my friends again and thrilled that they'd also had the opportunity to come to the West.

During this second summer school I met an eighteen-year-old girl from Florida called Elizabeth Mackey. At first I didn't notice her because there were so many people in each class, but then she sat right next to me during floor exercises. I felt self-conscious sitting so close. She wore her long hair loose and I noticed the subtle smell of her perfume, the sound of her breathing.

Throughout the summer school Elizabeth and I kept bumping into each other. Whenever our eyes met, my heart beat faster. I wanted to get close to her but I kept telling myself, "Don't be silly. Elizabeth is a nice girl. She looks at everyone this way. Remember the Bandit's unrequited love? Concentrate on your dancing. You are not worthy of such a beautiful girl."

I had other things to concentrate on then too. Ben called me one day and said, "Li, Billy has just injured his back. Would you like to replace him and dance with Suzanne Longley tonight?"

"Me? Dance with Suzanne? *Really?*" My heart leaped. Billy was a principal dancer in the company. He and Suzanne were guest artists that night, dancing Ben's pas de deux in the Houston Grand Opera's *Die Fledermaus* in an outdoor theater.

"But I don't know steps!" I shouted into the phone.

"I'll teach you. Hurry up, we'll wait for you."

I threw my practice clothes into my dance bag with shaking

hands and ran all the way to the studio. It took me just over three hours to learn every step of the grand pas de deux, and we didn't finish until late that afternoon. We barely had time to eat before going to the theater for our stage rehearsal at 6:30 p.m. I had never been so nervous in my life.

"Li, are you feeling all right about doing this performance?" Ben asked. "Because you can still say no."

"Yes, I like perform it!" I replied eagerly.

"Are you nervous?" asked Suzanne.

"No, not nervous," I lied.

I wasn't just nervous. I was petrified. What if I forget the choreography? What if the audience boos? Will they throw objects at me? Do Americans do that? Cunxin, just remember to breathe and let the music help you. And whatever you do, *don't* let Suzanne fall to the ground.

As the introduction music for our pas de deux was played, Suzanne looked at me with a radiant smile. I forced a smile back. This is it, I thought. The test of your seven years' training under Madame Mao. Remember your parents. Remember Teacher Xiao. Remember the Bandit and the Chinese people.

Suzanne and I charged onto the stage. My calves didn't cramp. I didn't forget any choreography. I was too nervous to know how well I danced, but Suzanne gave me the biggest hug after the performance and the audience screamed and yelled.

Ben read me the reviews the next day: America had discovered a new star, from China of all places, they said.

To celebrate, I was taken out to dinner after the second performance. So many well-wishers wanted to talk to me that it took me forever to finish my meal. The waiter kept asking me, with a pleasant smile, "Are you done, sir?" How nice, I thought, feeling rather proud. He's asking me if I'm a dancer. Even this waiter had watched my performance.

After my success with Suzanne, there seemed to be a magnet drawing me back to the academy. Secretly I was hoping to get a glimpse of Elizabeth. But hardly anyone was there because it was holiday time. Then, to my great surprise, as I passed a small studio, I saw Elizabeth practicing alone.

"Hello." She smiled and with my heart racing I timidly entered the studio. "I thought you had gone away with Ben for a holiday," she said. "Where did you go?"

"Something called gufton."

"You mean Galveston?" she asked.

"Yes, yes, Gulfston!" I shouted excitedly.

She giggled. "Why are you back here?"

"I have lumps."

"*Lumps?*" She frowned.

"Yes, lumps. Look."

She burst into laughter. "It's called a rash."

"Oh," I murmured.

"Do you want me to take you anywhere? I have a car."

"No, thank you." I replied politely. Then, suddenly I said, "Yes! I want go Chinatown, see Bruce Lee movie! You can take me?"

Elizabeth was eighteen then. I was nervous and excited, walking out of the academy with her. I was afraid someone might see us together and tell Ben, but I tried to look calm and casual.

We went into a Chinese café across the street from the cinema, the kind with small square tables and plastic tablecloths. For the first time in my life I found myself sitting opposite a girl, alone, of my age, a girl I liked. She looked so beautiful.

"You can call me Liz if you want. What about you? What do your friends call you?" she asked.

"Cunxin," I replied.

"It's so pretty," she said.

310

"It mean keep my innocent heart," I said.

"Cunxin, Cunxin, it's so beautiful," she murmured. "How old are you?"

"Nineteen," I replied.

"I'm eighteen. How many brothers and sisters do you have?" she asked.

"Sex brothers," I replied.

"Six, not sex." She laughed.

"Oh, I can't hear they are different. What sex mean?"

"Maybe I can explain it to you later."

I could sense she was uncomfortable. "English hard. In English, you say go, goes, gone. In Chinese we say will go, go and go yesterday, he go, she go, you go, I go and we all go."

She burst into laughter.

"Really!" I said. "English, change verb all the time. Is hard for Chinese person."

"But you're doing very well," she said. "We'd better go or we'll be late for the movie."

There were not that many people in the cinema, and I found it hard to concentrate with Elizabeth sitting next to me. I wanted to know her better, but I doubted Elizabeth would show me any special interest. So I was surprised when, after the movie, she agreed to have dinner with me.

We went to a small, cheap Chinese restaurant. We asked each other many questions and although we had difficulty understanding each other we managed, and we enjoyed being with each other. I ordered some authentic Chinese food—pig's intestines and sea slugs. That would impress her, I thought, but she seemed to have a rather small appetite. Still, I started to relax, and by the end of the evening I felt sad to part with her.

Before we approached Ben's apartment I told her to stop the car because I didn't want the security guard to see us. If he told Ben that I was having a relationship with an American, Ben

311

would be placed in a very difficult situation. He'd have to tell the Chinese consulate, and I would be sent straight back to China.

Elizabeth stopped her car one block away from Ben's complex. "When can we see each other again?"

"Don't know," I replied. I reached out and we touched hands. I felt her breath. I felt hot blood rushing through each vein. I don't know how long we kissed but the headlights of a passing car interrupted us. This was happening too fast. I needed time to think. So I quickly said good-bye and got out of her car.

"You'll call me, won't you?" she asked.

I nodded and walked back to Ben's apartment.

Elizabeth became my first lover. I felt liberated. I couldn't believe I could make love to a beautiful woman and that she could be mine. I felt a great sense of responsibility for Elizabeth, and great pride too. But I knew our secret relationship was dangerous and the only person I could think of to share my secret with was Lori. She'd sometimes tried to persuade me to stay in America but I had always said no. She felt sorry for me, having to go back to China.

A few weeks later, one Sunday, Lori invited me to her house for a barbecue. I met her husband, Dilworth, a Texas oil entrepreneur who chewed tobacco and drank bourbon. I told them how much I liked Elizabeth and the sorrow I felt about returning to China. I didn't expect them to do anything about it, but they took this matter to heart right away. Dilworth called the University of Texas and asked if they could recommend a good immigration lawyer. They suggested a man called Charles Foster.

The following day Lori and Dilworth took me to Charles Foster's office in downtown Houston.

Charles Foster said he had read about me in the newspaper. He said I could qualify for a green card on my own artistic merits. He also mentioned that the Chinese government recognized international marriage laws.

I remember feeling unsure, not about my love for Elizabeth, but Charles seemed very young to be so successful and I didn't really understand everything he'd said about the law anyway.

Lori and Dilworth tried to explain more, but I left that first meeting still very confused. I loved Elizabeth. And I couldn't go back to China and survive in a world with no freedom. Not anymore. But China was where my parents were, where my family and my friends lived. I could still contribute an enormous amount to Chinese ballet.

It was then that I realized I was torn between two possible lives. I didn't know what I was going to do.

二十一

21

ELIZABETH

I had been in Houston for eleven months, but my secret relationship with Elizabeth was only a few weeks old. Still, I had to keep focused on my work.

I'd been rehearsing the *Le Corsaire* pas de deux one day with Suzanne, experimenting with a new, one-handed lift, when just before the end of our rehearsal there was a jerk in my shoulder joint and a sharp pain shot through my right arm. I caught Suzanne with my left hand on the way down, but stars flashed before my eyes and for a few minutes I couldn't feel anything but intense pain.

Ben and Suzanne were immediately concerned. I went to the dancers' lounge and put an ice pack on my shoulder joint. I knew I had dislocated it, and probably torn some tendons and muscles too, but I didn't want to see a doctor. I didn't want Ben to think it was serious. He might take me out of the ballet.

My shoulder was swollen for days and I covered it up by wearing long-sleeved shirts. I couldn't do lifts properly and had to make different excuses. Then I developed severe tendinitis in my left Achilles tendon and a shinsplint in my right leg. I knew I was overworking myself, and I knew that by continuing to practice I might make my injuries worse. But I also knew I needed to work harder if I was ever to reach the standard of Baryshnikov and Vasiliev. There was no way I was going to let injury slow me down now.

Ben had also choreographed a circle of six consecutive double assemblé or double turns in the air, for my solo in *Le Corsaire*. I could barely do *one* well, let alone six. Every time my feet pushed off from the floor my body would twist in the air like a barbecued shrimp. "There is no point getting yourself injured," Ben said. "If it doesn't work, let's change it."

"No, Ben! Please, give me few days," I begged, despite the pain of the injuries. I was angry with myself for not being able to do what Ben had in mind but there was a weekend coming up and I knew I could use it to practice. I borrowed one of the dancer's keys for our studio and locked myself in for two whole days, practicing each movement and analyzing them in absolute detail—the angle of my leap, the timing, weight distribution, speed—everything. At times the pain was excruciating, but I remembered Teacher Xiao's mangoes. I yearned to taste each layer. I practiced over and over and over and fell many times, but then I thought of the bow shooter and how he'd persevered, and I practiced again and again and again.

I made the breakthrough late on Sunday afternoon. The angle and the speed of my first leg was the key.

I was elated. I truly believed, now, that nothing was impossible.

Le Corsaire was a huge success. My double assemblé and the difficult lifts worked beautifully. The audience demanded an encore. I didn't understand what an encore was then and I wasn't prepared, and the stagehands had already started to change the scenery for the next ballet. But then, quite unexpectedly, Ben came on stage with a microphone in hand. He stood in front of the curtain and made an announcement: he now had the Chinese government's permission for me to stay in Houston longer and had promoted me to a soloist position with the Houston Ballet.

This must be a dream, I thought. Senior Consul Zhang Zongshu from the Chinese consulate was in the audience that evening. He was very proud: I had brought glory to the Chinese people, he said, and he would do anything in his power to make sure my stay was extended. His report to the Chinese government would be most positive. In the end the Chinese government gave me permission to stay for an extra five months, and the dancers' union agreed to allow my promotion.

From then on in Houston I was a sort of celebrity. It was very strange. I was stopped by people in restaurants, shops, streets and even parking lots. But despite this instant stardom I knew I would have to work hard—I knew I couldn't lose sight of my aim. My injuries gradually got better, but nothing else changed. Zhang and I continued to stay with Ben, and I continued to meet Elizabeth in secret. I became increasingly frustrated at not being able to see Elizabeth more, but I also felt guilty. I felt like I was betraying Ben and China, both at once. I wished I hadn't allowed myself to fall in love with her. Living with both desire and guilt was becoming suffocating, but I had no choice. Anyone I told would be placed in a very dangerous situation with the Chinese government. I couldn't bear to put my family and friends in such a position. My only option was to stay quiet.

Soon it was April 1981 and I had less than a month to go before returning to China. The Houston Ballet's first major tour to New York was coming up, and both Zhang and I would perform.

I was the second cast for the lonely, arrogant prince in John Cranko's *The Lady and the Fool*. I had never even heard of this ballet before but one week before the performance in New York,

316

out of the blue, Ben asked me to do a full rehearsal with the first-cast dancers. I was stunned. I thought it must be a mistake.

The prince's first entrance was in the middle of a high-society ball. I had to enter at the far-back center stage and come down some steps with people on both sides of the stage standing back in silence and admiration. But walking down those steps was like walking on hot coals for me. Everything felt unnatural and awkward.

"Li, you're too sweet and too nice," Ben said and stopped the pianist. "Go back and do it again. I want more arrogance."

I was shaking with embarrassment. I was twenty, and I still had no idea what an arrogant prince would feel like. But Ben made me repeat it over and over again, and by the time he went on with the rest of the rehearsal my practice clothes were soaked with sweat.

But it paid off. My inhibitions went. I eventually enjoyed portraying this arrogant prince, a prince who would have been considered evil in communist China. And here I was, portraying him with pride. I had made a fundamental shift in my dancing.

The two weeks in New York allowed me to really taste that city. I fell in love with it. Everywhere I went I made new friends. New York was full of artists. So many wonderful classes to choose from. It seemed that ballet teachers and dancers were everywhere, even choreographers. One day when I was taking a class at the School of American Ballet, I bumped into George Balanchine and Jerome Robbins, two of the most highly regarded American choreographers in the world. The famous Danish teacher Stanley Williams taught class that day and many dancers from the New York City Ballet, including one of their stars, Peter Martins, were in that class. For me, a peasant boy from Qingdao, it was amazing.

Another day, I remember peering into the American Ballet Theater's studio and seeing Baryshnikov doing a barre. I couldn't believe my eyes! This was the man I had admired for so long! But

317

how little he was! How could such great dancing be coming from such a small body? Then the following day, in the same studio, there was Natalia Makarova sitting on the floor doing her stretches. And a day later I found myself standing on the same barre as Gelsey Kirkland, the very same Sugarplum Fairy who danced brilliantly with Baryshnikov in that *Nutcracker* video I'd watched in China. I would never forget her quality. Every movement was performed to perfection, every detail demonstrated with precision. I was meeting people and experiencing things that I had only dreamed about in China. It was magical, and New York was the focus.

During the two weeks I was in New York, Elizabeth and I communicated through just one secret phone call. I missed her the whole time. My feelings about leaving her and going back to China became unbearable. Duty toward my motherland, responsibility for my family, the desire for Western freedom—I thought I had made up my mind to go back to China, but now I was wavering. What does China have to offer you? *The Red Detachment of Women?* The dance world is yours to explore and conquer here. You have a beautiful American girl who loves you dearly. What more do you want? Don't go back. But then I thought of my parents, my brothers, my friends back in China. What about Teacher Xiao and Teacher Zhang? What about Ben and his relationship with China? You will destroy them all if you stay. And they have done so much for you.

It was in this confused, guilt-ridden state of mind that I returned to Houston, with only three days left before returning to China. Zhang and I spent the morning shopping for presents for friends and family back in China, and that afternoon I met Elizabeth two blocks away from Ben's apartment.

"I missed you!" she said, and immediately sensed my unease. "What's wrong?"

318

"Nothing wrong," I replied, but my heart was screaming. "Let's go to Chinatown and see a movie."

First we went to a gift shop where I bought Preston Frazier a decorative Chinese plate as a farewell present. Then I bought Elizabeth a Chinese jade ring. "For our friendship," I said.

She looked at me tenderly. "Thank you," she replied.

In the dark of the movie theater a Taiwanese film with English subtitles had already started. Forget about the movie, go to her apartment, a voice inside me said. No, you can't do that! Be strong or you will wallow in a greater mess, another voice replied.

Half an hour after the movie finished we were lying on the bed in Elizabeth's one-bedroom rented apartment, once more immersed in our passionate love. This was too much. You love her. Stay.

I called Lori. It was late afternoon. "Hi, Big Ballerina," I said. "I and Elizabeth, come talk with you?" I asked.

"Li, the Big Ballerino! Sure, when do you want to come?"

"Now okay?" I asked.

"*Now*? Okay," she replied.

Lori's apartment was half a block away from Elizabeth's and we were there in no time. "I want marry Elizabeth!" I said to Lori and Dilworth as soon as we walked in.

Lori gave Elizabeth and me a passionate hug. She was nearly in tears, she was so happy. Then she became more serious. "Have you told Ben yet?" she asked.

"No. I don't know how or when. He wouldn't like. He will kill me and Elizabeth when he find out, because he love China too much."

"Who cares about that," Dilworth barged in. "Let's have a wedding party!"

"In two days I go back China. No time for wedding," I said.

"Well, you could get married in a courthouse. It will only take a couple of hours. Dilworth and I can be your witnesses," Lori suggested.

So at ten the next morning in the Harris County Courthouse, Elizabeth and I made our vows as husband and wife, Lori and Dilworth by our sides. Elizabeth quickly kissed me, and Lori and Dilworth clapped.

After we signed the marriage documents, the four of us walked out of the courthouse into a beautiful April day. I'm married. I've married Elizabeth, I thought. And then immediately, what have I done to Ben?

"When are you going to tell Ben?" Elizabeth asked.

"Don't know. Not today. Big party tonight! Maybe tomorrow," I replied. Ben and the company had planned a farewell party for Zhang and me for our second-to-last night in America.

"We'll have our first night together tomorrow then. I can't wait," she said.

"Ben will be very angry. I don't know what he will do." I felt disoriented. I couldn't stop thinking of what I had done—I had done something behind Ben's back. Once more, happiness was overshadowed by guilt.

"Don't be afraid. We have each other," said Elizabeth. "You can dance anywhere. We can dance in Florida together, they will love you there!"

"Yes, we have each other," I repeated.

We did. We had each other. But neither of us knew how important that would be, only the very next day.

There were over a hundred dancers and friends at the farewell party for Zhang and me that night, held in the main dance studio. Elizabeth was there too. Everyone brought us presents and wished Zhang and me happiness. I felt like screaming, I'm married! I won't be going back to China tomorrow! Take your presents back! But I couldn't. Instead I put on a

pleasant face, thanked everyone for their kindness and continued the deception.

Elizabeth and I had our first dance together that night. "This
is our wedding dance," she whispered. "Are you happy?"

I nodded but I felt uncomfortable with Zhang and me being
the center of attention. Lori and Dilworth were there too, and
the four of us pretended nothing special had happened. Lori's
present to me that night was a badge. It said "Don't let the
turkeys get you down." It showed a turkey standing on a pile of
turkey shit with other turkeys standing threateningly around
him. I didn't really understand it, but I pinned it to my shirt all
the same.

The following morning, the day before I was to return to
China, I called Elizabeth at Dilworth's as soon as Ben and Zhang
had gone out. Elizabeth, Dilworth and Lori arrived and loaded
up my belongings. Then we went up to Lori's apartment to make
the phone call I dreaded most.

"Hello?" Ben answered.

"Ben, I want tell you something," I said straightaway. "I'm
married. I'm not go back to China."

Silence.

Eventually, "No, Li, you didn't. Who?"

"Elizabeth Mackey," I replied.

"Elizabeth? You can't be married!" he was virtually shouting
now. "You are going back to China! Tomorrow!"

"Ben, listen. I love Elizabeth, she is my wife. I take her to
China later when I have money, but not tomorrow," I said.

"Li, I can't *believe* this! You are destroying everybody's lives. I
won't *ever* be allowed back to China!"

My heart was torn by his words. I knew it was true. I alone
would be responsible for creating so much pain for others. I
knew Ben had been negotiating with the Chinese government to
take some dancers to China—now his plans would be ruined.

But I felt like I was being swept up into a whirlpool and only fate could determine the outcome. I wanted to worry about Ben and his plans, but I couldn't.

Ben changed to a more persuasive, softer tone. "Oh, Li, why are you doing this? China is where you *belong*. You *are* Chinese. You can't stay here! You don't even know Elizabeth!"

"I love Elizabeth, we are married. We are happy . . ."

"You are *not* married, don't be stupid!" he interrupted angrily. "Where did you marry?"

I felt our conversation was going nowhere. "Ben, I go now."

"Li, where are you?" he asked urgently.

But it was no use going on. I hung up and buried my head in my hands.

Elizabeth, Lori and Dilworth looked very concerned. "What did he say?" Lori asked.

I tried to repeat everything that Ben had said but everyone was becoming emotional by now. I knew one thing for sure. There wouldn't be a future for me at the Houston Ballet. It broke my heart. It was like waiting to be executed. The only comfort was Elizabeth's love and Lori and Dilworth's friendship.

The phone rang.

It was Ben.

"No, Li's not here," Dilworth answered.

"Can I speak to Lori?" Ben asked.

"She is not here either," and Dilworth hung up.

Another five minutes passed.

Then a loud knock at the door. It was Clare Duncan. "Hello, Dilworth. Can I have a word with Li?"

"Li's not here," Dilworth repeated.

"Are you sure?" Clare inquired.

"Do I look like a liar?"

Clare left.

Another five minutes.

The phone rang again.

"Dilworth, stop it, I know Li is there!" said Ben. "Clare saw his luggage in your car." He paused. "She's let the air out of your tires. Li's situation is serious. I need to speak to him urgently."

Dilworth gave me the phone.

"Ohh . . . Li!" Ben started to sob. "I'm finished! I've lost everything! Consul Zhang at the consulate thinks I've masterminded this whole thing. They think it's all my fault. You have ruined everything! I'll never be allowed back to China now!"

"I'm sorry, Ben. What you want me say?" I asked.

"I want you to say that this is all a mistake and that you *will* go back to China. Nothing will change if you go back now. I have spoken to Consul Zhang. You'll still be a hero if you go back to China now. You'll still be allowed to come back."

"If you want live in China, you go," I said.

"Li, the least you can do for me is explain all this to the consulate! Tell them I had nothing to do with it. Can you do this for me?"

"Yes, I will," I replied.

"Then I'll tell Consul Zhang that you will meet them at the consulate," he said and hung up.

"I don't think you should go," Elizabeth said, and Lori agreed.

"Already, I say yes to Ben. I don't want change my mind, I will go." I was determined.

"I think we should call Charles Foster," Dilworth said, and I knew this was the most sensible idea.

Charles was surprised to hear from me at first, because I hadn't spoken to him since our last and only meeting twelve weeks earlier. He congratulated me on our marriage, but when I told him that Ben had asked me to go to the Chinese consulate he strongly advised against it. "The consulate is considered Chinese territory. Better meet them on neutral ground, like at a restaurant."

"Is dangerous to meet in consulate?" I asked nervously.

"Yes, it could be dangerous," he replied.

I quickly called Ben back and told him I wanted to meet the Chinese officials at a restaurant instead.

"Li, if you want to change places, *you* call them."

So I did. I called Consul Zhang, and he sounded surprisingly calm and pleasant. "Cunxin, we're family, we understand what you did and why you did it. I only want to have a little chat with you. No more than five minutes. Then you will be free to go and enjoy your happy life with your bride."

So Dilworth drove Lori, Elizabeth and me to the Chinese consulate on Montrose Boulevard. When we arrived Charles was already there at the consulate gate, and as soon as we entered the big metal door clanged shut behind us.

My heart sank. I should have listened to Charles. I felt like a prisoner of China already.

二十二

22

DEFECTION

We were taken to a meeting room where Ben, Clare Duncan and Jack, the Houston Ballet's company lawyer, were already waiting. Consul Zhang was there, and his wife who was the translator, and several other consulate officials. The only one missing was the consul general himself.

I was surprised to see my friend Zhang there too. He looked tense and upset, and when our eyes briefly met he quickly turned away.

It was about six in the evening by now. Ben, Clare and Jack were all dressed in their evening wear ready for another farewell party at Louisa's house that night.

I looked around the room. I had been in this meeting room before, when I'd had to report to the consulate on weekends. It was a big square room with black-and-white Chinese landscapes and calligraphy on the walls. There were some sofas and chairs in the middle of the room and some extra chairs added for extra people. I still had Lori's "Don't let the turkeys get you down" badge on my jacket.

The atmosphere was tense. The Chinese host gestured for Elizabeth and me to sit. The consulate officials seemed relaxed and friendly, but Ben was clearly furious. He wouldn't even look at me.

We were offered tea and soft drinks, and there was a lot of small talk about China and the improving relationship between the two countries. Charles and I were perplexed: nobody was talking about why we were there at all! The officials seemed very content for everyone just to have a good time. I was perspiring and shivering. I was very scared. I could not stand the suspense much longer.

Then one of the officials asked Charles and Jack to speak with him, alone, in a room down the hall. I wanted Charles to stay but he gave me a reassuring look, and he told me later he'd thought it made sense anyway since he was effectively my attorney and Jack was the attorney acting on behalf of the Houston Ballet. They would engage in some serious talk about my situation and spare the rest of us from all the legal unpleasantries.

But it didn't seem like that to those of us left in the room. It seemed as though the consulate officials were deliberately keeping the conversation going, trying to distract us, while they gradually eliminated my friends from the room.

People disappeared one by one, and each time a friend left I squeezed Elizabeth's hand tighter and tighter. It wasn't long before only Clare, Zhang, Elizabeth, myself and two officials were left in the room.

Eventually Consul Zhang asked everyone, except me, to go to another room. He wanted a private conversation.

Elizabeth refused.

We begged Clare and Zhang to stay with us, but the two officials simply shoved Clare and Zhang out the door.

Then four security guards stormed in, heading straight for Elizabeth and me.

We screamed.

Clare and Zhang looked back and screamed too.

326

The building echoed. It took only a few seconds for the four Chinese guards to separate me from Elizabeth. I tried to kick them away but I was completely helpless against those highly trained guards. They quickly grabbed my arms and legs, carried me to the top floor and locked me into a small room, only big enough for two single beds and a small chest of drawers.

I was struggling to breathe. I was scared. Truly scared.

In the meantime, downstairs, Charles Foster realized what was happening. He demanded to see his client.

From then on, Charles said later, the atmosphere changed completely. In a very loud and strident voice the consulate official ordered Charles to sit. He was on Chinese territory, and he was expected to follow orders. The two employees who were serving drinks dropped their trays and assumed a defensive stance. They blocked the door. Charles charged forward but was pushed and shoved as he tried to get through. He could hear my voice yelling from above, "Help, they are taking me! Help, they are taking me!" By the time Charles and Jack got back to the main room everyone was there, except me.

From my room on the top floor I could hear the guards talking outside the door. "Could have killed that bastard!" said one of them. I was terrified. I remembered the executions I had witnessed as a child during the Cultural Revolution, and I saw my own death flash in front of my eyes. I felt desperately alone. Nobody could save me that night. It was just a matter of time before they stuck a gun to my head or forced me back to China where I would suffer an unbearably slow, humiliating death in the cruelest prison in the land.

I tried to think about my niang and her sweet laughter. I tried to think about my dia and his humble stories. I tried to think about Elizabeth, the smell of her perfume. I remembered the Bandit and our blood brothers' poem, but I couldn't hold on to any one comforting thread.

327

I looked out the tiny window and down at a pool on the ground floor. It was too far to jump. Escape was impossible. Death here, at least, would be simpler and quicker than the suffering and humiliation of a Chinese prison.

The door opened. Consul Zhang came into the room. He sat in front of me on the other bed and attempted a smile, but he seemed very sad. He looked straight into my eyes, like a chess player trying to figure out a strategy. I wanted to turn away but I thought this would suggest to him that I was wavering, so I forced back a smile.

We sat there just looking at each other. I was perspiring profusely. I couldn't stand this silence. If I sat there any longer, my heart would simply explode. I had to do something! What to say to Consul Zhang? What *was* there to say? I knew the outcome would be the same: I was scum, a defector, the most hated traitor of all.

Consul Zhang finally broke the silence. "Cunxin, what have you done?" he said calmly.

There seemed so many different ways to answer, but I knew none of my answers would satisfy him. "Nothing," I replied.

"Do you understand what you have done?" he asked, this time with more urgency.

"Yes, I love Elizabeth and I married her. Is this against the law?" I replied.

"Yes! What you have done is against your government's wishes and it's illegal in China! You're a Chinese citizen! *Your* government doesn't recognize your marriage. And you're too young to know what love is."

"Consul Zhang, my lawyer, Mr. Foster, told me that China *does* recognize international marriage law. I'm married here in America, and American law should be observed. As to my love for Elizabeth, it's a personal matter. I won't discuss it with you."

He was incensed. "Do you think a foreigner could really love

328

a Chinese? The foreigners will use you, abuse you, and dump you like a piece of trash!"

"How do you know what it is like to be loved by a foreigner?" I snapped back.

For a second he wasn't sure what to say. "Have you seen any marriages between Chinese and Americans?"

I couldn't think of any.

"It's not too late to change your mind. You can just tell Elizabeth that you have made a mistake and you want to walk away from it." It was as though he was encouraging me to do something immensely heroic.

"No," I said, "I don't want to divorce Elizabeth. I want to spend the rest of my life with her."

"We are not talking of divorce. As far as we are concerned, you were never married. We don't and won't recognize your marriage as legitimate. *You* don't decide what you're going to do with your life, the Communist Party does! You're a Chinese citizen. You follow Chinese laws, not American laws."

By now I was angry. "If you think Mr. Foster has informed me wrongly, let's ask him now," I said.

Consul Zhang looked perplexed. "Mr. Foster and your friends have left. They are disgusted with what you have done! You are alone. They are no friends of yours. *We're* your friends. Everything will be forgiven if you go back to China as planned. You will be loved and respected by all your people!"

I didn't believe for a moment what Consul Zhang said about my friends. But I did think they must have been thrown out of the consulate and that the Chinese government would promise me anything to get me back to China.

There was a knock on the door, and Consul Zhang left for a brief discussion with another man. I could hear whispers, but I couldn't make out what they were saying. Then Consul Zhang came back. He was trying hard to control his anger. "I want you to think about what we have just discussed, and I'll come back soon."

I felt a sense of relief when he closed the door. I needed to regroup, to gather my courage. I felt exhausted, but I knew this was only the beginning of a long and nerve-racking night.

A few minutes later the door opened again. This time one of the vice consuls general entered. He was an older, slightly taller man, and he spoke with a heavy southern-Chinese accent. He was very friendly and offered me something to drink. I politely refused. So he began to try to convince me to go back to China, listing all the benefits there would be for my family. "Think of your parents and all your brothers back home! How proud of you they must have been! You don't want to let them down. You don't want to create any problem for them, do you?"

This was my greatest fear. If anything terrible happened to my family because of what I had done, I would never forgive myself. But there was no reason to involve my family! The Chinese government was responsible for my education, not my parents.

"I left my family when I was eleven. I have nothing to do with them, and they have nothing to do with me," I tried. I couldn't implicate my family in all of this. My family had no idea what I'd done.

"You're the property of China," the vice consul general continued. "We have given you everything. We have the power to do anything that we want with you. We don't want to lose our star dancer! You simply *have* to listen to what we say. It is for your own good. The party knows what's good for you. Have faith in the party. Have you forgotten what the party has done for you? Have you forgotten what you have sworn in front of the Communist Youth Party flag?"

I remembered the years and years of lies about the West. I thought of Minister Wang who had refused to see me about my return to America. I thought of my lack of freedom in China, the desperate poverty that they had made sound so rich and glorious. "I don't want to talk about the party," I said.

"You don't expect the party will listen to you! *Do* you? The party listens to no one! Everyone listens to the party! Who helped you to get married? Is it Ben?" he asked suddenly.

"No. I made my own decision."

"Tell me the truth!" He raised his voice. "We already have the facts. Don't underestimate your government! Is it Ben? Someone in the American government? Someone in the Taiwanese government?"

Under different circumstances I would have burst into laughter. What he was suggesting was completely ludicrous. "No one has helped me. Would I have come to the consulate if I had a political agenda to hide or if the Americans or the Taiwanese had helped me? Would they have advised me to come tonight?" I asked.

"It's not for you to ask me questions! I'm asking *you*! Who helped you?"

"Nobody helped me. Didn't you hear me? I won't answer any more of your questions," I replied angrily.

The conversation with the vice consul general went on for another half an hour, but I spoke little. Then another consulate official replaced him for another half an hour of interrogation and persuasion. It was like musical chairs. Every half an hour another official would take over the interrogation. Each left without any progress. In a strange way, after the initial fear and despair, I felt calmer as time went on. What do I have to fear if I'm about to lose my life? I thought.

A couple of times during the interrogations I touched the scar on my arm, the one I received as a baby, the one that caused so much anxiety for my parents and that had now become a symbol of my niang's love. When I touched it I could feel her love.

331

It gave me comfort. It gave me courage. It reminded me of where I came from and where I wanted to be.

I didn't regret what I had done. In a strange way I felt at peace with myself. Elizabeth was my first love. Our marriage was not a marriage of convenience. I knew I could have stayed in America by qualifying on my own artistic merits. Charles had told me this at our very first meeting. But still I felt a strong sense of sorrow for my parents. I hadn't even sent them a single dollar yet.

I felt the tears pushing upward through my throat. My poor dear niang. She had suffered enough hardship already. I thought of her wrinkled face and the sorrow she would feel if she never saw me again. Oh, how much I loved her! She was the most innocent and loving niang on this earth. She had given me everything, yet I had nothing to give her in return. Would my niang ever recover from her despair at losing one of her beloved sons? This would surely kill her.

I thought too of my teachers who had invested so much of their time and effort in me, hoping that I would one day put Chinese ballet on the world map. Their hopes would be dashed. I would never see them again. But I was determined not to allow the consulate officials to see my tears or to sense my weakness.

Downstairs, in the main room, everyone was shaken. The consulate officials changed their approach and went back to their pleasantries again, offering everyone drinks and engaging in idle conversation. Charles told me later that he'd sat there, bewildered, but at last he could stand it no longer. "Wait a minute, my client was just dragged out of here and I don't know about the rest of you but I am not leaving until you have released him! You are in violation of U.S. law!"

"I don't understand, Mr. Foster," Consul Zhang spoke up with genuine surprise. "You just told us that you strongly supported good U.S.–Sino relations."

"Yes, I did and I do," Charles replied.

"Well, what is good for China and for the United States is for Li to return to China. If he does not, U.S.–Sino relations will be harmed. So will the Houston Ballet and their planned tour to the People's Republic of China."

Charles responded. "While we all may agree with you about what's good for U.S.–China relations, there's one problem with what you say. In the U.S., Li gets to make that decision."

They then proceeded to have lengthy, almost philosophical conversations about individual rights versus group rights. Charles later said he'd almost enjoyed it, except for the fact that he was concerned about my safety. He was working on the assumption that they would hold me through the night and then take me to the airport and fly me out of America the following morning.

But Ben and my friends would not leave the consulate without me. They refused to leave. So the consulate officials turned the lights out. The free tea, soft drinks and crackers were withdrawn. Only the use of the bathrooms was allowed.

About twenty minutes later the officials came back into the room. Kind and polite persuasion changed to cold, threatening words.

Ben and my friends continued to resist.

By now, rumors about my detention at the consulate had started to spread to Louisa's party. By 10.30 p.m. they suspected something terrible had happened. Two people in particular wanted to find out the truth: Anne Holmes and Carl Cunningham were dance critics for the *Houston Chronicle* and the *Houston Post*. They'd planned to interview me that night, but as time dragged on and I was still missing they eventually enlisted the help of some Houston Ballet board members and discovered that I was being held at the consulate against my will.

Hours had passed. People were beginning to gather at the side entrance to the consulate. Charles was asked by Consul Zhang to go and deal with them. That was ironic, he thought: the small crowd included a few newspaper reporters, and the Chinese officials seemed to be putting an unusual amount of faith in him, asking him to talk with the press.

Anne and Carl, the two dance critics, were among the small crowd gathering outside. Charles could only say to them that there was a discussion going on inside and they were about to resolve the situation. He believed that if he told them the truth it would make the situation even more inflammatory.

He went back inside. "Look, there are members of the press out there, and they are not going to go away," he told the Chinese officials. "They are going to make this into a big story." But to Charles's surprise the Chinese officials kept on insisting that, as a lawyer, he should know how to control the press. Charles laughed. This was America, he explained several times. In America even lawyers could not control the press.

At one o'clock in the morning, after many hours of interrogation, I was collapsing with hunger and exhaustion. My head was throbbing. I couldn't think anymore. I hadn't had anything to eat since breakfast the previous morning. I asked one of the consulars for something to eat. I didn't care if they put something terrible in my food like sleeping pills or poison. I just needed food.

They found me some leftover fried rice and a Tsingtao beer, a bittersweet offering—it reminded me of my parents back home. At least I would taste something from my hometown before I left this world, I thought.

After my fried rice and beer they wanted to resume the interrogation. I told them that my brain couldn't take any more. Please, just leave me alone, and if they wanted to kill me they should do it now. I had made up my mind. I wasn't going back to China.

To my surprise they agreed to stop their interrogation, and

they assigned one of the guards to sleep in the room and keep an eye on me. I thought I'd just feign sleep, so I pretended to snore. But the guard simply told me to stop it, and we both twisted and turned all night.

About the same time, Charles had his final discussion with Anne and Carl outside the consulate. They wanted to know all the details. They knew this was a front-page story. Charles asked them to withhold writing anything until the matter was resolved. They said they appreciated that, but they had a greater duty to the public and they had deadlines to meet. Charles went back inside and asked to use the telephone. First he rang Federal Judge Woodrow Seals, a feisty old guy who had been appointed by President John F. Kennedy.

"Charles, this better be good," he said. It was about two in the morning by now.

Charles briefly explained the emergency, and Judge Seals told him that he would meet him at the federal courthouse at 6 a.m. along with the chief justice of the Southern District of Texas, John Singleton. Charles then called his legal assistant to help draw up the documents.

Then, unknown to the consulate officials, Charles made another crucial call. He rang the U.S. State Department. He asked to speak to the duty officer for China. He said this was a critical matter. The U.S. government should act. Charles related the story of Simas Kudirka, a Lithuanian seaman who had been on board a Soviet trawler that was suspected of spying in U.S. waters in the early 1970s. Kudirka had jumped from the deck of the Soviet vessel onto the deck of a U.S. Coast Guard vessel. Soviet sailors forcibly removed him, and a long investigation followed. Everyone in the Coast Guard chain of command who had allowed Kudirka's removal faced the possibility of court-martial.

Kudirka eventually ended up in America. Charles had hosted him in Houston. He knew the U.S. State Department had internal

335

regulations about the forcible repatriation of foreign nationals, particularly when it came to communist countries. He knew he'd said enough.

The Chinese officials at this point became suspicious and told Charles that he could no longer use their phones. In any event, he knew he had to leave the consulate to help draft the legal documents. There were only a few hours left until morning, and he wanted to speed things along.

After Charles left the consulate, the Chinese officials had had enough. They demanded all the Westerners follow Charles and leave the consulate at once. But everyone was determined. They refused to leave until they saw me safe and sound. This irritated the Chinese hosts even more. They cut the phone off and turned off the lights once more.

When Charles left the consulate the morning papers were already out on the streets. Charles was shocked to see the headlines. "Chinese Consulate Holding Eight Americans Hostage." He returned to his office, then went to the federal courthouse with the finished legal documents, ready for signature.

Federal Judge Woodrow Seals and Chief Justice John Singleton were there as arranged. "Charles," said Singleton bluntly, "I hope you know what you are doing."

"Well," Charles replied, "there's not much time, so we just have to try our best."

Once the documents were signed, Charles rang Chase Untermeyer, executive assistant to the then Vice President George Bush. Charles cited the Kudirka story again and said this was a critical matter. "Chase," he said, "Vice President Bush's wife, Barbara, is a trustee of the Houston Ballet. The vice president should know the Chinese consulate is holding a Houston Ballet dancer, Li Cunxin, against his will." Charles knew the vice president would take appropriate action.

Chase in turn immediately contacted Vice President Bush, who had Chase call James Lilly, who was then the Asia specialist on the National Security Council and was later to become the U.S. ambassador to China.

Charles then returned to the consulate with a federal marshal to serve both orders, one ordering the consul general to produce me and the other enjoining the consul general from removing me from the country. The handful of people waiting outside had grown, and they were mostly press. One man, looking very much like Clark Kent with pad and pencil in hand, walked up to Charles and whispered in his ear. He was FBI. "The consulate is surrounded," he said. "We have the floor plans. There is no way they can take Li out."

Charles knocked on the door of the consulate, with the U.S. marshal, trying to serve the court orders. "Go away," said an official, "there is no one here."

For the rest of the day Charles went to and from the consulate, but he was not allowed back in. He received many phone calls both from the federal court and from Washington. FBI numbers outside the consulate began to grow.

Charles then received another call. It was from James Lilly in the White House. President Reagan was inquiring about the status of the case. Then the State Department called and asked Charles to go back to the consulate and tell them to reconnect their phones. The Chinese embassy was trying to contact them to give them instructions.

Charles returned to the consulate around 4 p.m., and by 5 o'clock he was again in a room by himself talking to Consul Zhang. Consul Zhang was almost in tears. He asked Charles again, did he *have* to release me? "Yes. The problem won't go away. If you don't release Li, it will only get worse."

The crowd outside now numbered around two hundred. All the major networks were there, television cameras in the back of flatbed trucks, cameras over the heads of the crowd, and the parking lot of Walgreen's drugstore next door had been turned into a mini–TV studio. In my room at the top of the consulate, I was, of course, completely unaware of these developments.

Soon after 5 p.m. Consul Zhang returned to my room. "Cunxin, for your own good, and for the last time, I'm going to ask you: will you go back to China?"

Here is the turning point of my life, I thought. I was prepared for the worst. "No, I won't go back. Do whatever you like with me."

He looked at me long and hard. Finally he said sadly, "I'm sorry you have chosen this road. I still believe you will regret it later. I'm sad we have lost you to America. You're now a man without a country and a people. But I want to warn you, there are many reporters outside. What you say to them now or in the future will have a direct effect on you and your family back in China. You should consider seriously anything you say or do. We will be watching you."

I could hardly believe what I had heard. I was going to be *free*.

All of sudden, I felt only compassion toward Consul Zhang. I understood that he only represented the government's desires, what was best for China and the Communist Party. But, unlike me, he *had* to go back and he would probably never manage to get out again. He had been kind to me the whole time I was in Houston. "I'm sorry, Consul Zhang," I said sincerely.

He looked at me with a barely detectable hint of empathy and led me downstairs to Elizabeth and Charles.

二十三

23

MY NEW LIFE

I kissed and hugged Elizabeth and told her that I loved her. I hugged and thanked Charles for saving my life. He was a man of great integrity. I couldn't have found a better human being—he had risked his reputation to save me.

I didn't want to say anything to the reporters, but Charles knew they wouldn't leave me alone until I did. So at 5.30 p.m. in front of a sea of microphones, flashing lights and cameras, with Elizabeth by my side, I managed a few simple words: "I am very happy to be able to stay with my wife and in America. I would like to do nice things for China and American art in the future."

All I could see was a mass of people and endless flashing lights. I could hear the clicking sounds of cameras, and reporters shouted questions at me from every direction. I held Elizabeth's hand tight. I could not think anymore. I wanted to get away.

At first some of the reporters' cars followed us, trying for an exclusive. But Dilworth drove his BMW very fast and managed to lose all the cars except one. That car followed us through every red light. Finally Dilworth had had enough. He pulled over and took a gun from the glove compartment. I was weary of drama by that stage. I imagined another headline in the newspapers: Chinese defector in shooting incident.

But then two men got out of the other car and approached us. They flashed their FBI badges. "Mr. Cooksin, the FBI would like to take you and your wife to a safe house for your protection. You are in a dangerous situation. The U.S. government has an obligation to make sure you are safe. The Chinese government may well choose to retaliate. Do you understand?"

I shook my head. "What's safe house?" I asked.

The FBI man smiled. "It's a comfortable house in a secret location guarded by the FBI. There will be someone to serve you twenty-four hours a day. It's as safe as the White House. You'll like it."

"Thank you, but I don't want go to safe house. I have my freedom now. Please, leave me alone," I replied.

"You're taking a big chance," the FBI man warned.

"I know, but I cannot live my life in fear."

The FBI man handed me a telephone number to call if I found myself in any kind of danger. "Just a precautionary measure," he said. "The FBI will have trailers on you until we feel it is safe enough."

"No, I don't want you follow me," I said.

He smiled again. "Don't worry, you won't even notice."

And, true to his word, if they did have someone trail me in those next few months, not once did I notice.

After my release from the consulate my story was flashed all over the TV networks, the newspapers and the radio stations. I received a flood of requests—Hollywood movie offers, books, TV, radio and newspaper interviews, magazine story offers and job offers from ballet companies all over the world. There were even offers in the Chinese newspapers that promised me lavish over-seas holidays to my choice of destination. Yes, well, I thought—any destination as long as it's in China.

The only offer I accepted was an interview on *Good Morning America*. I wanted to explain my situation once and for all, to correct any false stories. I didn't want my reputation as a defector to overshadow my reputation as a dancer.

Elizabeth's mother had flown to Houston from Florida as soon as she'd heard that her daughter and new son-in-law were locked up at the Chinese consulate. Now it was all over, Elizabeth and her mother and I were planning to drive to Florida to start our new lives together there. We didn't really know what we were going to do. We were simply shell-shocked.

On the morning we were to leave, Ben called. "Li, I've spoken to the Chinese consulate. They're not objecting to you working with the Houston Ballet, and the dancers' union has also given their permission. So I would still like to offer you that soloist contract."

I was overjoyed. I thought Ben would hate me forever! I thought I'd never work with him again.

"What about you and China?" I asked. I still felt immense guilt.

"I don't know, the consulate is very cold toward me. You were the last person they ever suspected of defecting. There's nothing more that I can do to convince them that I wasn't involved."

"Will you ever forgive me?" I asked.

"Yes, yes, I can. I wouldn't offer you a contract if I couldn't forgive you," he replied.

So Elizabeth and I abandoned our Florida plan for the time being, and I immediately joined the rehearsals for Ben's new creation of *Peer Gynt*. I was so happy. Everyone welcomed me back with open arms.

But even so, I didn't know another soul in America outside Houston. My English was still very poor, and now I was cut off from my own family. Elizabeth and I had only her one-bedroom apartment until the lease expired a few months later.

We eventually rented a two-bedroom fourplex, close to the ballet studios, as our first real home together. It was a run-down place with a noisy, inefficient air-conditioner and no mosquito screens on the windows. But we were happy.

Lori and Dilworth continued to love and care for Elizabeth and me. They often cooked for us: Dilworth even attempted a Chinese stir-fry once. He used a lot of oyster sauce. After that I cooked some of my niang's dishes for them, and Dilworth didn't try to cook Chinese for me again. Instead he stuck to American culture, taking me to cowboy bars and nightclubs and generally treating me like a little brother. We had such good times together.

It took awhile for Ben to feel comfortable with me again after the consulate incident. But now that I was a permanent member of the company, he started to give me more soloist and principal roles. My dancing continued to improve. A few months after my defection, Ben cast me in the technically challenging *Don Quixote* pas de deux for a national tour.

So it wasn't until Christmas that Elizabeth and I finally drove to Florida for our first holiday since our marriage. We stayed with her mother in West Palm Beach, and I met her father and his second wife.

I was sad to discover that Elizabeth's parents were divorced. Elizabeth had grown up in a comfortable, middle-class family. Her father had a small printing business, and her mother was a receptionist at the West Palm Beach Ballet School. It was worlds apart from the kind of life I had known.

But although I had Elizabeth's love, my job with the Houston Ballet and my precious freedom, I couldn't shake off a nagging dark shadow across my heart. I began to have nightmares. My family and I were being shot against a wall, just like the people from my commune back home. I would shout violently and wake up sweating and find Elizabeth leaning over me saying, "It's all right. It's all right."

I feared for my family and friends back in China. I feared the worst. I hated myself for putting my loved ones in danger. The pain to even imagine that I would never see them again! Everywhere I was reminded of my family. The good food that I ate every day in America would remind me of my family's struggle for survival. Seeing Elizabeth's mother reminded me of my niang. Tears would flood my eyes. Seeing children playing in the parks would remind me of my own childhood and all the games I used to play with my friends and brothers. And when the rain came, I thought of my family and wondered if they still rushed around to collect the flakes of dried yams from the rooftops before they got wet. I was homesick and guilt stricken and, without me realizing it, Elizabeth became the victim of my emotional suffering. My only escape was to dance.

Throughout this time I made enormous progress with my dancing, and Elizabeth worked hard as a scholarship student. But Ben never considered her a top prospect, and she gradually became disillusioned. She was convinced Ben didn't like her because she had married me. She was torn between her own dance career and mine.

I felt so very sorry. Elizabeth was such a courageous girl. She was strong-minded and gregarious. We saw ourselves as Romeo and Juliet, but we were convinced our story would have a happy ending. Yet no matter how hard we tried, life's intricacies always seemed to make our relationship worse. We avoided talking about the problem. We were afraid of hurting each other. I was still struggling to understand American culture, selfishly immersed in my own dancing world, arguing over unimportant things like unpaid bills and unwashed dishes.

One day, after a hard day's rehearsal, I walked into a dark apartment. "Hello, Liz?" I called out. No answer. She must be out, I thought. I turned on the lights—the dishes were still piled up in the sink after breakfast as usual. Anger started to simmer inside me. I looked to see if she had left me any messages, and I found none. I took a beer from the fridge and sat on a cheap folding chair and felt sorry for myself. Where is my wife? Where is my dinner? Why didn't she leave me a message? Why didn't she wash the dishes, with all the time she has during the day? Hunger made me feel angrier. I broke a couple of eggs into a bowl and was about to make fried rice when I noticed the rice was still sitting in a pot on the stove. I'd told Elizabeth to put it in the fridge so it would keep longer. Should I wait for her perhaps? Yes, of course. According to my family tradition, the family meal together was a sacred time. I should keep this tradition going.

I waited for over an hour. I started to worry. Maybe she'd had an accident. I picked up the phone and called Keith, the British boy who'd stayed at Ben's place and who was a close friend of Elizabeth's at the time. No answer. Please don't let anything happen to Liz, I prayed. I paced around our apartment with my heart hanging in the air.

Elizabeth eventually came home, in a happy mood, around nine o'clock. "Hello, my darling, have you had your dinner yet?" she said.

My anger flared up immediately. "Where you been?"

"I went out with some friends, and we had something to eat together. Why are you so angry?" she asked.

"Why I am angry? Look at these, dirty dishes in sink, like pigs' home, rice out on stove. No dinner, no message. I'm worried, hungry and angry!"

"Oh, you want me to cook for you? Is that what you're angry about? Let me tell you, you didn't marry a *cook*! I hate cooking!"

"I work all day and come home, see dirt everywhere! You

want me cook, clean, wash at seven o'clock? You have many more hours free, what you do?"

"You don't understand, do you? I want to dance, not cook! Dancing is something I've wanted to do since I was a little girl. It's the *only* thing I want to do. Your career is going from strength to strength, and you are happy with your leading roles. You go to sleep with sweet dreams. What about me?" she said, and by now she was in tears.

In my anger I could see nothing of my own selfishness. Sweet dreams? Had she forgotten my nightmares so quickly? She had no idea what I was going through. "In night, I think of my family in China . . ." But I couldn't go on. How could I express all my sorrow and guilt? "*You* don't understand!" I said finally.

"We don't understand each other!" she shouted.

We were still fuming the next morning. I'd gone out the evening before to walk off my anger, and Elizabeth had been asleep when I'd returned. My anger gradually gave in to remorse but we didn't speak for days.

That was the beginning of the end of our marriage. I wanted Elizabeth and Ben to get along. I hoped that he might accept her into the company. But eventually it was too agonizing for her to socialize with Ben, and she was convinced that as long as he was the artistic director of the Houston Ballet she would have no chance of getting a contract. I tried to teach her some of my techniques but with our close relationship and my poor English, our coaching sessions always ended in frustration. Our happiest moments were when we would dance together in our living room. I wished that I could give her this kind of happiness all the time, but I could see she was suffocating and I didn't know how to help. I encouraged her to continue her dancing career with other companies, but she thought I was pushing her away. She eventually tried the San Francisco Ballet and several other companies, but no

345

contracts were offered. She came back to Houston between tries, and over the months we communicated with each other less and less.

About a year after we married, she was finally accepted as a dancer by a small contemporary dance company in Oklahoma. She immediately started work. She was excited at last. She loved her new dancing opportunities. She loved performing. She was happy and alive.

Then one evening she phoned me from Oklahoma. "Li, I want a divorce."

I was shocked but not totally surprised. "If this is what you want, okay," I murmured sadly.

"I'll be back to get my stuff soon," she said shakily. "I'm sorry, Li, I really loved you."

I didn't blame Elizabeth for our failed marriage. I blamed myself. I had let Elizabeth down. I had failed as a husband. I didn't understand love in Western culture, and I shrank back into my own protective cocoon, withdrawing from many of my friends. I felt hopeless. I doubted that a marriage between East and West could ever work. Hadn't Consul Zhang told me this, that night at the consulate? What *could* I have done to have saved our marriage? We loved each other. We *had* each other, and now we had lost each other. I blamed fate. Fate had pulled a dirty trick on me. I thought of my parents' successful marriage and felt only more grief and shame.

Now there was no way back. I had no home to go to now, so I poured myself into my dance even more. Ballet was the only thing I knew how to do. It was my salvation as I tried to survive on my own in the Western world.

After our divorce, to help me pay my rent, I shared an apartment with another student for that first year. The second year I moved into a one-bedroom unit, and I finally had my own space.

346

By now it was May 1982, the year I would go to London for the very first time. Ben had choreographed a pas de deux using Vivaldi's *Four Seasons,* and he had especially created it for Janie Parker and me to perform at the Sadler's Wells Royal Ballet gala.

Janie had joined the Houston Ballet in 1976. She'd fallen in love with Ben's choreography and artistry and, despite the outrage of George Balanchine and the artistic director of her company in Geneva, she'd followed Ben to Houston.

Janie had the most beautiful long legs and pretty feet. When she stood on pointe her legs seemed to stretch on and on. She was very lyrical in her dancing and, like me, she loved the romantic ballets.

This was going to be our first partnership, and I was very apprehensive. She was one of the top two principal dancers of the Houston Ballet. In reality I was a little too short for her when she stood on pointe, but I made sure that I was strong enough and went through a physical-strengthening program to make absolutely certain.

I couldn't wait to get to London. I longed to see it. London, Paris, Washington, D.C.—the symbolic capitals of the Western world. I had seen some pictures of London but to be there in person, to experience the mood of this great city, would be awesome.

Like my first experience of America, I was shocked with what I saw in London. I'd guessed that the Chinese government would probably have lied to us about England too, but I was still overawed by its wealth and prosperity. The grandness of Buckingham Palace made me gasp with wonder. Where was the tragic poverty, the depressingly dark, unhappy London I had been told of in China? Britain should have made China look like heaven, but to my horror, it was the reverse.

It drizzled sporadically for the entire time we were in London but when the sun peeped out it was gloriously beautiful. The flowers in the meticulously maintained gardens, the café tables along the pathways, the wide busy streets. If only I could stay longer and enjoy all this! But our schedule was grueling, and we spent most of our time in the hotel and the theater. I did manage to see Piccadilly Circus, the changing of the guard at Buckingham Palace, and I marveled at the glorious detail of Big Ben and Parliament House. The history fascinated me. Ben even introduced me to rich clotted cream for afternoon tea one day, and I remember sitting there in that café and thinking of the London Festival Ballet dancing in Beijing that time in 1979, so long ago now, it seemed.

Back in Houston, before my defection, Ben had been negotiating with the Chinese government to take some Houston Ballet dancers to China. This was one of Ben's great dreams, but after my defection everyone including Ben thought this possibility was dashed. But to everyone's surprise the Chinese Government allowed Ben to proceed with his plan. The Houston Ballet dancers were paired with the Chinese dancers, and it was all a great success. As I had expected I wasn't allowed to go, nor would I have dared to return.

Ben's relationship with China mended after that trip and I was happy for him for that, but I still worried about the possible implications my defection might have had on my family and for several years I didn't write or call them, fearing I would get them into further trouble. When I eventually did dare to write, I received no reply and this just added even more worry to my already heavy heart.

It was now eighteen months since my defection, and the Houston Ballet was to do a six-week tour through Europe: Italy, Switzerland, France, Spain, Luxembourg and Monaco. It would be my first look at the Continent.

I loved the places we performed at. Epernay was one of them: our impresario had booked us there for two performances, and we were warned that the stage was small, uneven and raked. During the afternoon rehearsal it became apparent that the stage was far too small to accommodate the entire cast of *Etude*. Ben had to take some dancers out of a couple of the larger scenes. I was one of the principals and had to find the smoothest part of the stage on which to perform my difficult turns. After the rehearsal, Ben gathered all the dancers together. "I know we are in the city where the best champagnes are made, but I hope you are disciplined and responsible enough not to drink *any* before the show," Ben warned.

The audience enthusiastically received our performance. But I did see a few wobbly legs that night. Maybe it was the raked stage, maybe it was the champagne, but right after the performance the British consul general, a distant cousin of Ben's, provided the whole company with Moët & Chandon and Taittinger, passed around in flowery hand-painted glasses. It was consumed like water, and the party lasted into the early hours of the following morning.

From Epernay we traveled to Nice, with its beautiful Mediterranean beaches and turquoise water, where I would brunch in a beach café and watch the boats passing back and forth. I visited the Matisse and Chagall collections and at night dined with the dancers and friends from the ballet, tasting red wines I had never even imagined and eating superb cuisine in even the smallest and shabbiest of cafés.

While touring in Italy we had a few days free. I went to Florence with three of my Houston Ballet friends. I was awestruck by Florence. Endless monuments and sculptures, the history of the Medici family, masterpieces by Michelangelo, Brunelleschi, Donatello, Masaccio, the Piazza del Duomo and Piazza della Signoria. I was like a kid in a candy store. I was so excited that I missed my lunch appointment with my friends and my hotel checkout time, and had to rush to the train station to catch my train to Venice.

Venice was the place all of us were eager to visit. A friend had once told me that "to discover romance and beauty in Venice one must walk and walk." Well, at least that's what I thought she'd said. So I walked and walked, from one historical site to another. I stood there, in total amazement at the striking of the bell in the Torre dell'Orologio, at the incredible paintings, at the rich Venetian colors. This was romance and beauty in its ultimate form, I thought. I saw decay everywhere, part of the true beauty of Venice and its rich history. But this ancient city also made me sad—I thought of China and all that had been destroyed during the Cultural Revolution.

In the middle of all this glamour, I remembered, as always, my family and friends back in China. How I wished I could share this food with them! How I wanted to show them what I saw! But for them I knew the Western world and its affluence would remain completely out of reach.

二十四

24

A MILLET DREAM COME TRUE

After my failed marriage and that first amazing trip to Europe, my dance career moved rapidly forward. Ben's choreographic and teaching talents were immense—he became my mentor and I concentrated on my dancing with all my energy. I breathed ballet, I craved ballet. The freedom I now had allowed me to do anything I wanted to in America.

I was always surprised to hear others say I had a very strict work ethic, though, because for me dancing was fun. I wanted to practice during our fifteen-minute breaks—I could not allow such precious time to be wasted. I couldn't believe there were so many public holidays in America. And why were the studios shut on the weekend? We never had so many holidays in China. Other than going home for the Chinese New Year, the only holidays we had were 1 October for the birth of communist China and 1 May, which was dedicated to the workers of the world. Otherwise it was the strict routine of the Beijing Dance Academy, day after day after day.

Here in America I had freedom. But I knew I had paid a huge price for it. I had lost my niang, my dia, my brothers, my friends and my country, forever. Self-doubt often overwhelmed me. I was completely cut off from the first eighteen years of my life. Many times I wanted my niang to hold me, but I didn't even know if she was still alive.

I would have loved just to have heard their voices once again. In some ways, although I had escaped the communist cell, I had, in so many other ways, stepped right into a cell of another kind—a world of homesickness and heartache, of pain that was palpable, of sickness that was real. When I was alone, tears would fog my vision and drop like rain whenever I thought of my beloved niang.

Gradually, over the months and years, I learned to store my grief inside, and it flooded my heart with sorrow. I would remember my family's voices, their word-finding games, how we would pass food from one family member to another because there was never enough for all of us. I wondered, was my dia still telling his stories? How is my second brother? Did he marry the girl Big Aunt had introduced to him? Is he at peace with his life? How was the Bandit? The Chongs? Teacher Xiao and Zhang Shu? I missed my dia's stories. I missed making kites with him. I longed for my niang's warmth, her heartbeat, her love. At these moments, the distant memories of dried yams never seemed quite so bad.

And another thing concerned me—I didn't want to be like most of the Chinese people living in Houston, mixing only with other Chinese. I didn't want to be always on the fringe. So I tried to read books in English. My first was a book called *Black Beauty*. It was a Christmas present. An animal story, I thought. For children. Easy enough. But then, it was so hard! So many new words I didn't know. I turned to my dictionary and wrote down the meaning of each word in the book as I went. That killed the continuity of the story for me, but still I cried when Beauty lost his mother, just as I had. By the time I'd finished reading it, my tiny detailed notes covered each and every page of the novel.

I tried to fit in by dating American girls too. Once, I dated a young girl and we went to a wedding together. She asked me if I wanted some coke.

"No," I answered, "I don't like Coke, I am a beer drinker."

"I didn't mean Coca-Cola, I meant cocaine."

I had heard about cocaine. I'd heard it was bad. "No, thank you," I replied.

Then a friend of hers asked me if I wanted a smoke.

"I hate the taste of cigarettes," I said.

He laughed. "I wasn't offering you a cigarette, I was offering you some grass."

I was totally lost by then. Sounded like those horrible dried squash leaves I'd tried with my childhood friends back in China. But everyone assured me it would make me feel good, so I gave one of their grass cigarettes a try. Ten minutes later I didn't feel any different. So I tried another.

A few minutes later I felt like a hammer was pounding inside my head. Unhappiness overwhelmed me. My parents, my brothers, the Bandit, my friends, my failed marriage, the defection—all flooded into my mind. I was trapped. I had to go home. I don't remember which road I took or how I got there, but I do remember lying on my bed at one in the morning, alone with those painful thoughts. My head felt like someone had driven a long nail into it. Every joint of my body ached. I don't know what time I finally fell asleep, but when I opened the door the next morning, there was the girl I'd dated. Her face was red. She could hardly stand. The thought of what I'd just experienced made my head ache more, and I ended our relationship there and then.

All the way through rehearsal the following day, I thought I would lose my balance and fall at any moment. I was in a dreamland. Words just came out of my mouth without me thinking.

I performed the role of the jester in *Cinderella* at that night's dress rehearsal. All I could remember was the applause afterwards. Ben said it was the best solo I had ever done. Could I do it exactly like that on opening night? he asked. Repeat that? Of course I couldn't repeat what I'd done! I hadn't the slightest idea how I'd done it in the first place! That was the last time I would try anything that looked like dried squash leaves.

Aside from the drugs, though, I did want to experiment with nearly everything the Western world had to offer. I discovered Western movies, especially the John Wayne ones. I liked the courage he portrayed. I also liked movies such as *Star Trek* and the 007 films. I went to operas, symphonies, pop concerts and plays. Through Ben I met some extraordinary people—people including Liza Minnelli, Cleo Laine, Gregory Peck, Frank Sinatra and John Denver. I even went to discos, but I wasn't too fond of them. Still, I was like a bird let out of its cage, and I could fly in any direction I chose.

But I never lost my love for ballet. The Houston Ballet was my home now. The dancers were my family. I treasured each day and each performance as though it were my last. I looked to Ben for constant guidance and inspiration, and found it.

That year, I heard China was sending its first-ever delegation to compete in the International Ballet Competition in Japan. I asked Ben if I could go to the competition and represent China. Ben refused. Our performance schedule was too busy.

Later I asked Ben if I could enter the American International Ballet Competition in Jackson, Mississippi, the equivalent of the Olympics for ballet dancers. I wanted to get a sense of how my dancing stood up to international standards. And I told Ben I wanted to represent China. I owed China my loyalty as a Chinese dancer, or at least I owed my ballet teachers in China that loyalty.

Ben felt it would be good exposure for the Houston Ballet,

so he entered four of his dancers, including me, into the competition. I proudly registered as a Chinese citizen: it would be my way of returning something to all my teachers, especially Teacher Xiao and Zhang Shu for all they had given me in dance. This time, I wanted to make both Ben and China proud.

Over seventy competitors from all over the world would compete. As a soloist I would have to perform six solos, and we only had three weeks to prepare. I was inspired. To work with Ben so closely was a pleasure, and I didn't really care whether I won anything or not.

But at the registration desk on the first day of the competition, the Chinese delegation rejected me. I was a Chinese defector. They no longer recognized me as a Chinese citizen, whether I held a Chinese passport or not. Even worse, my former teachers and classmates from China were told by the Chinese government not to communicate with me. I had been so excited to see them, but now I was considered their enemy.

I was devastated. I wanted to go back to Houston at once, but the president of the organizing committee told Ben that he would be happy for me to represent America even though I wasn't an American citizen. I gratefully accepted, but I had to hold back my tears as my former teachers, classmates and friends, including Zhang Weiqiang, all avoided me during the course of the competition. I knew that they would have no choice but to follow orders from their government. Still, it didn't help my agony of sadness. Sometimes I would hear people call me "that bastard defector" or "that heartless turtle." I pretended not to hear, but privately I sobbed. I wished I hadn't come to the competition. How naïve had I been, wanting to represent China? I would wake up at night with tears in my eyes.

During the first round of the competition I simply couldn't concentrate. I fell on my hands in my final solo, the Bluebird from *Sleeping Beauty,* and I only barely qualified through to the second

355

round. I knew I had danced terribly. "Did you see him fall on his ass?" I heard some of the Chinese teachers say, and they laughed.

The second round of the competition required two contemporary solos. But by now I had a swollen right knee, a cricked neck, an injured left hamstring and the derision of my Chinese colleagues to cope with. I only had two days to recoup my mental and physical strength. I shrank into sorrow and suffered the pain alone. The rehearsals didn't go well at all, and Ben and my Houston Ballet colleagues noticed. I desperately searched for some strength from within. I kept asking myself, Do you want to swap places with your classmates from China? I thought of the fable of the frog, deep in the well, longing to get out. I began to realize that only one person could determine the result of the competition, and that was me.

The second round went much better, and I started to get my confidence back. But then, just before the third and final round, one of the Chinese competitors, Lin Jianwei from Shanghai, suddenly disappeared from the competition. Nobody could find him. Rumors began—perhaps I had helped him defect. My situation with the Chinese turned from bad to worse. Then some FBI agents approached me. They said the situation had become extremely serious. Five Chinese officials from the embassy in Washington were on their way to the competition. They recommended I leave as soon as possible.

"No, I won't leave," I said to Ben. "If I leave they will have more reason to think that I have helped in the defection."

"Li, this is serious!" Ben said.

"No, I will *not* leave. I will finish the competition!"

So, for the rest of the competition, either Ben or one of my Houston Ballet colleagues stayed with me the whole time. We moved out of the university complex and into a hotel. We used secret codes when opening our hotel room doors, and it was very intense.

In the middle of the third round of the competition one of the five officials from the Chinese embassy in Washington requested a meeting with me. It was Wang Zicheng, the former head of the Educational Bureau from the Ministry of Culture in China. He asked me if I'd helped Lin to defect. I said I had nothing to do with Lin's defection, and I felt he believed me.

To my great surprise, and despite the defection drama, I finished the competition with a silver medal. No gold was awarded to the male dancers because the judges could not agree on who should receive it. The best prize China received was Zhang Weiqiang's bronze, Ben received the gold for best choreography and Janie also received a gold medal.

I was happy, not just for myself but for Chinese ballet too, because deep down in my heart, I knew that without people like Teacher Xiao and Zhang Shu I would never have achieved this award. I dedicated my medal to Teacher Xiao. He was the one who had borne the brunt of the blame for my defection, who I learned much later had seen intense political attacks on the Beijing Dance Academy after I'd left. Yet Teacher Xiao had never lost faith in me. He had told me: the strength of your parents' character is in you. You can help your parents by becoming the best dancer you can.

I knew Teacher Xiao would have been happy and excited about my medal, but he'd also have to hide his pride. I was a defector and an enemy.

A few days after the end of the competition, the suspense surrounding Lin Jianwei's disappearance ended. Lin had sought political asylum with the help of a ballet teacher in Fort Worth. I was clean. And, secretly, I was pleased that this star from the Shanghai Ballet had followed in my footsteps. Part of me did feel sad for China, losing two of its dancers in just over a year, but the pursuit of our artistic dreams was paramount. When would the time come when we wouldn't need to defect to be able to work in the West? How long would this political and artistic suppression last? I had no answers. I wouldn't live long enough to see such freedom for China, I thought.

With the prize money from that ballet competition I put a down payment on my very first house. It was in a cheap and historic Houston suburb called the Heights, five minutes away from the theater district and ten minutes from the Houston Ballet studios.

I didn't know anything about termites then.

The house hadn't been renovated since the 1940s, and it still had cheap wood-veneer paneling and old smelly, worn-out lime-green carpeting. There was one small air conditioner in the living room, which had leaked and caused severe water damage to the supporting wooden beams. The roof shingles needed replacing, the foundation blocks were damaged by termites and the house leaned noticeably to one side. The wiring was exposed, the water pipes were rusted, there were leaking sewer pipes, cockroaches, mice . . . it was a disaster.

But I didn't care. I had purchased my first house. I had realized the capitalist dream. Suddenly a Chinese peasant boy and a former communist Red Guard had become a landowner in the Western world! I was amazed at how easily I had done it.

My fellow dancers at the Houston Ballet helped me with my renovations, and my house soon became a sort of dancers' meeting place during their free times. The whole house was turned upside down with renovations.

In hindsight it would have been easier and cheaper for me to have torn down the whole building and started all over again. I hadn't the slightest idea about wooden houses—my parents' house in China was built of stone and brick. But still I was very proud of my own house, and I loved entertaining my friends in it. Ben jokingly remarked to other people, "Communists make the best capitalists." I even got my driver's license and bought my first car that year, a secondhand Toyota. I felt a great sense of achievement about it all, but still I kept thinking about my family, the commune, the primitive house they were living in. What would my parents think about my own house? My own car? My Western wealth? I felt guilty for having so much.

After one year of being a soloist, Ben promoted me into the principal ranks. Gradually my reputation as a dancer spread both in America and internationally. My dancing career had gone beyond my wildest dreams, but still I was not satisfied. I knew I could improve even more—with the freedom I now had, anything was possible. I was the luckiest person in the world. Except of course for my only sadness, the one dark shadow that remained in my heart: that I could never see my parents again.

But then, in the middle of 1983, I met Mary McKendry.

I was performing with the Houston Ballet on a six-week tour through Europe. In London we performed at the Sadler's Wells Theater, and this time we were there for nearly two weeks. On one of our few free nights before the performance, Ben urged us all to see this Australian-born ballerina he'd seen perform with the London Festival Ballet. Ben rarely praised dancers from other companies: he always put his own dancers on a higher pedestal, but he had worked with Mary on several of his ballets and knew she was quite extraordinary. Out of curiosity I went to see her dance the lead in Ben's *Four Last Songs*. I was so impressed. I went back again the next night to see her in *Cinderella*. She was different from other dancers. There was a distinctive quality there, rare, lyrical and beautiful, with an intensity and commitment that transfixed me. I fell in love with her artistry immediately.

"Is there any chance of inviting Mary to join the Houston Ballet?" I asked Ben the next day. "She is such a wonderful dancer."

"I don't think she would leave London for Houston," Ben replied.

The following day, when we were rehearsing *Etude* on stage,

I saw Mary rush into the theater, her dark hair flying wildly around her face. She found a seat and sat quietly in the audience to watch our rehearsals.

I sneaked over to her during the first available break. "Hello, I'm Li," I said. "You must be Mary McKendry."

She nodded.

"I really enjoyed your performances!" I said enthusiastically.

"Thanks," she said briefly, then quickly turned her attention to the dancing.

I felt disappointed. I had wanted a longer conversation than that, but she didn't seem interested in talking to me.

I crept back onto the stage with my pride hurt. I had always been shy with girls and had problems communicating with them. But I didn't get another opportunity to talk to Mary again before we left to go back to Houston. I often thought of Mary and her dancing after that, but I wouldn't meet her again for another eighteen months.

After we got back to Houston, we began working on our major ballet for the year, *Sleeping Beauty*. Through Ben's Royal Ballet connections he had established a very special friendship with Margot Fonteyn. She had danced in some of Ben's earlier ballets and had tremendous respect for him, and Ben had periodically invited her to Houston for special coaching sessions or for special opening-night performances. Now she was coming to Houston again. I had loved and respected Margot so much ever since I had seen her in those videos in my Beijing Dance Academy days. I couldn't believe I would actually meet her.

Margot was an elegant lady. Her every mannerism represented grace. At Ben's place for dinner one night, she asked me about my family back in China. She was fond of the Chinese people and told me she had lived in Shanghai for quite a few years while she was a young girl.

"Did you like Shanghai?" I asked.

"Very much. I have a lot of fond memories. It was called the Paris of Asia then, and it was a place full of energy. But it's so different now," she said sadly.

That night, after my brief conversation with Margot about China, I lay in bed and tossed and turned. What Margot had said about China had stirred huge waves of emotion within me. I couldn't stop myself from thinking about my family and friends back in China. Special memories pushed their way back into my mind, and overwhelmed me once more with an ocean of sadness. I had made my career a success. I should be happy, but I wasn't. I wanted my niang, I wanted to hear her voice, I wanted to feel her love. This dream had slipped further and further away over the years. Now I felt despair beyond description. The hope of ever seeing my beloved ones again seemed gone. But how could I give up hope! I could never forget my niang's love, her strength of character. And my dia—the hardworking man with few words. My six brothers, my aunts and uncles. I could never forget my home.

The following year we took *Swan Lake* to the Kennedy Center in Washington, D.C. Two days before our opening-night performance, Barbara Bush invited Ben and me to the White House before our busy schedule began at the theater that morning. We met Barbara in one of the smaller White House reception rooms. Pastries, tea and coffee were already waiting.

"Hello, Ben, so nice to see you! Li, how nice it is to see you again." She opened her arms and gave us both a hug. She was still the happy, warm person that I remembered from my first meeting with her five years before. Nothing had changed, except that she now treated me like an old friend.

"Li, I keep hearing all about your wonderful achievements with your dancing, and I'm so happy that things have worked out for you," she said.

"Thank you, thank you and George for all you have done for me," I said.

"Oh, Li, we did nothing, really." She turned to Ben. "Tell me, Ben, how are all your China adventures going?"

"It's great, I love China. The Chinese people are so sincere. They pay me tremendous respect. I always feel reenergized when I go there," Ben replied. "It has changed a lot. Since Deng Xiaoping came along people seem to be happier. They have more freedom now. He has done an amazing job."

Then Barbara asked me what I thought of China's new direction. She caught me by surprise. I hesitated, and looked at Ben.

"Li hasn't been allowed back," Ben said, coming to my rescue. "I know he misses his family. I hope that one day he will be allowed to see them."

Barbara frowned and looked thoughtful. "Which city in China do you come from, Li?"

"Qingdao, where the beer is from."

"Nice beer and nice city." She smiled, and then turned the conversation to other things.

Before we left, Barbara showed us around the White House, and I felt honored and privileged to be given such a tour. I was surprised, though, to see how simple the interior decorations were. This was the center of American power, the center of world power. Where was the grandeur? The lavish palace of political might? Compared to Chairman Mao's monument in Tiananmen Square, the White House seemed very simple indeed.

Forty-five minutes later, Ben and I hugged Barbara good-bye and raced back to the theater for our rehearsals. But I was deeply touched by my visit to the White House and by this elegant, kindhearted, approachable lady. I thought of the minister for Culture in China—the comparison was ridiculous.

Two days later, at our *Swan Lake* performance, Vice President

George Bush and Barbara Bush invited the Chinese ambassador and the cultural attaché, Wang Zicheng, to be their guests. I was performing the prince, the same role that had so eluded me back in China. I felt like a prince and danced like a prince now. I approached the role from within. Gone were my peasant inhibitions and inadequacies. I didn't need to perm my hair to make me feel more princely, and I felt a wonderful rapport from the audience.

After the performance, the Bushes came on stage to congratulate us. Mr. Bush stopped in front of me. "*Ni hao*, Li. Congratulations. You were wonderful tonight," and he introduced the Chinese ambassador and Wang Zicheng, who had briefed Zhang Weiqiang and me at the Ministry of Culture in Beijing before our first trip to the U.S., and again at the Jackson Ballet Competition.

"We're old friends. Hello, Cunxin!" he shook my hands excitedly. "Congratulations, you have made us proud tonight! Would you have time to come to the embassy tomorrow, for tea in the morning?" he asked.

I was so surprised by his praise. I was even more surprised at the invitation. "Yes, I would love to come," I said.

Ben accompanied me to the Chinese embassy the next morning because I was too scared to go there by myself, given my last experience at the consulate in Houston. We were welcomed and congratulated by Wang Zicheng, and he proudly showed us the reviews of our performance in the *Washington Post*. He congratulated me for my contribution to the ballet profession and for adding glory to the Chinese people. Then he told me something else. He told me that he had favorably reviewed my situation, and that Vice President Bush had intervened on my behalf with regard to my parents. He said that the possibility of my going back to China was still remote, but that he would instead try to

363

obtain the Chinese government's approval for my parents to come to America for a brief visit. He made no promises.

I knew Barbara Bush would have been the one who had told her husband of my homesickness and longing to see my family. I was deeply touched. I could never repay her for such generosity and kindness.

Knowing China, though, the process of trying to get my parents here could take many years. I held little hope. Wang Zicheng was simply trying to pay Mr. Bush some lip service and trying to shut me up. I thanked him, but didn't think he could ever deliver. So as time went on, the hope of seeing my parents after five long years gradually faded from my heart.

But I was wrong. A few months later I received a letter from Wang Zicheng. He had indeed obtained the Chinese government's permission for my parents to leave China for a visit to the United States.

I held the letter in my hand, and tears streamed down my face. I was shaking with joy.

二十五

25

No More Nightmares

I stayed home and cried. I didn't know how long I cried for, and I didn't care. I just wanted to be alone to enjoy this overwhelming happiness.

Those tears washed out six long, unbearable years of sadness and grief. I wanted to stand on top of New York's twin towers and yell out, let the entire world know how happy and how lucky I was.

I had no idea what my parents would look like after six years of hard, hard living. That night, trembling with excitement, I dialed my old village phone number. "Hello, can I speak to Li Tingfang, please?"

"Who is calling?"

"Li Cunxin, his sixth son," I replied.

I could tell the man on the other end was hesitating. I was afraid he would hang up, so I quickly added, "I have the central government's permission for my parents to come and visit me in America."

"Wait a minute," he said. I could hear him talking to another

365

man in the background, and then I heard a voice shout over the village's loudspeaker, "Li Tingfang! Li Tingfang! Phone call from *America!*"

I could hardly control my joy. My heart sang. Five minutes felt like five hours. I was anxious beyond description. I had a Tsingtao beer in my other hand and took a big gulp, but my hands were shaking uncontrollably.

Then I heard the sound of rapid footsteps. "I go first!" Then, "All right! All right! Hurry up!" Then I heard my second brother Cunyuan shouting into the phone. "Cunxin!"

"*Erga . . .*" My throat choked with tears.

"Are you all right?" he asked.

"Never better!" I managed to reply.

"Dia and Niang are coming to the phone! Your brothers are all here, except our big brother. He is still in Tibet . . ."

Before Cunyuan could finish, suddenly the voice of my third brother, Cunmao, interrupted.

"*Ni hao*, Cunxin!"

"I'm so happy to be able to hear your voice. How are my fourth uncle and aunt?" I asked.

"They're good, but they're getting old," he replied.

"Please tell them that I love them and miss them," I said.

"I will." Cunmao handed the phone to my fourth brother, who then passed it on to my fifth brother and finally to my youngest brother.

"Jing Tring!"

"Where are you?" he asked.

Before I could answer him, I heard my fifth brother saying in the background. "What a stupid question! Where do you think he is? In *America.*"

"I'm in Houston, in my house," I replied.

"What time is it there?" he asked.

"Seven-thirty in the evening," I replied.

"Oh, we are on different times!" he said unbelievingly.

I heard more of my brothers' laughter in the background. "Sixth brother, we all miss you so much! We are so happy you are alive!" he said.

"Jing Tring, I miss you all too . . ."

I was about to go on, but then another voice spoke urgently into the phone. "Jing Hao!"

I was overjoyed. I couldn't speak.

It was my niang. At last.

"Jing Hao, Jing Hao?" she kept asking, over and over again.

"Niang . . ."

"Is it really you, my sixth son . . . ?" Her voice choked and she started to sob. "Ohh, my son!" She sighed. "I never thought this day would come before I leave this world. How happy I am. Gods have mercy. I can die peacefully now," she murmured.

"Niang, I have the central government's permission for you and Dia to come to America! We will see each other soon!"

"Jing Hao, please don't talk of such false hope . . ."

"But Niang, it is true! I have the permission letter in my hand! Now! You can start to apply for your passports!"

"Ohh . . . Ohh . . . Jing Hao said we can go to America to see him!" she said to the rest of the family, and I heard a roar of cheers in the background. Then she added, "Jing Hao, your dia wants to talk to you."

"Niang . . . before you go, I just want to tell you . . . I love you," I said.

This was the first time that I'd ever told her that. How many times I'd wished I'd said it to her before I'd left China.

There was a silence.

Then all I heard was the sound of my niang's quiet sobbing.

It took several months for my parents to obtain their passports, but once they did, the U.S. visa was quickly granted. Charles Foster helped with all their applications, the U.S. State Department was already well-informed about my situation, and knowing the vice president of the United States was a very helpful way of speeding things up.

While all this was going on, I had to prepare for the Japan International Ballet Competition in Osaka. After my success in Jackson, Ben encouraged me to enter with one of the rising stars of the Houston Ballet, Martha Butler, who was only seventeen. At first I had reservations about Ben's selection: I thought Martha was too young and inexperienced to perform in such a high-pressure competition. But once again I was proven wrong . . .

Apart from my brief stop at the Tokyo airport to change planes on my first trip to America, this was my first experience of Japan. Once again I was confronted with a prosperous and industrial country, but because of limited studio space in the host city of Osaka we had to take a fast train every day, for over an hour, to Kyoto for rehearsals.

Kyoto was one of the most beautiful and peaceful cities I'd ever seen: Buddhist temples, beautifully maintained gardens, the meditative rock gardens with their musical sounds, dripping water, bamboo and tranquillity. And the food—so delicately beautiful, like small artworks. The sushi was almost too pretty to eat. Some of the Japanese traditions reminded me of the Chinese customs that I had grown up with. I remembered too my dia talking about the Japanese occupation of Qingdao during the Second World War. Here in Kyoto I was so close to China, to my family and my friends only three hours away, yet still I felt so distant. Nothing would change, I thought. I would never be allowed to return to my homeland again.

Martha and I were placed twenty-sixth after the first round of the competition. I thought this was amazing, considering Martha had never performed in this kind of professional environment before: she hadn't even performed a full classical pas de deux in her entire life. She was so nervous that she kept her mouth open the whole time she was on stage. One of the judges said she looked like a goldfish.

In the second round we performed a contemporary work Ben had choreographed for us. I had to carry Martha in my arms, with her body sadly curled up. We were searching and struggling for a way out, but were pulled back by a powerful, invisible force everywhere we went. After all our hopes of survival had been crushed, we finally ended our performance with a slow, deathlike movement, both of us entwined together. All through our performance I pretended that I was carrying the last beloved survivor of my family after our village back home in China had been destroyed. No home to go back to and no loved ones left. All we had was each other. Sometimes my thoughts were too painful for me, and I prayed that my family back home would never suffer the same fate as the fate we danced that night.

Martha's standard improved on a daily basis for those two weeks at the competition. She was a fast learner, with great mental strength and beautiful physicality. I knew she would one day become a wonderful artist, and to our astonishment we were awarded a silver medal by the international jury. Ben again received the medal for best choreography. It was a great feeling, to receive such an honor. We had danced against competitors from the Bolshoi, the Kirov and the Paris Opéra Ballet: we learned so much from them, and Martha and I had formed a close partnership.

After our return from Japan, Martha and I went straight into rehearsals for *Nutcracker*. I'd been told by Ben that my parents would be arriving in about a month's time, so one evening Preston and Richard came over to help me begin to get my house ready.

"What's all *this*?" Richard yelled, pointing at a pile of stuff in the middle of my living room: there was some timber, a spare toilet seat, some tiles, bags of cement, and tools . . .

"They are my treasures. They are very useful," I replied.

"I know they are useful, but are you going to use them before your parents come?"

"I'm not sure," I replied.

Richard rolled his eyes. "Out, out, throw them all out!" he shouted.

Richard and Preston went through each item in that pile and chucked out almost all of my "treasures." Then they organized a working party of dancers, stagehands, an electrician, carpenter and plumber, even some board members. They painted, cleaned, fixed . . . and by the end of the week my house was transformed. There wasn't even any sawdust left on the windowsills. But they hadn't finished yet—Richard lent me two bamboo plants in huge flowerpots. Ben bought a pair of antique Mandarin chairs and Preston gave me an antique Mandarin skirt, which he'd had framed by the Houston Museum of Fine Arts. By the end of it all my house looked like a million dollars.

Ben and Preston had taken over the arrangement of my parents' travel too. They wanted me to leave everything to them: just concentrate on *Nutcracker*. So I did.

A couple of days before my parents' arrival, I went crazy with shopping. I bought so many different kinds of food, all the rare and precious things we could never dream of having in China when I grew up: eggs, tree fungus, dried mushrooms, seafood, pork, chicken, rice, even Tsingtao beer and the best rice wine called Maotai which, in China, was only available to high government officials. I bought fruit—apples, pears, oranges, bananas, grapes and a whole watermelon and stacked them into two big plates on the dining table. My small fridge was overflowing. I also bought a futon bed for my parents to sleep on because I was concerned they wouldn't be able to sleep on a bouncy Western mattress after so many years of sleeping on a hard earth bed. I bought them thick cotton shirts and sweaters too. I was beside myself with excitement. I wanted to buy them everything the Western world had to offer. I knew they would be blown away by what they were about to see.

The final rehearsals for *Nutcracker* would usually have taken an enormous physical toll, but not this time. I had so much energy. My feet were light. I was filled with music and color, and my heart blossomed like a lotus flower. Just thinking about my parents would bring tears to my eyes, but now they were tears of happiness and joy.

I wanted this opening-night performance to be magic, not only for the general public, but also for my parents. This would be the first time they would see me dance, the first time they would see a live performance, and I would be dancing the prince. The anticipation was agonizing. And, at the back of my mind, I was still afraid that the Chinese government might change its mind at the last minute and prevent my parents' coming.

For several nights I lay in bed, eyes wide open, thinking about my dia and my niang. I wasn't sure what they would think. Would they like America? Would they handle the culture shock and be able to enjoy their time here? And how would they cope while I was working?

18 December 1984. The day my parents were due to arrive. I spent the entire day in the studio and theater. I had to concentrate on the performance. It was the only thing that helped my anxiety. Eventually I ran out of things to practice, so I started my makeup early that afternoon. My makeup brush was very unsteady, my hands trembled and I could hear my heart thumping loudly. Everything felt strange and new. I tried to concentrate but it was impossible to chase away the images of my parents, brothers and all the people I loved back home.

The last thing I had to do to finish my makeup was to spray some silver glitter into my hair, to suggest snowflakes. As my dresser helped me put my jacket on, I glanced at myself in the mirror and wondered what my parents would think of all of this. They were coming from another world.

I went on stage and felt the intense heat of the spotlights. How would my parents react to these bright lights, to the thousands of people clapping in the audience? I wondered, would they be proud of me?

It was time for the performance to begin. My lips felt dry, and I was breathing fast. As the time ticked away, my anxiety and nervousness rose. "Why aren't we starting? What's wrong?" I asked the stage manager.

"Nothing. We're just delaying the performance by a few minutes—people are stuck in traffic," the stage manager replied.

The truth was, however, that my parents' plane was an hour late. By the time they arrived it was about twenty minutes past curtain time, and I was a nervous wreck. They'd been met at the airport by my friend Betty Lou and escorted by police car through the rush-hour traffic.

Word spread quickly through the audience about my parents' arrival. Houstonians were well aware of my story, so when my parents were finally ushered into the theater the whole audience burst into applause.

My poor niang! My poor dia! They had never been away from Qingdao before. They had just had their first car ride, train ride and airplane experience all in one day, and now here they were, suddenly faced with the blinding lights of a grand theater and a sea of people applauding them.

"Six years! Six long years!" my niang kept saying. "Finally I'm going to see my son. My heart is so hot, it burns with joy and pride!"

I was told of my parents' arrival only moments before the applause erupted from the audience. My whole being burst with happiness. I wanted to soar into the air. I wanted to cry. I wanted to see them then, at that very moment, but the performance was about to start and I knew I would have to wait.

The audience was ecstatic. People applauded even when I just came on stage. They too wanted me to dance well, to dance for my parents.

My partners were Janie Parker and Suzanne Longley that night, and they shared my excitement. Ben's pas de deux were challenging, some of the lifts were difficult and often created problems for us in rehearsals. But not that night. Everything was seamless. The lifts felt light, the partnering effortless: I felt my partners' every subtle movement, and they felt mine. My nerves were there, yet under control, and they became my endless source of energy. My leaps were high: I was flying like a bird, gliding through the open sky. If the music had allowed it, I would have leaped into the air all night. There was no hard work, only sheer joy.

The audience seemed totally captivated. I could taste the excitement. All the hopping up and down stairs, the pirouetting in the candlelight, the torn hamstrings and the painful injuries of the past twelve years—it all felt worthwhile that night. When the curtain came down at the end of Act One, I knew I had completed one of my best performances—and I had done it in front of my parents. The dream I had once been too afraid to dream had come true.

During intermission, Ben brought my niang and my dia backstage.

It was six years since I had set eyes on them. They wore Mao's suits buttoned all the way up to their necks, my niang in gray and my dia in dark blue. They looked so proper, so stiff. My memories of them didn't match. They looked older too, especially my niang. Her black hair had turned to gray, and the many years of harsh living had obviously taken their toll. Her face was more wrinkled, and now she wore a pair of black-rimmed oversized glasses.

The three of us, in tears, simply hugged each other tight. Nobody spoke for a long time. My niang took her handkerchief out, and it was already soaked with tears. "Don't cry! Don't cry! It's all right now!" she kept saying.

I wanted that moment to linger on and on and on. I had longed for her comfort for so many years.

By the time I went back to my dressing room to change for the second act, nearly all my makeup had been wiped off by my niang's handkerchief. I didn't care. I had felt my niang's adoring love and tender touch once more.

After the performance, my niang and my dia came backstage again. They watched people congratulate me and I could see the pride in my parents' eyes.

Finally, my dia, the man of few words, could contain himself no longer. "Why didn't you wear any *pants?*" he said. He had never seen anyone wearing tights before.

Ben and some of my other friends had wanted to arrange a big party in honor of my parents that night, but I wanted to spend that first night alone with them, in my own house.

My parents felt on top of the world as we drove back to my own place, in my own car. They couldn't believe their eyes when they saw where I lived.

"Is this *your* house?" my niang asked in utter disbelief.

I nodded.

"This is a *palace!*" my dia gasped.

I cooked a couple of my niang's favorite recipes for dinner that night, and afterwards we sat around the dining table with a pot of their favorite jasmine tea. We talked and talked. Sadly, I discovered that my niang had developed diabetes and a weak heart condition. Her incredible eyesight had also deserted her. My dia, however, was still as strong as an ox, despite being hard of hearing.

So many years of missed events to catch up on, so many

beloved memories. I wanted to know it all, everything about each one of my brothers, their families, their lives. All my brothers except Jing Tring were married by now. I was an uncle: I had nieces and a nephew. My parents told me Deng Xiaoping had done wonders for the Chinese economy. "If it weren't for Deng Xiaoping's open-door policy, our lives would still be in ruins," my niang said. She told me how their living standards had improved, how my brothers were each allowed to buy a small piece of land, cheaply, from the commune, to build their own houses on.

My parents told me how scared they had been when someone in the commune had heard about my defection. They'd heard it on the Voice of America on a shortwave radio. China has really changed, I thought. No one had a radio, let alone a shortwave one, in the village when I grew up, not even while I was in Beijing.

The people in our village had told my parents that I had turned my back on China. Some officials had paid a special visit to my family two days after my defection. My dia had been at work that day. "Do you know what your son has *done*?" an official howled at my niang. "Your son has defected from his motherland for the filthy America! You, as his mother, should be ashamed, bringing up such a bastard!"

But the officials had underestimated my niang. "How could you blame *me*?" she replied angrily. "You, the government, took my innocent son away! From the age of eleven *you* were responsible for his upbringing! Now, you are asking me what have *I* done? *You* have lost my son. *You* are responsible!"

The officials were speechless. "You will hear from us again" was all they said.

My parents had lived in constant fear and despair ever since then. They had been prepared to go to prison and lose everything they had to defend my honor. Some of my relatives and friends had distanced themselves from my family, for fear of being implicated in my defection, but the officials never contacted my family again.

"Your niang developed nightmares after your defection," my dia added. "If there were any loud noises at night, she would be terrified. For many nights she sobbed and sobbed."

"My heart would have bled to death if it weren't for my desire to see you again!" my niang cried. "So many times I prayed to see you one more time. Now I can finally close my eyes and die in peace. My dream has come true! I am the happiest person on earth!"

"Dia, what about *you?*" I asked.

"I had to be strong," he said. "But I was scared of losing one of my sons, a son we are proud of!"

This was the first time he'd ever actually said he was proud of me. I knew it wasn't easy for him to say, and my heart was light and happy.

"Your dia lost so much weight during that time!" my niang continued. "His face was as long as his own shadow. Only sadness and agony. He spoke even less. Can you imagine your dia speaking *less* than usual! He let more noise out from his bottom end than from his top!" She laughed.

My niang then told me of a dream she'd had, one that kept recurring for years and years. Just before I'd been accepted by the Beijing Dance Academy, in late 1971, she'd dreamed of a huge crowd, gathered in a cloudlike mist. Through the mist she could see many gorgeous dancers, like goddesses, dancing in the sky. Rainbows were their costumes, and the shining stars were the light. She told me that her dream had come true tonight, watching me dance. She had flown by airplane up to the ninth heaven. She'd seen the goddesslike dancing of the Houston Ballet. Her heart had been filled with pride and happiness. Now she could die in peace.

"What you did on stage looked very difficult," my dia said.

"I was dizzy just watching you spin! I couldn't believe you were still standing afterwards."

We talked and talked. So many questions, questions that had been stored in our hearts for so many years. "How many times your dia and I questioned ourselves," my niang confessed. "Did we do the right thing, letting you go to Beijing at such a young age? I cried for days after your first letter. For days and days. When you said you had to wash your own clothes, I thought, What have I done?! Why did I encourage you to go? You were only eleven! We grieved for years. I knew you were homesick. I knew you tried hard to hide it. And I knew you would be even more homesick if we told you how *we* felt."

I began to tell them then how devastating my homesickness had been in those first two dreadful years at the Beijing Dance Academy. How hopeless I'd felt about my dancing. How afraid I was of being sent back home and bringing shame to the Li family. How I'd hidden in the weeping willow trees. And how, many times, I had clutched onto my niang's quilt and sobbed myself to sleep.

"How did you recover from this?" my dia asked.

"Remember the pen you gave me?"

My dia laughed. "That was the only way I knew how to encourage you to study hard, to reach your potential. I'm sorry if I hurt your pride."

"No, I'm grateful. Grateful for what you have done for me. I only wish I still had that pen. I lost it, on tour, during my first year with the Houston Ballet. I loved that pen."

"Do you still have the quilt I made you?" my niang asked.

"After my defection the academy officials burned it along with all my other belongings."

My niang just sighed, but there was enormous sadness in that one short sound.

I told them many things that night. I told them about my

marriage to Elizabeth. I told them about Ben and what happened the night of my defection, and their jaws dropped with shock. They spoke not a single word until I had finished my story.

Then they asked me about Elizabeth, but there was no judgment in my parents' words. "Elizabeth must be a courageous girl to marry a Chinese boy so young," my niang said simply. "There is a god who has looked after you and steered the course of your life. You are a fortunate boy."

That night, with my parents sleeping just a few meters away, I tucked myself under the blankets and slept like a baby. No more nightmares now.

二十六

26

RUSSIA

Later that week, Ben invited my parents and me to his house for dinner one night. My good friend Betty Lou, who'd picked my parents up from the airport, would also be there.

That evening at Ben's, as soon as Betty Lou and I kissed each other on the cheek, she handed me a folded piece of paper. At first I thought it was either another review about our *Nutcracker* performance or a news article about my parents' visit to America.

The letter had been written on Christmas Eve. In the top right-hand corner I saw the emblem of the United States of America and the vice-presidential title underneath.

Dear Betty Lou,

Thanks for making me aware that Li Cunxin's parents, Li Ting Fong and Fung Rei Ching, were planning to apply for visitors' visas at our embassy in Beijing. I contacted officials at the Department of State and asked them to ask our embassy in Beijing if Mr. Li's parents had applied for their visas. I was pleased to hear that their visas

were issued on December 13. I hope that they have a safe journey and
enjoy their visit with their son.

   With warmest wishes,
   Sincerely yours,
   George Bush

Tears blurred my vision. My hands shook. I gave Betty Lou an enormous hug. I couldn't believe she had asked for help from the vice president himself. I couldn't believe the vice president would actually take the time to inquire about a personal affair of mine. I thought of the minister for culture in China. In China I wasn't worth one minute of his time.

I told my parents about the letter. They too were speechless. *"Zhi, zhi, zhi . . ."* was all my niang could say, and she shook her head in disbelief. "Be serious, Jing Hao! An American vice president inquiring about two Chinese peasants?"

My dia also shook his head and smiled in agreement with my niang. "Jing Hao is kidding. George who?"

I nodded my head and pointed at Betty Lou.

She smiled and nodded back.

Eventually it sank in. The vice president! Of America! My parents rushed to Betty Lou, and they too hugged her tight.

While I was at work over the next few weeks, my parents were often taken out to see the sights of Houston by some of my friends. Or they simply enjoyed staying home. My niang continued to sew, even though her eyesight was poor, and she cooked most of the meals while my dia cleaned and fixed things around the house. They had great fun gardening too. I had a large backyard, and they ended up planting over fifty roses. They weeded and watered them every day without fail. Never in their lives had they even imagined the luxury of being able to plant *flowers*.

My parents were forever grateful to Ben for what he had done for me. One day my parents invited Ben over for dumplings, and much to my niang's utter astonishment Ben showed up with a top-of-the-line Singer sewing machine. Just for her! She was deeply moved by such generosity and thoughtfulness. But she was too scared to touch it. Eventually she was persuaded to give it a try and she began to practice, following the instructions carefully. But she nearly fed her fingers into the machine instead. "I'm no good at this modern stuff. It took me a lifetime to learn how to sew. It will take me another lifetime to learn how to use this machine." But my niang did eventually take the sewing machine back with her to China—and gave it to one of her daughters-in-law.

My parents simply couldn't get over so many things about living in America: the fact that people had hot water in every home, that I had a dishwasher, washing machine and dryer. But still my niang insisted on washing everything by hand. She had hot running water, after all. What more could she want? Hot water was everything! One of my parents' most favorite things to do was to help each other wash their backs in the bath. And my dia spent a lot of time crawling in the attic or under the house inspecting the plumbing, the hot-water heater, the central heating, the air-conditioning units: he was like an awestruck child.

The refrigerator was another fascination, and my dia and niang were surprised at how long food could be kept fresh. My niang had to shop for food almost every day in China, but here shopping was completely different. "There is more Chinese food here than in China!" she said, aghast. "Many of these ingredients I can't even get in China at all!"

One weekend I took my parents to Macy's department store. "If this isn't heaven, I don't know what is!" my niang gasped. So many clothes to choose from! So much of everything everywhere! We stepped onto an escalator and she nearly lost her balance. Moving stairs!

The three weeks of my parents' stay were disappearing fast. I watched their reactions to America and relived some of my own reactions from when I'd arrived in America five years earlier. What a shock these three weeks were for them. They would reflect on this trip for many days, weeks, months, even years after they returned to our village in China.

I didn't want them to go back. I simply hadn't had enough time with them.

For their last few days in America I took them to Charles Foster's condominium, an elegant high-rise in Galveston about forty-five minutes from Houston. The condominium was part of a five-star hotel, and the hotel staff serviced Charles's apartment. My parents felt so guilty having the hotel people do all the work that my niang and dia made their own bed every morning instead. The staff thought no one ever slept in it. And my parents would go to one of the local piers and buy fish or shrimp from the fishing boats, and we'd cook them ourselves in the apartment.

Two days before my parents' departure another friend of mine kindly let us use his lakeside town house too, and to get around the complex my parents had to drive golf carts—the same kind I'd crashed into the ditch in Disneyland. At first I drove them to show them how, but my dia was quick to learn. He'd been working with trucks for so many years back in China, after all, so he was a natural driver. Even my niang reluctantly agreed to have a go. We spent only two days there, but on the last day when I woke up I found both my parents gone. When I looked out of the window I saw each of them driving a golf cart and chasing each other around like children playing tag. They laughed and giggled and laughed and giggled, and it was one of the happiest moments in their lives.

My parents were in constant shock during their stay in America, but they took everything calmly, storing it in their memories so they could savor it all when they returned home to China.

They had never expected to see such prosperity. They had never expected such kindness from the people of another country.

I gave my parents some money before they left, so they could at least improve their lifestyle when they went back to our village. For all my brothers, sisters-in-law, nieces, my nephew, relatives and friends, I bought gifts. There was something for everyone, no matter how big or small. By the time they were ready to leave, my parents had many suitcases full of gifts: watches for my brothers, clothes for my sisters-in-law, picture books and nylon jump ropes for the children, mugs and T-shirts with the Houston skyline on them for friends and relatives, a couple of bottles of Maotai for my grandfather and oldest uncle, and Ben's sewing machine too. "We left China poor, but will return so rich!" my niang exclaimed on their last night in America. "I don't mean the material things. It's the richness I feel in my heart. How well you're doing here and how much you're loved and respected! We will savor this trip for the rest of our lives. We're *truly* fortunate."

"Do you still remember the story about the frog in the well?" my dia asked all of a sudden.

I nodded. I remembered.

"Thank you for showing us what is outside our well. If it weren't for you I would die an ignorant man. We may be going back to our well, but at least we've experienced the kind of life that Deng Xiaoping might lead us to in China one day. Now we will carry only fond memories and all the goodwill of your American friends home with us," he said.

We talked way past midnight. We were so afraid that some important things might be left unsaid. The uncertainty of whether we would ever see each other again weighed heavily on our minds. It was during our conversation that night that I suddenly realized my dia had become quite talkative.

I took them out to the airport the following day.

"I don't know when we will see each other again," I said, close to tears.

"But now we have seen you and met your friends we can lay all our worries to rest," my niang reassured me. "We will go home feeling happy about your life here in America. I only wish you'll be allowed to see your brothers again one day. They all miss you."

"I don't know if I'll ever be allowed to go back home."

"With Deng Xiaoping's open-door policy," my dia added, "you never know. Who could have imagined that we would be allowed to come here?"

"I will miss you," I said to him.

My niang hugged me tight. I felt her warmth, her love.

Finally I watched them disappear behind the customs checkpoint. I stood there for a long while afterwards, just staring at the wall.

After my parents' visit to America I could telephone them in China and write to them, freely, without fear of reprisal, and I could send them money too. But I was still not allowed to go back. There was a considerable amount of resentment among Chinese government officials for what had happened that night at the consulate in April 1981. But at least I had seen my parents, and the heavy weight of sadness had lifted from me.

Now it was back to ballet and another competition was coming up, this time in Moscow in June. I knew there was a lot of politics involved in these competitions, and my experiences in China had made me wary of going to Russia. But Russia had always had a certain allure ever since I'd watched so many brilliant Russian dancers in those videos back at the Beijing Dance Academy. I *longed* to go there. I was not a U.S. citizen, however, and the Russian government had problems with me, a Chinese defector to the U.S. who still held a Chinese passport and who wanted to represent America. The Russian government hated defectors with a passion. They had lost some of their best dancers to the West that way—Nureyev, Baryshnikov, Makarova and others too.

Faced with a dilemma, Ben and Charles started a massive campaign to lobby both Congress and the Senate to pass a special resolution, to change my status and allow me U.S. citizenship a year ahead of the usual qualifying time.

The task was huge. To me it was inconceivable. Only rarely in American history had this been achieved before, mostly for Olympic competitors. Charles thought we had a chance, though, because we had the George Bush connection, so we lobbied on the grounds of a possible gold medal at the Moscow International Ballet Competition. Americans love gold medals of any sort, even ballet ones, and I received many, many letters of support. Time was critical, though, given the bureaucratic process. Charles contacted congressmen, senators, anyone and everyone who had any political connection at all, and we eventually gathered enough support to have the bill passed by the immigration subcommittee of Congress. But we ran out of time to get the necessary approval in the Senate. Fortunately, however, the American International Ballet Competition Association persisted and eventually the Russian authorities relented. They would allow me to represent the U.S. Ben and the Houston Ballet's pianist would go with me, and before long I was on my way to Moscow.

I was of course aware that the people of the Soviet Union were still living behind the Iron Curtain, but nevertheless, once there I was surprised at just how much the Russian people were starved of freedom. It was worse than I had imagined. The fear of the KGB seemed to be on everyone's minds.

One day I went to Red Square to see Lenin's preserved body, not because I was interested in him as a communist forefather or anything, but just like the other tourists I went out of curiosity. By then I had totally abandoned my old communist beliefs.

I entered the mausoleum, following all the other tourists in single file. As we descended into the depths of the tomb, I noticed the polished black and red granite that covered the floor, the walls and the ceiling. It was awesome. Guards everywhere stood motionless, as though we didn't exist. And there was Lenin, lying in his sealed glass coffin. A ghostly white figure. He didn't even look real. He was so small: how surprising that just this one small man could have such an impact on the world. His communist ideals formed the background I grew up on, and his influence was felt in nearly every corner of the earth. I looked at him and remembered Chairman Mao. I had seen Chairman Mao's preserved body in its glass coffin once also, on a trip organized by the Beijing Dance Academy, and I remembered thinking he looked pretty ugly. But Lenin's distorted face was even worse. I thought of my na-na, displayed in her coffin in the middle of her living room, when I was just eight years old.

I was surprised to see how many similarities there were between China and Russia. The harsh lifestyle, the lack of food, the drabness of people's dress, the discrepancy between the official exchange rate and the black market. The food at restaurants was limited too. I'd had Chicken Kiev in America on a couple of occasions and I thought, since this was Russia, Chicken Kiev would have to be much better here—like having Peking Duck in China. But I was terribly disappointed. It was nothing like what I'd had in America. The only thing that wasn't disappointing was the marvellous Russian caviar. I smeared it over toast, I ate it all the time. To me it was inexpensive, but for the Russians it was nothing but an extravagance.

For the competition in Moscow we competed on the historic Bolshoi stage. It was huge, but it was also raked. When I jumped up the stage it felt like I was pushing uphill. When I did my turns my weight fell toward the audience. Becoming accustomed to this type of stage takes two to three weeks, but this entire competition only ran for two weeks. American stages were all flat. Most European stages were raked, but the Bolshoi was famous for its very steep rake, and it proved disastrous for me. Two minutes before the curtain went up on my first round, I slipped just as I was taking off for a grand jeté. My body crashed to the floor and I landed hard on my back. Stars flashed in front of my eyes. A sharp pain traveled down my neck and lower back. I knew at once that I had a serious injury, but when I thought about the huge efforts Ben and the Houstonians had put into getting me to Moscow, I knew I had to continue. I couldn't possibly let them down.

I tried to regroup. I tried to concentrate. But before I could really assess my injury, I was called to places. The performance was about to begin.

My legs felt weak, especially when I pushed off for jumps, and my turns were wobbly. I heard the music but my mind could think only of the pain in my neck and back. All I can remember was trying to get this first solo over with. How I wished I'd had some painkillers with me. But I'd left my anti-inflammatory pills at my hotel, and anyway, I doubted there was enough time for the medication to work. The *Giselle* solo went like a blur and before I knew it I was on stage for my second solo—from the *Coppelia* wedding scene.

I got through the first round but in the second round my back worsened. I went to see a Russian doctor. He said I just had a muscle spasm—it would go away with some massage. But it didn't. I'd had muscle spasms before. This wasn't like anything I had ever experienced. I couldn't even tie my shoelaces. I tried to remember the pain of my torn hamstrings during my Beijing Opera Movement classes back in China. I tried to remember that at least here I had the freedom to choose whether I would perform or not. Here I could simply stop the competition, pack up and go back to America.

Because of the injury Ben had to modify my classical solo for the second round. It was so simplified that the judges must have thought I was deliberately avoiding the difficult steps. However, for my contemporary solo, I had never received so many curtain calls in my entire dance career. But then the Russian judges complained that this ballet was politically motivated. It was anticommunist, they said. Ben and I were astounded.

By the time I finished the second round I was having trouble even getting up from my bed in the mornings. The pain had started to travel down my legs and the heavy-duty painkillers I was taking did nothing but make me drowsy and my muscles numb. I challenged myself to finish, despite my injuries, but decided this was going to be my last ballet competition. I'd had enough of the politics and dramas and, although the medals gave me some international recognition, they would never make me a better dancer or a better human being.

There were other things to worry about during that competition too. Disturbing things. During the course of that week both Ben's room and my room were trashed. Some of Ben's belongings were missing, and my alarm clock had been smashed to pieces. I remember feeling uncomfortable, unsafe. It was as though we were being watched.

Then, just as the competition ended, the Russian authorities asked to check the entry visa in my passport. They said there might be problems. The U.S. delegation said they thought it would be safer for me to go with them to Leningrad and leave Russia from there rather than from Moscow.

I was happy to go home via Leningrad. Leningrad was where the Kirov Ballet and the Vaganova Ballet School were based, so I would have the opportunity of visiting the Mariinsky Theater where the Kirov Ballet performed and of visiting the Vaganova Ballet School. I remember watching the Kirov Ballet perform *Sleeping Beauty*, and I remember paying homage to the inventor of my ballet training method, the great Vaganova Ballet School. I was eternally grateful for that wonderful training.

In the end I received a bronze medal from that Moscow competition. The judges normally sign all the certificates before they are handed out, but when I received my competition certificate it was unsigned. I could not help but think about the Russians and their hatred of defectors and I knew that, in their eyes, I was no different.

By the time I left Russia my back had completely seized up, and the pain was increasing. But as soon as I returned to Houston two things happened. Janie Parker and I went to Chile to perform in a gala, which was already scheduled, even though my back was getting worse by the day. And Mary McKendry from the London Festival Ballet came to join the Houston Ballet as a principal dancer.

"Jeano, is it true that Mary McKendry is coming?" I asked our general manager eagerly.

"Yes, a real coup," he replied, beaming. "Make sure you treat her well. We can't afford to lose her."

After Janie and I returned from Chile I met Mary again in class the following morning. She and I immediately started to rehearse the leading roles in *Sleeping Beauty*. It had been eighteen months since I'd met her in London. I was so happy that Ben had paired us together. But I wasn't sure whether my back would hold up.

I didn't know what to make of Mary at first. She struck me as brutally honest in her opinions—and in her dancing. She was a perfectionist, as I was.

One movement we had to rehearse in that first week was a sequence of three "fish dives," where Mary had to do a double turn on one pointe and then I would pick her up by her waist and she would dive forward and finish with her face inches away from the floor, both of her legs high in the air. It was one of my favorite movements to practice and perform.

389

My back pain, however, prevented me from rehearsing this with Mary. She urged me to see a doctor. But I didn't want to: I didn't want to lose my first opportunity to dance with her. So we continued to work together for another week, but by then the pain was excruciating and after a CT scan the doctors informed me that I had two, possibly three, herniated disks in my lower back.

The doctors immediately ordered me to stop dancing. Bed rest only, for as long as it took my injury to heal. Otherwise, they said, I might have to have surgery, with less than a 50 percent success rate.

I was devastated. I had lost my first opportunity to work with Mary, and frighteningly, I faced the possibility of never being able to dance again.

That night I lay in my bed and thought of all that this might mean to my life. Ballet was all I knew, all I had known since the age of eleven. It was my passion, my identity. How could I, once again, be left on my own with an unknown future? Now I was the soaring bird suddenly shot down. I was a caged tiger once more. My frustration and despair were enormous.

I knew the only way for me to recover was to be as disciplined and dedicated with my rehabilitation as I had been with my dancing. So I taught myself to meditate. I taught myself to control my frustration and pain. I had no choice but to overcome it.

I wouldn't let my insecurity overwhelm me, but during this time I missed my niang dreadfully. I didn't want my parents to worry about me, so I didn't tell them about my injury. Instead I asked them to apply for visas and come to America for a second time.

Mary visited me during that period, even though she didn't really know me very well. It was then that she asked me if I had books to read. She loved reading and was appalled when I said I read very little. I told her about my reading experience with *Black Beauty*.

"Read something shorter and easier to start with! Don't worry about what each word means exactly. It's hard even for Western people to understand every word. English is a difficult language. Just try to get the *story*, even if you have to guess to start with. You'll get so much pleasure out of reading, I promise!"

So for nearly three months, friends and fans brought me food, videotapes—and books. I took Mary's advice. I just started to read short things: newspaper articles and short storybooks. Then I tried longer books: *Romeo and Juliet* was one of my favorites. I even attempted *The Hobbit*, though I found the language in both these books hard to comprehend. But still I found it fascinating, and I especially loved Tolkien's extraordinary characters.

So Mary introduced me to literature and once I started reading I couldn't stop, couldn't believe the stories I had been missing out on. I worked hard at keeping my mental focus over those three months as I was lying on my bed. I had a secret plan— the Houston Ballet was going to perform in New York City in October. That was less than four months away. Ben and my doctors doubted I would make it back by then. But I never lost hope. I had acupuncture treatments, homeopathy, Chinese herbal medicines, and a wonderful masseur who Mary called "Mad Charles" and who worked with me constantly. He kept telling me that I would make it back to the stage, but the strengthening program seemed slow and painful, and many times I had my doubts.

Eventually, however, my injuries gradually started to mend. The disk herniation never went away completely, but the strengthening program helped me build stronger abdominal and back muscles to support it and I had to do continual exercises to keep the injury in check.

But finally I had made it back to the stage.

二十七

27

MARY

Mary and I were back dancing together again, and we quickly became good friends. We trusted each other's tastes in dancing and each other's opinions in other aspects of life too.

After a rehearsal one day, Mary invited me to her apartment for dinner. I arrived with a six-pack of beer in hand just as Mary was in the middle of making spaghetti carbonara.

"Can I help?" I offered.

"No, thank you! Just relax! Enjoy your beer. All is under control!" she replied a little too cheerily.

I peered into the kitchen—and saw total chaos. There was a huge pot on the stove *full* of spaghetti which was all glued together. There was so much of it. Enough to serve at least ten people, I thought.

"How many are coming for dinner?" I asked casually.

"Oh, just the two of us!"

I laughed. "It looks like you have enough food here to feed all of Mao's army."

When the dinner was served the spaghetti was a lump and the sauce was very bland.

"How did you learn to cook?" I asked.

"I *can't* cook! I'm hopeless in the kitchen! Can't you tell? My mother is a good cook, but I never paid any attention while she was cooking. I'm sorry this is a bit gluey. It's my first attempt at carbonara sauce," Mary said apologetically.

"Still tastes good though," I said, trying to comfort her.

"Would you like more? There's plenty left!"

"I know," I replied. We looked at each other and burst into laughter. We laughed and laughed. Her first attempt to impress me with her cooking had definitely failed the test for a perfect Chinese wife. But her efforts and her honesty won me over completely and I liked her even more after that disastrous carbonara.

My parents didn't come back to America until February of 1986, four months after our New York tour I'd worked so hard to recover for. By then my relationship with Mary had gone beyond just being friends. Her love of literature had become a major influence on me, and I loved her open-mindedness and her curiosity. She constantly searched for new knowledge, not only in dance but in all aspects of life, and her tremendous inner strength and high principles seemed to be a match for my stubbornness. Mary could put me back in my place and set me straight anytime.

We stayed together at each other's places often by now. However, we decided that to avoid any unnecessary shock Mary shouldn't stay overnight with me once my parents were here. Traditional Chinese marriage values couldn't possibly allow us to sleep together without being married. My parents would never approve.

Charles Foster got my parents a six-month visa this time. They were just as thrilled to see me and, though it still took them awhile to get over their culture shock, they were much more familiar with America this time around and enjoyed every bit of it. Their kindness and their love of life made them the center of attention among my friends. They were so well liked, and I was going to have them with me for the whole six months.

After a performance one night I brought Mary home to have dinner with us. My niang cooked some of my favorite dumplings. It was almost midnight by the time we finished dinner, and before my parents went to bed my niang stopped and said, "Jing Hao, tell Mary, don't go home tonight, it's too late."

"But we only have two beds. Where is she going to sleep?" I asked innocently.

"You're a man now, do I have to tell you where she should sleep?"

"You don't mind if we sleep in the same bed?" I asked, red faced.

"As long as you love each other, we don't care what you do," she replied. My niang looked at Mary. Then she whispered to me, "Of course we would prefer you to marry a Chinese girl who can look after you and cook for you as a Chinese wife could, but we know that we are old-fashioned. I can tell there is something special between you." She paused. "We made a mess of arranging your second brother's marriage. We will not interfere again."

Then my niang turned to Mary, who was just about to leave. "Mary, don't go home tonight, it's too late," my niang said to her in Chinese.

Before I could translate for her, I saw Mary's face. She had understood.

My parents' liberal thinking surprised me greatly that night. I knew they liked Mary but I also knew that deep down they would have strong reservations about their son marrying another Western person, especially after my failed marriage with Elizabeth. Still, they left the matter entirely to my own judgment.

But even *I* wasn't completely sure whether Mary and I could cross our cultural boundaries successfully. Memories of my marriage to Elizabeth haunted me often. But then, Mary was like no other woman I had ever met. She had an unusual understanding of Eastern culture. She had the most generous spirit. She endlessly bombarded me with questions about my childhood, my family, about China and especially about my life at the Beijing Dance Academy. I asked about her family and childhood too, and about Australia in general. I had learned about Australia in our geography classes back at the academy and was always puzzled that such a huge country like Australia only had a population the same size as Shanghai's. It was almost inconceivable.

Mary had been in Houston for nearly a year by now. Our friendship grew stronger all the time, and my parents liked her more and more. Mary even began buying me clothes. "Do you like this?" she asked one day when we were out shopping, and she pulled a shirt off the rack.

"No, no, don't be ridiculous! I'll never wear this! It's too . . . colorful," I said, horrified. The shirt was a mess of gaudy colors and hectic patterns, way too loud for me.

"No, you will look so handsome in it! Let's try it on," she said enthusiastically.

I put the shirt on and looked at myself in the mirror. I gasped.

"There, you look like a colorful artist now," Mary continued. "I knew you would look beautiful with a bit of color. It's done. The shirt is yours."

I continued to study myself in the mirror. Gradually I got over the shock. The longer I lingered, the more I liked it. Maybe she was right. A bit of color did suit me. But there were so *many* colors and patterns! Compared to what I wore in China—the Mao jacket, the plain colors—this is very daring, I said to myself.

A couple of days later Mary and I were invited to a post-performance dinner party. I decided to be brave and wear the shirt.

"Where did you get this shirt? It looks great!" Ben said.

"Mary bought it for me," I replied proudly.

That shirt became my favorite thing to wear. Later I even wore it to the White House to meet Vice President and Barbara Bush.

Mary and I had formed a rapport, a chemistry, but we both knew that getting involved with someone within the same profession was going to be difficult. A dancer's life was hard enough. Two dancers together would be impossible, especially two ambitious principal dancers like us. But there seemed to be a certain force drawing us closer all the time. I knew she was fond of me, and I knew she was special. I quietly wondered if I loved her, but still I wasn't sure.

Ben had paired Mary and me together for the leading roles in *Peer Gynt* at around this time. I vividly remember rehearsing a scene one day: Peer had been informed by Solveig's little sister, Helga, that his mother was dying. Peer was torn between going back to his mother or staying with his beloved Solveig. Mary and I had to do this romantic, agonizing pas de deux together just before we parted on stage. There was a long phrase of beautiful, intensely sad music. Mary and I looked at each other and kissed each other good-bye.

At that moment, we both had tears in our eyes. We stood there and looked at each other. We had no sense of time. We both knew, instantly. Our destiny together was inevitable.

After that fateful moment I decided I would ask Mary to marry me. In fact I decided many times after that, but every time I managed to talk myself out of it. In the end I felt like I was fighting against an irresistible force.

One day not long after our *Peer Gynt* rehearsal I was guest-performing with the Pittsburgh Ballet in *Giselle*, and I knew that Mary was having dinner with my parents back in Houston that night. I spoke to my parents over the phone, and made sure everything was all right. "Mary is looking after us. She is such a nice girl!" my niang told me.

Then I spoke to Mary. "How is everything in Houston?" I asked.

"Fine, your parents are adorable! I've just bought them some Chinese cabbage and pork, and they have made me some delicious dumplings!"

"Mary, I miss you. I want to ask you something . . ." My heart thumped as I spoke. I was so nervous and so hopelessly backward in trying to find the appropriate words. I just wanted to say, "Will you marry me?" but I was too scared. What if she said no?

My fumbling continued, my voice shaking. "Mary, you are such a special person in my heart and the most beautiful person in the world. I feel that you are a much better human being than I am. Sometimes I don't feel that I deserve you. Would you still love me the same when I have a long silver beard at the end of my life?"

"Li." Mary sounded impatient. "What are you trying to say?" I knew she was thinking, for god's sake just get on with it! "Are you trying to tell me that you want to spend the rest of your life with me?"

"Yes! Do you think we can be happy together, for the rest of our lives?" I still couldn't say what I wanted to say.

"Li," she said matter-of-factly, "you are the dearest person in my life. I will love you until I die. Of course we can be happy together for the rest of our lives."

Asking Mary to marry me was the hardest, the bravest and the luckiest thing I had ever done in my life. My heart soared into the air. Now I had found my soul mate. My niang was ecstatic. Even my dia was happy, though his reaction wasn't quite as spontaneous as my niang's.

Mary told her parents about our engagement immediately,

and of course they were happy, but being Catholics they were somewhat uneasy about their daughter not being able to have a traditional wedding because of my previous divorce. So one of my friends, who was also Catholic, set up a meeting for me with a priest, Father Monaghan.

Father Monaghan was a chubby, friendly person. He wore a pair of spectacles and a priest's robe. I hesitated in front of this rather ordinary-looking man—he didn't look like a messenger of God to me. "Nice to meet you, Father Mon . . ." I struggled with the pronunciation.

"Monaghan," he said helpfully. "Tell me about your problems."

I told him everything—my failed marriage with Elizabeth, my defection story, which he knew well enough already, my love for Mary, her parents' sincere wish that their daughter could be married in the Catholic Church.

"Does Mary love you as much as you love her?" he asked.

"Yes," I replied.

"Do you believe in any religion?" he asked.

"No, I was never allowed to believe in any religion. Except Mao's communism," I replied.

"Do you believe in God?" he asked seriously.

This was the first time anyone had asked me this, and I had never given it much thought. I remembered looking up into the sky as a child and imagining the gods above, whoever they might be. I remembered flying my kite back home in my village and imagining my secret communication channel up to the gods, saying my prayers and sending up my secret wishes. I thought of every turning point in my life, and I knew I'd felt a great force guiding me, but I could never put a finger on what that was.

"Yes, I do believe there is a god," I finally replied.

Then Father Monaghan said, "I'm going to ask you the last and most serious question of all. I want you to take your time to consider this."

I started to feel nervous.

"To be able to marry Mary you have to become a Catholic. Are you prepared to adopt the Catholic religion as your only religion for the rest of your life?"

I sat there like a statue. Communism had been my religion for over eighteen years. Ever since I'd turned my back on it, I hadn't questioned myself about other religious beliefs. I had no idea what kind of differences there were between other religions. Perhaps Catholicism was like communism, I thought. But as long as I believed in God, the one God for all people in the whole world, then surely Mary and I would be able to share the same religion. So I agreed there and then to become a Catholic.

Both Mary and her parents were overwhelmed with this news. Mary's mother couldn't figure out how on earth Father Monaghan would get the Catholic Church to agree to have my first marriage annulled. But Father Monaghan assured us that because my communist background had denied me any religious freedom, our marriage within the Catholic Church would be perfectly possible.

I was supposed to have five religious education sessions with Father Monaghan, and I was given a Bible to read. I still had such difficulty understanding how Jesus could possibly have been born to a virgin. "How do we know that Jesus wasn't Joseph's child?" I asked Father Monaghan. But Father Monaghan was very patient and after just three lessons I was baptized, at the age of twenty-six. It was 1987, and our marriage date was set for October.

Two nights before our wedding, I learned all about the tradition of the bachelor's party. I was reassured by my friends that this was one tradition that we simply *had* to have.

That same night I was invited to a lavish black-tie party in honor of the beautiful and glamorous Isabella Rossellini, daughter of Ingrid Bergman. But first my friends took me to an

Irish pub. They gave me vodka. They all drank water, but I thought they were drinking vodka too. By the time we got to Isabella's party, my head was spinning.

Then it was on to our final stop, a men's club. We were ushered to a private VIP room. During the course of the evening, twenty-dollar, fifty-dollar, sometimes one-hundred-dollar bills were exchanged as the men were entertained by topless dancers. This was the Western version of the Chinese wedding's "chaos night," I thought. Mary's brother Matthew, who was with me, was horrified. By one o'clock in the morning, I was exhausted and told my friends that I'd had enough of the wiggly topless dancers and I just needed to go home. But I was too drunk to drive.

"I'll drive you home!" my friend John volunteered.

"No, I will. *I'm* not drunk," said Matthew. But all the way home he forgot he wasn't in Australia still, and he habitually drove on the wrong side of the road.

Mary's mother was so worried about our bachelor party. She nearly called the police to see if there were any reports of dead Chinese and Australians in any car accidents that night.

By the time of our wedding Mary and I had bought a new house with a large front yard that we could use for our wedding reception. Since my parents had just left America—they'd arrived more than six months ago—none of my family members could be there, but we had invited over fifty of our friends. How I wished my parents could be present too.

We decided to have our wedding in the little Catholic chapel where I had been baptized. The wedding rehearsals were like getting ready for a major performance. But the wedding ceremony itself was no ordinary performance: it was the defining moment of our lives.

With Charles Foster standing by my side as my best man, I nervously waited for the sound of the music that would signal

Mary's entrance into the chapel. Then I saw her, the princess of my life being led down the aisle by her brother Matthew. I had feelings in my heart like never before. For a brief moment I thought I was in another time altogether. For a brief moment I could see only the image of a young and innocent eighteen-year-old Chinese girl, way back in 1946, being carried with her entourage toward her future husband's village. But then suddenly that image vanished and I saw in its place Mary's beautiful, loving face.

We went to Acapulco for our honeymoon and shared the most intimate time of our lives together. The more we understood each other, the closer we grew.

But our marriage didn't change our commitment to our dance, and although we loved to dance with each other we respected Ben's artistic decisions too. As the Houston Ballet's reputation spread, more and more choreographers came and staged their works, and we continued to progress and develop as artists. Christopher Bruce came with his *Ghost Dances,* a beautiful work choreographed to South American music. I learned so much from him. His choreography was breathtaking. He even created a new work especially for Mary and me, called *Guatama Buddha.*

Another British choreographer, Ronald Hynd, the choreographer of *The Sanguine Fan,* which the London Festival Ballet performed in China back in 1979, came to Houston to do a full-length version of *The Hunchback of Notre Dame.* The whole company was abuzz with this new creation. There was a lot of speculation about who would be chosen for the title roles of the Hunchback and the gypsy girl, Esmeralda. Ronnie Hynd walked around the studios for days watching classes and rehearsals before making his final decision. When the casting sheet went up, Mary was Esmeralda and I was the Hunchback.

The whole choreographic process for *The Hunchback* was

fascinating, and Ronnie's theatrical skills allowed me to perform a role that was totally different from my usual princely roles. There wasn't much dancing and Mary and I didn't dance together as partners, but it was a great acting experience for me, and in the end Mary stole the show.

Glen Tetley was another choreographer I loved working with, and he was arguably one of the most highly respected modern ballet choreographers in the world. His legendary pursuit of excellence and his moderate temperament made dancers work beyond their usual physical limitations. He came to stage one of his most technically challenging ballets, *Le Sacre du Printemps* or *The Rite of Spring*. Even Baryshnikov had found it a challenge, I was told.

Glen came into the studio in the middle of our class one day and sat by the mirror with his friend Scott. I watched as Glen's eyes darted around while he whispered to Scott, who scribbled down some notes in a notepad. I was nervous. I wanted so much for him to like me and choose me to be in his work.

To my joy, I was his first cast for the lead in *Le Sacre du Printemps*. When I walked into the studio on the first day of rehearsals I was shaking with excitement. I couldn't believe I was going to work with one of the world's most creative choreographers. But from the start of that rehearsal I knew this was going to be one of the most challenging times of my career. Glen was certainly demanding. Nothing escaped his experienced eye. Every subtle detail had to be right. He expected total concentration and total dedication. Sometimes, when a dancer didn't give 100 percent, he would stop him in the middle of his dance and simply say, "Okay, that was a warm-up. Now let's do it again for real." There were no protests, no screaming or yelling, only recognition of his high expectations.

I had several physically difficult solos in this ballet, and they required enormous stamina. Glen understood exactly what it would take. Many times, after hours of endless jumping and turning under Glen's strict and watchful eye, I felt there was not another breath left in me. Every muscle in my body was wasted with fatigue, and my back injury still gave me problems. Often I just wanted to lie down on the floor and die. But then, just as I felt I was at the end of my physical capabilities, he'd say, "Let's do it again for the road."

Is he mad? I would scream inside. But I knew I had to start these solos again with whatever was left inside me. No one complained. We knew that without this kind of work our stamina would not improve.

Sometimes during the rehearsals, when Glen would ask me to do it for "the last time," I would feel sick from extreme exhaustion, but somehow Glen kept pushing me beyond my physical boundaries. I discovered those rare moments when the power of the music took over. It was refreshing, almost spiritual. By the time of the performance, I felt full of energy, ready to explode on stage.

Then came *Romeo and Juliet*. Ben had planned to choreograph a new version for the Houston Ballet to be staged at the newly completed Wortham Center in Houston. It would be one of the most lavish and expensive productions in Houston Ballet history. Both scenery and costumes would be designed by David Walker, the famous ballet and opera designer from The Royal Ballet in England. Everything was going to be made in London and shipped to Houston. Ben had chosen Janie Parker and me as his first cast and Mary was paired with Kenneth McCombie as second cast.

I loved the story of *Romeo and Juliet* and the Prokofiev score, but the rehearsals were grueling. Ben often threw out certain sections of his choreography, even though we had been rehearsing for days, and then he'd start all over again. We'd try many, many different ways of doing a particular lift, of partnering, jumping or performing turns, over and over, until Ben would finally shout, "That's it! I like that." It was a tough schedule: there were detours, setbacks, endless challenges, but our enthusiasm was always sky-high.

But for a ballet that told a story like *Romeo and Juliet,* I had to gather all my experiences together so I could somehow make the Romeo role more real for myself and for the audience. Some aspects of Romeo's character I found easy to portray, but others were difficult. I read Shakespeare's play over and over and watched as many *Romeo and Juliet* movies as I could get my hands on. I wanted to create my own version of Romeo, to make it *my* role. I remembered my feelings toward Her Junfang in that dark room in the Beijing Dance Academy. I remembered my first love, Elizabeth, and my love for Mary. I remembered portrayals of love, from literature, film, anything that would help me in my creation of Romeo.

The opening night of *Romeo and Juliet* was one of the biggest events in the history of the Houston Ballet. The air was full of tension. I couldn't make myself calm down. I heard the applause for the conductor. Just listen to the music, I told myself. Just listen to the sound of the music.

That night, from the very first note, I knew I had not only heard the heart and soul of the music but I had felt it as well. I leaped joyously and I lifted my Juliet high in the air. I ran wildly around the stage to celebrate our soaring love. And when Romeo mistakenly believed that Juliet was dead, all the sorrow and despair I had ever experienced in my life overwhelmed me. I thought of the years of separation from my parents, of fearing for my life in that small room in the Chinese consulate. I thought of life without Mary, I thought of the greatest sacrifice one could make, to take one's own life for the sake of love. When Juliet finally plunged Romeo's knife into her heart and closed her eyes forever, there was not a sound from anyone in the entire theater, only the soul-wrenching music playing to the end.

Then suddenly the audience erupted into applause. I didn't want it to end. I'd tasted the delicious feeling of the ultimate performance; the performance of my life. Another moment to treasure forever.

I was invited as guest artist to dance with a number of companies worldwide after *Romeo and Juliet*. La Scala in Milan, steeped in history, was one of the most thrilling and inspirational. But along the way I still kept striving for one distinction. I didn't want to be just a technically good dancer: I wanted to be creative, emotionally powerful, artistically mature. I'd made many breakthroughs in my dancing already, and had a number of offers from other companies, but my loyalty was always with Ben and the Houston Ballet and I still often remembered the old Chinese fables, such as the bow shooter, and drew on them for inspiration. I kept telling myself that I had only tasted the mango skin, not the flesh. I kept reminding myself of the painful leg-limbering exercises that Teacher Gao had made us do all those years before. Constantly I reminded myself of where I had come from—my peasant roots, the starvation, the desperation of being trapped in the deep well, of my Chinese heritage—all this I used as my internal driving force. And as my standard of dancing improved, my ambition of becoming one of the best dancers in the world was never forgotten. I worked even harder. I kept Nureyev, Baryshnikov and Vasiliev always in my mind. I had overcome so many obstacles in my life. Nothing could stop me now.

But no matter how successful I would become as a dancer, there was always one last unfulfilled dream. So, in early 1988, with Mary holding my hand, I went back to the Chinese consulate in Houston.

It was still in the same building where I had been detained, nearly seven years earlier. This time I was there to ask the Chinese government's permission to allow me back into China to visit my family. To go home. I wasn't sure what kind of reaction I would receive.

The entrance to the consulate was now much grander. A big round emblem of the People's Republic of China had been erected high above the gate. Once inside we were warmly greeted by the cultural consul, Mr. Tang, who led us to a meeting room and offered us some Chinese tea. He didn't have any idea that this room was the very same room where Charles, Elizabeth and I had been detained back in April 1981.

I was nervous and uncomfortable sitting there. Images from that night seven years before flashed through my mind. I felt claustrophobic. My heart began to race.

Mary sensed my apprehension and gently reached for my hand and held it tight. Almost exactly like what Elizabeth had done on that dreadful night.

Consul Tang was easygoing and friendly but, even so, I wasn't sure what to make of him. Should I trust him? I'd walked into a trap here before. I didn't want that kind of nightmare again. I guessed that he would have been well-informed of my past, but Consul Tang didn't mention that. Instead he began to tell us how the Chinese now had more freedom and a much higher living standard under Deng Xiaoping. He emphasized that China today had an open-door policy toward the rest of the world. It had been nearly nine years since I'd left China. Things had changed.

"Cunxin," he said, "I've read your file and I know quite a bit of your past. We want to forget what has happened, but there still could be considerable opposition within the Chinese government to your return to China. But I will try my best to help you because I believe that what you have achieved in the last nine years has only added glory to the image of the Chinese people. I hope Beijing will grant you permission, but I can't guarantee that they will."

I left the consulate feeling vaguely optimistic, but the waiting over the next few weeks was unbearable. A month passed. No word from the consulate. I called Consul Tang.

"Nothing yet. I'm sorry," he responded.

With each passing day my hopes became dimmer.

Two months later I had just about given up hope altogether when, after a rehearsal one day, I found a message in my pigeon-hole at the studios: "Please call Consul Tang at the Chinese consulate."

With a trembling hand I dialed his number and prepared myself for bad news.

"Cunxin! Congratulations! You have been granted permission to go back to China. You and your wife can come to the consulate any time to apply for your visas."

At last. I was going home.

二十八

28

GOING HOME

Mary and I had to finish our May performances in Houston before we could depart for China. Two months more of waiting. By the time we were ready to leave, we had five suitcases full of gifts and had organized to send two refrigerators on ahead for my family back home. Mary couldn't quite understand the gift-buying frenzy. In her mind, giving them money would have been far better. But for me, the gifts were part of the Chinese tradition I was accustomed to.

The thought of seeing every one of my brothers, my uncles, aunties and friends from my childhood, and especially my friends in Beijing—the Bandit, Teacher Xiao, Chong Xiongjun and Fengtian—made me overwhelmingly restless. These loved ones had only existed in my dreams for the past nine years. Now, each passing day seemed like a month. I grew impatient. I tried meditation to distract me from my obsessive longing, but I simply couldn't wait a day longer.

I usually had no trouble sleeping on planes, but the trip home to China was different. There seemed to be a spring in my eyelids, and every time I tried to close them they just popped right open again.

Even though I'd already told Mary so much about everyone who was important to me in China, she wanted to know more, always more. She asked me so many questions, and she was just as excited as I was. We had so little sleep on that trip. But we didn't feel tired. We lived on adrenaline and excitement.

Beijing Airport, 3 June 1988. It was around seven in the evening when we landed. It was summertime, and the weather was warm. My blood brother, the Bandit, and my violinist friend, Fengtian, were to meet us. And there they were, waiting in the crowd outside the baggage carousel. I rushed toward them, each of us with eyes full of tears, arms outstretched ready to shake hands, which was the correct thing to do for Chinese people in public. But instead, in a split second, I pulled them toward me and we hugged and hugged, sobbing on each other's shoulders.

"It's been a long time," the Bandit finally murmured.

I said nothing, only hugged him tighter.

I wanted to say so much, but no words could describe my joy. I had imagined this moment over and over, incessantly, for the last nine years.

The airport in Beijing was the same one that I'd left from in 1979. But now it was much grander, with a massive extension. By the time we hauled our luggage onto the minibus it was nearly 10 p.m., but the place was still crowded and there were long lines of taxis busily loading people in and out. Things *had* changed, I thought. When I'd left, air travel was well out of the reach of most Chinese and a taxi was a rare sight indeed.

Our minibus sped onto a dimly lit road toward a hotel in the city where the Bandit had booked a room for us. We talked nonstop. So many questions to ask each other. It was impossible to cram the past nine years into the two hours of this minibus trip. The only times the conversation paused was for me to translate for Mary.

Mary looked on in amazement all through the trip. She was speechless. This reunion. The long-lost friendship. She couldn't believe how much love there was between the Bandit and me.

By now both the Bandit and Fengtian had married. The Bandit's wife, Marji, was a manager in a foreign joint-venture four-star hotel. She spoke fluent English, so she could translate for Mary too. Fengtian's wife, Jiping, was a Chinese folk-dance teacher at the Beijing Dance Academy. On that bus trip to our hotel, Marji, Jiping and Mary immediately became good friends.

But just before we arrived at our hotel, the Bandit told me something else. Something unsettling. The Chinese secret police wanted to see me.

Not again, I thought to myself. But they were already waiting for me when we arrived at the hotel. Two men and a woman. They wanted to talk to me, alone, but Mary refused to leave me. She said she couldn't understand Chinese anyway, so what difference would it make? That wasn't entirely true: by then Mary could speak and understand some Chinese, but the officials didn't know that so they relented and let her stay.

The Chinese secret police asked me a lot of questions, mainly about the defection in 1981. They asked me again if there was any Taiwanese or American government involvement. There were two conflicting reports, they said, from the consulate in Houston and from the embassy in Washington. They wanted to know which was closer to the truth. They were very polite and I never really felt in danger, but they did say that, for my safety, they would provide me with discreet protection. I knew what that meant. They were going to keep an eye on me.

Mary and I stayed in Beijing at first and spent every minute with my friends. The Bandit told me all that had happened since I'd left: he was now a soloist at the Central Ballet of China. Both Fengtian and Chong Xiongjun had been selected by the Song and Dance Company of China. Chong was married too, to a nice lady who worked at a clothing factory in Beijing. Much had happened. I had been away so long.

So, on the back of the Bandit's and Fengtian's bikes, Mary and I traveled around Beijing. Sometimes we ate at their homes and other times I tried to show Mary some of the small eateries that had existed during my youth, but many places I had once known had either been torn down or had changed ownership as China had gone through rapid change. I was surprised. And impressed. Even though there were signs of prosperity everywhere and the progress I was witnessing far exceeded my expectations, still, the massive number of bicycles, the polluted air and the millions of pedestrians were all so familiar to me. There seemed to be much more freedom. People were happier. The influence of Mao and the grim shadow of the Cultural Revolution had begun to lift. Now Deng Xiaoping's "Get rich is glorious" slogan was on everyone's lips, and was splashed around on enormous billboards everywhere.

We had been in Beijing for a couple of days when I asked the Bandit if I could visit my former teachers at the Beijing Dance Academy. The Bandit was my liaison with the academy officials, but it wasn't until our third day in Beijing that I finally received permission to go.

It was a hot summer morning. Mary and I rode through the narrow backstreets with the Bandit and Fengtian, and I breathed in and savored the familiar Beijing smells: there seemed to be a food stand on every corner. Street merchants were shouting, everyone trying to compete with each other for attention. By the time we reached the Beijing Dance Academy it was around ten o'clock.

There it was. The small windows of our three-story sleeping quarters—the building with the blocked toilets, the building where eight of us slept on four-bed bunks in one small room.

411

There was the metal gate, its familiarity immediately triggering vivid memories of the years I spent inside it. The discipline, the 5.30 a.m. wake-up bells, jogging in Taoranting Park, the early-morning exercise sessions, rush hour for the toilets, waiting in line for our food in the canteen, the self-criticisms, the endless political study sessions, the nights when I climbed over this gate after my desperate attempts to see Minister Wang. And I remembered most of all the two people who were instrumental in helping to create the success I now enjoyed: Teacher Xiao and Zhang Shu.

Suddenly, before I could go on with my thoughts, I saw them. Both of them—Teacher Xiao and Zhang Shu—waiting for me on the other side of the gate.

My heart was full of emotions that I wanted to express, but I couldn't speak a word. Teacher Xiao and Zhang Shu opened the gate and rushed toward me.

We could only shake hands and look at each other through tear-filled eyes. It was like a dream. I couldn't think of anything to say: my tears had flooded my brain. So instead I put all my love, gratitude and years of unspoken words into our passionate hand-shaking. It was only when the Bandit reminded me that I should introduce Mary to them that I was jolted back to the present.

The academy looked exactly the same as when I had left it nine years ago. There was the guardhouse by the gate, and the small sports ground. There were the canteens, the hot-water heater room, the studio building and the Ping-Pong tables beside it. Everything was there. Nothing had changed, except that the buildings seemed even more run-down than I remembered.

Within only a few minutes a small crowd of familiar faces surrounded me. Most were teachers, among them my first ballet teacher, Chen Lueng, and one of my Chinese folk dance teachers, Ma Lixie. They all wanted to talk to me and asked many questions. Eventually Teacher Xiao and Zhang Shu had to remind me that all the other ballet teachers were eagerly waiting for me too, and that we should make our way inside.

We walked into a roomful of faces. The teachers of the ballet department had prepared tea for us, with roasted peanuts, sunflower seeds, even some cut-up watermelon. We sat around and talked. Zhang Shu, I discovered, was still the head of the ballet department. I also found out that they knew of some of my achievements and that they were especially impressed by the medals I'd won at the international ballet competitions. We talked and talked. I thanked every one of them for what they'd done for me. I asked what they would like me to do for them while I was there. "Dance for us!" Teacher Xiao said.

People cheered at his suggestion and I understood then how much they wanted me to show them what I'd learned in the West in the past nine years. I had no dancing gear with me, so Teacher Xiao lent me a pair of tights and some ballet shoes. But they had to keep the teachers from the other dance departments and all the academy students away—China might have changed, but in the officials' minds I was still too much of a Western influence.

My audience gathered in front of me, in that old dance studio once more, the same one where I had endlessly practiced my pirouettes and had left dents in the wooden floor. I noticed the familiar smell of mildew mixed with sweat and saw again the dust motes floating in the air through the beams of sunlight. It was all still there, in every detail. Here I was, standing in front of my former teachers, nervous to dance in front of those familiar, critical eyes. It felt like my very first exam in my first year at the Beijing Dance Academy. I felt like I was eleven years old again.

I decided to dance the prince solo from Act Three of *Swan Lake*. There was no music, so I danced while my audience hummed the tune. Without the costumes, the makeup and the music, it felt so bare and disjointed. How I wished I could show them one of Ben's awesome productions. But I could tell from my teachers'

413

eyes that they were proud of what I had achieved in dance—their long-lost son had finally returned.

I also danced one of the solos from Glen Tetley's *Le Sacre du Printemps* and Christopher Bruce's *Ghost Dances* while Mary obligingly hummed the tunes. We chatted in between my demonstrations, but they asked me so many questions and were so hungry for Western knowledge that after two hours I was exhausted.

"All right, all right, let's not kill Cunxin off!" Teacher Xiao said finally.

We left the old dance studio and went to Teacher Xiao's little apartment in the academy grounds. His wife cooked us a beautiful lunch and we continued to talk and talk. There was so much to catch up on. Teacher Xiao was now the co-head of the choreography department and had been promoted to professor.

"Cunxin, I couldn't tell you how many times I have dreamed about your dancing!" Teacher Xiao said. "I always wondered if I would ever see you dance again before I died. I'm *honored* to have been your teacher! You have done Chinese ballet proud, all over the world."

We hugged each other tight. I had been so afraid that I would disappoint him. Teacher Xiao was the person whose opinion mattered most to me. He was the one who had shown me how beautiful ballet could be. He was the one who'd encouraged me to taste the mango. He was my mentor, my friend, the one man to whom I owed so much.

After our lunch, I showed Mary the stairs where I had done my hops and the studios where I had worked and sweated for all those years. She was shocked. Compared to what she was used to the conditions were very primitive. We sat in the dimly lit school theater where she had watched our performance that time, back in 1979. Our paths had crossed then, in this very place, and now here we were again, sitting on the old splintered wooden seats.

I closed my eyes. Into my mind flooded so many memories. My performances of Madame Mao's model ballets. Teacher Xiao's unattainable pirouettes. The theaterful of teachers and students chanting Mao's political slogans . . .

I don't know how long I sat there dreaming of the past, but when I opened my eyes Mary was looking at me intently. "I can't *believe* this is really where you have come from," she said.

Before leaving Beijing I wanted to host a party at my hotel restaurant for all of my old teachers and classmates. It was a wonderful reunion, but bittersweet as well. There were many happy tears that night. One of the academy officials delivered a speech, welcoming me back to China, and I was urged to respond. I introduced Mary as an exceptional dancer in her own right and went on to say that this was one of the most exciting days of my life. "To be able to see you all is a millet dream come true. How many times I wished to be able to see you all! Sixteen years ago, thanks to Madame Mao, I was selected to join the Beijing Dance Academy. I was just a peasant boy. I knew nothing of ballet. I was homesick, a lost cause. But over those seven years you taught me and cared for me and befriended me. You have given me things I can never repay. I don't know where I would be today without you."

"You would be back in Li Commune!" the Bandit shouted, and there was much laughter.

Yes, I thought, I would be back home in Li Commune, eating dried yams and drinking northwest wind.

二十九

29

BACK IN MY VILLAGE

The next day Mary and I were on an old prop-driven plane flying to Qingdao.

I was finally going home. I would see all my brothers, their wives and children, after all these years. But I wasn't sure what to expect. What would my village and commune look like now? Would there be as much change there as I had seen in Beijing? How were my uncles, aunts, cousins and all my childhood friends? What would they think of Mary? All my friends in Beijing had adored her, and I wanted my family to feel the same. I wished the plane would fly on just a little bit faster.

Mary understood exactly how I felt. She held my hand the whole way.

As the plane was descending toward Qingdao, Mary said, "Li, take a deep breath and enjoy your family." But still I wondered what she would think of the harsh conditions she was about to encounter.

The landing was rough. Our plane slid toward a simple

two-story building. I looked out the window at my first glimpse of home.

But . . . where is *this*? The surroundings seemed familiar, but unfamiliar too. Then suddenly I saw a line of large trees in the distance, and I realized with a thud in my heart exactly where we were. This was the old airport, the very same airport where I had dug the half-burned coal from under the runway when I was a small boy. I remembered being there with my brothers, of being shot at by the army guards, of dropping my basket and spade and running, terrified, for my life. Now the two-story building stood where the old guardhouse used to be, and smooth runways spread out in different directions. The vision from my childhood days vanished in an instant.

All of my brothers, except my fourth brother, were at the airport waiting for us, with their wives and children, over twenty family members in total. I shook hands with all of them. I wanted to hug each one just as I had done with the Bandit and Fengtian, but I was afraid that this would embarrass them too much. This was not Beijing. This was just a small country town.

All of my brothers looked older than I remembered. We met all the sisters-in-law, and all the children immediately called Mary and me Sixth Mother and Sixth Father, but Mary attracted the greatest attention. Even strangers at the airport asked my brothers who this Western girl was. "Our sister-in-law!" my brothers proudly replied, and they all fought to carry our suitcases.

My family had borrowed two trucks to take us home. Mary was pushed into the front seat of one, next to the driver, and I was pushed into the other, and the rest of the family members piled into the back of each truck.

Along the dusty road on the way to my old village I once again smelled the familiar country air—full of the scent of human waste still used as fertilizer in the fields. Childhood memories returned once more. I loved this distinctive manure smell. It was

417

the smell of my own town, and at long last I knew I was really home.

As our trucks slowly rolled down the old streets, people lit up firecrackers to celebrate my return. All the villagers had come out to greet us, standing on both sides of the streets, waving at us as we passed. Some I recognized, many I couldn't. After nine years, the countless older uncles and aunts, younger uncles and aunts, great-grand-uncles and grand-aunts, grand-nephews and their wives, had all gotten mixed up in my mind, with the exception of a very few. I couldn't even remember what their proper titles were. All I could do was nod my head, smile and repeat "*Ni hao*," "*Ni hao*," "*Ni hao* . . ."

As soon as my family saw our truck turn into our street, my fourth brother, who had stayed home to help Niang prepare food, lit a long string of firecrackers. More firecrackers! It was just like it was when I was a small boy—the noise, the light, the smoke, the smell of gunpowder and the flying fragments of red paper.

Our trucks stopped, and a sea of people gathered around us.

And then, through the crowd, I glimpsed my parents. They were standing by our gate with my fourth uncle and aunt, happy and proud. I rushed to them. I hugged Niang. I shook hands with Dia and Fourth Uncle. Just as I was going to shake my fourth auntie's hand, Niang threw herself at me and hugged me tight. "Oh, my sixth son! I missed you!" she sobbed.

Mary had gotten down from the other truck by now, and immediately people's attention turned to her. As she walked toward me, the villagers parted the way for her, whispering about the color of her hair, the size of her nose, the pattern of her shirt, the height of her heels. Mary was the first Westerner to come to the village since 1949. She was a sensation.

In the shady courtyard of my old home, a small square wooden table, knee-high, had been placed. Many little wooden

418

folding stools were carefully positioned around it. A big floral teapot and teacups sat in the center of the table, and one of my sisters-in-law began to fill everyone's cups. Plates full of roasted sunflower seeds, peanuts and sorghum sweets were passed around. We popped open the sunflower seeds with our teeth and cracked the peanut shells with our hands. I remembered the sorghum sweets I used to take to Beijing with me. Every object was drenched with memories.

It was late in the afternoon by now. The sun was setting and had painted the sky a beautiful orange color. I watched Mary—she was surrounded by my sisters-in-law and nieces. They seemed to understand each other without me having to translate for them at all. It was almost as though Mary had always been a part of this family.

Mary and I had brought some American cigarettes and candies, and these were passed around and shared. The children feasted on the chewing gum and sweets, and loved the American jump ropes that we'd also brought for them. But the thing that excited and astounded everyone was our Polaroid camera. They were beside themselves with amazement. How could their own images, pictures of *themselves*, come out so quickly! It was thrilling. I was sad to discover, however, that the children in my village no longer seemed to play the simple games from my childhood, such as marbles or one-legged fights. Instead, they were crazy about small Japanese electronic gadgets, just like children in America. I was amazed that these sorts of sophisticated games were available in my village at all. How times had changed.

The children in my family welcomed Mary and me by putting on a singing and dancing show. We cheered and laughed as they each did their little numbers. The younger ones, from two to five years old, did their best trying to keep up. My two-year-old niece was knocked over a few times by the older children, but after a piece of candy and some encouragement she was participating once more. Then, just before dinnertime, many of the villagers returned from their work in the fields and popped their heads through the windows to get a glimpse of Mary and me. I could see they were too embarrassed to come in, so I took Mary outside instead. Within minutes a large crowd had gathered and an old man, whom I accidentally called Great Uncle instead of Great-Grand-Nephew, asked us to dance.

"Yes, please! Dance for us, please!" the crowd urged.

Mary and I looked at their eager faces. We exchanged a glance and Mary nodded.

"Are you sure?" I asked.

She nodded again. "Let's do an arabesque lift from *Nutcracker*."

So a small space in the middle of the street was cleared for us and the crowd gathered around. I lifted Mary high above my head, then flipped her down into a fish dive. The crowd gasped, then cheered and roared with applause. *"Zailai, zailai!"* More, more! they demanded.

I picked Mary up with one arm and twirled her around in circles. The villagers screamed with delight.

By the time we went back inside, my niang and my fourth brother had prepared a tableful of colorful dishes. It was too hot inside so they set two more tables up in the shady courtyard, so there was one for the men, one for the women and a third for the children. Big bottles of local beer were popped open under the tables, and there were many *gan bei*s that night. All of my brothers could cook, and each of them cooked his favorite dish.

So many questions were asked about our life in the West. My parents had told them something of it, but still they wanted more and hung on our every word. They had little idea, of course, of the ballet world from which Mary and I had come. But they were not celebrating the famous dancer that night. For them, they were just happy that their sixth brother had finally returned. I fitted back into my sixth son position just as though

420

I had never left, nine years earlier. So much had changed, but what endured was love and trust.

My family bombarded Mary with questions. They wanted to seat her at the men's table as a special honor, but she insisted on sitting with the women even though she only spoke very limited Chinese. She told my parents that she just wanted to be treated like everyone else in the family. She wanted no special privileges.

Rather than stay in a hotel, Mary and I had decided to stay with my parents, but I worried that Mary would find it hard living in such poor conditions. There was still no bath or shower and no hot water. The hole-in-the-ground toilet outside was exactly the way I remembered it from my childhood. And although Mary liked Chinese food, I wasn't sure she was really ready for three weeks of it in our village.

But Mary took everything in her stride, and everyone loved her. I translated for her as much as I could that night, but when I eventually lost my voice through talking too much she stopped asking me questions.

Then, within days of our arrival, the local police came. They took our passports. We became suspicious, worried. They told us it was for registration purposes. We could only hope that we would get them back before we were due to leave.

Everywhere we went in the commune in those three weeks, people's eyes were fixed on us. They couldn't stop talking about Mary—her hair, the color of her eyes, her white skin. They watched her every move. Only when she said *"Ni hao"* to them, did they remember that Mary was a person too and they would burst into laughter.

My parents' house was still much the same as when I had left. Only a few changes signaled to me that now it was nine years later. The pigsty, chicken yard and vegetable patch were gone, replaced by a clean, paved courtyard, but the inside layout of the house was exactly the same. I was disappointed to see that my beloved newspaper on the walls and ceilings had been replaced with bright flowery wallpaper: I would have liked another word-finding game with my brothers. The earth kangs were still there, but now the windows had big panes of glass and there were even electric fans to keep the house cool. Now we wouldn't have to rely on the breeze to blow the mosquitoes away. Small motorized blowers for fire making replaced my beloved wind boxes. There was clearly a huge improvement in my parents' lifestyle. "And it's all because of your financial help," my niang said.

We got to know my six nieces and one nephew while we were there too. There was only one boy among my four brothers' children. My parents would have liked more grandsons, but the one-child policy had now been strongly enforced in China. My second brother and fourth brother were the only two of my brothers classified as peasants, so only they were allowed to have a second child if their first wasn't a boy. My other brothers were salaried people and so were considered in the same way as city folk—one child only, regardless of gender.

"But what happens if you do become pregnant with a second child?" Mary asked.

"The government will force you to have an abortion," one of my sisters-in-law replied. "Even if you run away, they will track you down, force you to have an abortion, and you'll be penalized."

Mary thought it was nothing short of barbaric.

"Mary, can you have six extra boys and give us one each?" another sister-in-law asked, and everyone laughed. Deep inside, however, I knew how they felt. Not producing a son to continue the family line was considered the worst betrayal of your ancestors. I looked at my third brother while he was cooking and I realized that what my parents had done, all those years ago, giving him to my fourth uncle who couldn't have children, was one of the greatest sacrifices they could have made. I looked at my third brother's beautiful daughter, Lulu, then looked at my nephew and my other nieces. I felt sad that they, like most of the next generation of children growing up in China, would have no brothers or sisters. We had survived through generations of dark and impoverished living because of this one strength, because of the unconditional love and unselfish care of each other within our family unit. It was all we'd had.

During our three weeks in Qingdao, Mary and I spent a day each with every one of my brothers' families. We started with my big brother, Cuncia, and his wife and son, who lived in a small two-bedroom apartment provided by the Laoshan Post Office where he was now a senior manager.

Cuncia had spent over sixteen years in Tibet, one of many Red Guards who had responded to Mao's calling. He had worked hard and been promoted to the head of the Communist Youth Party in the Tibet Post Office.

It was then that my brother had met and married another native of Shandong Province, and they'd had their son. But then, in 1981, the Chinese government suddenly changed its policy toward Tibet. All Chinese living and working in Tibet were ordered to return to their home province.

Cuncia told us that he had first been promoted to the position of deputy head of the post office in a large county called Jiaoxien. He was loved and respected. But one day, in 1983, he was suddenly called into his boss's office and swiftly demoted. To his utter surprise, one of the opposition party Red Guards had become jealous of his rapid promotion and still held a grudge against him—he had lodged a complaint to the government about an incident where my brother had slapped a party leader during a heated argument at the height of the Cultural Revolution. It was an incident that had happened over twenty-five years earlier.

"I'm only one of millions of victims," my brother explained to

Mary. "I am, like so many people in China, still amazed at how badly I was manipulated and betrayed by Mao and the Gang of Four. The Red Guards of yesterday were the epitome of the communist spirit. Now we are searching for answers. We have to live with our injured pride and our lost beliefs."

I felt so much sorrow for Cuncia. I knew what he said was true—he had spent the best part of his youth pursuing nothing but propaganda. But the Cultural Revolution didn't just rob him of his youth; it crushed and destroyed his spirit and his soul. His trust in his society had vanished. Even his sacred family values had been called into question by Mao and the Cultural Revolution.

The brother I became most concerned about, however, was my second brother, Cunyuan. He had built himself a two-story three-bedroom house on commune-provided land, and although his marriage wasn't his choice, he had learned to love and care for his wife and their two daughters.

Then in 1986, so he told us on the night we visited him, he was working for a lumber company and was on one of his business trips to a northern province called Dongbei. He had been walking back to his hotel when he'd found a newborn girl abandoned and crying on the roadside. There was a simple note attached to her blankets: "If my daughter has luck on her side," it read, "she will be rescued by a kindhearted person who will love her as his or her own child. May the gods bless you—my beloved child, and bless you—the kindhearted person." It was signed, "The child's mother."

Another abandoned, unwanted baby girl. There are many such stories from China.

Cunyuan brought this little girl home. He and his wife loved and cared for her like one of their own. Now they had three daughters. She grew up to be a beautiful girl, with a sparkling personality, and the Li family adored her. The local government at first refused to recognize her as a legitimate child, but after several years of persistence from my brother and his wife, the county officials finally allowed them to adopt her and register her as a local citizen.

I had asked my second sister-in-law to cook us some typical peasant food that night, such as dried yams and corn bread, for Mary to experience. "Brother, you've been away too long!" Cunyuan said. "Some of the food we used to hate is now back in fashion—like corn bread."

"Even dried yams?" I asked.

"Not dried yams. People feed that stuff to their dogs, and even they hate it," he replied quickly.

Mary did try the dried yams that night, but I noticed she mostly ate the dumplings.

After the meal, while Mary was playing with my brother's three girls, I asked Cunyuan to show me the farmland he had been allocated by the commune. But what I really wanted was a chance to be alone with him. I remembered our heart-wrenching conversation, years ago, on the way to the train station. I eagerly wanted to know how he saw life now, and I desperately hoped that he was happy.

As we walked I noticed that we were heading in the direction of our na-na's burial place. I felt a rush of shame. I hadn't visited her grave yet and promised myself that I would take Mary there the very next day.

"Here is my land." My second brother pointed to a small area, no bigger than four meters by six.

"Is this *it*?"

"Yes, this is ours. It is not *really* even ours. It's on loan from the government." He gestured for me to sit down.

I sat next to him on the edge of his precious land and looked at the layered fields in front of us.

"See those buildings over there?" Cunyuan pointed at rows of newly built ten-story apartments on the east side of our village.

"Some of our land was sold to state-owned companies to build apartments for their employees. I'm afraid I will lose even this land soon." He shook his head.

"Won't they compensate you?" I asked.

"All land belongs to the government. They can take it back any time they want to."

"Is there any kind of central planning?"

"None whatsoever. Soon we will have no land left to farm. We are forced to put our faith, and our future, in the hands of a few government officials. I'm so afraid they will swindle our land away, and our livelihood, all in the name of reform," he replied.

I asked him about his marriage next.

"I love her," Cunyuan said of his wife. "She is a nice person with a kind soul. She's a good wife and a wonderful mother. She wasn't my choice and I have struggled to come to terms with it, but I have learned to love and care for her, just as I have learned to accept life as it is." He paused. "Do you remember our dia's story about the frog in the well?" he asked.

I nodded.

"Even though life is better now, I still feel like the unfortunate frog trapped in that deep well," he said. "The only joy in my life is my beautiful children. My wife and I pour all our love into them. We hope they will be better educated and have a happier and better life than ours," he said. "It's a shame that I will never have the privilege to see the world out there. Maybe my children will one day."

At that point we saw Mary and my sister-in-law coming toward us, the children with popsicles in their hands, and we left our discussion at that.

The following morning our dia led all of his sons, his grandchildren and Mary, to our na-na's grave. We carried stacks and stacks of yellowish rice paper with gold bars stamped on it, several boxes of incense and a bottle of water.

I was sad to see that there was not much of the grave left. Years of rain had washed away part of the hump of earth, but my family had prevented the weeds from becoming overgrown. Our dia knelt in front of our na-na's grave and murmured, "Niang, your seventh son is here with all my sons, Jing Hao's wife, Mary, and all my grandchildren to give you our love. We've also brought you money, food and drinks." He then kowtowed three times. Cuncia followed him, then my other brothers from eldest to youngest.

When it was my turn, both Mary and I knelt down in front of the grave together. No words could express what I felt. I remembered na-na's kind face, her toothless smile, the way she would hobble around on her bound feet and the sweet, kind deeds she did. I remembered the time I broke six of my niang's precious new plates and she pretended that she'd been the one who had broken them instead. She was still so vivid in my mind, even though it was over nineteen years since she'd died. I kowtowed, and kowtowed, and kowtowed, to make up for the lost years, and Mary followed in turn.

After all the children had finished their kowtows, our dia placed a stack of paper money and eight pieces of incense on top of our na-na's grave. He secured the paper money with a piece of rock so the wind wouldn't blow it away. Then we lit all the paper and incense and our dia poured the bottle of water around the grave. We will never know if her spirit knew we were there, but it satisfied something deep inside me, this tribute to my beloved na-na.

This was also the day Mary and I were to spend with my fourth brother, Cunsang, and his family. True to his word, as soon as he'd finished his four-year term in the navy, Cunsang had come home and married Zhen Hua. My parents tried in vain to persuade him to serve for longer, but he didn't want to be apart from Zhen Hua. Now they were happily married with two children, and living on a small egg farm that they'd started on a piece of rented land up on the Northern Hill. When Mary and I went to visit, he proudly showed us his fifty hens and about a hundred chicks. He cooked us many different chicken and egg dishes—and they were all delicious.

Cunsang's family lived simply and happily. He was so proud of his achievement with this farm. He so desperately wanted to expand it, but he had no money. So Mary and I gladly gave him some to help him realize his dream. Cunsang was overwhelmed by this. He couldn't speak for several minutes, just held the money in his shaking hands, and looked from me to Mary and back to me again. Eventually he put his hand on his heart. "Thank you!" he murmured.

The following day, it was my third brother's turn for our visit. Cunmao had married a beautiful girl he'd met at high school, and they dearly loved their six-year-old girl, Lulu. They lived in a two-story house, similar to my second brother's, and by now Cunmao was a successful businessman. He did all kinds of business deals, and his wife was an accountant in the Qingdao Carpet Factory. Cunmao had remained a kind and considerate son to his adopted parents—my fourth uncle and aunt. I was relieved.

Cunmao cooked us a tableful of food for lunch that day, and after many *gan bei*s, Fourth Uncle and Aunt went to bed for a rest. When my third sister-in-law and Lulu took Mary for a walk to the village shop, I took the opportunity to quietly ask Cunmao how he was.

"I'm fine," he replied.

"Have you made peace with your adoption?" I asked.

He was surprised, and for a while he just looked at me. Then tears slowly gathered in his eyes. "No, I don't think I ever will." He shook his head and wiped the tears from his face. "There always seems to be something missing in my heart. For all these years I've longed to be part of my real family, which is only next door.

I wanted to go back, but I couldn't. I will always have to push my sadness far away from my heart and mind. It is a constant battle."

It was only then, after so many years, that I told him I'd overheard his conversation with our niang that day, the day he'd begged her to take him back.

"How did you cope with it for all these years?" I asked.

"It has been hard, sometimes impossible, especially in my teenage years. At times I blamed my real parents for giving me away, other times I blamed my adopted parents for not giving me back, but most of the time I blamed myself."

"Why blame yourself? It's not your fault."

"But I did blame myself. I blamed myself for all the desire and guilt in my heart. I felt bitter that my life and destiny had been decided by two sets of parents, but I loved them all. I could do nothing but be a faithful son to my adopted parents. If I hadn't, I would have hurt everyone. I would have torn the Li family apart. What is done is done."

I tried hard to swallow the hot ball of tears in my throat. "Third Brother, I've always loved you like one of my other brothers. We all feel the same way," I said.

He nodded then, and we raised our glasses and drank a toast to happiness.

Mary and I went to visit my fifth brother, Cunfar, next. He was now married to a lovely lady who loved him dearly. They had no children, but secretly wished for a son.

Cunfar and my fifth sister-in-law took us to a restaurant on the Laoshan mountain, a place I had always wanted to go to, but could never before have afforded. In front of a spectacular view over the blue ocean, we sat and watched the fishermen row their small boats in and out of their sea farms.

Cunfar told me that he had replaced my dia at the Laoshan Transportation Company when our dia had reached retirement age—that was the rule: one of his children was to replace him at his work and, had I stayed in Qingdao, I would have been the one, not Cunfar. But even as a child, Cunfar had dearly wanted to be the one to replace our dia. He too wanted to get out of the well, and becoming a truck driver or a factory worker was his only way. He loved the transportation business. He worked hard and was quickly promoted to a director's position. Now he was in charge of a large fleet of trucks.

My brother and I exchanged many childhood stories. "Remember the dead champion cricket you kept for me?" I asked.

"How could I ever forget!" he said.

After lunch we all walked along a rocky mountain path toward a small Buddhist temple, an old one built high on a hill, one of the few that had survived the Cultural Revolution. Suddenly, Cunfar and I stopped. "Listen! Did you hear it?" I asked excitedly.

"Yes! But I heard it first!" he shouted.

"No, I heard it first!"

"What is it?" Mary walked up from behind us with my fifth sister-in-law.

"A cricket!" I answered.

My fifth sister-in-law laughed. "You brothers and your crickets, you never change, do you?"

三十

30

ANOTHER WEDDING
QINGDAO, 1988

The time for Mary and me to return to America was fast approaching. But before we left, there was an important event to attend. During our last week in Qingdao, my youngest brother, Jing Tring, was to marry. His bride was a beautiful woman, the younger sister of one of my close friends from the local school.

It was mid-June and a very hot day. Everyone was busy decorating my parents' house for the wedding. Many different shapes and colors of double happiness papers were glued onto the walls, the doors and the windows. Even the chests of drawers were covered with them. Now, instead of using sedan chairs for the bride and groom, my family had hired two cars and decorated them with big red silk flowers and ribbons.

Around eleven o'clock the wedding cars slowly rolled into our narrow street. Cunsang and Cunfar immediately lit up long strings of firecrackers. I was the official photographer, with a video camera in one hand and a still camera in the other. The groom helped his beautiful bride out of the first car. She was

431

dressed like a Western bride in a long white dress with a lot of frills and a floral veil. She even wore high-heeled shoes. My little brother wore a cream suit with a red silk rose pinned over his heart. A huge crowd of people gathered around, and everyone murmured lucky words: "Handsome dragon attracts beautiful pheasant," "Arrival of daughter with many sons to follow," they would say. In this wedding there would be no kowtowing in front of a fire, no stepping over a horse's saddle, no three-day sitting for the bride. But the bride and groom did get a bowl of "widen your heart" noodles and the dates and chestnuts were still tied to their chopsticks, just as they were for my parents so many years before.

The two refrigerators that Mary and I had sent on ahead for my family still hadn't arrived, so there was nowhere to keep the food cool on the wedding day. Everything had to be bought and cooked fresh. Cunmao and Cunfar were the designated chefs, and Cunsang was the kitchen hand. Both lunch and dinner receptions were held in my parents' house. The courtyard was crammed with tables and chairs: fifty guests, five tables of ten, and my brothers did all the cooking on one coal burner. Endless dishes were served. It was a feast. And since Mary and I hadn't had our wedding in China, everyone insisted that Mary too should dress up like a bride. Somewhere they found her a Western wedding dress. It was pink and she looked beautiful.

To say everyone had a merry time that day was an understatement. Many of the old traditions might have gone, but excessive drinking was one they'd certainly kept. Guests were falling on their faces from overdrinking. Some of the new traditions helped here, like trying to pick up hard-boiled eggs from a flat plate with a pair of chopsticks. Mary and I, and the bride and groom, had to walk around carrying trays laden with glasses of wine to give to each guest as lucky drinks. Before each of them could take one, they had to say something lucky to us, such as "wishing you a happy life with many sons" or "love each other until the silver beard touches the ground." They were not allowed to repeat other people's lucky wishes or more penalty drinks would be awarded. Trouble was, the more they drank the more likely they were to forget what others had said before. And so it went on.

Suddenly, in the middle of the drinking binge, my big uncle, my niang's eldest brother who was head of the propaganda department for the Qingdao Building Materials Bureau, made a request and everyone cheered him on. He wanted Mary and me to dance. We happily agreed and decided to dance one of our favorites, the second-act pas de deux from *Giselle*. We'd had a few drinks too, but it didn't matter. We just hummed the music and danced while our adoring audience clapped and cheered our every lift and movement. It was one of our most rewarding performances ever.

After our dance, our dia spoke as the father of the groom. I'd had no idea this was part of the new custom. "Welcome, dear relatives and friends," he said. "This is one of the happiest days for the Li family. As you all know, I don't talk much. My wife always takes the words out of my mouth."

His audience laughed and our dia looked over at our niang at the ladies' table. She gave him a happy, loving smile.

Our dia continued. "When I was twenty-one years old, my niang told me that I was to marry a nice girl aged eighteen. I told her, 'I don't want to marry anyone, I don't know how to be a husband.' She replied, 'All you have to do is love her. She will teach you the rest about life.' Little did I know then, but by fate I had married a rare jewel, the most precious jewel I could ever wish for. I treasured and loved her from the time I lifted her veil. I still love her today and will love her for the remainder of my humble life. My niang was right. My wife took care of everything. She taught me everything I needed to know. She made me a better man." He paused. "We have been through tough times together. Sometimes we felt like we couldn't go on, but then some sparks of life reminded us why we *should* go on. These sparks gave us such pleasure. These sparks are our children. We are fortunate . . ." Our dia hesitated. He was finding it hard to speak. "We are fortunate to have seven sons," he said, holding back tears. He looked at his fourth brother. They held hands and my dia continued. "We are proud of each and every one of our sons. The fact that you are all still alive today is such a miracle. Each one of you is so fortunate to have survived through those harsh years, and now all of you have married nice wives and four of you have your own beautiful children. All I want to say to you today is . . . love and treasure your wife and children with all your hearts. It doesn't matter what happens in the world around you. As long as you have your family, everything will be all right."

There was silence. I had never heard him speak so much, so eloquently. I quietly went over to the ladies' table and told Mary what the man of few words had just said.

Mary got up. She walked over to our dia and kissed him on his cheek. She raised her wine glass and shouted in her best Shandong dialect, "To Dia, to Niang! *Gan bei!*"

Everyone stood and raised their glasses high. "*Gan bei!*" they roared in response. This was the last thing they'd expected from a Western girl.

There were only a few days left now before Mary and I were due to leave Qingdao. Yang Ping, the boy whose arm I'd broken when we were only nine years old, had organized a class reunion in my honor. Over thirty of my old classmates were there. Many childhood stories were retold, some happy, many sad. Teacher Song was there too. She immediately recalled the moment she pointed me out to the auditioning teacher from the Beijing Dance Academy. "Strange how things happen," she said. "I wondered so many times what your life would have been like if I hadn't tapped on that person's shoulder that day. You know, I so very nearly didn't."

Three days before our flight back to Beijing and America, I sat by my niang's side on the kang, watching her sewing furiously. She was making a cotton quilt for Mary and me. We'd told her that there was no more room in our suitcases for a quilt. But, she'd said, to give newlyweds a quilt was a Chinese tradition, and she'd wanted to make me another ever since I'd told her that the officials of the Beijing Dance Academy had burned my precious quilt. "Jing Hao, I know, for all these years, how much guilt you must have felt for having more than your brothers, how much responsibility you must have felt carrying your entire family's dreams on your shoulders, how much burden you must have put on yourself by realizing that you had to succeed. I also know how much you loved your family and how much you wanted to help us. Now you've seen how well your brothers are doing, you should let go of all your worries. You have given all of us so much already. The one thing your brothers will always treasure is what you've done with your life. Your success has given them hope, courage, pride. It will be their inspiration to move forward. You have no idea how proud of you we all are!" Just then I noticed Mary walk in with my youngest sister-in-law, but when she saw my niang and I engaged in such an intimate conversation she quickly led my sister-in-law out.

"Mary is such a nice girl," my niang went on. "I hope you will treasure her, respect her, forever. Never take her love for granted. I hope you will love Mary like your dia loved me. We love her! I have no doubt you will make a happy family together."

That afternoon, after my conversation with my niang, Mary suddenly became ill. We suspected food poisoning, so my brothers and I took her to Laoshan Hospital and a doctor prescribed intravenous medicine for her. There was no room in the hospital for Mary to stay, so the doctor allowed us to take the two intra-venous bags, the tubes and the needles home with us. My third sister-in-law called a friend who was a nurse in her factory and they helped set the treatment up in our house, hanging the bag from a windowsill while Mary lay on the earth kang, pale faced, watching the fluid dripping into her blood. I looked at her beautiful, peaceful, sun-darkened face and remembered my dia's words at the wedding, and my niang's that morning.

The treatment soon worked, and Mary quickly recovered and was well enough to make the trip back to Beijing. "Mary has become a commune girl," my niang said during our last dinner together. At first my parents had been worried that Mary might not get used to the harsh commune life and wouldn't enjoy her experiences in China. But Mary loved the whole thing, except perhaps the food poisoning and the hole-in-the-ground toilet. She fought to wash the dishes with my sisters-in-law. She became the favorite sixth niang of my nephew and nieces. She even remembered what to call the many uncles, aunties, great-grand-nephews and other relatives.

We had only been able to buy one-way tickets to Qingdao. We were told in Beijing that they didn't sell domestic return tickets. So my brothers had to use some personal connections to get us the return tickets back to Beijing. And, just a couple of days before we were to leave, the local police gave us our passports back. We were to take my youngest brother and his bride to the capital with us, for a honeymoon, and they would stay and explore Beijing after we left.

When the final moment came for Mary and me to bid farewell to my niang, my dia and my brothers, my heart was a twisted knot. It felt just like the first time I'd left for the Beijing Dance Academy sixteen years earlier. Leaving my beloved niang would always be hard. I watched the tears flood down her face. Even the family rock, my dia, tried hard to control his emotions

436

when we finally shook hands in farewell. As our truck pulled away, I saw he too was wiping tears from his face.

It was time to leave China, time to bid another farewell, this time to my little brother, Jing Tring, his bride, the Bandit, Teacher Xiao, Fengtian, Chong Xiongjun and all their wives at Beijing Airport. By now Mary and I were totally incapable of holding back our tears. We were constantly touched by my friends' kindness. All of them would have given us their hearts and more, and by the time we found ourselves sitting on the plane we were both emotionally drained.

I was going home. But I was leaving home too. I was closing a full circle within my heart. I thought of my beloved ones. Now they didn't have to eat any more dried yams. Now they had better food to eat. Now their living standard had improved considerably.

But Mary and I couldn't stop comparing our life in the West to theirs in Qingdao, and at times I was again overwhelmed with guilt. Ever since I had been selected for the Beijing Dance Academy, I had felt this guilt, this burden, this sense of responsibility for my family. I wished all of my brothers could have had the opportunities I'd had, but deep in my sad heart I knew it was not to be. I was the one who had to fulfill my niang's, my dia's and my six brothers' dreams. Mary and I had given each of them as much money as we could afford, but I knew that it didn't matter how much I gave them; it would only ever provide them with temporary help. What they needed most was the one thing I couldn't give them—opportunity. Maybe, just maybe, now for the first time in their lives, there was a glimpse of hope under Deng Xiaoping's leadership. I had gone back home and had expected to leave them feeling light and optimistic. Instead I was leaving with a confused heart.

I sat on the plane and watched the thick clouds pass beneath. I had no desire to sleep. I could think only of my family, my family and friends who lived so simply yet made their happiness in their own ways.

Mary was sleeping now. I looked at her kind and peaceful face. I felt truly blessed to have found her, to have her by my side.

I had no idea what would happen next in our lives, but my guilt at leaving my family in China began to be replaced with excitement. The road I had traveled so far had had so many detours. Nothing had been smooth or easy. I knew the road ahead wouldn't be smooth or easy either, but what I could see was possibility. The possibilities of the world were so vast. And no matter what lay ahead or behind, I always had my niang, my dia, my brothers and friends, and Mary as my lifelong companion.

I looked out of the aircraft window into the darkening sky. I saw myself as a small boy, running barefoot through the commune fields. I saw myself as a Red Guard, and I saw myself once again as Mao's last dancer endlessly practicing in a dim and dusty dance studio in Beijing. I thought of my journey toward the most precious thing I had, my freedom, and of what had always propelled me forward—my dia's pride and dignity, and my niang's extraordinary courage and unlimited love.

AFTERWORD TO THE
ORIGINAL EDITION

Melbourne, 2003

Mary and I visited my family in China many times after that first visit in 1988. The speed of economic reform there and the improvements in people's living standards greatly impressed me each time.

Over the years, both Mary's dance career and mine continued to flourish. We were invited by companies internationally to guest-perform, and both of us felt we were at the height of our dance careers.

Our first child, Sophie, was born in 1989. She brought such happiness and laughter into our lives. My parents came back to Houston to help us look after Sophie so Mary could go back to dance again. They adored Sophie, especially my niang. Sophie was the daughter she had always longed for. They talked to her in Chinese endlessly: they knew she would be an important link with her relatives in China when she grew up. So Sophie had four adults showering endless love and care onto her, and for us life seemed perfect.

But then something happened that changed everything. Sophie was just eighteen months old, and we had brought her and my parents to Australia while Mary and I were guest-performing with the Australian Ballet. One day, a birthday balloon Sophie was playing with suddenly popped. The noise was so loud that it took all of us by surprise. All of us except Sophie. We became suspicious and had her hearing tested as soon as we returned home to Houston.

Sophie was diagnosed as profoundly deaf. We were in total shock. We couldn't believe our beloved daughter would never hear music, would never hear all the sounds we took for granted.

We did everything in our power to find the cause and a cure. From Western medicine to Eastern treatment, nothing helped.

Just ten days after Sophie's diagnosis, Mary decided to give up her dance career and devote all her time to teaching Sophie to speak. We were devastated just thinking of what Sophie would miss in life and the enormous task ahead of us. I knew Mary's sacrifice would end her dance career. To lose Mary in dance was like losing my shadow. It took me a long time to recover.

But for Mary, her journey with Sophie was just beginning. She poured every ounce of energy she had into Sophie. Each discovery of a new sound, each word uttered by Sophie, was an enormous milestone. But her progress was extremely slow.

When Sophie was four years old we were told about a new Australian invention called the cochlear implant or bionic ear. After extensive research, we decided Sophie should have the implant.

I still remember Sophie's eyes lighting up with excitement when she heard sound for the first time. With Mary's total dedication and the bionic ear, Sophie made rapid progress in her hearing and speech. She is now in a normal school, learning piano, ballet, jazz and tap. It's impossible to adequately describe how we lived through this difficult ordeal. Sophie truly is our miracle child.

In 1992, our second child arrived. Thomas was born with normal hearing and so was our third child, Bridie, who was born in 1997.

In 1995, after dancing with the Houston Ballet for nearly sixteen years, I decided to join the Australian Ballet as a principal artist and move to Melbourne. I had guest-performed with the Australian Ballet on several occasions and enjoyed working with them, but to leave Ben, who had been my mentor for sixteen years, who was instrumental in the success of my career, was not easy. To leave America, the country that had granted me my freedom, was very emotional. But what helped me through this decision was that the Houston Ballet had been invited to perform in China at the end of that year: I would finish my career with the Houston Ballet in China, the place where it had all started.

I was excited beyond description about this trip back to China. Finally I would perform in front of my people, show them what I had achieved in the West over the past sixteen years. All of my brothers, sisters-in-law and relatives, over thirty of them, took the long train trip from Qingdao to Beijing to see me dance.

I performed in the same theater where I had danced my first *Swan Lake* before I'd left China in 1979. I danced Romeo in Ben's *Romeo and Juliet*, and Janie Parker was my Juliet. The Central TV of China broadcast the opening night live—to five hundred million people throughout the country. To see the pride on Teacher Xiao's face, the excitement in the Bandit's eyes and to hear Fengtian and my former teachers, classmates and the entire audience cheering was all I needed. My only sadness was that Zhang Shu wasn't there—he had died from a heart attack a few years before.

The Australian Ballet was a new challenge for me. I knew that at thirty-four years of age it wouldn't be easy, but with twenty-three years of artistry in me, with the love and support of Mary, with the unconditional love of my parents, with my newfound freedom, I had nothing to fear. Some of my most satisfying performances happened in those last three years with the Australian Ballet. I felt a sense of ultimate satisfaction, of perfect harmony between artistic and technical knowledge. And the Australian audiences embraced me warmly from the very beginning.

During my last few years of dancing I began to study finance on the weekends and in my free evenings. It took me three years to complete a diploma with the Australian Securities Institute, and I was offered a job at a major stockbroking firm in Australia. However, the Australian Ballet wanted me to continue to dance. But I was thirty-six years old by then. Most dancers would have retired well before that. So in the end, a compromise was reached: I would be trained as an investment adviser and would continue to dance as a principal artist for a while longer.

I danced and learned about the stockbroking business for the next two years. But the workload eventually forced me to make a final decision—to permanently retire from dancing. I was thirty-eight years old.

Ben came to my last performance in Sydney and brought along with him the fondest wishes of everyone from the Houston Ballet. My last performance was as Basilio in *Don Quixote*. When I had danced this role at eighteen, I bashed through the performance, focusing only on the technical aspect of the role. At twenty-eight, I put all kinds of pressure on myself: I had to perform better than Baryshnikov or Nureyev, but I always came well short of my own expectations. But now, at thirty-eight, I was my own master. I had finally tasted Teacher Xiao's mango.

And where are all the others in my story now? Ben retired as the artistic director of the Houston Ballet after twenty-seven years at the reins. I attended his farewell gala in Houston—he had especially choreographed a solo for me to perform. Mary is still the love of my life and is currently teaching and coaching at the Australian Ballet. Elizabeth, I'd heard, remarried and her husband is a pilot. Charles Foster remains a close friend: we are godfathers to each other's children.

My friend Dilworth, sadly, died in a car accident in Texas in the mid-eighties, and Lori has since remarried.

Consul Zhang eventually left the foreign ministry and became deputy mayor of a large Chinese city.

Zhang Weiqiang also left China for the West, but he didn't have to defect. Under Deng Xiaoping's open-door policy, he became a principal dancer with the Royal Winnipeg Ballet and has now retired.

Teacher Xiao has retired from the Beijing Dance Academy but still teaches, coaches and judges international ballet competitions. The Bandit and Fengtian have left their artistic professions and become businessmen in China, like a billion others there. All my brothers are doing well in their own businesses, and their living standards continue to improve. They all wish for more children and envy Mary and me for having three. And my dia in China has just celebrated his eightieth birthday.

Recently I made a surprise visit to my family in China and showed up at my parents' doorstep quite unannounced. My niang was cooking in the kitchen. Upon seeing me, she dropped her wok flipper and could only manage to utter, "Ah! Ah! You! It's you!" She threw her arms around me and hugged me tight.

PART FOUR

MY STORY CONTINUES

2003–2009

三十一

31

KEEPING HEARTS WARM

It is now over six years since I made that surprise visit back to see my parents, when Niang dropped her wok flipper in surprise and hugged me tight. Since then I've taken my own family to China many times. I'd always wanted my children to keep their links with China, but each time I went to see my parents, I couldn't help wondering if it would be the last time I'd see them. Niang would say things like, "Your dia and I have lived incredible lives despite the hardship of our earlier years. If it wasn't for you we would not be so lucky! We have no regrets."

During one of my trips home in 2004, my family in China was excited about the planned rebuilding of the village where I'd grown up. It was a two-year project, and on average each villager would receive two or three newly built apartments in exchange for their old dwellings. But there were many different opinions about the value of their properties. Even my six brothers argued among themselves about the offer from the developer.

I thought they should take the offer and run! I knew China was in the middle of the biggest property boom it had ever seen, but to get everyone in the village to agree, and to issue building permits through various government agencies, and to actually build a whole lot of apartments to house around five thousand people was going to be a monumental undertaking. "It'll never happen!" I said to my brothers.

To my surprise, however, two years later, the primitive commune village I'd been born in had indeed gone forever: replaced by rows and rows of six-storey Hong Kong–style apartments. Now it's a complex with its own security guards, underground parking, and even small gardens full of greenery and trees. But the ugly security screens and bars on the windows and doors seemed odd to my eyes. My old village had had no need of those.

The villagers clearly enjoyed their newfound comfort and wealth. They loved all the modern conveniences: air-conditioning, heating, piped water and natural gas. Unthinkable in the old village. And now most families even had extra apartments they could rent out for more income.

My parents *loved* their apartment. It was a spacious two-bedroom with wooden floors, a sitting room and dining area. It had a good-sized refrigerator, air-conditioning and heating, and a twenty-inch color TV opposite a comfy L-shaped sofa. Their kitchen had a big, deep sink and a gas cooktop—even an electric kettle and rice cooker! Not as many gadgets as Ben's kitchen back in Houston in 1979, but they sure were catching up fast in China.

The apartment was well lit by large windows in each room. My brothers and I had wanted to make sure that Niang and Dia would have the best of the modern amenities: their very own toilet, shower, washing machine and dryer. I'd called my parents the day they'd moved in. I was so happy for them. "*Never*, in all our lives," Niang said, "did we dream we'd be so lucky!" She was ecstatic with pride.

But not everything went smoothly. My second brother, Cunyuan, told me that some villagers had refused to accept the developer's offer, and saw their houses become a pile of rubble overnight. The local government controlled all the permissions, and no one could do anything about it. From the expressions on the faces of my other brothers, I guessed that Cunyuan had been one of those who hadn't agreed with the offer, but overall he too was happy with his three new apartments. Cunyuan and his three girls could live in one and rent out the other two for much-needed income.

The rebuilding of our old village had other consequences for families though. In spite of this modernization, the older generation moaned about the loss of community feeling in the new complex. The traditional strong family unit used to be the backbone of the Chinese community, but with the disappearance of our village and others like it, that too was going. One elderly widow from our village received her three brand-new apartments in exchange for her old commune house, and was elated about her sudden change of fortune. Finally, she could live comfortably for the rest of her days! Then the trouble came . . .

The widow had three daughters and a son, all married with their own families. Traditionally, her son would inherit most of her wealth and care for her in her old age. So of course she transferred two of the three apartments to her son's name. Her three daughters could divide up the remaining apartment between them. But the daughters were enraged. In their more modern way of thinking, the three apartments should have been shared equally. They blamed their brother for manipulating their mother into this. Soon they stopped talking to each other. Now they are completely estranged.

This was just one of many unhappy stories from my old village. Many other things have also changed for my parents in this new, rapidly changing China. One day, four years ago, my niang and dia were getting ready for their usual after-lunch nap. Dia always preferred to sleep on a hard wooden bed, a little like the kang we'd slept on in the old village. Soon after he'd gone into the bedroom, my niang heard a loud thud. "What are you doing?" she asked from her comfy L-shaped sofa.

There was no answer.

That old deaf thing, my niang thought. In recent years, my dia's hearing had gradually become worse.

"What was that sound?" she asked with a louder voice.

Still no answer.

So my niang opened the bedroom door, and found her husband of fifty-nine years struggling on the floor, gasping for breath.

She screamed and rushed over to him, and quickly realized she needed to phone for medical help. But for years she'd relied on her husband to make the phone calls. She hadn't bothered to remember any of her sons' phone numbers!

Out of desperation, Niang ran and knocked on her neighbors' door. With their help she got my dia up, and called my seventh brother, Jing Tring. Together they managed to get Dia into the hospital: he was there for two weeks in the end, receiving medication, some acupuncture and also some massage to relieve his condition. And with the improved medical care in China, Dia did recover much of his mobility, but not his speech. He had suffered a stroke.

Throughout his life, Dia was known as a man of few words. Even so, losing his ability to speak was devastating. He'd never had the opportunity to learn to read or write. By losing his speech he'd effectively lost all forms of communication. Before his stroke, my parents would spend their days socializing with

450

their fellow villagers, or go on day tours to nearby scenic places. But mostly they would enjoy endless discussions, all the gossip of the world news they heard on TV programs, and they would chat over tea, happily together, about local events. As my niang's eyesight and health had worsened, my dia gradually took on the basic cooking too, so somehow their roles in the household reversed. It was such an ideal and happy environment they'd created for themselves. But how would their lives be from now on? Dia's stroke was a warning bell for the rest of the family. His health was deteriorating and we all knew it.

Back in Australia, my family and I now live in a rambling, Federation-style house in Melbourne, opposite a beautiful park. So unlike my first termite-infested home in Houston! And it's walking distance to our children's schools.

Our eldest daughter, Sophie, successfully completed her final-year subjects at high school, even Chinese. It had always been my dream for my children to speak Chinese, but because of Sophie's deafness, I'd given up that dream for her. Mary and I thought that if she could just speak English properly we'd be happy. I'd never spoken Chinese to my children over the years, fearing it would disrupt and confuse Sophie's learning of English, so I didn't really expect her to follow through with this. I knew how difficult the Chinese language was, even for Chinese people, let alone a foreigner, and a profoundly deaf foreigner as well. Sophie's cochlear implants do give her some hearing, but she hears mechanical, imperfect sounds. For her to differentiate the many intonations of Chinese would be extremely difficult. But Sophie persevered, completed her course, and is now fluent in Chinese.

Sophie also told us that she wanted to complete one of her Year 12 subjects ahead of time, so she'd have fewer subjects to concentrate on in her final year. "So which subject would you like to tackle?" Mary asked.

451

"Dance," Sophie replied.

Mary and I looked at each other. Oh dear me! Not dance. Anything but dance, I thought. We knew that would be difficult, too. Sophie would never be able to hear the subtleties of the music. But again, she was determined. And to our astonishment and pride, she received the Victorian Premier's Award, and one of the highest scores in the state, for dance. We were overjoyed. Sophie was beginning to making her dreams a reality.

Mary is still coaching at the Australian Ballet, teaching the next generation of great dance talents, and she has also been a guest teacher with other ballet companies and schools around the world. Mary has well and truly reclaimed her passion for dance, but our children have always come first in her decision-making. Her love and devotion toward them have been simply incredible. She has always been the strength behind my success, and the success of my family.

Our son Tom started Year 11 in 2009, too. Mary and I always thought he had a dancer's physique, but we never managed to get him into ballet. Sport was the thing for him. He loved playing sports: Australian Rules football, soccer, tennis, and even basketball, which he'd picked up in America when he'd gone on a six-month scholarship three years ago to St. John's School in Houston. He'd made great friends there, both in and out of school, and he'd joined the tennis team and loved American sports like baseball and basketball. He's followed the Houston Rockets, his favorite basketball team, ever since. But tennis was the sport he worked hard at and was most passionate about.

Tom had always known of the positive influence America had had on me—and now he too was gaining a fondness for that country. Mary and I were both so pleased that Tom had learned much about discipline and independence from his time in Houston. He'd suddenly grown up. It had been such a self-assuring experience for him. And one day, as if to prove this,

452

about a month before we were to leave for China, I heard a commotion in the kitchen. "Li! Come here, Li! Quick!" Mary was shouting excitedly.

Recently we'd placed a height marker on our kitchen wall for each member of the family. For years we'd waited for Tom to grow taller, but he'd always been one of the smallest boys among his classmates. Even my brothers in China had given up hope of him ever challenging my title as the tallest man in the Li family.

But that day I rushed into the kitchen and there was Tom, smiling broadly with his boyish face, standing against my marker on the wall. He was taller than me. He'd just turned sixteen.

Our younger daughter, Bridie, had just turned eleven by then, and had started Year 6. She was the most agile of all our children, born with unusual flexibility, and for this reason Mary enrolled her in gymnastics when she was six. She quickly rose to the higher levels and was placed in the elite group of young gymnasts. But what to do with Bridie's gymnastics became a constant dilemma. We wanted her to realize her full potential in something she enjoyed, but as dancers we knew just how time-consuming and lonely a life of professional gymnastics could be. We didn't know if she would want to continue, so Mary and I decided to pull her out for a while, and if Bridie was still pining for gymnastics after two weeks, we would let her continue. Bridie, however, quickly moved onto ballet, tap, jazz, and tennis: all the things she'd never had time for, and was back to her old, lively self, full of energy.

And what about my brothers in China? How have their lives altered since 2003?

My eldest brother Cuncia suffered a second stroke two years after his first one, which he'd had at the age of fifty-five. His black hair had turned completely gray. He blames himself for his health, eating too much fatty food and not getting enough exercise when living standards had improved in China. He and his wife spend most of their days looking after their son Jing Jing's only child, as both of his parents have to work to earn a living.

My second brother Cunyuan's relationship with his siblings has become strained in recent years, mainly due to his lingering bitterness toward our parents for not allowing him to marry the girl he'd wanted to marry, and for not letting him go to Tibet, all those years ago. Just for my sake, Cunyuan and my other brothers gather together when I come home for visits, but they have little to do with each other apart from that. Like all bad relationships, it inevitably started with misunderstandings, lack of communication and unspoken feelings.

Cunyuan knows that I still love dumplings, so he and his wife always invite me to his home for a meal. Besides my niang's dumplings, my second sister-in-law's dumplings are the next best. Over dinner once, Cunyuan told me about his family, how his second daughter Lili had fallen in love with a transient worker from the south of China, and how she'd followed him to the Canton area. She'd become pregnant, but her excitement quickly turned to bitter disappointment when she discovered he had no intention of marrying her. Nor did he want anything to do with their child. She was heartbroken. But Lili was determined, so with the family's support she became the mother of a very cute little girl. In my parents' time, to have a child without being married would bring only bad luck and shame. Lili would have been despised by society, and her family would bear the disgrace. How China has changed!

My third brother Cunmao has taken good care of his adoptive parents—my fourth uncle and aunt—over the years. Cunmao always secretly longed to go back to his true parents. But he couldn't, for fear of destroying two families. That was until my fourth uncle's death. Cunmao properly farewelled him, as a good son would do. He then called his birth father "Dia" for the first time in his life. Cunmao had waited for this moment for nearly fifty years. A few years later, my fourth aunt also passed away, and Cunmao could finally call his real mother "Niang." What emotional moments for him! He felt he'd come home, and today he has found true peace and harmony.

My parents suffered more pain and guilt than anyone, knowing that Cunmao had wanted to come back ever since, as a teenager, he'd found out who his true parents were. It gave my parents some comfort to see him grow into a loving and caring son to his adoptive parents. And now, their third son could finally return to the family he'd always belonged to. There were no celebrations. No ceremonial traditions. He just naturally took up that long-vacant place in the Li family. But he never forgot his first "Niang" and "Dia" and the depth of emotions they'd experienced for nearly fifty years.

Cunmao is the general manager and shareholder in a very successful building materials and home furnishing supermarket in Qingdao. His wife owns a tea shop, and five years ago their daughter Lulu came to study in Australia. She subsequently fell in love and married a chef, and they have just bought their first home in Melbourne.

My fourth brother Cunsang is a chef, too. His cooking is not fancy, but basic and delicious. Niang calls it "honest and homey." Recently he discovered a hidden passion and talent for wood carving. His apartment is full of carved objects: birds, wild boar, flowers, fishermen. Most of these he carves from tree roots.

"Why tree roots?" I asked him.

"Tree roots are tough and challenging, but they will last in time," he replied wisely.

Cunsang's wife, Zhen Hua, told me that Cunsang had taken nearly six months to complete one particular carving. I truly admired such patience and skill.

"Which one is it?" I asked to see the masterpiece.

"I gave it to a friend," Cunsang replied.

"But why didn't you keep it?" I asked, amazed.

"Because my friend liked it better," he said.

Cunsang has not changed. He always had a generous soul.

Since 2003 my fifth brother Cunfar has built up a thriving transportation business, a real estate business and a sea cucumber farm. Sea cucumbers! Those ugly slug-looking things that taste like rubber! Some Chinese people swear they are good for fighting the flu, or for keeping one young and virile. Every time my brothers try to convince me to eat one, I tell them I'd rather be gagging on dried yams again than eating that grotesque creature!

Jing Tring, the little brother I'd once taken to the village grain grinder to find a cure for our warts, has his own human resources and recruitment company. It's a new and growing area in China. His daughter Rong Rong is studying in Australia, and Mary and I have taken on the role of her Australian parents. Jing Tring and his wife came to visit us in Australia in late 2008. It was their first trip out of China. They were very impressed by many aspects of Australian life—the deep clear blue sky and clean air—but they found the rhythm rather slow compared to China. There was less hectic traffic, fewer stops and starts, fewer crowds, and the restaurants were quieter. People's lifestyles seemed more orderly to him.

Jing Tring had been asked by friends in China to bring back things like Swiss watches, expensive fishing rods and rare wines. They had to be the genuine Western article. Jing Tring and his friends are the new breed of Chinese entrepreneur—eager to buy and able to afford true Western luxuries.

So much, then, has happened since 2003, not just for my families in China and Melbourne, but for many others in my story. In America, which had been such an enormous part of my dancing life for so many years, Houston is still like another home for me. I go back as often as I can.

One time I met my former wife, Elizabeth, during one of my book tours near Boston. She'd contacted me soon after she'd read my book, and we agreed to have lunch for old times' sake. Both of us were nervous—we hadn't seen each other for over twenty years! We met at a Japanese restaurant in Northampton, Massachusetts, and talked freely about our marriage, and how young we'd been, and put to rest some unanswered questions we'd buried deep ever since our divorce. We both had the maturity to accept the past. There was no animosity, no blame, no bad feelings, just mutual understanding and respect.

I met up with Charles Foster, too, on that trip. No matter how far apart we live or how long it's been since we last saw each other, we are still very close. Today Charles is widely recognized as one of the foremost immigration experts in the United States. He is still happily married to his Chinese wife, Lily, and they live with their two teenage sons in Houston.

As for my mentor, Ben Stevenson . . . well, after retiring as director of the Houston Ballet, he became Artistic Director for the Dallas and Fort Worth Ballet, now the Texas Ballet Theater. He was in his element, excited about the extraordinary talents he'd found, and he still had the passion to build another world-class company, that same passion that had inspired me immeasurably when I had first met him. Our shared history has kept us close. Ben even hosted a book-signing event for me in Dallas, and has probably purchased more copies of my book as gifts than anyone else I know!

And as my book took me all over the world again, much as ballet had once done, I began to reconnect with my past in so many ways. Meeting people like Elizabeth, Charles and Ben again brought back vivid memories of my defection and of how I'd thought I would never see China or my family again.

I remembered, too, the various movie offers I'd rejected from Hollywood studios after the defection in 1981. My initial inclination was always to say no to such offers. It was truly scary to think of my life as a motion picture! I worried that the movie industry would be littered with intrigues and scandals and ego-driven executives. But I did secretly hope that, like the book, a movie might perhaps give people new hope and courage in their lives. Keeping hearts warm, like I'd longed for, all those years ago.

So I was encouraged by friends to consider this idea of a movie more carefully. Things are different now from 1981, they said. There's no need to worry about any negative implications a film might have on your family back in China. I began to relent, and after meetings in Hollywood and London, at the beginning of 2006, a new development began . . .

三十二

32

"NOTHING IS IMPOSSIBLE"

Nine months after the publication of my book, at my office in the stockbroking firm where I worked in Melbourne, I received a phone call from someone who introduced himself as Jan Sardi. Was he a client of mine, I wondered. The name sounded familiar . . .

Sensing my hesitation, he quickly told me he was the screenwriter for the film *Shine*, about the life of the pianist David Helfgott. I'd seen that film. It was one of my favorites!

"Please tell me you haven't given your film rights away yet," Jan said.

I told him that no, I hadn't, but I was negotiating with a London producer.

"Can you hold off until we meet? I only need half an hour of your time," he asked.

Jan and I met the following day. The planned half-hour session turned into a two-hour meeting. He came armed with a copy of *Mao's Last Dancer* and a notebook full of ideas for a movie. It was uncanny, as though he'd been working on the project for years. He seemed truly passionate about my story.

A few days later, Jane Scott, the producer of *Shine*, came and met me too. She was just as passionate about her vision for the movie, and at the end of that meeting I asked my film agent to negotiate with them. Even though they were not offering huge sums, my instincts told me that they would take good care of my story. Here were people who would make a movie with integrity and class.

One thing I learned about filmmaking from these meetings was the importance of a good screenplay. A good screenplay is the foundation of any successful film. Jan gave me his screenplay for *Shine* to read, to get a sense of his writing style. He wanted me to help in the writing process, and I agreed. He would spend over a year reading through the 680,000 words of my original manuscript, looking at dance videos, dance reviews and interview footage. Then he'd travel to China and America to meet people like Teacher Xiao, Ben Stevenson, Elizabeth and Charles Foster. He'd often arrange meetings, on a weekly basis at first, and he'd ask endless questions, and always came prepared with a thick stack of cards for different scene ideas.

During all the time we spent together, Jan always showed incredible respect for my story. His challenge was the same as that which had confronted my book editors with the original manuscript: what to keep in and what to let go. He had to reduce a book of over 400 pages to a screenplay of 108 pages, without losing the emotional impact of my story.

A year later, after many drafts, Jan showed me the final screenplay. I felt its authenticity, its emotion: it had stayed true to my original story. I was happy.

Of course, a film can't go ahead without securing funding— one of the biggest hurdles for any filmmaker—and though Jane had some potential investors, there was a long way to go yet, and she wasn't sure if they would come through for her in the end. Perhaps I could help, I told her. From time to time, at my speaking engagements, business people would ask me if there'd ever be an opportunity to invest in my film, and a colleague at my stockbroking firm, Damien Silk, wanted to be involved too. I thought that Jane might not want to put this in the hands of a couple of stockbrokers—after all, it is notoriously difficult and risky to raise film finance from the private sector—but after meeting with us to discuss possibilities, that's exactly what she did. And within twenty-four hours of our opening offer there was enough demand from potential investors to assure us all that we would eventually raise most of the film's budget. There was now a film!

Not long after that, another incredible thing happened. I'll never forget it. It was Jane on the mobile. "Li, I have some very good news to share with you!" she said.

"What is it? Tell me!"

"Bruce Beresford has agreed to direct our film!"

"Bruce *who*?" I asked in disbelief.

"Bruce Beresford . . ." Jane repeated. "He directed *Breaker Morant* and *Driving Miss Daisy* and . . ."

"I know, I know! I know who he is!" I interrupted excitedly. I simply could not believe such wonderful news!

Jane said that Bruce wanted to go through the screenplay with me in detail, and ask lots of questions about my past experiences.

So I met up with Bruce and we spent an entire weekend working together. He had an intimidating stature, but was such a gentle beast: easygoing, with a contagious sense of humor, and a curious and inquisitive mind. I asked him if he'd have a professional actor playing me, and maybe a dancer double for the ballet scenes.

461

"No, I don't think that'd work. I was hoping you'd have a dancer in mind," he replied.

"Well, yes, but I don't know if he can *act*," I said.

"Well, as long as he's not totally stupid, I think I can teach him how to act," Bruce said confidently.

Ever since word got out that there'd be a film of *Mao's Last Dancer*, I'd been inundated with CVs, pictures and DVDs from actors, hoping they could play me. Then one day a good friend at the Australian Ballet told me he'd seen a wonderful Chinese dancer at the Birmingham Royal Ballet. His name was Chi Cao.

I knew that name! He was the son of two of my former Beijing Dance Academy teachers! Like me, Chi had graduated from the academy at the age of eighteen, and was now a principal dancer, and a great possibility for the role of me in the movie. John Meehan, the then director of the Hong Kong Ballet, also said there were several wonderful dancers in his company that could play a part in the film. So in October 2007 Bruce, Jane and I flew to Hong Kong to audition them, and then on to England to meet Chi Cao.

Chi had injured himself just before his audition, but he'd taken painkillers so he could continue. And Chi's performance was electrifying: Bruce and Jane knew they'd found their star.

Then another brilliant dancer who'd just joined the Australian Ballet School from Beijing was discovered. His name was Chengwu Guo and he was only seventeen. I watched his impressive display of strong technique and astonishing skill. Chengwu had also graduated from the Beijing Dance Academy. So many parallels! I invited Bruce, Jan and Jane to see him perform and, like Chi, Chengwu was immediately offered a role, as the teenage me. And finally, a boy was found to play the young me from an athletics school in Beijing. He was a nice-looking boy: I would've definitely been selected for more roles at the Beijing Dance Academy if I'd been as cute as him!

I was amazed at the coincidences that were emerging. Chi, Chengwu and I were all from the Beijing Dance Academy, and we'd all won similar awards and danced at similar ballet companies. Maybe there's more to coincidence in life than we truly know.

Filming was due to begin in early March 2008. First there was filming in China, then it was on to film in Sydney on April 21 and after that filming in Houston.

With such a large cast and crew, the Chinese locations were always going to be the most challenging. Early in 2008 the script was sent to the China Film Bureau, where it was painstakingly examined by the officials. Some of their objections seemed simply ridiculous: Madame Mao's name couldn't be mentioned, though they didn't mind if we used an actor who looked and dressed just like Madame Mao, as long as we called her "Government Leader." But despite their suggested changes, everything seemed to be progressing smoothly and Jane was confident things would go well. So locations were secured, sets were built, costumes made and actors and crew contracted. By early March everything was ready to begin.

Then things started to unravel.

We began to hear that several other film permits, which had already been issued to Western films due to shoot in China, had just been pulled. Then they stopped issuing foreign film permits altogether. The official line was that the bureau was "reorganizing their thoughts and establishing new procedures."

Enormous efforts were made by various Australian government departments; all lobbied the Chinese authorities on Jane's behalf to obtain the permit. But the Chinese government were clamping down: they never officially denied the permit, and they never officially issued it either. One would think things couldn't get any worse for our film, but they did. Most of the camera equipment was seized at Customs and wasn't released on time for the start of filming! So local equipment had to be hired instead, which made things even harder.

It was a terrible dilemma for Jane and her Chinese producer. They had a cast and crew of over three hundred people, and to abandon filming in China would have disastrous consequences for the film. But to go ahead meant risking the anger of the Chinese government. More equipment could be confiscated, people arrested—even deported!

I couldn't possibly guess what Jane went through in making her decision to continue. It would take an incredibly strong person to endure the nightmares of filming in China even with a permit, let alone without one. Such tenacity at times could border on hardheadedness and was a source of our occasional disagreements. But go ahead she did, and on March 17, 2008, I was finally on my way to the film set—a redecorated warehouse in the countryside about an hour and a half outside Beijing.

When I walked onto the set, I was suddenly overwhelmed by emotion. I could hardly believe my eyes. It was my family home in the village. There was the room from my childhood! The woks, the windbox, the cupboards on the wall . . . I lost all sense of where I was. I could see myself as a boy once more, with my niang and dia and all my brothers. The production team in China had done a remarkable job—everything looked absolutely authentic. Many of the Chinese team would have grown up in China in the 1960s: they knew how to make it real.

Bruce Beresford introduced me to some of the cast, including "me" as an eleven-year-old, and the glamorous Chinese actress Joan Chen who would play my mother. I also met another wonderful actor, Wang Shuang Bao, who'd be my dia. I returned to Australia feeling confident about the filming, but was still worried that it might never be finished because of all the dramas with the permits!

Later the following month, Mary and I went up to Sydney to

464

see Graeme Murphy choreograph the dance scenes. Watching Chi in some of my favorite ballets such as *Don Quixote* and *The Rite of Spring* brought many memories back, reviving some of the glorious highs but also the heartbreaking lows. Chi was a brilliant dancer. It was exciting to watch him. We shared some thoughts together when Chi asked me for advice, and Mary too shared her insights with Camilla Vergotis, the dancer who would play her in the film, a dancer Mary herself had taught at the Australian Ballet.

The whole filming schedule in China was to take five weeks. The trials and tribulations would be many, and nerve-racking. Even when the filming was complete, the post-production phase would take about seven months, and the release date would still be many months away, perhaps even years. A distributor would have to be found, a musical score written . . . but I knew I had to be patient. And that year would bring many other things for me to experience . . .

2008 was also the year of the Chinese Olympics, an opportunity for China to showcase its progress to the world. It seemed funny to me—after years of trying to stamp out old superstitions under Mao's communist rule, when it came to the Beijing Olympics, even the Chinese government couldn't let go of them. Their insatiable fascination with lucky numbers, especially the number eight, drove them to choose the eighth day of the eighth month, at 8 p.m. of course, for the opening ceremony, and it was nominally the eighth year of the new millennium too.

My son Tom and I went to Beijing for the last week of the competitions. I'd wanted to take Tom to the Olympics so he might gain inspiration and motivation from the world's top athletes, and to experience this once-in-a-lifetime historical moment. He loved sports so much that it just seemed too good an opportunity to miss.

We'd marveled at the breathtaking design of the Bird's Nest Stadium on the TV, but to actually stand in front of it was something else! We had to shuffle through massive crowds of desperate ticket sellers and heavy police security, but we were awestruck as we moved closer. The sun had set through a haze of pollution, and the bright colors of the Watercube swimming center illuminated the surroundings. I saw the wonder in Tom's eyes as he looked up at the majestic Bird's Nest. The imposing grandeur of its intertwining steel structure was too much to absorb. Tom usually hated having his photo taken, but now he just had to stand in front of the camera, with the Cube and the Nest in the background, with his excited smile and his games ticket waving enthusiastically in the air.

It was an unbelievable experience for both of us. I was immensely proud to be Chinese, even as an overseas Chinese now. There were many memorable moments: when Jamaican-born Usain Bolt broke the men's 100 meters world record and the 200 meters world record; watching Steve Hooker compete in the pole vault; and when Tom and I were invited into the Athletes' Village. There we met some of the world's greatest athletes. I was surprised when a few of them knew me as "Mao's last dancer."

"I can't *believe* Steve Hooker has read your book!" Tom whispered, amazed, after the tall, curly-haired Olympic gold medalist had finished talking to us.

While we were in China we stayed with my best friend, the Bandit, and his family.

The Bandit and I always pick up where we leave off every time we meet. He and his son Qihan, my godson, met us at Beijing airport, and we were soon catching up with news and laughing and punching each other on the arms. I asked him how he was, and how his health was going.

"You know *me*," he said with a broad smile, "I love good food, and enjoy my beer and wine."

"But what about your smoking?" I asked. His wife, Marji, and I had been nagging him about giving up for years.

The Bandit shook his head and pointed to the cigarette butts in his car. "Can't stop. Old habit," he said. I love my "blood brother" the Bandit. I wanted him to live a healthy life. I really couldn't comprehend how hard it must have been to try to quit.

The Bandit, fortunately, was a good driver. I watched him weave through the dense, dangerous traffic on the Beijing highways. You had to be a good driver in Beijing, because even though there were strict traffic laws and clear signs, no one seemed to obey them. It was chaotic. My heart nearly leapt out of me when I thought a collision was inevitable, but then both drivers would curse and honk their horns, and drive off as if nothing had happened.

"How can you do this every day?" I asked the Bandit after yet another heart-stopping near miss.

"Everyone drives like this! You get used to it!" he replied, and honked his horn again at a driver who'd cut into his lane. "You just hope not too many people drive like that *idiot*!?"

I could hear Tom and Qihan talking to each other in Chinese in the back seat. Tom had been learning Chinese at school for over four years by then. I was pleased too, to see Qihan becoming a tall and handsome young man. He was in his second year of high school.

The Bandit was staying in his father-in-law's apartment inside the Beijing Dance Academy complex: he and Marji had just bought an off-the-plan apartment in a new residential building project, and they proudly drove me there to show me a model of it: it had seven stages of development and over 800 apartment buildings! It was like a small city.

The Bandit had done well over the years. He had a souvenir business and traded in collectable stamps and rare coins. Marji was working too, as a general manager in a large foreign-owned hotel chain. Recently the Bandit had invested in shares, but sustained a big loss. He asked me for some trade secrets—how to make a quick profit—and was disappointed when I said there was no quick way to make a fortune in shares. It would take discipline, patience and hard work, just like dancing. But the Bandit's attitude to the stock market was common in China. How to make fast money was a common conversation topic.

The residential project the Bandit had bought into was one that truly reflected China today. New building constructions were sprouting everywhere. No wonder the majority of billionaires in China were all in property. But these years of booming manufacturing, building, mining and consumption had also created gross environmental neglect. Air pollution in Beijing was the worst I'd ever seen, despite the government's efforts to clean things up before the Olympics. A permanent haze of pollution hovered above the city, blocking the sun and obscuring the sky. Olympians were concerned about their health. Even I got a throat infection after only a day, and the stuff I coughed up was black. After years of living in the West, I simply took clean air for granted. Many young people in China now were becoming increasingly concerned about environmental issues such as this, and they knew things would have to change.

Despite the pollution, however, the 2008 Olympics were spectacular. This gigantic nation of over 1.3 billion had finally emerged onto the world stage. People everywhere seemed to have plenty of cash to splash around. Tom and I saw booming conditions all over Beijing: shoppers crammed into enormous shopping malls, long queues waiting to get into restaurants. "Dad, people have so much money in China now!" Tom said. "Not like when you were living here thirty years ago."

But underneath this façade of prosperity I could see troubling signs, and wondered how my family would be affected.

468

I'd often thought that the level of growth in China couldn't be sustained, and it seemed to be as I'd feared. In Qingdao many foreign businesses had shut their doors. There were horror stories of workers throughout the city who'd turn up for work, only to find the gates of their workplace locked, while the foreign owner of one particular factory had even sold everything and fled, owing months of workers' salaries and entitlements, leaving behind crippling bank loans and several hundred jobless workers.

China today has a market of over a billion consumers, and the population of Qingdao is rising at an alarming rate, with a rapidly increasing gap between rich and poor. Millions of migrant workers leave their rural towns and flock to Qingdao to find better jobs. Qingdao had been the host city for the Olympic boating events too, so it had received a large amount of funding to beautify the city for visitors. The airport was now large and modern, with spacious lobbies and new check-in counters, a soaring ceiling, and many restaurants and shops. Unimaginable from the days when my friends and I dug half-burnt coal from under the runway and had been frightened away by the soldiers' bullets. Now, many of the wealthier Chinese fly from Qingdao to Hong Kong, in droves, to purchase their dream products. Even some of my old friends and classmates now wear expensive sunglasses and carry Gucci bags and wear Prada shoes! Coca-Cola and McDonald's are everywhere. Now people don't want the brand-name products sold in their local stores, because they might be buying fakes instead of the real thing, so they have a genuine distrust of their authenticity and quality. Even I, who've lived in the West for many years, was surprised by the kind of money people were earning and spending in China. Traditionally, the Chinese are the world's best savers. My parents' generation saved as much as they could for their children or their old age. But now Western consumer culture has spread like wildfire. I guess no one can blame them: China endured such hardship throughout the last century, and today people are finally able to taste the same wealth and consumerism that had so amazed me when I'd first seen it in America back in 1979.

Corruption, though, seemed to be everywhere. Money could buy anything—high positions in the military, the police force, in government and even in schools and universities. I'd often hear about dishonest business dealings. Everyone knew the saying: the only way to be successful doing business in China is to have strong "*guan xi*"—to have good relationships with officials or their relatives. Without "*guan xi*" you'll have little chance of success unless you're a multinational company willing to buy your way into China, and even then you have to have the officials on your side.

The Bandit reminded me about my first investment in China: I'd met a successful business friend of his, and started a joint venture in plastic toys, with the Bandit's friend and a local factory in Beijing. Little did I know that my invested money would be used for expensive restaurants, spas and a luxury U.S. car, and the rest went into the personal pocket of the man the Bandit had trusted as a friend. When we discovered what was happening, the man simply cut the Bandit and me out, and all we got back from our investment was a broken-down van. "It was shocking back then, but now it is just common business practice," said the Bandit. I hated that terrible experience, and I was glad that my friendship with the Bandit had stayed strong.

The observations I'd made, the disquiet I felt, all seemed to be highlighted during my stay in Beijing with Tom. It worried me that the Chinese people's psyche, their values and perhaps their happiness, were changing too quickly. Making money fast became an obsession for many, and their old, good values were forgotten. Some thought nothing of selling their ancient antiques to buy new, cheaply made furniture; people moved away from child-centered families because of the strict one-child policy that, to me, seems to have created a nation of young emperors and empresses with little understanding of tolerance or compassion. Never before had I seen people behaving with such impatience and disrespect. People pushed to the front at taxi and bus stops, with no courtesy for others. But when we were young we had to be polite and respectful to the elderly and to foreigners. I did not see this now, in the new China.

Jing Tring told me there was instead a sense of frustration and emptiness. He said that he and his wife and five other couples took an annual pilgrimage to a Buddhist temple about two and a half hours by air from Qingdao. They went to pray for their families' health, happiness and prosperity.

"Why go that far?" I asked Jing Tring.

"It's one of the very few temples in China that we are still allowed to go to," he said. "It makes me feel good that maybe a god up there will look after us."

"Do many people go?" I asked.

"You should see it! Sometimes it is difficult to get a spot to pray! All the good spots and best times are taken by the officials, and people who can afford to pay. We get what's left. People burn incense, paper money . . . I even saw some crazy people burning *real* money!"

"*Real* money?!" I shook my head in disbelief. A trip like that could easily cost the average worker two months' wages, all for a sense of spiritual belonging. I couldn't see how anyone could afford to burn real money!

That trip with Tom opened up all sorts of new thoughts for me about the country of my birth. My experiences on that trip, during the August of 2008, highlighted just how many differences there now were between the China I remembered from my childhood and the China I was seeing now. I thought of my

471

film and of how that would portray my old China and the lives of all the people I'd grown up with.

It was wonderful too, that on that same trip to Beijing, I met up again with my old ballet teacher, Teacher Xiao. He'd gathered together a small group of my former Beijing Dance Academy classmates. Many had gone overseas by now, or couldn't be contacted, but all except two were still involved with ballet, either teaching or in administration at various dance companies.

We had such a great time reminiscing about our days at the academy. How long it's been since I was that small boy hugging my niang's quilt and crying myself to sleep on that first night in Beijing! How hard it was to fill the thirty-year gap since I'd first left China! But after a couple of *Gan bei's*, we found ourselves sharing many memories. "Teacher Xiao is some kind of teacher!" one Qingdao classmate shouted. "Just look at his students from the famous 1972 class. Nearly half went overseas to pursue their dreams, including our star guest of honor today!" She jerked her chin at me, and everyone laughed. "Now there is even a successful stockbroker!" More laughter. This classmate had since become the director of the academy's ballet department.

Teacher Xiao was now seventy-one years old, but he looked ten years younger than that. "Teacher Xiao, you still look like a Woa Woa!" one of my classmates teased. "Woa Woa", meaning "baby," had been Teacher Xiao's nickname when he'd taught us at the academy.

Teacher Xiao had been so kind. He'd organized an authentic Northern-style meal—lots of dumplings and noodle dishes—at a restaurant near the academy. The restaurant was new, built with the feel of old Chinese courtyard architecture. A goldfish pond wound through the courtyard, and an exclusive banquet room was reserved for us on the third floor.

The restaurant manager seemed very attentive to Teacher Xiao. "Does the manager know you?" I asked.

"Who doesn't know the famous dance professor?" another of my classmates replied. Indeed, the Bandit told me that Teacher Xiao was now one of the most highly respected ballet choreographers and coaches in all of China.

There were many questions directed at me that day, about my family, whether my children danced, and what Mary was doing. Everyone was especially interested about the movie and seemed to know much about Bruce Beresford. They were incredibly excited when I told them Joan Chen would play my niang.

"And I heard Chi Cao is playing you in the movie!" Teacher Xiao said. "I hope he will do you great justice."

"You will be very pleased," I said. "He's a wonderful dancer."

"I am happy!" Teacher Xiao said. "He was like you, a hard worker."

Toward the end of the meal, Teacher Xiao raised his glass: "You all know how proud I was to be your teacher. I am proud to hear of your successes in life. Remember what I used to tell you, Cunxin! Nothing is impossible! No matter what you have become, whether you teach ballet or raise pigs or do stockbroking, you have all adapted to the changes life has thrown at you. I am so happy for this gathering. I hope we will soon gather again. And finally, a toast to Cunxin's film!"

三十三

33

Paper Wishes

It is 2009. The Year of the Ox. Chinese New Year comes earlier than usual, falling in January rather than February. This year, it will be a happy occasion for the Li family. My dia was born in the Year of the Ox, in 1924, so it will be his "Own Life Year" as the Chinese would say. But it will also be a challenging twelve months for those born that year. For our family, though, all we can think of are the coming celebrations. It's been four years now since Dia's stroke, and although he's lost his ability to speak, we've still planned an enormous family gathering for him. We've been planning it for over a year. So we were all counting the days, weeks and months, with eager anticipation, until we could gather again to celebrate. My parents always enjoyed these family gatherings, especially when the entire family was there: four generations under one roof! They would be so proud!

I could hardly contain my excitement about seeing everyone again. This excitement never lessened over the years, even though I visited regularly. As I ticked off each day in my diary, I found myself becoming anxious and impatient. I imagined what a happy occasion it would be for all of us. I could almost smell the gunpowder from the firecrackers, and see thousands of tiny little blown-up pieces of red firecracker paper. I could see the beautiful colors of the fireworks, filling people's hearts with joy, and I could imagine the children's delighted faces. I tried to guess what tricks my brothers and sisters-in-law would play on Mary to get her to drink those gut-burning Chinese spirits. How Mary would try any excuse to get out of that!

But most of all I thought of my mother's delicious dumplings. They would be the highlight of the Chinese New Year. It's not just the wonderful taste—it's what they symbolized: a reminder of her love, an unbreakable link to my earliest childhood memories. But my sixth sense was beginning to tell me that this might be the last time for our entire family to be together again. I was worried about my parents, and their health in particular.

So here we were in January 2009, all ready to go, plane tickets purchased months before, visas obtained, clothes and gifts packed. My life was surrounded with the busy routine of family life.

Then, just weeks before our departure, I received an urgent call from my fifth brother. "Our dia is gravely ill," Cunfar said. I could hear despair in his voice.

"How ill?" I asked anxiously.

"The doctor is not sure, but he's in intensive care, at Qingdao Hospital. You'd better come home, quickly," he replied.

I asked many more questions, desperately wanting to know what happened. Did Dia collapse? Where did it happen? Was he resting comfortably now? But all Cunfar would say was that he would tell me more when he saw me. He urged me to come home, and quickly.

"How is our niang taking it?" I tried imagining my poor niang trying to cope in her apartment on her own.

Cunfar paused. "She's had a stroke, a few days ago . . ."

At that moment I felt like some enormous force had struck me. I felt numb. A couple of days earlier, Jing Tring had called and told me that Niang had gone to hospital, but he hadn't said anything about a stroke, just that she was all right and not to worry. She'd been in and out of hospital quite frequently in the last couple of years, so it didn't cause undue alarm, just made me more anxious to get home.

"The doctor said she is out of immediate danger," Cunfar added, trying to reassure me.

I told Mary about Dia's precarious situation and Niang's stroke, and she urged me to leave at once. "I wish we could come with you, but tell your brothers and sisters-in-law that you are bringing our love and thoughts with you. And we'll be there very soon," she said.

Barely twenty-four hours later I was on my way to China. My mind was like a rough sea on that flight. Nine hours until I would even get to Hong Kong! So many memories of my parents flooded in: their sweet voices, their larger-than-life personalities, childhood moments that were deeply imprinted in my heart. The thought of both of them fighting for their lives was simply terrible, and immensely frightening. What if Niang also lost her ability to speak? What if it was much more serious than I'd first thought? I didn't understand. They'd always been so strong, dependable, like solid unshakeable rocks. And when my sadness threatened to swallow me up, I could only think: death is inevitable. They've been on a great journey. They're good people, and they will rest in peace.

These thoughts gave me some comfort until I arrived in Hong Kong, where I immediately called Jing Tring while I waited for my connecting flight to Qingdao.

"How is Dia?" I asked, almost too terrified to hear the answer.

"He has slipped into a coma."

My heart sunk. It was as I had feared.

"And Niang?"

"We haven't told her yet. We're not sure if we should. What do you think, Liu Ge?"

I understood their concerns about not telling Niang about Dia's condition, but I felt the alternative was worse. "We need to tell Niang. She deserves to know. She should see him before anything happens."

"Yes, I will tell our brothers what you say," Jing Tring replied.

Third brother Cunmao, fifth brother Cunfar and Jing Tring met me at Qingdao Airport.

We shook hands. "Good trip?" Cunmao asked as he grabbed my hand tightly.

What could I say? It was the worst trip home I'd ever had, filled with dread. I was about to say so, but I thought it would be inappropriate, disrespectful to Dia. So I simply shook my head and got into Cunmao's black Honda sedan.

On the way to the hospital, my brothers' faces were grim and sad: none of the cheery happiness I'd pictured a week before.

"How is Dia?" I asked hopefully, as Cunmao drove through the smog and heavy traffic.

"Slipping away," Cunfar replied from the back seat.

"Did you tell Niang?" I asked Jing Tring after a moment's silence.

"Yes, soon after our phone conversation. She was still in her hospital bed."

"How did she react?"

"Just closed her eyes . . . and silently sobbed." I could hear Jing Tring's choking voice behind me. Then my brothers began to tell me what had happened. Since that first stroke of Dia's over four years ago, they'd all rotated on a weekly basis to take care of our parents. Last week was Cunmao's turn. One morning, his wife had come to help prepare breakfast and asked, "Where is our niang?"

"I told her she was still asleep," Cunmao said, "But we knew Niang never slept this late, so she went to check on Niang in her bedroom, and found Niang on the floor, all twisted, by the window. It was like she'd suffered great agony. So we rushed her to the hospital, and she was in a coma for two days. Then she recovered consciousness, but she'd lost all feeling on the right side of her body, and some of her speech ability as well. The doctors told us she'd had a severe stroke," Cunmao said, and looked sadder than I'd ever seen him.

Then Jing Tring told me what happened to Dia, only a few days later. Jing Tring had been cooking a lunch of bread and stir-fried vegetable dishes for Dia, at our parents' apartment.

"I was fixing Dia tea, and was just telling him about how well Niang was recovering, and that she'd soon be home. Dia just nodded, like he always does. Then I asked him if he'd like some tea, but he just shook his head, and pointed towards his bed. I thought he wanted a nap, so I took him into his bedroom, but just minutes later he rushed out again, and seemed to be in pain." The emotion in Jing Tring's voice was starting to distress me even more.

"I didn't know what was wrong!" Jing Tring's voice quivered. "Dia just pointed at his stomach. But you know our dia never complains." Jing Tring was right. We'd always marveled at Dia's toughness.

"So we drove him to the same hospital where Niang was," Jing Tring continued. "The doctors did many tests, a CT scan too, I think, but they couldn't find out what was wrong. They said they'd have to do exploratory surgery."

Jing Tring looked at me, and paused to get control of his emotions. "The surgeon came out after the operation—a couple of hours later. He said there was little hope. He said Dia's organs were shutting down. He urged us to prepare for his funeral . . ." By now Jing Tring was sobbing.

"And then we asked the surgeon how long they could keep Dia alive," Cunfar added emotionally, "because one of our brothers lives in Australia, and he'd want to be here . . . before our father . . . He said we should tell you to hurry. That was when I phoned you in Australia—as soon as we knew . . ." Cunfar's voice faded into silence.

As our car sped along, nobody spoke. We were all lost in our own emotions.

"Did Niang see Dia?" I asked eventually.

"Yes," Cunmao replied. "She called out Dia's name, but she got no reaction. She tried touching his forehead. Then she said, 'Go. Wait for me,' and just sobbed."

At the hospital we were met by my three other brothers, their wives and some of their children. The hospital was one of Qingdao's finest, less than three years old, with a large lobby, but still not big enough to accommodate the massive number of people going in and out. And we had to wait over five minutes for an elevator. Every time one arrived, impatient people would push their way on, and there were no queues. The over-the-weight-limit warning bell would go off constantly! So everyone would scream and curse, and the last person or two to squeeze in would have to get off again and wait for the next elevator.

I saw many doctors and nurses hurrying by, all wearing white medical coats over Western-style clothes, and all with photo IDs around their necks. China has moved on from the days of Mao's barefoot doctors, I thought.

The head surgeon, a friend of Jing Tring's, took me into Dia's room, where he lay with tubes sticking out of his nose and wrists. His breath was short, and his face seemed swollen and green.

479

"Dia, I'm back," I said gently. His eyelids flickered very slightly.

"Uncle, uncle, your sixth son is back to see you!" the surgeon added in a much louder voice. His eyelids flickered again, but Dia just couldn't open his eyes.

"Your father heard you, and knows you're here," the doctor said kindly.

"Dia, you rest. I'll be back soon."

I asked the doctor to explain my dia's illness and if there was any way at all we could revive him. But the doctor was definite. "No, he is too far gone. His entire system has shut down."

"What now?" I asked.

"We can sustain him with medication, or pull the life support and relieve him of his agony."

These were not the words I wanted to hear. I wanted him to say there was still hope, that there was a magical cure for my dia, like there'd been for me when I'd burnt my arm as a baby, or when Jing Tring and I had been cured of our warts. I thought of the time, long ago now, when Dia had nursed Niang through her terrible illness, the day I'd found her collapsed on the Northern Hill, her pile of washing scattered all around her. If only my parents could recover again, just as miraculously.

After conversations with the surgeon, all seven of us sat together, and made the hardest decision we'd ever had to make: to allow our beloved father to die in peace. We did not want to prolong his agony. Pain and sadness were etched on everyone's face, but we all knew it was just a matter of time, his time. We had to let him find his final resting place.

That evening, only twenty-four hours after I'd left Australia, Jing Tring took me back to our parents' apartment. "Why don't you stay with us tonight?" he suggested.

"No, thank you. I want to stay here."

"I will stay with you, then. You shouldn't be alone."

"That's all right. I want to be alone," I reassured him.

I sat down on the L-shaped sofa, and felt numb. I began to think about how I'd wanted to be alone when I was a small boy at the Beijing Dance Academy, and of how I used to hide in the willow trees. But I could not hide in the willow trees now. I could not hide from what was happening to my parents.

The apartment was cold. January is normally cold in Qingdao, but that night the temperature dropped to eighteen below zero. I didn't care though. I felt only a vast emptiness in my heart.

I called Mary, and woke her up. It was early morning back in Australia. "I'm so sorry, Li!" she said. "I wish I could be there. I know this is painful, but it's a sensible decision, and it's for the best."

I wished Mary was there too. Talking to her was comforting, but it made me miss her and the children even more. I wanted them to come as originally planned. But we'd decided that it would be better to wait. Everyone would be busy with funeral matters. "Without us there," Mary said wisely, "you can give your full attention to Dia and Niang."

The only other person I called besides Mary was my blood brother the Bandit. I knew he'd want to know. Over the years he'd become part of the Li family. "I'll be there as soon as I can," the Bandit had said, and he caught a flight to Qingdao the very next day.

It had only been five days since Jing Tring had taken Dia to hospital. Now everything had changed. His life would end, I knew that. But I just couldn't accept it. A miracle might still happen! A phone call from the hospital to say that Dia was awake. He'd nod and smile when he saw me like he always did. The man of few words! And I'd chat to him about Mary and our children. He liked to hear about Sophie. He'd always had a soft spot for Sophie. After all, Niang and Dia had taken care of her in Houston for the first two years of her life.

I wished only that this dreadful nightmare might end.

I walked around the apartment, first into Niang's room where I tried to imagine exactly where she'd been when she'd suffered her stroke. I crouched near the window where my third sister-in-law had found her that morning. I sat on the bed and it was still warm. It was really a modern version of the old kang, with electric heating underneath it, and with all that had happened no one had noticed that the heating was still on. Then I went and sat on the edge of my dia's wooden bed.

There were pictures everywhere in the apartment: on the walls, under the glass tops of the chests of drawers, in picture frames: photos of all their seven sons, their grandchildren and great-grandchildren's smiling faces. And photos from their foreign adventures with me—in America, Australia, Hong Kong and Mexico. These photos were my parents' pride and joy. My brothers and their wives would tease Niang and Dia about having too many pictures of their sixth son and his family. They accused them of playing favorites, but my parents always laughed happily and said, "We will gladly take pictures with you in all those places, if you take us to those countries too . . . !"

I went out onto the small patio, where they would often store food in winter. Except for the refrigerator, it was the coldest part of the apartment by far. Now it was stacked full, in preparation for the Chinese New Year. This year my brothers had stored extra food, foods my parents and I especially enjoyed. I noticed there were also a lot of sea cucumbers. But there were many other things, delicious things: roasted peanuts and sunflower seeds, Chinese cabbages the circumference of a grown man's waist, smoked duck, marinated pheasant, dried shrimp, and eggs of several kinds—quail, chicken, duck. And of course, there were many of those big, round Chinese bread rolls called mantos. I thought of Niang kneading the dough to perfection as I'd watched her when I was a child, and of the

482

unforgettable aroma of the food on Chinese New Year: the Li family smell.

Everything was familiar in this apartment, except for my parents' absence. Without them it was empty, lonely. I sat for a long time, just staring into the darkness. The wind outside pelted a few leafless branches against the building. My emotions swept me everywhere, through all my memories of my parents. Time after time, I wiped away tears.

I must have finally fallen asleep. I had no idea what time I'd dozed off, but it was now about five in the morning, and I'd woken to a world of brilliant white. Snow had fallen overnight, and was still coming down furiously. The world outside looked pristine and majestic. I'd danced in thick snow like this, thick fake snow, as the Nutcracker Prince. I remembered dancing that ballet in front of my parents, when they'd first come to Houston to see me perform. I could still hear my dia say, astonished, at the end of the show, "Why didn't you wear any *pants*?" That moment seemed like yesterday, a moment that belonged to Dia and me, always occupying a special place in my heart. I thought of the Nutcracker snow that accompanied Clara and me to the Land of Sweets. Now the real Qingdao snow outside would accompany my dia to the Land of Paradise.

That morning, we arrived early at the hospital. No one said much. We all understood that Dia's life would slowly slip away, but we went in and talked to him as though he were going to live on regardless. We would not say anything sad or unlucky.

That whole day we waited in the hospital. I visited Niang a couple of times, and she asked me how her husband was. I said he was doing fine. It pained me to lie, but this time I thought it best. There was no need to alarm her further. But Niang simply shook her head. She knew.

Hour after hour we waited, dreading that the doctor would

come with the news. With so many members, the Li family occupied a very large section of the waiting room, which was also used as an overnight sleeping room for patients' families and relatives. There were foldable chairs and stretchers, rolled-up mats, blankets and quilts crowding the tiny twelve-foot-square room. There was a peculiar smell, too, which reminded me of the Beijing railway station back in 1972. I could smell fruits, sweets, fish and dried shrimps, body odor and unwashed clothes, and the modern familiar smells of McDonald's and KFC. People ate their meals on their knees, and hovered around so they wouldn't miss being called to see their loved ones.

My dia's breath became shallower each time I visited him that day. At the beginning I loathed the thought of him going, but on my last visit, before I went home that evening, to my horror, I found myself wishing him gone.

I felt immensely guilty, but that was my honest feeling. Why should Dia suffer at the end of his life like this? Later, I found that my brothers shared the same feeling; they too, had wished for my dia's agony to end.

Just before midnight, on January 9, 2009, the phone rang back at my parents' apartment. It was Jing Tring. I was just about to go back to the hospital for my turn to sit in the waiting room.

"Liu Ge, our dia is gone."

The entire Li family, and friends as well, over thirty people, converged on the hospital. Everyone was wide-eyed and white-faced.

The seven of us very quickly crammed into Dia's ward. Only the sons were permitted in with Dia when his body was dressed. No tears were allowed to be shed, so we all tried hard to hold back our emotions. By tradition, the daughter of the deceased would prepare the funeral dress, but since our parents had seven

484

sons and not one daughter, we had to hire a professional dresser to help. To my surprise, Niang had already hand-sewn all of Dia's, and her own, funeral clothes, years ago, when her eyesight had still been good, in preparation for this very day.

We washed Dia's body with a brand-new towel, shaved him and combed his hair, and the hired dresser gently put on Dia's beautiful clothes. All were made of pure cotton or silk. The inner shirt and pants were beige, the outer mandarin gown was dark blue silk, his favorite color. In his hand we placed a small bag containing some dried bread. Chinese legend has it that a magical dog will guard the divide between the human world and the new world our dia was about to enter, but it would not let him in unless he gave it some food. Finally a small piece of silver, called *ya kou yu*, was inserted into Dia's mouth. He looked serene and peaceful.

We were allowed to cry only after Dia was properly dressed. Still, we had to be careful not to shed tears onto his body, as this would take undesirable things to his pure new world.

The seven of us quietly discussed whether we should tell Niang of this dreadful news. After everyone had expressed his opinion it was decided that we had no choice but to tell her the truth, no matter how devastating for her it might be.

So all of us, Niang's seven sons, went to her room around two in the morning. We were dreading to wake her, but the hospital was eager to take Dia's body away from the ward. To our surprise, Niang was already wide awake. She must have felt the loss.

"Niang, Dia has gone to a better world," Cuncia said. Niang gently nodded. "Take me," she said.

We wheeled her to Dia, two floors up. She looked at him tenderly for a long time, then made a despairing sound, and heartbreaking sobs and tears followed. Her body heaved uncontrollably. I went to her and held her tight. "Niang, Niang . . ." was all I could say.

By local tradition, our dia's body would be taken back to his home and placed in an open coffin in the living room for the three-day waiting time. But because of his surgery, the doctors advised us to keep his body at the crematorium. So we carried a piece of cardboard bearing our dia's name and his date of birth, written in black ink, all the way to his apartment, and placed it on a table in the living room. His soul would follow his name and all of us home, until we placed the sign in his permanent resting place three days later. A picture of Dia's kind, honest face was also put in the middle of the table, and in front of it were three burning incense sticks, and tall candles on either side. There was Dia's favorite food: cooked fish, vegetables, meat, eggs, wine, fruit and of course roasted sunflower seeds and peanuts. There were also two small glasses of the harsh Chinese liquor called Maotai, and Dia's favorite Western drink, the Drambuie that I'd brought home for him. A clay basin was placed on the floor to contain fire and ash from the burning of paper money, the traditional gold paper bearing the symbols of a gold nugget and an old coin: only this sort of money could be used in Dia's next world. And with China's new prosperity, there were some other items added to the list of things to be burned—paper cars and houses, paper refrigerators and even paper televisions, so Dia could enjoy all these modern luxuries in his new world.

I didn't cry much, though. I couldn't. It wasn't because I wasn't heartbroken. Maybe it was because I was so overwhelmed, worrying about Niang. I felt exhausted and had intense headaches. I found my emotions suppressed without really knowing why.

On the last day, a large entourage of the Li family, friends and relatives arrived at the crematorium. It was early, a freezingly cold morning, with strong chilling winds. Snow had frozen into thick layers of ice on the paths. Everyone wore plenty of clothes: layers of sweaters and woollen pants, heavy jackets, gloves and scarves. Even with my overcoat I was still shivering uncontrollably. I felt frozen in my heart.

Since our na-na's death over forty years ago, this was only the second funeral I'd ever attended, and to my surprise the old funeral traditions of Na-na's day were returning. Chairman Mao's efforts to destroy the old traditions hadn't worked. People still lavished their loved ones with affection, bringing paper money and lighting incense, kneeling and kowtowing three times. In the old days, all the sons would have to wait by the dead for the entire three days, without sleeping at all, burning the incense and the paper money to allow the loved one as much wealth as possible in their new world. The sons would kneel, kowtow and cry, along with all the visitors. Funerals were an expensive and exhausting experience.

The seven of us met at the crematorium's ash-box shop. There was a lump of a crowd outside. At 8:30 we were finally allowed to cram into the shop, but inside the variety of ash-boxes to choose from was overwhelming. It had to be the right size to fit into the small cement slot at the cemetery, but then there were lucky shapes, and colors, and would redwood be better than stone, or perhaps a carved or painted one? After much discussion, we eventually settled on an expensive, ancient-looking carved redwood box for our dia's ashes.

At 9:30 it was time to enter the spacious display hall. It was a big square room, and our dia lay serenely in his coffin, on a raised platform in the middle of the room. Bouquets and baskets of flowers and wreaths bearing his name surrounded the coffin and leaned up against the walls. The whole room echoed with wailing and weeping. It was then I realized that this would be the very last time I'd ever see my dia. I could no longer contain my grief, and tears at last flooded out. My legs felt weak, and a pair of strong hands grabbed me from behind and supported my shoulders. "You are all right. I am here," the Bandit whispered.

"Your attention, please, while I read the eulogy," the ceremony master yelled over the incessant wailing. He tried several times before the crying quietened down, but still the sobbing persisted and I couldn't concentrate on his words. I murkily remember hearing Dia's name, his date and place of birth, a list of his achievements, and that he'd been eighty-five. I remember hearing, "Li Tingfang always regarded himself as a lucky man by marrying his beloved Fang Reiqing. He was most proud of his seven sons. All are present today. As we see, he was loved, admired and respected by his family, his friends, fellow villagers and colleagues. He worked hard all his life. He provided his family with love, comfort and food . . ." At this moment Cunfar cried out, "Dia!" and a chorus of crying followed. The ceremony master asked for calm and continued. "Li Tingfang was a good man, who lived a proud and dignified life. Today we farewell him on a safe journey to a magical world, to live a better life for ever after." Then he called us all forward and we circled around Dia in a final farewell. As the Bandit supported me by the coffin, I tried so hard to get a good look at my dia through my tear-fogged vision, but I couldn't see clearly. I wiped away my tears with a handkerchief, and took one last look at my father, a vision that would forever now live in my treasured memories.

We'd purchased a double slot at a scenic cemetery not far from our village for Dia's ashes: one slot for Dia and another for Niang's when her time came. The slots were side by side in the ground. I thought of Na-na, who hadn't wanted to be buried next to my grandfather because his first wife was buried next to him. It was always our parents' wish to have their ashes buried side by side, to spend their next lives together.

The cemetery was in a small valley surrounded by mountains, with a little manmade lake and some lovely pagodas, and there we had another ceremony. Since Dia's death, each family member, young and old, had made some little nuggets of shiny gold and silver paper. There were sacks of them, and lots of yellow rice paper with the money symbol stamped on them, all prepared over the three-day waiting period.

Dia's ash-box was placed in the cement slot, and my eldest brother carefully arranged seven pieces of willow branch around it. They had to be from the same branch, as straight as we could find, and evenly cut. They represented Dia's seven sons. Miniature jewelry, food and money were also buried in the slot. It was sad to see the waiting slot next to Dia's. I thought of Niang, still in her hospital bed, struggling for her own life. It was a terrifying, harrowing feeling.

Once the marble top was sealed, we knelt one by one in front of Dia's resting place and kowtowed three times. We burned the gold and silver nuggets, the paper money, the incense, wine and firecrackers. On our way out we stopped at a temple with a gold god of death sitting cross-legged in the middle, and there we burned the rest of what we'd brought, praying aloud for the god to look after our dia. How I prayed and prayed that he would.

It is a week after the funeral. Jing Tring and I pick Niang up from the hospital. On the way, we stop to buy her a wheelchair. Two and a half weeks after her stroke, and only ten days after Dia died, Niang is coming home.

Niang has recovered some sensation in her right leg, but not her right arm. The doctors cannot tell us whether she will ever walk again. Niang, however, is in better spirits today. Jing Tring and I take her back to her apartment, and as soon as she comes into the living room she notices Dia's picture still sitting there on the table. "Take me there!" she points frantically. So we wheel her close and she looks at him for a long time. Her eyes are moist. "He was a good man," she says simply.

I spend as much time with her as I can over these next few days. I massage her every day, praying she will regain her mobility. I watch her determined face when she tries to move her paralyzed arm, and feel her frustration when she can't. How fragile she's become! Even speaking seems to drain her energy, and often she will close her eyes and rest.

Our much-anticipated Chinese New Year hasn't turned out as we'd hoped. There are no fireworks, no brightly colored clothes, no happy visits to friends and relatives. Instead it is a sobering, reflective time. We gather around Niang on New Year's Eve and kowtow and wish her a speedy recovery. We kowtow to Dia too, but there is an empty feeling without him that night. The delicious food doesn't quite taste the same. There is no laughter. Our niang eats her food in her room as usual, because she is more comfortable there, but when she hears us discussing whether we should drink alcohol that night, she says very definitely, "Drink! Your dia would want you to be merry tonight!" Dear Niang, even after all she's been through, she still thinks only of others.

That night I realize just how much our dia had meant to us over the years, how much of his character we have all taken on. I feel immensely fortunate to have had a father who instilled in us good morals and principles. He was always a tall person, nothing to do with his height, but with the dignified human being that he was. "Pride is the most precious thing in our lives," he'd said when I was five. "Never lose your pride and dignity, no matter how hard life is." In my mind I can still hear his stern voice and see his serious expression the day I'd stolen my friend Sien Yu's toy car.

I truly believe that the ultimate measure of one's success in life is not what position you have occupied or how much money you have, but what kind of person you have become, what difference you have made to the people around you. My great fear is that at the end of *my* life, I won't measure up to my dia's extraordinary success.

Each day that passes is a day closer to going back to my own family in Australia. How I long to be with Mary and the children, but how can I leave Niang? Leaving my niang is always painful, but now I wish never to part from her. I wish I could take her back to Australia with me.

"You need not worry about me!" she says when she senses my reluctance to leave. "You go now. Take good care of your own family. I'll be fine with your brothers and sisters-in-law." And it is true. I do take great comfort in knowing that Cunsang and my other brothers will take care of her, and that I will return as soon and as often as I can.

After three weeks, the time finally comes for us to say goodbye. I hug Niang with all my heart. Suddenly she flings her good arm around my shoulders with surprising strength and hugs me tight, just like she'd done after she'd made me return the toy car to Sien Yu. At this moment now, I feel her enduring love once more, that same love that had given me strength and confidence as I was leaving home at the age of eleven to go into the unknown, that same love that had given me hope and courage at the Chinese consulate in Houston when my life was hanging by the thinnest of threads. Her love would always be the reason for overcoming my toughest challenges and impossible odds. I would never forget it, and it would sustain me to the end.

Soon after I get home I relive my story in another form. Jane Scott arranges a private screening of the film *Mao's Last Dancer,* for me and my family in Melbourne.

I am tense and nervous when I enter the cinema. I have stomach cramp before I sit down.

Mary's mother, Coralie, comes with us. Our children are the most excited of all. Jan Sardi and Jane Scott are also there with the film publicist and, except for Jane, everyone is seeing the film for the first time.

I close my eyes and try to calm myself down before the screen lights up.

It is strange, that first time my name is called out in the film. Watching someone being me is very surreal. But my unease is quickly dispelled by the unfolding story, as I am taken back in time to those experiences I'd endured as a child, experiences that stretch far, far beyond the film footage itself. And then, seeing my beloved niang and dia in the film, after I'd only just said farewell to Dia and left my niang back in China! It is so difficult. I wish my dia hadn't gone. I wish with all my heart they were sitting beside me in this cinema, proud and happy once more.

I remember those paper wishes I'd sent up to the gods when I was just a small boy in the fields of Qingdao. I remember daydreaming about all the beautiful things in life I would never have. I remember begging the gods above for food for my family, for a way out of the deep dark well. My imagination then, as a small boy, had traveled far beyond that world, into my own special land. Now my dia has traveled far beyond our world, into his own special land. It is 2009. Perhaps the story of my dia and my niang won't end here, but will continue to keep hearts warm and hopes alive for many more years to come.

THE LI FAMILY TREE

FATHER'S SIDE

MOTHER'S SIDE

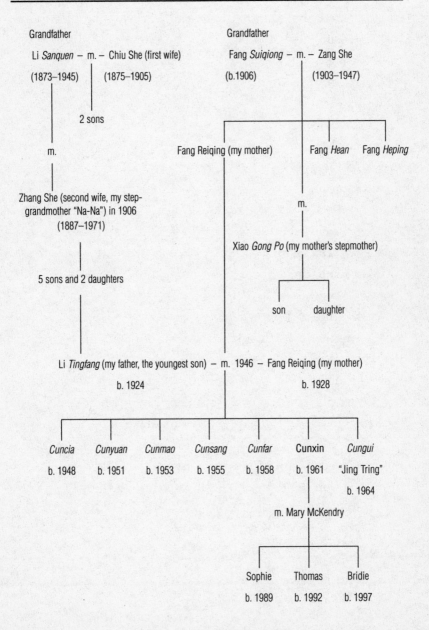

Grandfather

Li *Sanquen* – m. – Chiu She (first wife)

(1873–1945)　　　　(1875–1905)

2 sons

m.

Zhang She (second wife, my step-grandmother "Na-Na") in 1906

(1887–1971)

5 sons and 2 daughters

Grandfather

Fang *Suiqiong* – m. – Zang She

(b.1906)　　　　(1903–1947)

Fang Reiqing (my mother)　　Fang *Hean*　Fang *Heping*

m.

Xiao *Gong Po* (my mother's stepmother)

son　　daughter

Li *Tingfang* (my father, the youngest son) – m. 1946 – Fang Reiqing (my mother)

b. 1924　　　　　　　　　b. 1928

Cuncia	*Cunyuan*	*Cunmao*	*Cunsang*	*Cunfar*	**Cunxin**	*Cungui*
b. 1948	b. 1951	b. 1953	b. 1955	b. 1958	b. 1961	"Jing Tring"
						b. 1964

m. Mary McKendry

Sophie	Thomas	Bridie
b. 1989	b. 1992	b. 1997

ACKNOWLEDGMENTS

To embark on writing my autobiography was an enormous challenge. At times I wondered if I was insane ever to agree to write it in the first place. Then again, I had the privilege of working with two of the most sensitive, caring and creative editors at Penguin Australia. They skilfully pulled the story out of me and guided me through it in a most fascinating and rewarding process. My publisher, Julie Watts, and my editor, Suzanne Wilson—they are not only two of the best editors one could ever dream of working with; they are also two people with high principles and integrity. Without the sound advice of these two special women and the highly professional team at Penguin, *Mao's Last Dancer* would never have happened. Also to Cathy Larsen, the designer of my book, for her creativity and wonderful design work.

A special thanks to my dear friend Charles Foster, to whom I owe my life and more. He has made an important contribution to this book. The Bandit, Teacher Xiao, Fengtian and others in China have also helped. And to my beloved parents and all of my brothers back in China who allowed me to tell their stories. They helped me with their recollections of our hard, hard childhood. They endured my endless bombardments—phone call after phone call, letter after letter. To ask them to reflect on those years was like asking them to relive them. They provided me with enormous emotional support in the writing of this book.

And thank you to all my other friends and relatives who helped me with my book and who so enthusiastically supported me.

Li Cunxin

DISCUSSION GUIDE

1. How are fate and destiny shown as common themes throughout the book?

2. Do you think Li did so horribly in his first year at the Beijing Dance Academy because he lacked talent or because he was homesick?

3. When the Bandit wanted to make Li his Blood Brother (page 182), Li was hesitant at first because he didn't think he could live up to the Bandit's expectations of him as his brother. Do you think it was their shared emotional need to feel like part of a family at the Academy that made him finally agree? Why or why not?

4. The hardships of commune life seem exhausting and relentless, but Academy life was not much easier. Which would you choose and why?

5. Some of Li's teachers at the Academy were very encouraging and motivational to the students and some were not. Discuss some of the varied teaching styles and why you think they differed so much. Do you think this had to do with the Cultural Revolution or different personalities?

6. Li is a very emotional boy, often breaking into tears when he is sad or unsure of things. How does this differ from Western preconceived notions about people, especially men, in communist China?

7. Discuss Li's first trip to Houston and his defense of, and eventual confusion about, Chairman Mao's Cultural Revolution.

8. Do you think personal or artistic freedom was Li's main objective to return to America?

9. Was Li's harrowing experience at the consulate in Houston, prior to his defection, a necessary move by the Chinese government, especially its threatening to harm his family? Even with China's updated "open-door policy," do you consider this a scare tactic, or required for the country's communist ideals?

10. When Li's marriage to Elizabeth ends in divorce, Li blames himself, saying he ". . . didn't understand love in Western culture . . ." (page 346). Do you agree? Discuss how Li's guilt plays a role throughout the book.

11. Discuss Li's conflict with his freedom and the price he paid for it.

12. Do you think Li would have been as disciplined and dedicated to ballet if not for the intense work ethic instilled in him in China?

13. "Taste the mango" was a phrase that Li followed from his days at the Academy, when Teacher Xiao mentored him to excel. Discuss some of the important things in Li's life and career that would not have been possible had he not made that phrase one to live by.

14. Li's fourth brother, Cunmao, has a very different sense of duty to his family from Li (page 429). How so? Why do you think these brothers handled their family situations so differently? Did Li's leaving for the Academy have everything to do with it, or was it something else entirely?

15. Li's *niang* and *dia* instilled pride, courage, dignity, and love in him. How do you think his life would have been different had he not done everything for his family? Discuss how this mentality in China is different from Western culture. Do you think this is still the way of thinking in China, which is more heavily Western-influenced now?

PHOTOGRAPHIC CREDITS

Every effort has been made to trace copyright holders of the photographic material included in this book. The publishers would appreciate hearing from any copyright holders not here acknowledged.

Front jacket and spine: Li Cunxin as a boy, and the New Village, Li Commune. Photographs courtesy Li Cunxin.

Inside front jacket: Li's mother and her seven sons. Courtesy Li Cunxin.

Inside back jacket: Li's family today: Mary, Sophie, Tom and Bridie. Photograph by Julian Smibert, courtesy Li Cunxin.

Photographic insert:

"My classmates," "The New Village," "Proudly wearing Mao's army uniform," "My beloved niang," "My first lonely day in Beijing," "The Beijing Dance Academy" (photo by Sarah Darling), *"Hai Luo Sha"* and "Rehearsing *Hai Luo Sha*," all courtesy Li Cunxin.

"First contact with the West" and "On the steps of the Vaganova Ballet School," photographs by Ben Stevenson, courtesy Li Cunxin.

"Defection," photograph courtesy Charles Foster, Houston.

"*Sleeping Beauty*" photograph © Jim Caldwell.

"With Barbara Bush," courtesy George Bush Presidential Library.

"Applying my makeup," photograph by Leticia London, www.leticia london.com.

"*Rite of Spring*" photograph © Jim Caldwell.

"The Esmeralda pas de deux," photograph by Branco Gaica, courtesy Australian Ballet.

"My beloved family," photograph by Chris Beck, courtesy Melbourne *Age*.

ABOUT THE AUTHOR

LI CUNXIN was born in 1961, in the New Village, Li Commune, near the city of Qingdao on the coast of northeast China. The sixth of seven sons in a poor rural family, Li's peasant life in Chairman Mao's communist China changed dramatically when, at the age of eleven, he was chosen by Madame Mao's cultural advisers to become a student at the Beijing Dance Academy. After summer school in America, for which he was one of only two students chosen, he defected to the West and became a principal dancer for the Houston Ballet.

Li went on to become one of the best male dancers in the world. He is now a senior manager in a major stockbroking firm and lives in Melbourne, Australia, with his wife, Mary, and their three children, Sophie, Tom and Bridie.